CW00502465

THE WORLD READERS

Series edited by Robin Kirk and Orin Starn

THE ALASKA NATIVE READER

Edited by Maria *Shaa Tláa* Williams

THE BANGLADESH READER

Edited by Meghna Guhathakurta and Willem van Schendel

THE CZECH READER

Edited by Jan Bažant, Nina Bažantová, and Frances Starn

THE GHANA READER

Edited by Kwasi Konadu and Clifford C. Campbell

THE INDONESIA READER

Edited by Tineke Hellwig and Eric Tagliacozzo

THE RUSSIA READER

Edited by Adele Barker and Bruce Grant

THE SOUTH AFRICA READER

Edited by Clifton Crais and Thomas V. McClendon

THE SRI LANKA READER

Edited by John Clifford Holt

THE LATIN AMERICA READERS
Series edited by Robin Kirk and Orin Starn

THE ARGENTINA READER
Edited by Gabriela Nouzeilles and Graciela Montaldo

THE BRAZIL READER
Edited by Robert M. Levine and John J. Crocitti

THE CHILE READER
Edited by Elizabeth Quay Hutchison, Thomas Miller Klubock, Nara B. Milanich, and Peter Winn

THE COSTA RICA READER
Edited by Steven Palmer and Iván Molina

THE CUBA READER
Edited by Aviva Chomsky, Barry Carr, and Pamela Maria Smorkaloff

THE DOMINICAN REPUBLIC READER
Edited by Eric Paul Roorda, Lauren Derby, and Raymundo González

THE ECUADOR READER
Edited by Carlos de la Torre and Steve Striffler

THE GUATEMALA READER
Edited by Greg Grandin, Deborah T. Levenson, and Elizabeth Oglesby

THE MEXICO READER
Edited by Gilbert M. Joseph and Timothy J. Henderson

THE PARAGUAY READER
Edited by Peter Lambert and Andrew Nickson

THE PERU READER, 2ND EDITION
Edited by Orin Starn, Iván Degregori, and Robin Kirk

THE RIO DE JANEIRO READER
Edited by Daryle Williams, Amy Chazkel, and Paulo Knauss

The Ghana Reader

THE GHANA READER

HISTORY, CULTURE, POLITICS

Kwasi Konadu and Clifford C. Campbell, editors

DUKE UNIVERSITY PRESS *Durham and London* 2016

Printed in the United States of America on acid-free paper ∞
Typeset in Monotype Dante by BW&A Books, Inc.

Library of Congress Cataloging-in-Publication Data
The Ghana reader : history, culture, politics /
Kwasi Konadu and Clifford C. Campbell, eds.
pages cm—(World readers)
Includes bibliographical references and index.
ISBN 978-0-8223-5984-5 (hardcover : alk. paper)
ISBN 978-0-8223-5992-0 (pbk. : alk. paper)
ISBN 978-0-8223-7496-1 (e-book)
1. Ghana—History. 2. Ghana—Civilization.
3. Ghana—Politics and government.
I. Konadu, Kwasi, editor. II. Campbell, Clifford C., editor.
III. Series: World readers.
DT510.G47 2016
966.7—dc23
2015030360

Cover art: Adzewa, a Fante women's group. Photograph by
Clifford Campbell, Accra, September 2009.

produced with a grant from
Figure Foundation
publication of the global nation

Contents

Acknowledgments

The completion of this book was made possible by a multitude of individuals and institutions on all sides of the Atlantic Ocean. We thank our families for their never-taken-for-granted love and support. There are a number of people to whom we owe a debt of gratitude. We are deeply thankful to the various writers, artists, photographers, and institutions that have kindly granted permission to publish extracts of their work. We owe special thanks to Martha Rhule Nyanyi Akorful Tamakloe, Kwame Essien, Adwoa Opong, Kofi Tamakloe, Gertrude Nkrumah, J. H. K. Nketia, Sarah Quarcoo, Dennis Howard, Quweina Roberts, Andrews K. Agyemfra Tettey, Helen Yitah, Kofi Baku, Jean Allman, Kwesi Yankah, Ann Brower Stahl, Kwame Dawes, Msia Kibona Clark, Benjamin Talton, Dela Tsikata, Gerard L. Chouin, Rebecca Wrenn, Ole Justesen, Seestah IMAHKÜS, Kosi Kedem, the late Selena Winsnes, George Abugri, Sally Welsh, Kwabena Akurang-Parry, Bayo Holsey, George M. Bob-Milliar, Akoss Ofori-Mensah, Michael Dwyer, Akosua Adomako Ampofo, Emmanuel K. Sallah, Diana Owusu Antwi, Kassahun Checole, Maria Czop, Perry C. Cartwright, Hannah Bannister, Joseph Bruchac, Hakimah Abdul-Fattah, Peter Froehlich, Harriet Tagoe, Frank Koorevaar, Claire Smith, Adam Hirschberg, Teresa Krauss, Charlotte Cooper, Georgia Glover, Brigid Hamilton-Jones, and David Aremu.

We are grateful for the insightful critiques of the manuscript provided by several anonymous reviewers. We also thank Duke University Press editors Valerie Millholland and Miriam Angress for their support and meticulousness, as well as interns Candela Marini, Mackenzie Cramblit, and Isabel Rios-Torres. Finally, we thank you, the reader, for choosing this book. The usual disclaimers apply.

Introduction

"We put ourselves under the protection of . . . the [local] king and the viceroy, and the next day . . . we set about to begin our sales. . . . The merchants in this country were alerted to our arrival, and then we saw [them make] their way down from the hills and came to buy our goods," wrote a Flemish-speaking merchant who traveled to the Gold Coast (present-day Ghana) around 1479–80.[1] Unlike in most of the Americas, the encounter between the region that became Ghana and Europe was not one of conquest and colonization; rather, it was one where European nationals competed with each other for the good favor and "protection" of indigenous leaders and merchants at a time when the commerce that brought Europe to West Africa was based on gold. Europeans found a vast territory of forests and lagoons connected by the politics of commercial and social networks, peoples residing in sophisticated social and cultural orders and skilled in the arts of trade, agriculture, and gold mining. Gold, in the minds of the interlopers, become shorthand for the region, hence, the Gold Coast. Centuries later, the global trade in gold would be eclipsed by the trafficking in human captives and then a cash crop economy centered almost exclusively on cocoa and other commercially viable resources. Today gold is still a valuable commodity as one of Ghana's largest exports, but the nation of Ghana is also known throughout the world by another commodity that shines—their national soccer team, the Black Stars.

The name "Black Stars" comes directly from pan-Africanist Marcus Garvey and his well-intentioned but ill-fated Black Star Line shipping enterprise, which sought to demonstrate, against the prevailing racism and economic injustice of his time, that (diasporic) Africans could manage their own affairs and compete with others on the world economic stage. Inspired by Garvey, Ghana's first prime minister and president, Kwame Nkrumah, not only consolidated local unrest into a nationalist movement for independence from British colonial rule, but also sought to strengthen its pan-Africanist position and unify the various peoples of emergent Ghana through a national soccer team—the Black Stars. Soccer, therefore, has not so much surpassed the commercial and cultural endowments of Ghana as it has consolidated the identity and resources of a nation that increased its global stock with each Black Stars victory in the team's widely noted performance in the 2010 world cup of soccer.

In the world of sports and for an event that occurs every four years, 2010 is old news. So why invoke Ghana's performance in the 2010 FIFA World Cup? We use soccer, which both unifies and divides Ghana, as an appropriate metaphor for the larger hopes and disappointments a continent and the world outside of it has and continues to invest in Ghana and its resources, and to foreground Ghana's pan-African legacy, its partnership with the United States and Eurasia, and its relations to diasporic groups within and outside its borders. The 2010 World Cup brought all these factors into focus, precisely because it was the first time an African nation hosted the "world's game" since 1930 and because the host South African team was eliminated in the first round, allowing African and world spectators to shift their attention to the Black Stars—not as Ghana's national team, but as Africa's team. En route to the quarterfinals, the Ghanaian team defeated the U.S. national team for the second time and looked poised to be the first African team to reach the finals—with all of (diasporic) Africa behind it! But this moment was not entirely new: Ghana has served, on several critical occasions, as a barometer for Africa and an inspiration to Africa's and Ghana's diaspora in the Americas and in Europe. Ultimately, two European teams advanced to the finals, but the important point here is not Ghana's disastrous exit from the competition after a blown penalty kick; rather, it is that Ghana achieved global visibility on the geopolitical map, highlighting her established status as a strategic international partner of Europe, India, China, and the United States. Barack Obama's much-publicized first presidential trip to Africa—or Ghana, to be exact—further projected Ghana as a "model democracy," and thanks to its relative political stability, Ghana has served strategic military interests for the United States and as a West African base for a myriad of multinational corporations and nongovernmental organizations. In addition, North American– and European-based oil prospectors continue their search for and consolidation of oil resources discovered off the Ghanaian coastline, while Chinese entrepreneurs seek out new markets in Ghana for "African" textile products and engage in (illegal) gold mining. Both its stability and its oil have once again placed the Gold Coast / Ghana in a global economic order not of its own making or choosing, with all of Africa and the world watching their performance.

Since the days of the trans-Saharan trade network from West and North Africa to the lands bordering the Mediterranean and the commerce centered on the Atlantic, the Gold Coast / Ghana has been an active participant in international commerce, politics, and culture, whether the contribution is gold, human captives, cocoa, *kente* cloth, or pan-Africanism, diasporic culture and politics, or the former secretary general of the United Nations, Kofi Annan. In short, the overarching theme throughout Ghana's history and more or less throughout *The Ghana Reader* is the enormous symbolic and pragmatic value Ghana continues to have in global relations relative to its size and place. Of course, taken together, the snapshot of Ghana as a democratic, oil-bearing, and soccer-playing power in West Africa has an array of uneven consequences. For one, many in Ghana view the possession of oil ("black gold") as both a blessing and a burden that regional states like Nigeria have managed poorly, and much of the potential profits from oil would find a home in North America and Europe—a historical condition all too familiar to the former Gold Coast, when gold and human captives were the principal commodities between Europe, West Africa, and the Americas.

Whether their country is a potential oil or soccer giant, Ghanaians view their histories and themselves in diverse ways, and their hopes invested in the Black Stars are no less conflicted than those invested in offshore oil, Pentecostalism, diaspora tourism, or the "elite" tendency to send their children to U.S. and European universities. Like most postcolonies, Ghana has had to grapple with becoming a nation with many histories—indigenous, Islamic, European, migrant African, and Asian—and the different meanings those histories hold in a republic that has yet to adequately balance local, continental, and global concerns. Unlike most postcolonies, Ghana captures the ills and aspirations of Africa; it has done so since 1957, when it became the first sub-Saharan African nation to receive its political independence and its leader, Kwame Nkrumah, articulated a continental vision of a unified and sovereign Africa. But the abrupt end of Nkrumah's tenure as president, the coups that followed, the decline of Ghana's pan-Africanist tradition, and the evolving self-understandings of its people underscore the fascinating yet conflicted nature of the former "model colony" of Britain and the current "model democracy" of the Western world. With all its cultural wealth, endowed ecologies, and historic value, Ghana continually attracts scholars, multinational corporations, Peace Corps and Fulbright participants, a bevy of nongovernmental organizations, and study-abroad and postgraduate students from Europe, Asia, and the Americas. Yet most who are transients may not fully appreciate the intricate subtleties of Ghana's peoples, their cultural histories, or how their dialogue with global and local perspectives, forces, and hopes unfold in their worlds. The editors hope *The Ghana Reader* will facilitate that fuller appreciation for those who come to Ghana through study or travel.

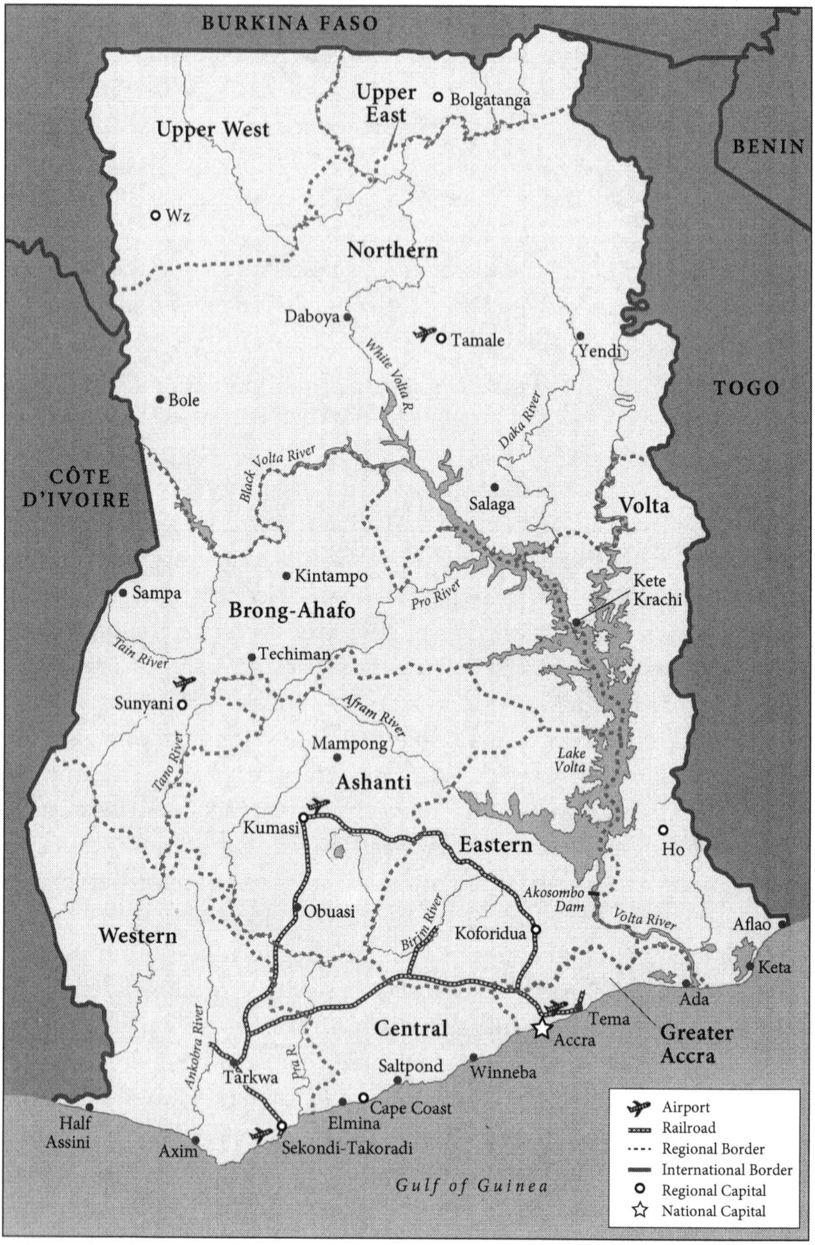

General map of Ghana.

Ghana lies near the equator in West Africa, along the Gulf of Guinea. Its 348 miles of shoreline range from mangrove swamps and coastal sand dunes to freshwater and sandy beaches that border the Atlantic Ocean, while Burkina Faso to the north, Togo to the east, and Côte d'Ivoire (Ivory Coast) to the west forms its political boundaries. Thousands of peoples from these neighboring countries, inclusive of an area between the Gambia and Nigeria, make Ghana their seasonal or permanent home. The moist, semi-deciduous forest of Ghana's southern half gives way to savanna woodland and grasslands in the northern and in some coastal parts of the country. The Tano and Volta Rivers provide natural but not exact markers for the western and eastern ends of the country, respectively, while several other rivers crisscross a landscape dotted with hills, a few mountains, and, in the east, the Kwahu plateau and other highlands. Lake Bosomtwi, Ghana's largest natural lake, is dwarfed in size and importance by the world's largest artificial lake, Lake Volta. Lake Volta is navigable for about 245 miles—carrying goods and people between the north and south—and its Akosombo dam provides hydroelectricity to Ghana and several adjoining countries.

The topography and peoples of Ghana are divided into ten administrative regions, each with its own capital: Greater Accra (Accra), Central (Cape Coast), Eastern (Koforidua), Western (Sekondi-Takoradi), Asante/Ashanti (Kumase), Brong-Ahafo (Sunyani), Northern (Tamale), Upper East (Bolgatanga), Upper West (Wa), and Volta (Ho). Regional ministers and coordinating councils are responsible for the plans and programs of 110 district administrations within the parameters of national development policies and priorities. With a total area of 92,100 square miles, the country is most densely populated in the coastal areas, particularly in the capital, Accra, with about 2.3 million inhabitants, and in the Ashanti (Asante) region, with some 1.8 million inhabitants clustered in and around the regional capital of Kumase. The Ashanti region, with its variant of Akan culture and its well-known history as a former empire, is dominated by tropical rainforest, agriculture, and gold and cocoa production. About half of Ghana's estimated 25 million people fall under the cultural-linguistic group known as Akan, thus they and their language are found largely in the central and southern half of the country, whereas the Mole-Dagbon, Gurma, and Guan and their subgroupings and the Ewe and Gã-Adangme, respectively, populate the northern and southern coastlines of Ghana. Certainly there are links between these cultural groups and their varying and overlapping ecologies of habitation. We have to be careful not to assume a static link, however, between cultural specifics and geography. For instance, in southern Ghana the staple foods are cassava and plantains, and in northern Ghana they are millet and sorghum; however, all eat the major staple foods of various yams and corn (maize), though these crops grow in specific ecologies and among specific (and culturally predominant) groups of people. We tend, therefore, to favor the view that many of these cultural specifics (e.g., clothing, cuisine, art) developed over time and across specific geographies, rather than accept the idea that where people live and what they eat today is the same as, say, three hundred years ago. Thus in terms of the locale of "ethnicities," we included and allowed selections in this *Reader* to talk about cultural groups and their locales throughout the volume rather than in one place.

Many of these peoples migrate within Ghana, intermarry, and transcend cultural and religious boundaries established within each group, as much as some choose to remain within those boundaries, almost purposely setting or perceiving themselves apart from the general populace. An example of this latter phenomenon include, but is certainly not limited to, *zongo* communities, also known as "stranger's quarters," found throughout Ghana, but mostly in urban centers such as Takyiman, Kumase, Accra, and Takoradi. These communities are predominantly, though not exclusively, Muslim, and they are usually found in central and southern Ghana, where large parts of the urbanite population are Christian and where zongos are situated on the periphery of urban centers and are densely populated, with attendant sanitation challenges. Currently almost half the total population lives in cities, and as urbanization increases, no doubt these zongos will grow too, especially in the competitive urban landscapes of Greater Accra and the Ashanti region.

In all ten regions, most people farm, on either a subsistence or a commercial basis. More than half the total population is under age twenty-four, and though urbanization is on the rise, half of the population still lives in rural areas, 80 percent of these in villages. Naturally, rural peoples are the backbone of the national economy; the agrarian sector, for instance, employs approximately 60 percent of the total Ghanaian workforce, which averages about 10 to 11 million. The agrarian and natural resources sector, with the exception of fisheries, produce cocoa (second in value only to gold as the largest export), rice, coffee, timber, industrial diamonds, manganese, bauxite, wood products, textiles, pineapples, cotton, plantains, and coco-yams for some indigenous markets, but largely for export.

Though Ghana abounds in natural resources and has 33.6 million acres of arable land suitable for crops or livestock, only 12 percent of all arable land is used. This paradox between ecological endowment and abandonment also plays out in the social and economic divisions within the country. The line from poverty to prosperity flows from the largely Islamic northern to the increasingly Christian southern parts of Ghana, where one finds other paradoxes too: some four thousand manufacturing industries are concentrated in the coastal zone but with attendant pollution (via hazardous chemicals), waste management, and migration issues, whereas villages tend to be cleaner than cities but enjoy a lower quality of life due to the asymmetrical distribution of resources and investments made outside of coastal enclaves. The dichotomy between northern and southern Ghana has its origins in the early formation of the region through its indigenous polities and settlements, when and how Islamic and other migrants moved into the region Europeans referred to as the Gold Coast, and, of course, with whom these European interlopers developed relations and the paths by which the Gold Coast became a British colony and then a self-governing nation.

The historical processes by which Ghana became a nation have been detailed elsewhere, but some general outline is necessary.[2] There is no agreement on how and when the region that became Ghana was first populated and by whom, but the archaeological, biomedical, and oral-historical evidence for early societies in central and southern Ghana points to food-producing mixed economies based on hunting and farming (e.g., oil palm and high-calorie root crops) that facilitated population and settlement growth, communal labor for forest clearance with stone (and later iron) tools, reproductive strategies during periods of malaria adaptation, and the development of a spiritual culture tied to the ecological cycles of the forest and its fringes and sacred ancestral sites.[3] Akan- or Twi-speaking agriculturalists and hunters are the only ones that claim to be indigenous to the region, and their migration stories and ancient sites of ancestral beginnings—in sharp contrast to others with much *later* migration histories—place them all within the modern boundaries of Ghana. These peoples populated and then exploited the water, wood, gold, iron, salt, kola, oil palm, root crops, and botanical and animal resources of the dense forest and its savanna and coastal peripheries over the past two millennia. They designed cultural and sociopolitical structures to deal with diseases, power and authority, land and labor, and the growth of durable settlements, which, in time, became polities of varying sizes and complexities. For the northern part of Ghana, the archaeological dates for a number of excavated sites show later occupation than those for the edge of the northern forest—a forest that covers the central and southern half of present-day Ghana—and within the dense tropical forest extending southward to the coast, where we find much later evidence for coastal peoples, such as the Eti/Etsi, and the Akan, or specifically Fante, migrants who would displace, conquer, or absorb them.[4]

Between the fourteenth and fifteenth centuries, Islamic and non-Islamic

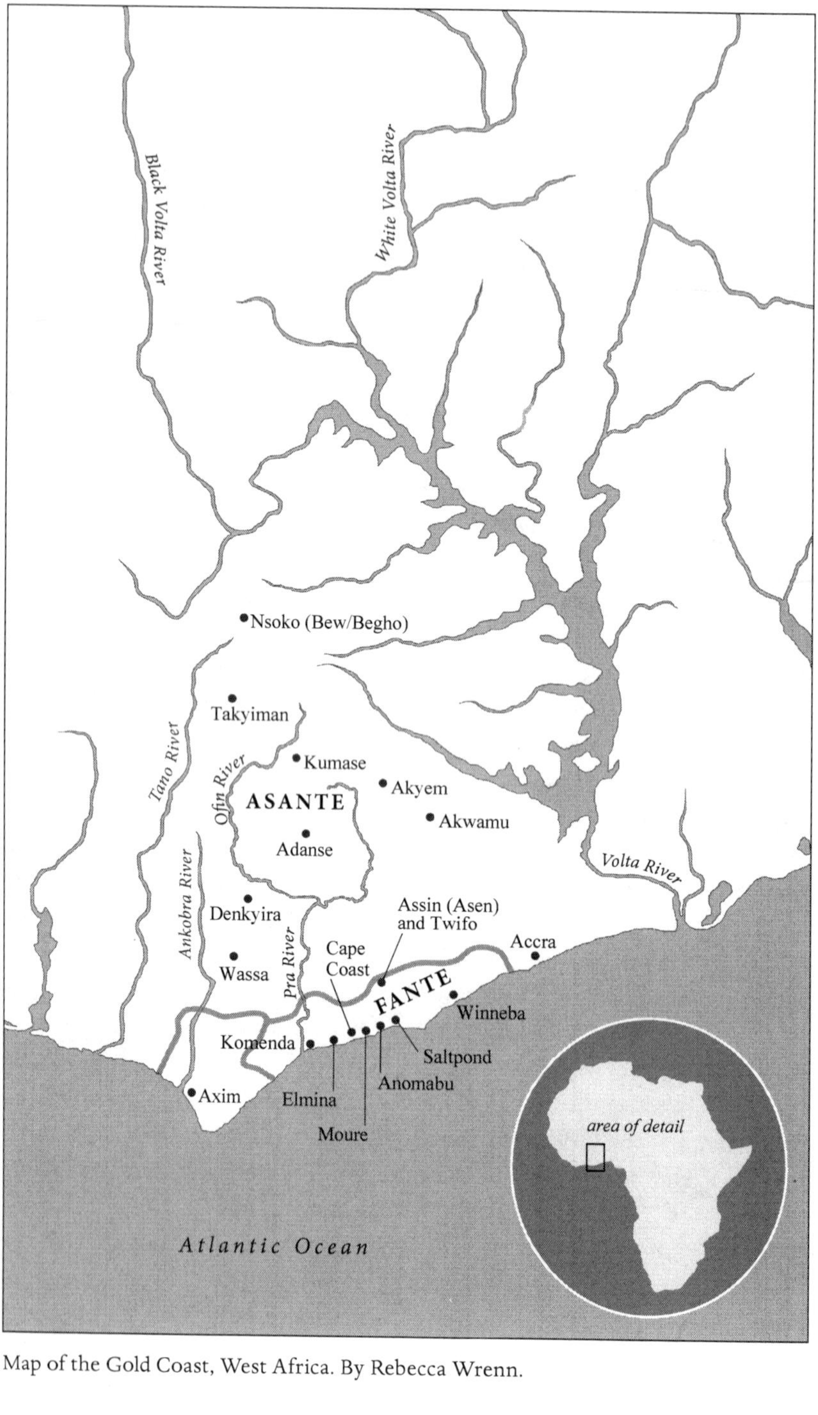

Map of the Gold Coast, West Africa. By Rebecca Wrenn.

migrants settled the northern and northwest savanna and perhaps the northeast region, while peoples such as the Gã and Ewe began to settle along the southeastern littoral. By then, Akan(Twi)-speaking peoples dominated much of the region, subjugating and trading with those to the north and northwest of the forest and both African groups and European nationals along the coastline. The Akan were not a singular people but rather various groups that came to fall under a shared cultural-linguistic umbrella, thus their polities—Bono, Akani, Denkyira, Akwamu, Akyem, Fante, and Asante—controlled much of present-day Ghana and competed with one another over land and valued resources, only to come under Asante hegemony in the eighteenth century. Subjugated local polities paid tribute to their overlords in form of captives, gold, and other valuable commodities that would ultimately find their way into the hands of private and national European companies, beginning with the Portuguese in the late fifteenth century. These companies or the governments under which they operated paid "rent" to various local rulers for land on which their fortified bases were constructed and provided gifts to facilitate trade or the opening of trade routes. Once the various European merchant companies established their coastal holdings (i.e., forts, dungeons, trading posts) and developed trade relations with and, at times, against indigenous polities, commerce that formerly flowed through the northern corridors via trans-Saharan trade was reoriented to the Guinea coast, privileging the burgeoning Atlantic commerce. New coastal settlements and polities emerged, and the urbanization and militarization of states increased along the littoral and in its hinterlands.

The commerce in gold, metals, cloths, beads, firearms, and enslaved peoples also increased, especially in the seventeenth and eighteenth centuries, when the Asante empire controlled an area approximate to much of present-day Ghana and extending into Togo and Ivory Coast and where Fante merchants served as middlemen in the commerce of imported goods and exported captives between the coast and forest. The European demand for African commodities and captives simulated a kind of political cannibalism in the forest and on the coast, whereby African polities vanquished one another for coveted foreign trade goods, including ammunition and arms, as Europeans competed and warred against each other for the dominant polity's good favor. At the beginning of the nineteenth century all the peoples along the coast and in much of northern Ghana were under Asante rule, as part of "Greater Asante," which exercised its authority through the Asante capital of Kumase.

By the end of the nineteenth century, the once dominant Asante Empire had spent much of its energies maintaining control over its subjugated peoples, quelling rebellions, and enduring a bitter and deadly civil war, before capitulating to British overlordship and becoming a Crown Colony in 1901. The process of British colonialism—armed with commercial and Christianizing interests—began on the coast, first among those African communities who had been trade partners and anti-Asante allies, and then proceeding into the arid savanna region under the pretense of trade while offering northern societies treaties of "protection" and finally invading Asante in the dense forest. Throughout the nineteenth century Asante and Britain remained at odds, signing various treaties of peace that only forestalled the inevitable. The March 1874 Anglo-Asante Treaty of Fomena was the beginning of the end of the Asante Empire: it allowed the Asante heartland to remain independent, but ceded those conquered territories south of Asante to the British, who by August converted these "protected" territories into its Gold Coast Colony, with a colonial governor and legislative council. Soon the British would sign treaties of protection with Asante's northern territories, not only to seize these grassland territories away from a destabilized Asante but also to fend off the Germans and the French, who both expressed imperial interest in the area in the 1890s. By 1901, the former Asante Empire or Greater Asante was effectively divided into three British colonial dependencies—the Gold Coast Colony, the Crown Colony of Asante, and the Protectorate of the Northern Territories—and these three entities pursued distinct policies that were often at odds with each other. By systematically severing the southern and northern parts of Greater Asante and then seizing Asante proper at a time when it sought to "modernize" along industrial lines and even seek British protectorate status through negotiations, the British imperialists simply reconfigured a politically united region under one empire (Asante) into the colonial Gold Coast under another (Britain). At the conclusion of World War I in late 1918, Britain was awarded German Togoland; the British, for administrative purposes, added German Togo's northern districts to the Protectorate of the Northern Territories and its southern districts to the Gold Coast Colony. Nonetheless, the peoples and the geography of former Greater Asante remained approximately the same as the colonial Gold Coast, extending into the republic of Ghana in 1957.[5]

Though the coast became the locus of the colonial government and the influential local intellectuals and radicals seduced by its ideology resided in the southern half of the colony, the dichotomy between the north and the south had already been laid over the preceding centuries and through the presence and predation of the Europeans and their forty-plus slaving forts, which still dot the Ghanaian shoreline. It is not surprising, therefore, that a local elite or intelligentsia developed in the southern part of the Gold Coast / Ghana and that its members were almost all trained in British law, literature, religion, and cultural or ideological values (all of which we can call "the colonial package")—in contradistinction with the "Northern Territories," as northern Ghana was called. The missionary and colonial classroom and its book depots were the laboratories in which both elite and nonelite (and their children) encountered the "colonial package" and through which socioeconomic aspirations were shaped in colonial society.[6] A large number of those aspirants were newly schooled young men as well as ambitious but socially powerless young men. Hence men became the local clergy, clerks, legislative council members, lawyers, intellectuals, and urbanites—all conditioned by Christian beliefs, teachings, and literature and predominantly along the coast. These men also shaped matters of morality and colonial policy, and often responded to political crisis in the colony by producing early nationalist works of history. This literary activism had the aim of sharing power with the colonialists rather than ending colonialism, wherein nationalists sought to make the case for their competencies in both indigenous and British culture and establish that they were thus best qualified to mediate between the colonial administration and the colonized peoples. Fante intellectuals like John Mensah Sarbah and Casely Hayford epitomized such "colonial middlemen." Both were trained as lawyers in British jurisprudence but had to be equally competent in Akan "customary" law, enabling them to become influential intermediaries in the bevy of local court cases in which political aspirants viewed themselves as more "civilized" and "modern" and to become intellectual nationalists who could argue for a united Gold Coast within the British Empire. In fact, it was such intellectuals and a group of Asante radicals or refugees domiciled in the Gold Coast Colony who made the case for a united Gold Coast Colony with the Crown Colony of Asante and the Northern Territories, albeit under British rule.

Other than the old "divide-and-rule" tactic, Britain had no clear colonial strategy for the Gold Coast, so it turned to local institutions and officials that could be used to facilitate its economic interests (including the labor needed to produce or acquire valued resources), the creation of new markets for its industrial goods, and its diffusion of a colonial ideology centered around ideas of Christian morality, civilization, and modernity. The result was the awkward policy of "indirect" rule, where the colonizers depended on the local institutions and officials of the old (now colonized) and where the colonizers were themselves divided in implementing their own policy of divide-and-rule. For instance, when British "indirect rule" experienced a crisis in the 1920s, British colonial anthropologist R. S. Rattray's *Ashanti*

Law and Constitution (1929) was used as a blueprint by colonial officials, who restored the Asante Confederacy—the political framework of Greater Asante—along "traditional" lines, essentially giving it authority over its former imperial divisions, in 1935.[7] Asante proper, as a Crown Colony, only fell under the jurisdiction of the Legislative Council of the Gold Coast in 1948. But from the early twentieth century on, there continued to be much conflict between the British colonial governors of the Gold Coast and the chief commissioners in Asante over whether Asante proper should be integrated into the Gold Coast Colony or remain independent of it. In effect, the implementers of divide-and-rule were themselves bitterly divided.

The policy of "indirect" colonial rule certainly had its troubles, and in some ways it created its own demise by subverting indigenous structures of authority, which generated a morass of succession and land dispute court cases for which lawyer-nationalists like Sarbah and J. B. Danquah gained greater notoriety and influence, and Danquah's influence in coastal politics would shape the formation of an independent Ghana. It was Danquah who claimed (falsely) that the Akan—who populated the central and southern half of the colony—migrated from the former Ghana Empire of old. And in 1957, after some struggle with political allies and then enemies such as Kwame Nkrumah, Danquah proposed the name "Ghana" for the independent nation.[8] Danquah used history to engender national and "race" pride, thus during the era of decolonization, the name "Ghana" was more than symbolic in importance for the nationalist movements of the Gold Coast. History was a key political force in a colonial Gold Coast, where mass movements and riots prompted accommodations, since the colonial administration was unable to curtail or crush the mass urban and rural upheavals that pushed for reforms of the 1940s. The former instruments of "indirect rule" (that is, the so-called traditional officials) provided little leadership, and because they could not facilitate the goals of the various upheavals, they were discarded by the colonial state in favor of the urbanized nationalists, such as Danquah, who positioned themselves as the solution to the crisis of the state. Indeed, "decolonization in the late 1950s did not follow either from the failure of reform or from loss of control. The nationalists were simply easier to persuade—indeed did not need to be persuaded—that political independence was the solution to the economic and social problems of colonial society."[9]

On the eve of political independence, the political divisions were clear. In 1947, Danquah founded the United Gold Coast Convention (UGCC) political party and invited Nkrumah to join; two years year after joining the UGCC, Nkrumah split with Danquah over the appropriate path to independence and founded the Convention People's Party (CPP), which embraced the idea of a united Gold Coast with a unitary constitution that would include Asante proper. Some in Asante favored this approach, while others, such as the National Liberation Movement (NLM), founded in Kumase in 1954, struggled with Nkrumah's CPP and it demanded Asante self-determination in the form of an autonomous Asante within the Gold Coast configuration or Asante secession. This demand clashed with the anticipated blueprint of a Ghana republic that did not afford Asante "special" parliamentary consideration, a blueprint worked out with the British government.[10] In the end, the Asantehene (leader of the Asante), officeholders, and intellectuals "usurped the leadership of the 'young men' within the NLM and transformed it into a parliamentary party that reached a compromise solution with Nkrumah's CPP; articulated the position of the *amanhene* [divisional leaders of territories within Asante] in the republic's constitution; and provided Asante with a semblance of regional autonomy. This marked a key victory for the established order within Asante, and the workers and farmers who supported NLM remained aliens to the contemporary state, muted and without political recourse."[11] In sum, the polities, politics, and peoples of old became, more or less, the factors and forces that shaped the new nation of Ghana in the mid-twentieth century.

But over that century of gestation, Ghana was also influenced by those whom we often do not consider in the typical colonial equation of the colonizer (Britain) and the colonized. For instance, diasporic African groups, especially those from the Caribbean basin and North America, have lived and made significant contributions to the Gold Coast / Ghana since the early to mid-nineteenth century, with continuous streams of settlers and visitors since the 1960s.[12] Lebanese merchants and their families—those they came with beginning in the late nineteenth century and those they spawned in subsequent generations—are also an important part of Ghana's domestic economic past and present. The Lebanese and Indians have thrived in hospitality and commercial merchandising, thus their presence has been formidable, especially in tourism and, more recently, heritage-tourism.[13] Finally, Chinese laborers also came to the colony in the late nineteenth century, and although their numbers were insignificant, Ghana's oil and industrialization and China's broadening role in Ghanaian affairs, especially its economy, suggest that China will play a more significant role in the future of the Ghanaian nation and the weight of its past and present worlds.

The Ghana Reader aims to introduce readers to the many worlds of Ghana and how political and cultural views have moved the nation through its histories. Though it is not designed as an all-inclusive text, we hope readers will find *The Ghana Reader* engaging, providing key insights and a set of perspectives about Ghana. While introductory notes will place each reading in its historical context, we are less concerned with chronology than with ambience and deeper resonances. Readers will meet and hear the voices of many arresting characters in the market women, farmers, itinerant traders, migrant workers, intellectuals, politicians, clergy, musicians, artisans, and folks who constitute Ghana's citizenry. Readers will encounter the absorbing debates and dialogue of the subjects and authors of each reading. They will take in the impressions of Ghanaians, foreign travelers, and modern scholars. In the end, we hope that the reader—whether a student, a traveler, or merely an interested general reader—will finish the book with a sense of having experienced an extraordinary country firsthand. We also hope that the themes and controversies explored by our writers will provide substance for discussion and debate. At the core of the volume lies an attempt to convey something of the multiple histories of Ghana's development as a nation. *The Ghana Reader* seeks to show how these histories intersect, illuminating the tension between long-standing processes of national state formation and the responses they have produced at Ghana's rural and urban grassroots. We hope that *The Ghana Reader* will introduce many to the study of Ghana in a way that will make them at once sympathetic toward Ghana's birth and its subsequent challenges (and, in a way, Africa's challenges), as well as more appreciative of its cultural richness and transformative potential.

Our criteria for selecting pieces for inclusion in *The Ghana Reader* have been relatively straightforward. First, we have sought to evoke a variety of voices, so that the worlds of Ghana will emerge vividly. Second, we have put a premium on pieces that are of critical importance but not usually accessible to lay readers. Third, we have made every effort to present selections that can be easily appreciated by readers without background experience in African/Ghanaian history, even though some of these selections come from academic sources. Most of the pieces chosen were originally written for a general audience; each, we hope, is successful in clarifying issues, piquing interest, and stimulating thought. Finally, we have privileged brevity in some instances and where we thought appropriate to the content chosen and substantial excerpts in others to allow for as many integral voices as possible. Numerous works that have made essential contributions to our understanding of Ghana have been omitted simply due to considerations of space. Many of these materials will be included in a supplemental list of readings for those who wish to delve more deeply.

The Ghana Reader is organized into six parts. Each part focuses on a particular subtheme, consisting of multiple perspectives flowing from it while enlarging the reader's perspective on the ways in which the cultural groups and historic polities of old came together and continue into the present as the nation of Ghana, including major nuances accompanying such processes. Against this backdrop, part I is thus concerned with the question of the origins of the nation of Ghana, using oral and archaeological sources to explore its "precolonial" polities and settlements and the peoples who eventually became the citizens of Ghana. Part II continues the story into the sixteenth and early eighteenth centuries, focusing on the coastal relations between Gold Coast societies and European nationals, and what that interaction tells us about the peoples and places on the Gold Coast littoral as well as in the forest-savanna interior. The perspectives in part III graphically illustrate how the aforementioned encounters and the sociopolitical transformations embedded in the transatlantic slave system created the climate for so-called legitimate trade and the colonial Gold Coast by the end of the nineteenth century. Part IV explores Ghana's rather brief but influential colonial past. Colonialism was not simply territorial occupation and an exploitation of valued human and material resources, but also an ideological occupation of the psyche that would shape Ghana's tenure as an independent republic. As the first African nation south of the Sahara to receive political independence from British colonial rule, Ghana became a beacon of pan-Africanism and the nationalist movement pushing for an independent Africa under its charismatic leader and first prime minister and later president, Kwame Nkrumah. Part V examines the Nkrumah and post-Nkrumah years, a period characterized by initial and great optimism but soon besieged by coups, corruption, violence, and socioeconomic instability that continued until the late 1990s, when Ghana began to rebound. In part VI, we look ahead facing the past and exploring the near future through a range of critical matters: relations with the African diaspora in Ghana and Ghanaians abroad, the rise of Pentecostal Christianity, the prospects of oil revenue against the backdrop of poor living conditions for many, the place of cell phones and related gadgets and the ideological baggage these tools bring from outside Ghana, and more.

In sum, we hope *The Ghana Reader* will not only introduce many to the study of Ghana in a way that charts the dynamic formation of Ghanaian society and culture, but also allow them to simultaneously appreciate the pain and beauty of that (trans)formation and the potential that lies in Ghanaian peoples' hands. Indeed, only the peoples of Ghana can and should shape what time will ultimately tell.

Notes

1. Eustache de la Fosse, *Voyage a la Côte occidentale d'Afrique, en Portugal et en Espagne (1479–1480)*, edited by R. Foulche-Delbosc (Paris: Alfonse Picard et Fils, 1897), 12.
2. Interested readers should consult, among other works, Kwasi Konadu, *The Akan Diaspora in the Americas* (New York: Oxford University Press, 2010), esp. chaps. 2, 3, and 7; D. E. K. Amenumey, *Ghana: A Concise History from Pre-Colonial Times to the Twentieth Century* (Accra: Woeli, 2008); Roger S. Gocking, *The History of Ghana* (Westport, CT: Greenwood, 2005); Ivor Wilks, *Forests of Gold: Essays on the Akan and the Kingdom of Asante* (Athens: Ohio University Press, 1993); and Ray A. Kea, *Settlements, Trade, and Polities in the Seventeenth-Century Gold Coast* (Baltimore: Johns Hopkins University Press, 1982).
3. See Gérard L. F. Chouin, "The 'Big Bang' Theory Reconsidered: Framing Early Ghanaian History," *Transactions of the Historical Society of Ghana*, n.s., 14 (2012): 13–40; Konadu, *Akan Diaspora*, 27–54; Gérard L. F. Chouin and Christopher DeCorse, "Prelude to the Atlantic Trade: New Perspectives on Southern Ghana's Pre-Atlantic History, 800–1500," *Journal of African History* 51, no. 2 (2010): 123–45; A. Norman Klein, "Toward a New Understanding of Akan Origins," *Africa* 66, no. 2 (1996): 248–73; P. Shinnie and A. Shinnie, *Early Asante* (Calgary: Department of Archeology, the University of Calgary, 1995); A. Norman Klein, "Slavery and Akan Origins?," *Ethnohistory* 41, no. 4 (1994): 627–56.
4. Ann B. Stahl, "Early Food Production in West Africa: Rethinking the Role of the Kintampo Culture," *Current Anthropology* 27, no. 5 (1986): 534–35, and "Reinvestigation of Kintampo 6 Rock Shelter, Ghana: Implications for the Nature of Culture Change," *African Archaeological Review* 3 (1985): 146–47. For the coastal and eastern parts of the region, see E. K. Agorsah, "Before the Flood: The Golden Volta Basin," *Nyame Akuma* 41 (1994): 35, and D. Calvocoressi and N. David, "A New Survey of Radiocarbon and Thermoluminescene Dates for West Africa," *Journal of African History* 20, no. 1 (1979): 1–29.
5. For more on these matters, see Kwasi Konadu, "Euro-African Commerce and Social Chaos: Akan Societies in the Nineteenth and Twentieth Centuries," *History in Africa* 36 (2009): 265–92; Ivor Wilks, *Asante in the Nineteenth Century: The Structure and Evolution of a Political Order* (1979; reprint, New York: Cambridge University Press, 1989), and *One Nation, Many Histories: Ghana Past and Present* (Accra: Anansesem, 1996).
6. See Stephanie Newell, *Literary Culture in Colonial Ghana: How to Play the Game of Life* (Bloomington: Indiana University Press, 2002).
7. Wilks, *Asante in the Nineteenth Century*, 124.
8. Ray Jenkins, "William Ofori Atta, Nnambi Azikiwe, J. B. Danquah and the 'Grilling' of W. E. F. Ward of Achimota in 1935," *History in Africa* 21 (1994): 180.
9. Richard C. Crook, "Decolonization, the Colonial State, and Chieftaincy in the Gold Coast," *African Affairs* 85, no. 338 (1986): 83.
10. Jean M. Allman, "The Youngmen and the Porcupine: Class, Nationalism and Asante's Struggle for Self-Determination, 1954–57," *Journal of African History* 31 (1990): 264, 267.
11. Konadu, "Euro-African Commerce," 281.
12. Konadu, *Akan Diaspora*, 205–12, 228–33.
13. Emmanuel K. Akyeampong, "Race, Identity and Citizenship in Black Africa: The Case of the Lebanese in Ghana," *Africa* 76, no. 3 (2006): 297–323.

I

One Nation, Many Histories

An understanding of Ghana must begin with the cultural groups that came to populate the region later called the Gold Coast (renamed Ghana in 1957), and with a recognition of the historical axes of commonality and diversity that caution against unitary readings of Ghanaian identity. The concept of a Ghanaian nation is not a fairly new innovation that originated in the nationalist context of the 1950s, but a product of the country's multiple local histories and its uneven historical relations with the world within and the world beyond its forest-savanna boundaries. Indeed, the idea of "one nation, many histories" underscores the multiple histories and historic pathways through which the Ghanaian "nation" was born in the mid-twentieth century.

In part I, we have taken a chronological approach to the early peopling of Ghana. The ultimate origins of any group of people is often buried under the soil on which their ancient ancestors lived and traveled, and because our most advanced techniques can only tell us partially what people did, we have few ways to know who they were and why they did what (we think) they did. Our goal, therefore, is not to resolve these vexed questions of origins but rather to introduce you to the known peoples and places of the deep past—that is, the trailblazing women and men, sacred places and matrilineal structures, and sociopolitical developments that have all shaped our evolving understanding of early Ghanaian societies. Archaeological and oral data dominate the means by which we trace how early societies moved through their histories. Taken together, archaeological and oral sources simultaneously expose and fill in each other's gaps, especially where documents do not exist and where the key methodological and theoretical assumptions of historical linguistics remain under revision and debate.

There is much that we do not know and will never know about the lives of the ancients—called *tetefoɔ* in the Twi (Akan) language—who made the semideciduous forest and the grassland and coastal environs their homeland. But our current knowledge of this region and its peopling suggests the central and southern areas have been populated for at least the last two millennia, and in the process of movement and settlement its peoples created relatively large and long-lasting settlements in the forest and on its fringes. Who were they? There is no way to know with any certainty. They, however, were certainly kindred or coalesced groups of peoples who came to see themselves as farmers and hunters (and pastoralists in the northern regions) with a food-producing economy, producers of gold and iron in the interior and on the coast (by at least 600 CE [Common Era]), merchants engaged in local and regional commerce, spiritualists with a holistic understanding of spiritual and temporal realities (based on the high correlation between sacred groves and ancient settlements), and forgers of settlements and polities of varying complexities.

The above profile of the ancient designers of early societies is a composite sketch that is not without lingering questions. Accumulative research of the past five decades suggests these peoples were in fact proto-Akan culture bearers, but there is no scholarly consensus, and other candidates—such as the Guan or the peoples of ancient Kintampo settlements—are peoples about which we know relatively little to nothing. If there is a bias in this portrait, it is in the collective evidence and where or to whom it points. By the fifteenth century, there is little doubt, the various peoples who became known as Akan or Twi speakers dominated the forested and coastal regions, and these groups (organized into large family groupings or matriclans) claimed to be autochthons and thus adopted a "vertical" migration story to their place(s) of settlement—either emerging from "holes in the ground" or descending from the sky via golden chains—thereby making them ineligible as immigrants. Other groups that settled the Gold Coast / Ghana, such as the coastal Gã-Adangme and Ewe or northern Islamic societies, have documented migratory histories of a later date and therefore do not claim to be indigenous to the region. What the Akan claim to land and settlement reveals is not the veracity of their accounts but that the remembered versions of ancient migratory stories were by those who were already settled in unoccupied or conquered lands, hence a homogeneous claim across a wide geographic area and where their major polities and peoples dotting sixteenth- to early twentieth-century European maps remained consistently in place. Finally, these claims are not about origins of peoples per se, but for our purposes, they point to what might have been some of the earlier processes of social and cultural integration among groups of strangers eventually creating composite identities. This was "nation" building then; much later, the mid-twentieth century would have its own version.

Ancestral Faces

Kwesi Brew

Kwesi Brew (1928–2007) was educated at the University of Ghana and worked in Ghana's civil service, serving as a longtime diplomat and as an ambassador to Mexico and Senegal. One of West Africa's most significant twentieth-century poets, Kwesi Brew was born in 1928 in Cape Coast, Ghana. Cape Coast lies on the Atlantic Ocean and was an important site of early encounters with European merchants and later colonialists. It is therefore not surprising to find in Brew's poems the themes of encounter, recollection, ancestry, and careful attention to the rhythm of local cultural understandings and practices. In Ancestral Faces, *Brew reminds readers of the intimate connection between the living and those who came before them; this thematic link remains a core understanding for many in Ghana. Brew also reminds us it is appropriate to introduce readers to a place (Ghana) and its peoples by beginning with those ancient ones who shaped what eventually became Ghana in the mid-twentieth century.*

They sneaked into the limbo of time
But could not muffle the gay jingling
Brass bells on the frothy necks
Of the sacrificial sheep that limped and nodded after them;
They could not hide the moss on the bald pate
Of their reverent heads;
And the gnarled backs of the *wawa* tree;
Nor the rust on the ancient state-swords;
Nor the skulls studded with grinning cowries;
They could not silence the drums,
The fiber of their souls and ours—The drums that whisper to us
  behind black sinewy hands.
They gazed
And sweeping like white locusts through the forests
Saw the same men, slightly wizened,

Shuffle their sandaled feet to the same rhythms,
They heard the same words of wisdom uttered
Between puffs of pale blue smoke:
They saw us,
And said: They have not changed!

The Holocene Archaeology of Ghana

Ann Brower Stahl

We know comparatively very little about the earliest peoples of the region that became Ghana. Matters concerning the ancients appearing in Brew's poem remain obscured by our inadequate techniques and the deep gaps in our knowledge. Archaeology, however, has helped to fill some of these important gaps in Ghanaian prehistory by interpreting material culture to tell us something about the advent of sedentism, agriculture, iron technology, urbanism, and long-distance commerce. In The Holocene Archaeology of Ghana, *anthropological archaeologist Ann Brower Stahl, professor and chair of the Anthropology Department at the University of Victoria (Canada), focuses on the Holocene epoch (i.e., the past ten thousand years) in the archaeology of Ghana. As a scholar who has studied daily life in the rural Banda area of west central Ghana since the mid-1980s, Stahl offers important insights into the relationship between material culture and identity against a series of dramatic changes. In those changes, mobile hunting-gathering gave way to increased sedentism and agricultural production; iron metallurgy was added to the technological repertoire; and societies became enmeshed in interregional exchange networks, resulting in changes in social complexity and foreshadowing the European presence in West Africa.*

We have a better understanding of variability in the Later Iron Age (LIA). Long-distance trade linkages were forged and complex polities emerged, first in the wooded savanna and subsequently in the forest. . . . Northward-looking exchange relations dominated the first half of the first millennium BP [Before the Present]. A gradual but crucial shift in the gravity of exchange accompanied the arrival of Europeans on the West African coast beginning in the fifteenth century. Trade that formerly moved northward across the Sahara was increasingly funneled southward to European middlemen. As a result, the importance of forest polities grew. Our understanding of how LIA societies were affected by these external connections was initially based on Arab and European documents; however, archaeological evidence has come to play an increasingly important role in our efforts to reconstruct

Paramount Chief and Attendants, oil on canvas by Kofi Antubam, from *African Art: The Years since 1920*, by Marshall Ward Mount (Bloomington: Indiana University Press, 1973), 126.

LIA Ghanaian societies. Drawing on both historical and archaeological sources, [Merrick] Posnansky suggested that the growth of trade was accompanied by movements of people into uninhabited areas. He identified several factors that may have contributed to the southward shift in the focus of settlement and exchange: an increased demand for gold in Europe; two centuries of drought that followed a period of increased humidity from the eleventh to the sixth centuries BP; and the Black Death, which may have spread across the Sahara in the sixth century BP. The growth of towns may also relate to the increased importance of slaves in the Gold Coast economy as previously dispersed peoples aggregated as a means of protection. I begin by considering the forging of trade relations with the middle Niger and its impact on savanna woodland societies, then consider sites that postdate European maritime contacts with the Gold Coast. . . .

The trans-Saharan caravan trade that linked Arab North Africa with the Sudanic zone was well established by the eighth century BP. Islamic scholars left written accounts of Sudanic kingdoms, and historians relied heavily on these documents to reconstruct the complex history of successive

Sudanic kingdoms [ancient Wagadu (Ghana), Mali, Songhai]. Documents provided an Arab-centric view of these societies and suggested that they developed as a result of Arab contact. Recent archaeological research along the middle Niger demonstrated that interregional trade in raw materials and food predated Arab contact, suggesting that contact with Arab North Africa stimulated, but did not necessarily initiate, the growth of complex societies in the Sudan.

Early historians were intrigued by documentary references to a place variably identified as Bighu, Biʿu, or Biku, reputed to be a source of Sudanic gold. Most scholars agreed that Bew was located somewhere in Ghana, and historians linked the name with the site of Begho on the northern margins of the Ghana forest. Both Goody and Wilks argued that Begho was an entrepot where Akan gold from the southern forest was exchanged for northern commodities—salt, cloth, and copper alloys. Historical sources suggested that Mande-speaking traders (Wangara, Dyula) led caravans laden with Saharan goods south to Begho, beyond which they could not penetrate due to dense forest and the ubiquity of trypanosomiasis (sleeping sickness), which affected their pack animals. Here they exchanged their wares for gold transported by human portage from the forest goldfields. Documents suggest that Begho was sacked by Asante armies early in the eighteenth century, and scholars believe that the town was abandoned as a result.

Oral histories describe the organization of the former town into distinct residential quarters. The Brong quarter was home to Akan-speaking Brong peoples, presumed to be the ancestors of Brong [Bono] who live in the area today; the Kramo was home to Mande-speaking merchants whose origins lay in the Niger bend area; and a third quarter, Dwinfuor, was occupied by artisans. Archaeological evidence suggests that a fourth quarter, the Nyarko, predates the occupation of other residential districts. Oral sources suggest that it was home to a group of mixed origins. The archaeological site consists of approximately 1,500 low mounds, many presumed to be the remains of collapsed compounds. These mounds are clustered into four areas, each separated from the others by a distance of a kilometer or two, thought to represent the discrete quarters described by oral-historical accounts. The term Begho may refer to an area larger than the site near Hani, and neighboring towns may have shared in the Sudanic trade.

Excavations by West African Trade Project personnel between 1970 and 1979 tested all residential quarters, as well as several neighboring industrial sites. The resultant sequence, based on radiocarbon dates and datable imports, suggests an occupation from the eighth through the second century BP. Full publication of excavation results is awaited; however, the sequence has been outlined in several publications. They emphasize several themes: (1) The site is older than was expected based on historical sources; (2) there is considerable evidence for artisanal activity, which appears to be influenced by connections with the middle Niger; (3) the decline of Begho is related to the rise of Asante in the southern forest; and (4) there is continuity in ceramic style from the main period of occupation at Begho to the present.

Documents suggested that Begho developed in response to Mande traders moving south from centers on the middle Niger (i.e., Jenne) in the thirteenth or fourteenth centuries; however, radiocarbon dates suggest that part of the site predates the trans-Saharan trade by two to three centuries. Ceramics from the Nyarko quarter were distinctive and included a high proportion of red, design-painted pottery. Two radiocarbon dates from this area of the site point to an initial occupation in the eighth century BP. Thus it appears that Mande traders probably came into contact with people already resident in the area who were exploiting locally available gold resources. Posnansky has stressed that Begho was a merchant center, not a state. Excavations at the Brong, Kramo, and Dwinfuor quarters document the period of peak occupation from the fifth to the second centuries BP, a period of intensified contact with societies of the middle Niger. These contacts are evidenced in exotic goods including beads, copper, a piece of glass, and several pieces of sixteenth-century Chinese porcelain.

At its height, a variety of artisanal specialties was practiced at Begho, several of which probably derive from Sudanic societies. Textile production is attested by numerous spindle whorls, many of which were painted and resemble spindle whorls from the important merchant town of Jenne Jeno on the Niger River. Today much of the cloth woven in Ghana is produced on narrow strip looms. Strips are sewn together to create large cloths. Historians of textile production suggest that strip weaving is Sudanic in origin and was introduced to Volta basin societies through mercantile connections. A brass foundry located in the Dwinfuor quarter yielded hundreds of crucibles and probably signals northern influence. Finished brass vessels, often adorned with Arabic script, were imported into the savanna woodland area and may have provided the inspiration for several innovations in ceramic forms including the sharp angles or carinations between rims and necks, neck and body, or body and base that appear as new elements on medieval pottery at Begho. The medieval Islamic brassware that was its inspiration is included in the state paraphernalia of modern Volta basin chieftaincies.

There is also evidence for ivory working at Begho, and two examples of ivory side-blown trumpets were found in third- and fourth-century BP contexts. Side-blown trumpets are important regalia among contemporary and historic Akan peoples (e.g., Asante). Again, Posnansky traces these instruments to the north. Ceramic weights are another indicator of northern influence. Chipped, shaped potsherds from Begho conform quite closely to the Islamic system of weights used to measure gold and silver [*mitkal* and *uqiya*]. A final innovation that probably reflects northern influence are flat-roofed houses evidenced by ceramic drain tiles at Begho. Thus Begho is viewed as the conduit through which artisanal skills later elaborated by the historic Akan states (e.g., Asante) were introduced to Ghana. Posnansky posits "a steady, albeit gradual stream of influence from the Mali area, probably accelerating from the late fourteenth century as world trade expanded."

The enigmatic Komaland sites in northern Ghana provide tantalizing insight into the influence of Sudanic culture on medieval Volta basin societies. The sites are known for their terra-cotta figurines, which appeared in urban art markets. This prompted an investigation that identified low mounds concentrated in a twenty-square-kilometer area associated with large, often spectacular, terra-cotta figurines. Excavations at Yikpabongo revealed that the mounds were funerary structures with similar stratigraphic profiles: A circle of stones was underlaid by deposits rich in domestic pottery, grinding slabs, and terra-cotta figurines. Beneath this layer of mixed deposits were the remains of a daub burial chamber or platform associated with human remains. Small numbers of cowries and copper ornaments were recovered from the burial overburden. Burials were associated with whole pots and animal remains interpreted as sacrifices. Larger mounds yielded multiple burials, while smaller mounds appeared to represent individual interments.

More than five hundred intact and fragmentary terra-cotta sculptures have been recovered from excavations at Yikpabongo. Countless more have been looted, illegally exported, and sold by private art dealers. The size and subject of the sculpture are diverse. Most of the terra-cottas depict humans, often with multiple heads or faces. Local hunters report finding life-size naturalistic sculptures of humans. Other sculptures are small (less than ten centimeters) and depict animals including crocodiles, snakes, hippos, and lions. Several of the figurines from Yikpabongo were embedded with gold dust. The terra-cotta art of Komaland exhibits some similarity to the terra-cotta art of Jenne Jeno on the middle Niger. Two thermoluminescence dates on terra-cottas recovered from surface contexts suggest that they date to the fourth century BP. Although there is little evidence from which to reconstruct the economic or social parameters of the Komaland sites, Anquandah suggested that they represent a kingdom involved in the trans-Saharan trade. An alternative view, grounded in oral-historical sources, is that they represent a diaspora of skilled craftspeople who were descendants of Mande-speaking immigrants (Kantonsi) from the Niger bend.

Publication of the Komaland finds fueled demand for these unique objects on the international art market. The destruction of sites by looters diminishes the possibility that we will ever have a clear understanding of their role in the cultural development of Volta basin societies.

Begho's decline is attributed to the shift from the Mediterranean to the Atlantic world economy. European traders provided an alternative market for Akan gold, and mid-eighteenth-century Arab documents suggest that Mande traders diverted trade from the Sudanic entrepots as a result. Sudanic rulers responded by mounting a campaign against Begho intended to reestablish the northward flow of gold. The expedition was led by the historical figure Naba'a (Jakpa), who subsequently withdrew to the north of the Black Volta, where he established the overkingdom of Gonja (see below) through a series of brutal conquests. Begho's position as an important trade center was further eroded by the rise of Asante, a forest state that dominated the Ghanaian scene from the terminal seventeenth through the nineteenth centuries. Scholars assumed that hostilities with Asante early in the eighteenth century dealt the fatal blow to Begho, but archaeological research suggests that Begho was occupied into the late eighteenth century or early nineteenth century. Nevertheless, the movement of artisans away from Begho to the Asante capital at Kumasi further eroded the economic basis of Begho. Degradation of the surrounding environment probably also contributed to Begho's decline. Dapaa, a large iron-smelting complex (twenty-six slag mounds) on the margins of Begho, dates to ca. 300–550 BP, and the amount of charcoal consumed by the furnaces required the harvesting of some three hundred thousand mature trees.

Although Begho's role in long-distance exchange declined, archaeological evidence suggests continuity in the material culture of everyday life, including building style and ceramics. Local potting is today dominated by Mo-speaking peoples in the village of Bondakile, roughly twenty kilometers from the site of Begho. Crossland and Posnansky noted similarities between contemporary Mo pots and that from the Brong quarter at Begho and suggested that Mo people supplied utilitarian pottery to the occupants of Begho. Yet significant variability is encompassed within the supposedly homogeneous Begho ware. Moreover, neighboring sites that postdate Begho's demise show considerable change in the ceramic inventory during the nineteenth and early twentieth centuries. Thus the emphasis placed on continuity from Begho to contemporary Mo potting may have obscured some important changes in ceramic production.

In-progress excavations of a metallurgical workshop in the Banda region of Ghana. The burned features and clay pot in the foreground were associated with the forging of copper alloys and iron in the fourteenth and fifteenth centuries CE. The large stones across the area served as anvils and as grinding stones for the shaping and finishing of metal objects. Photograph by Ann B. Stahl, 2009. Courtesy of the author.

Although Begho has received most attention in the literature, control of the Volta basin was divided among several polities from the sixteenth century. Each has a rich oral-historical tradition but limited reference in archival materials. They include Bono Manso, an early Akan state centered on the contemporary town of Techiman [Takyiman]; Gonja, with its capital at Yagbum and centers at Daboya, Bole, and Dakrupe; Dagomba, with its capital at Yendi Dabari; and Mamprussi, centered on the Gambaga plateau. Although the extent of research varies, each polity has been the subject of archaeological investigations. A site that may rival Begho as an early town on the southern margins of the wooded savanna is Bono Manso. Bono is thought to be the earliest state among Akan-speaking peoples. The history and archaeology of the Bono state were the focus of [Kwaku] Effah-Gyamfi's research, which was brought to a halt by his premature death in 1983.

The earliest phase of occupation at Bono Manso is thought to date to the sixth or seventh century BP. Relatively dispersed wattle-and-daub structures were associated with locally produced ceramics, minimally decorated with grooving, incision, or fine cord roulette. The second phase represents the peak occupation dated to the fourth century BP, during which an estimated ten thousand people lived at the site. Houses were made from more substantial swish (mud coursing) and dwellings are larger than during Phase I. Phase II ceramics were distinguished by the presence of burnishing, superimposed by cord roulette and grooving on vessel bodies. Carinated vessels were interpreted as imitations of brass vessels. Bono Manso experienced a period of decline during the second century BP. This occupation is less extensive and presumably indicates a smaller population [ca. eight thousand]. Phase III ceramics are distinguished by mica inclusions in the paste and greater use of curvilinear grooved decoration. Quatrefoil-based pipe forms were common. A small percentage of ceramics at Bono Manso resembled pottery from Begho, Ahwene Koko, and New Buipe and was cited as evidence for regional exchange. Although trade items were not recovered, there was evidence for craft production (weaving, brass-casting, and ironworking) that suggests involvement in trade with the Middle Niger.

The kingdom of Gonja is well-known from oral-historical and written accounts. Gonja controlled the western Volta basin from the sixteenth century to the colonial period. A striking feature of the Gonja kingdom is the diversity of ethnic-linguistic groups subsumed within it, including speakers of Guan and Voltaic languages. Oral sources and the Kitab Ghanja, a mid-eighteenth-century Arab text, agree that Gonja was founded by mounted soldiers who invaded from the north. [Ivor] Wilks links this to the punitive expedition mounded against Begho in an effort to reestablish the flow of gold to markets along the middle Niger.

Until recently, the only excavated site known to span the period of the Gonja incursion was New Buipe, the site of an extensive salvage excavation by [Richard] York during the Volta Basin Research Project. York noted simple, red-painted pottery (Silima ware) throughout much of the New Buipe sequence but found that more complex, geometrically painted pottery was common in levels dated between the fifth and the third centuries BP. Painted pottery was thought to reflect Mande influence from the north based upon parallels with the painted pottery from Koumbi Saleh, the capital of an ancient Sudanic state in southern Mauritania. Thus archaeologists linked the appearance of red-painted pottery to the historically documented expedition led by Naba.

[Peter] Shinnie's research at Daboya was designed to test the idea that the arrival of the immigrant Gonja would correlate with changes in material culture. However, the results of four seasons of excavation at Daboya and testing of sites in western Gonja indicate that changes in the ceramic inventory (including the advent of painted pottery) precede the historically dated incursion of the Gonja by several centuries. Red-painted sherds, comparable to York's Silima ware at New Buipe, appeared in contexts radiocarbon dated to the eighth century BP at Daboya. Shinnie and [François] Kense support the idea that these design-painted wares represent early Mande influence from the north but question the linkage with the founding of Gonja. There is significant continuity between pre-Gonja Phase C ceramics and those of Phase D (Gonja). The only distinctive material culture associated with Phase D is iron objects that resemble contemporary horse regalia. Despite the oral-historical evidence of long-distance connections with the north, the authors conclude that there was little impact on the day-to-day activities of indigenous peoples. Further, they see no substantial changes in material culture associated with the imposition of Asante hegemony over Gonja in the eighteenth century.

We know very little about the archaeology of the Dagomba and Mamprussi states of northeastern Ghana. Early excavations at Yendi Dabari, the ancient capital of Dagomba, revealed part of a complex structure comprised of rectangular rooms that were distinct from the circular buildings built in the area today. A large sample of tobacco pipes dominated by double-angled forms suggested a seventeenth-century occupation based on comparison with pipe sequences in southern Ghana. The archaeology of the Gambaga escarpment has only recently been explored. This was the center of the historic Mamprussi kingdom, another polity forged by an immigrant group who imposed their hegemony on an existing population. Two seasons of survey and limited test excavation suggest that the area was sparsely occupied prior to the last five hundred years. The number and diversity of smelting sites suggest that northeastern Ghana shared in the florescence of iron production documented for adjacent areas in Togo.

Quest for the River, Creation of the Path

Kwasi Konadu

The archaeology of Ghana suggests that for at least the last thousand years, much of what is now central and southern Ghana was occupied and culturally shaped by Akan peoples. These peoples came to include Bono (Brong) inhabitants near the edge of the northern forest, Asante and others in the central forest, and the Fante and others, including later arrivals such as the Gã-Adangme and Ewe, on the Atlantic coast. Other indigenous groups—some of which became Islamic—occupied the northern savanna just above the semi-deciduous forest, but this area would not be incorporated in the region that became Ghana until the end of the nineteenth century and beginning of the twentieth. Thus the polities and peoples we know best and the ones with which the various European merchants interacted were largely, though not exclusively, constituted by Akan language speakers and culture bearers. Recently, both archaeologists and historians have taken renewed interest in the origins of peoples, and in this excerpt Kwasi Konadu offers an important (but highly condensed) view on the early formation of a composite Akan culture and those influenced by it, taking cues from recent research in Ghana archaeology and oral histories. He emphasizes the forest-savanna context and the place of the Tano River in how the Akan conceptualized their beginnings and the shape of their communities and composite culture.

The question of Akan origins owes much to the structure of their histories and the cultural claims made with regard to settlement, custodianship of land, and the prerogative of establishing and maintaining social order. . . . Renewed interest in the origins of Akan social orders and institutionalized cultural practices . . . has yielded new insights and prompted critical questions about old data and established interpretations. . . . In *Forests of Gold*, Ivor Wilks explains that various events and processes that occurred between the fifteenth and the seventeenth century came to define the Akan as, essentially, sedentary agriculturalists, socially distributed between matriclan and matrilineage, politically organized into "states," and culturally bonded by language, religion, and a common sense of shared history. The processes from which those characteristics originate were the cumulative outcome of the transformation from forging to an agrarian economy involving large-scale forest clearance. Therein the *abusua* (matriclan structure) evolved in the context of a political authority based upon manipulation of the demands for gold and supplies of enslaved labor, and the *ɔman* (state) political structure in the forestlands emerged as the Akan peripherally participated in both the old Mediterranean economy and the expanding "Atlantic economy." Wilks's uncertainty about whether there was an era of massive land clearance or a piecemeal process extending into antiquity and his argument for "slave labor" clearance of the Akan forest have prompted at least one historian to question Wilks's model. Others may also question his certainty that the Akan were driven out of the savanna and into the forest by a northern incursion. The general strategies of defense or responses to hegemony, particularly with the advent of western Sudanic polities and then Islam in the West African savanna, varied from fighting, finding refuge, withdrawal to remote and defensible areas, creating structural defenses, and conversion to Islam with the hope that this would offer some measure of protection. There is no evidence that one or a combination of these responses either contributed to Akan movement into the high forest or was a causal or facilitating factor in Akan settlement and cultural development. Precisely who subdued and expelled the Akan from the savanna if this was their "homeland," and when and how this happened, are left unattended by Wilks, though his model for the emergence of Akan polities still continues to enjoy wide, uncritical acceptance.

In his review essay of *Forests of Gold*, A. Norman Klein argues that slavery was the "unifying idea" that informed Wilks's thinking on Akan origins and the Asante polity, the most notable Akan society in eighteenth- and nineteenth-century documentary sources. According to Klein's reading of Wilks's "unifying idea," enslaved persons were imported (in exchange for gold) to clear the forest, and this led to a population boom, a "new class formation" led by "slave-owning entrepreneurs," and an agricultural revolution that initiated the formation of southerly Akan states. For Klein, this is an "academic myth" that has uncritically received wide acceptance. The backbone of Wilks's myth, according to Klein, is anachronism in that Wilks used nineteenth-century data to make fifteenth- and sixteenth-century interpretations; that is, Wilks "project[ed] well-known historical conditions into an unknown past," particularly by using oral histories. In response to Klein and in the end, Wilks remained unconvinced by Klein's argument and by archaeological research that casts doubt on his chronology for the emergence of southerly Akan polities in the forest and suggests a much earlier presence. The issue here is the lack of specific historical data, since the number of enslaved persons imported by Portuguese and Mande (Juula) traders to clear the forest and engage in farming and gold mining is unknown, details concerning the formation of the matriclan structure in which they were incorporated is lacking, no data exists for the size or productivity of seventeenth-century (or earlier) peasant or "slave-worked" farms to support a population boom, and the forest fallow system believed to have been part of an "agricultural revolution" only appeared in the historical record in the early nineteenth century.

In an effort to offer a counternarrative to Wilks's, Klein has argued instead (based upon archaeological and biomedical data) that for millennia the Akan forest was inhabited by agriculturalists, who responded to later Eurasian diseases and slave raiding by clustering into denser populations, which placed a greater emphasis on fertility (especially of imported women) as a weapon against social dislocation, slavery, and disease in the late fifteenth to early eighteenth centuries. Klein dates the early Akan in the southern forest of contemporary Ghana to approximately two millennia ago. Indeed, Klein's approximate dates for forest occupation are consistent with the archaeological record for Ghana. They also suggest that those early Akan settlers were embedded in the economies of a forest-savanna mosaic prior to Islam, that commerce and mobility were cornerstones of society, and that an early Akan agrarian order existed, one based upon egalitarian and "classless" principles, as was found among Akan societies such as the Eotile on the Ivory Coast around 1000 CE. . . .

The archaeological record on Akan settlements and Kintampo sites in the forest, at the forest-savanna nexus, on the coast, and in neighboring regions to the east and west of contemporary Ghana, in addition to biomedical and ecological factors, tells a story that casts serious doubt on much of the received knowledge about early Akan society and settlement. The coastal and eastern parts of Ghana have received less treatment, and, as a result, archaeological findings for the coastal sites must be considered tentative until further investigation. Of the twenty-seven known Kintampo archaeological sites in Ghana, most are located in the forest or on its fringes, and approximately six exist in the true savanna. The major archaeological sites of the forest interior—most of which are positioned east, south, and north of Kumase as an axis—show overlap in occupation and evidence of settled life and of advanced social and cultural development. A number of these archaeological sites were substantial in size and had permanent structures that suggest large populations and long-term occupation. The age of the majority of those sites ranges from 3500 BCE [Before the Common Era] to the nineteenth century in terms of occupation and include the Bosompra cave on the eastern forest fringe, Bono-Manso and Bɛw (Begho) on the northern forest fringe, Nkukua Buoho, Boyase Hill, Asantemanso, Adansemanso, Dawu-Akwapem, Akwamu, and the Krobo mountains of inhabited caves.

Oral and archaeological evidence from two of the oldest Akan towns in the forest interior, Asantemanso and Adansemanso, indicates continuous occupation from 700 BCE to the present and 393 to 1650 CE, respectively, although Adansemanso was occupied mainly in the first half of the second millennium CE, a long dry period in West Africa and the second major regression in the levels of Lake Bosomtwe. The excavated material culture of Asantemanso and Adansemanso supports the oral-historical sources, which are consistent with Akan spiritual, ideational, and material culture through a constellation of evidence of iron smelting, ritual and festival practices, indigenous medicine, functional and artistic wares and figurines, social organization, and trading activities. At both sites, we find sacred groves and forests with shrines in close proximity to streams, ancient roadways, and fields indicative of agriculture. Although Peter Shinnie, who carried out excavations at Adansemanso and Asantemanso, seems certain "there was permanent settlement [with a population of several thousand] at Asantemanso as early as the last few centuries B.C.," he, however, would rather speculate on the presence of Guan speakers in the central Ghana forest than where the evidence points—to a proto-Akan presence.

In the northern and northwest parts of the forest, areas associated with Akan origins are generally dated from the fifth century CE onward, and, in addition to continuity in pottery styles, rock shelter sites show the use of microlithic industries and ground-stone artifacts into the first millennium. Like Asantemanso and Adansemanso of the forest interior, the two best-known sites of the northern and northwest forest are the Akan settlements of Bono-Manso, capital of Bono polity, and the township of Bɛw (commonly referred to as Begho). All of the sacred sites associated with Bono settlement in the northern forest and on its fringes are located either next to inselbergs—as was the case with early sites in and around Kumase—or in caves and rock shelters, of which the Amowi rock shelter of the Bono was inhabited no later than 400 CE. Some archaeologists date Bono-Manso to 1000 CE despite the early occupation of Amowi, iron smelting at Abam in Bono-Manso (ca. 300 CE) and in the eastern limits of Begho (ca. 100 CE), and the rock shelter of Atwetwebooso and the Nseserekeseso ancestral site in southeastern Begho. The archaeology of these ancient sites confirms the frequent references in Akan oral narratives of founding settlers emerging from "holes in the earth." The archaeological record also provides no evi-

A pathway paved with stones in the semideciduous forests of Ghana. Photograph by Kwasi Konadu, 2005.

dence of an intrusive northern people moving into the region, but it does support the claim that several Akan societies were autochthonous to areas where Kintampo cultural sites on the fringe and in the forest interior are found. . . .

The clearing and occupation of the dense forest by proto-Akan settlers and agriculturalists who cultivated oil palm and high-caloric root crops through communal labor and used efficient reproductive strategies helped to sustain population during an era of aridity and adaptation to malaria. These processes shaped a proto-Akan culture that achieved levels of development concomitant with an agricultural cycle and a calendrical matrix that regulated daily life and rituals associated with the identification of an Akan Creator as manifest in a myriad of ways—expressed as *abosom*, "children" of that Creator—in the natural order. In this context, the ritual consumption of yams—harvested in *kitawonsa* and *ɛbo* (July and September)—and palm oil likely developed during harvests and periodic ceremonies where both indigenous crops were prominent and became staple offerings to ancestors. These cycles informed the calendrical matrix (*adaduanan*, calendrical cycle of forty-two days) that ordered patterns of Akan activity and behavior in short cycles and placed greater emphasis on peace, cleansing, sacredness, contentment, settlement, balancing strength and compassion, and the drive to temper human feelings and actions based upon arrogance and warlike aggressiveness. Temporally, the *adaduanan* might have been a calculated response to the potential of conflict, sabotage, tyranny, and self-interest over group interests, and thus it ordered society in terms of travel and (social) transactions, cleansing when chaos or transgressions occurred, peace rather than long-term war, avoidance of the overuse of the earth and its resources, and compassion and courage in the face of the inescapable human realities of death, pain, and suffering.

In the natural order, the forest and the farm were afforded respect as homes to spiritual and human occupations (the latter as tenants who used rather than owned these life-sustaining areas), and the restrictions placed upon farming on specific days (via the *adaduanan*) illustrate the translation of that respect into cultural practice. Thus, out of a respect for such restrictions and to meditate on the meaning of temporal life within the natural order through offerings and the pouring of *mpaeɛ* (libation), one would receive the appropriate *nhyira* (blessings) and be empowered by the spiritual presence of the ancestors, or *abosom*, invoked. Many trailblazing hunters explored new territory beyond the recognizable *asasetepa* (barren land), established frontier zones in cooperation with other hunters, and became custodians of such land and the various types of *abosom* they encountered in the forests and rivers and on the mountains. Those spiritual entities were then "domesticated," imbued with spiritual meaning, and deemed to be facilitators of life and its human dimension. *Ohyeɛ* denoted "boundary land," and the *ɔ-de-hyeɛ* (*ɔdehyeɛ*), usually rendered as "royal," were actually those who knew the boundaries as descendants of the principal hunter (*abofoɔ*, master hunters) who became the ruler of the new settlement. These hunters not only paved the way for new settlements and provided leadership to them, but the very pathways they created connected towns and villages and would be crossed and recrossed by other hunters, merchants, farmers, and travelers. In doing so, hunters helped address common problems encountered in the moist forest—inadequate transportation, communication, and food supply—and, rightfully, became integral actors in shaping society.

Though they were forest dwellers, most of the integral and oldest *abosom* of the Akan were and still are water and not forest derived, and the highest *ɔbosom*, Tano or Taa Kora, came to be embodied by the sacred Tano River, which originated inland near the edge of the forest in [the Bono state of] Takyiman and merged into the southerly *ɔbosompo* (ocean) near Assinie. In a "standard text" played on the *atumpan* drums, the creation of Tano and the world of the Akan [are] symbiotically revealed: *ɔkwan atware asuo, asuo atware kwan, ɔpanin ne hwan?* (The path crosses the river, the river crosses the path, which is older [or which came first]?) The response: *yebɔɔ kwan no kɔtoo asuo no* (We created the path to meet the river). And thus the river was created not only before the pathways in the forest, but before the humans who created the paths! How could this be? The drum text continues: *Asuo no firi tete, asuo no firi ɔdomankoma ɔbɔadee, konkon Tanɔ* . . . ([The] river is from ancient times, this river is from the beneficent Creator, sacred Tano . . .). A hunter found Tano, or Ta Kora, in a cave; a town, Tanoboase (Tano under the rock), was founded and the hunter became the ruler and the custodian of Ta Kora. This scenario recurred as often as the paths in the forest were crossed, and as the Tano River and Akan societies stretched from the edge of the forest to the coast, Tano provided life facilitators in the form of the *abosom*, and many gold-producing settlements emerged on or near the river. Rivers and streams also marked the internal divisions of settlements and demarcated frontiers, and, in their crossing, hunters and other trailblazers often encountered and later revered those water-derived *abosom*. Rivers and streams held added significance, for they were sites for retrieving life-sustaining water, washing clothes, bathing, and periodic purification and meditation rituals—rituals that were more or less regulated by the *adaduanan*. The pioneering hunters (*abommofoɔ*, "one who creates something new") who established new settlements were referred to as *ɔhene*, a term indicative of the hunter's itchy body in terms of his ability to create pathways and settlements in the forest; hence, *ne ho ye hene* (his or her body is itchy). The phrase *ne ho ye hene* connotes a person well versed in the lie of the land and is usually the first person on that unoccupied land, who thus has rights to be custodian of the land and the spiritual agencies embedded in its environs. The Akan matrilineal clan and political system likely evolved through these processes of scouting, settlement, and custodianship. . . .

The hunter's duty, like that of other trailblazers who preceded him and became the custodians of lands and the spiritual agencies thereof, "was to study the land, and to report whether it would be suitable for farming and yield enough food to feed the population. . . ." The streams and rivers often noted in the traditions of origin . . . also lent themselves to key *abosom* that guided the polity and provided a means for its people to actualize their spiritual concepts and practices. . . . In early agrarian settlements, hunter-trailblazers and their descendants played integral roles in finding unsettled land, assuming custodianship of that land, and developing a sociopolitical order. Indeed, there might be a greater correlation between food production in early and present-day Akan societies, trade activities, the growth of towns, and the women who have not only traditionally dominated local food-trading activities but were also key in the founding of new settlements. . . .

On the evidence for early society and culture in the forest and on its borders, a likely scenario is that the clearing of the dense forest began by at least 1500 BCE, using stone tools just after the forest reached its farthest expanse and during a suitable period of aridity between 2500 and 300 BCE. The concomitant prominence of oil palm pollen, which is indicative of human occupation, suggests that the dense forest was being settled by a proto-Akan people with a food-producing economy based on oil palm cultivation and the exploitation of high-calorie root crops, which facilitated population growth. This society also made use of communal labor and reproductive strategies needed for forest clearance and settlement during a period of malaria adaptation. In addition, it utilized an agrarian sociopolitical order where hunters and their descendants played key roles in finding unsettled land and assuming custodianship. These processes must have shaped the proto-Akan culture of settlements both within and on the periphery of forests. Indeed, there is a direct correlation between food production, trade activities, the growth of towns, and the women, who have traditionally dominated local food-trading activities and allowed for both population growth through procreation and matrilineal processes for assimilating others into the cultural order. These forest and forest-fringe dwellers achieved levels of cultural development, and their spirituality became linked to an agricultural cycle, sacred ancestral sites, and so-called totemic association and the identification of an Akan Creator as manifest in a myriad of ways in the natural order.

Proto-Akan societies and culture were largely an indigenous development, and this interpretation of early culture and society is well supported by the archaeological, historical, and linguistic evidence. The combined evidence does not support the Mande myth or the idea that integral Akan cultural practices were the product of Mande cultural or linguistic diffusion. On the contrary, a process of Akanization has occurred in settlements that had contact with non-Akan cultures, and the Akan have for the most part remained linguistically and culturally unaffected by those cultures. Though the Akan have adopted minor foreign elements over time, those same non-Akan cultures have imported and adopted much from the Akan. The Akan had many commercial and cultural contacts with Muslims, yet they were never Islamized and remained largely unaffected in cultural and commercial terms. The Akan also rarely if ever settled in towns controlled by others in the forestland and on its edges, including areas where Muslims took up residency, such as the town of Begho. Those towns, which were established principally for trade, were on the northwestern edge of the forest, and Mande traders made it clear that they rarely entered the high forest; in fact, in Begho and Bono-Manso, these traders remained in distinct quarters or on the periphery of each capital. Even when Islamicized Africans took up residence in the Akan forest in later periods and in places like nineteenth-century Kumase, they resided in separate living areas.

The Akan remained largely unaffected by Islam, and one key reason is that Akan societies were built on spiritual agencies (e.g., *abosom*), foundational ideas, and emblematic objects (e.g., sacred swords, stools). Those agencies functioned as facilitators of the social and natural order and shaped the cultural self-understandings, settlements, and the polities as sources of identification and belonging on the later Gold Coast. In the late fifteenth century and early sixteenth century, the Portuguese came upon Akan societies who exhibited sophisticated cultural knowledge, spiritual understandings of divine and social order, and commercial skills after centuries of experience in local and regional trade and were able to approach these Europeans with tact. The Portuguese, like other Europeans to follow, were invariably limited to the Gold Coast littoral, but the nature of the Portuguese encounter with Akan societies set the pace for other Akan-European interactions, particularly Akan response to Christianization. As with Islam, the Akan thwarted others' efforts to convert them to Christianity, for their social orders were facilitated by a spiritual culture attentive to the *abosom* and structured toward agriculture and regional commerce. Where commerce and (spiritual) culture were at odds, the apparent inconsistencies or contradictions were perhaps accurate reflections of those encounters and the consequences thereof.

A Creation Story and a "Beautiful Prayer" to Tano

R. S. Rattray

The collective work of British colonial anthropologist Robert S. Rattray (1881–1938), in particular that published during the 1920s, is well known to students of the Akan and the Asante. In his first volume, Ashanti *(by the time of its publication "Ashanti" meant "Greater Asante"), Rattray retells a widespread creation story about the beginnings of a world preceding humans and inhabited by spiritual agents (*abosom*), and then supplies us with a "prayer" to the first of such agents, Tano (or Ta Kora), infused with historical events. Rivers are sources of life, providing water for cooking, consumption, and cleansing. Ta Kora is embodied by the sacred Tano River; as the Creator's first "child," it is the only ɔbosom with direct divine origins. Tano, also called Ta Kora (Ta is the shorthand for Tano), is viewed as the Creator's primary and most ancient intermediary on earth (Asase Yaa). The Bono Manso region is not only one of the oldest centers of Akan culture, it is also the source of the Tano River. As the culture of the Akan expanded into the forests and down to the coasts of present-day Ghana and Cote D'Ivoire, this expansion seems to follow the path of the Tano River, where both it and the Bia (Bea) River take their origins from the Bono area and eventually flows in a southerly direction into the Aby Lagoon and the Atlantic Ocean (*ɔbosompo [Opo]*). In its southerly flow, the Tano River passes (to the east) Lake Bosumtwe, a large natural lake southeast of Kumase, before terminating in the ocean. The following account charts the importance of the Tano River in the cosmological and cultural life of those it continues to serve.*

There is known, from one end of Ashanti to the other [i.e., Greater Asante], a popular myth, which I shall here only outline very briefly. . . . This myth recounts how 'Nyame—the [Creator, among the Akan]—had various sons [i.e., offspring] of whom one in particular was a *bayeyere* (favorite son). 'Nyame decided to send these children of his down to the earth in order that they might receive benefits from, and confer them upon, mankind. All these sons bore the names of what are now rivers or lakes:

Tano (the great river of that name)
Bosomtwe (the great lake near [Kumase])
Bea (a river)
Opo (the sea)

and every other river or water of any importance. Thus in diagrammatic form we have:

The Supreme Being (Onyame or Onyankopon)

Tano, river. Bosomtwe, lake. Bea, river. Opo, the sea. Other rivers.

The tributaries of these again are "their children."

In Ashanti, any water that dries up in the hot season is known by the title of a "dan 'Nyame" water (a rely-upon-God water).

Returning to our myth, I need not go into the whole story of how, owing to the machinations of the goat (an animal hateful of this [*ɔbosom*] and taboo to his priests), the final resting-place of all the waters was not as really intended by 'Nyame. What has been said is sufficient to show that waters in Ashanti, some in a greater, others in a lesser degree, are all looked upon as containing the power or spirit of the divine Creator, and thus as being a great life-giving force. "As a woman gives birth to a child, so may water to a [*ɔbosom*]," once said a priest to me. . . .

Early next morning, Friday, the 5th May 1922—a sacred Friday [*fofie*]—we all met in the court-yard of the Ta Kora [Tano] temple. . . . The old priest, who had three lines of clay upon his shoulders and arms, and several other of the priests now set down their stools before the altar upon which stood the shrine of Ta Kora. A cloth was spread upon the floor a little to the left of these men, and another priest set his stool upon it and seated himself. The rest of us ranged ourselves facing them. . . . This priest, settling himself firmly on his stool, arranged his feet upon the cloth so that only his heels rested upon it. . . . The old red priest, who was sitting near, just on the left of the priest carrying the shrine . . . now spoke in a low voice as follows:

Odomankoma obosom, ankobi na huni
Nkadomako okyere abrane.
Ohene Ame Yaw obosom
Asante 'hene obosom

Woye sa kum nkora miensa
Obosom a ofiri bomu

Wo na wokum Adinkira
Ohene a yede kosua fufuo guare no
Wo na wo nkwanta aye hu
Ope wo afwe asei wo, asai wo a nsai
Nokware obosom, ose na ewom
Won a odawuru bo Nyamefrebere
Wo ko babi a, bra
Kwampiri asu o yiri a, na ye fre wo
Abiridi abrade ete 'Nyame so
Wo na wonwene akwan tene mu
Nne Fofie, na ye re pe wo anim afwe
Na waba abetie die ye re ka akyerewo

Creator's god, who sees even though he is not present.
Nkadomako (a title) who seizes strong men,
God of King Ame Yao [ruler (*ohene*) of ancient Bono kingdom]
God of the King of Asante [ruler of the Asante kingdom],
You did such and such a thing [i.e., battled] and slew Nkoransa
 [a rival state].
God who [emerges] from within the rock [the source of the Tano River],
You who slew Adinkra [ruler of the Akan state of Gyaman]
King, whom we bathe with white eggs.
You, the crossroads leading to whose dwelling are a fearful place.
He who would see you in order to destroy you, with that destruction be
 not destroyed.
God who is truthful, when you speak there is truth in what you say.
You, whose [sacred bell] sounds even to Mecca
If you have gone elsewhere, come (hither).
Kwampiri (a title), upon whom, when the waters are in flood, we call.
Shooting stars that abide with the Creator
You weave (as it were) a thread (in a loom) across a path stretching afar.
Today is a sacred Friday and we wish to behold your face,
So come and listen to what we have to tell you.

Folk Songs of Ghana

J. H. Kwabena Nketia

The organization of early societies and those that came after them share some foundational features, though not as constants over time. Nonetheless, some of those features included, for instance, the types of leadership structures which emerged and the ways in which spirituality, politics, and polity converge in the personnel occupying those structures. As we have seen thus far, the cultural and social roles played by both male and female leaders have been central to a range of Ghanaian societies, and these leadership roles and the deeds of rulers are often preserved in songs. Throughout present-day Ghana, indigenous music communicates the culture, beliefs, and attitudes of its bearers. In the following excerpts J. H. Kwabena Nketia (1921–), the world-renowned musicologist and composer, provides us one Nnwonkorɔ and one Adowa musical style featuring a male and female ruler, respectively. Adowa music is practiced primarily by quasi-professional performers and usually (though not exclusively) at funerals, while Nnwonkorɔ is performed chiefly by women at various occasions and thus less formal than Adowa.

Song No. 12

ɔnam oo, ɔnam oo,
ɔnam nsaa so na ɛredi ahim e.

ɔnana e, na yɛrebɛdi ahim e.
Agyei Kofoɔ aboro nsa,
ɔkyereben Aduesare,
N'ani ye hu oo.
Ee Agyei Kofoɔ,
ɔnam nsaa so na ɛredi ahim e,
Agoo!

ɔnam oo, ɔnam oo,
ɔnam mpaboa so na ɛredi ahim e.
Yee ɔnana e, na yɛrebɛdi ahim e.
Adum Agyei aboro nsa,

Village Women. Mosaic by Martin Numadzi, 2009. Courtesy of the artist.

ɔkyereben Aduesare,
Afaafa Adu oo.
Ee Agyei Kofoɔ,
ɔnam nsaa so na ɛredi ahim e,
Agoo!

He is coming, he is coming,
Treading along on camel blanket [denoting wealth or nobility] in triumph.
Stranger, we are bestirring ourselves.
Agyei, the warrior, is drunk [i.e., manliness, daring],
The green mamba [symbol of beauty and ferocity] with fearful eyes.
Yes Agyei, the warrior,
He is treading along on camel
blanket in triumph,
Make way for him.

He is coming, he is coming,
Treading along on sandals [i.e., people].
Stranger, we are bestirring ourselves.
Adum Agyei is drunk,
The green mamba,
Afaafa Adu.
Yes, Agyei, the warrior,
He is treading along on camel
blanket in triumph,
Make way for him.

Song No. 24

Yiadom Konadu Mansa ee,
Na frɛ no ma me oo, ɔhemmaa.
ɔboɔ ba de Konadu hemmaa ee,

Na frɛ no ma me oo, ɔhemmaa.
Woyee-e!
ɔhemmaa dada ee,
ɔhemmaa dada ee,
Frɛ no ma me oo, ɔhemmaa.

Yiadom Konadu Mansa,
Please call the Queen for me.
A child of *ɔboɔ* [i.e., a particular town] is called Konadu,
the Queen,
Please call her for me.
Hurrah!
The Queen of old [i.e., ancient line of succession],
The Queen of old,
Call her for me.

Bono-Takyiman Oral Traditions

Dennis Warren and Owusu Brempong

Dennis Warren (1942–97) was a medical anthropologist who first traveled to Ghana as a Peace Corps volunteer teaching science classes to people like former student and later colleague Owusu Brempong, who, while completing his PhD in folklore at Indiana University, collected hundreds of hours of oral histories among the Bono peoples of Takyiman between the late 1960s and the early 1970s. Out of Warren's and Brempong's efforts came a series of significant oral historical data among one of the earliest societies, residing in and around the northern edge of the dense Ghanaian forest. We have chosen two interviews, which include only the responses of the interviewee but covers a range of subjects, allowing the reader a fuller picture of Bono society and history as interpreted by its elders and indigenous officials. The first interview focuses on questions of origins, early sociopolitical formation, and the cause of the Bono kingdom's decline at the hands of the Asante, whereas the second interview focuses squarely on aspects of Bono culture from the perspective of a former ruler of Takyiman (Techiman).

Interview with "Local Historian" Nana Kwame Nyame, ca. 1969–1970

THE EARLY CHIEFS AND NYAME

It is not true that in the early days Techiman [Takyiman] was ruled by women (queenmothers), or that women led the soldiers in time of war. From time immemorial, Techiman has had chiefs; men have always ruled. Nor is it true that in the early days Techiman served Nyame [the Creator], which was the moon, a female [*ɔbosom*]. It is also not true that the men rebelled against the women, therefore the women chose one of the men to be a chief (Krontihene) to run the affairs of the state while the queenmother's council still worked. Techiman has never been ruled by women. The person who told this history did not learn history from his father; it is a fabrication of his own mind. When an Omanhene dies, the Krontihene is the next chief in power to rule the state. Nana Kwame Nyame does not understand the reason why [the London-based researcher Eva] Meyerowitz wrote that

Nyankopon was *owia* ("the sun") and Nyame was *bosome* ("the moon"). He does not know where Meyerowitz got these materials. Nyankopon, Nyame, and Odomankoma are the same [Creator].

WHO ARE THE FANTI [FANTE]?

It is not true that the Fanti brought the [*abosom*] Taa Kora and Taa Mensah from the *sarem* [savanna]. All these [*abosom*] were picked in Techiman. Nana Takyi Firi [the founder of Takyiman] was not a Fanti from the *sarem*. The Fanti migrated from Techiman. If the Fanti claim that they migrated from the *sarem* then it can be said that Techiman people came from *sarem* but their origin is Techiman not the *sarem*. It was war that sent the Fanti away [to the coast in the fourteenth or fifteenth century].

YAM FESTIVALS

It is not true that when chiefs celebrate yam festivals it means their soul is dead and they want to revive it. Nor is it true that when [the] *abosomfo* celebrate yam festivals it means the [*abosom*] are dead and they want to revive them. The yam festival is a tradition; every state celebrates one. It is like the Christmas celebrated by Europeans. During yam festivals they first give food to the [*ɔbosom*] Taa Mensah because the soul of the state is in the hands of this [*ɔbosom*]. After the yam is given to the [*ɔbosom*], the elders (the chiefs) also celebrate their yam festivals one by one.

DIALA AND THE SAHARA

It is not true that Techiman people came from a place called Diala. Nana Kwame Nyame was not there when this history was told [to Eva Meyerowitz]. Techiman people came from a hole at Amowi [in the adjacent district of Nkoransa]. It is not true that the ancestors of the Akan were white people living at the *sarem*. There were no white people living at the *sarem*.

NANA BREMPONG KATAKYERA

He was a very old chief. His nephew was Kwakye Ameyaw, a handsome young man. All the young men and the chief's servants loved him very much. Nana Katakyera was very old and would not die to leave the stool vacant for Kwakye Ameyaw. The servants always loved debating. One evening they sat beside an open fire in the courtyard of the palace. They began to debate the topic "Who can face hunger for thirty days?" Some servants declared that some people could do it, while others said that no one could do it. Nana Katakyera was there. He was moved by the topic and told them that, although he was old, he could face hunger for thirty days. This was the time when the Techiman capital was at Maaso. Maaso means "that town which is big."

All the subchiefs lived in their villages, and only the chief and his servants lived at the Maaso palace. The subchiefs had elected some of their elders to take care of their Maaso wards in their absence. These elders did not go to the chief's palace, but stayed within their wards. They went to their farms every day and stayed in their houses. The chiefs came from their villages and went to the palace only when there was trouble, or during Monokuo when they wait to celebrate the Adae. After the Adae they went back to their villages leaving the elders behind to take care of their wards. Nana Katakyera Brempong promised to face hunger the next day. He would stay in a room without any food or drink for thirty days. He did not know that it was a trick that Kwakye Ameyaw and the servants were playing to kill him. He was not forced to do it, but it was a trap into which he fell. He began the fast. Every morning talking drums were beaten to call him to make sure that he was not dead. They beat the drums, "Brempong Katakyera Wobetumi ne kom adi abemerese?" (Brempong Katakyera, can you face hunger?). The chief answered, "Maadi maawie" (I have already faced it). This went on for twenty-nine days. On the twenty ninth day, the chief's voice became very small and dry. He could not answer the call of the talking drums properly. On the last day, the thirtieth, no answer was given to the call of the drums. Nana Katakyera had died and the stool was vacant for Nana Kwakye Ameyaw.

The death of the chief brought silence in the palace. The other chiefs were in their villages and the servants kept it hidden from the elders in charge of the Maaso wards. Later, they informed some of the linguists secretly. The announcement of the chief's death brought disorder to the capital. The Krontihene was informed in his town. Men began to ride about on horses. Killings began simultaneously in all directions. The riders used their big cutlasses on the head of every person they met. They went to the palace at Maaso to see the dead chief. All the chief's servants, about three thousand, were killed in the presence of the Krontihene. Nana Kwakye Ameyaw succeeded. The spirit of his predecessor was not satisfied with him; it was during Kwakye Ameyaw's time that Techiman was destroyed [during the 1722–23 Bono-Asante War].

Interview with Nana Akumfi Ameyaw, Ex-Techimanhene, ca. 1970

BONO CULTURE AND TRADITIONS

It is not true when people say that Techiman had no culture or tradition of its own. Techiman taught the Asante how to wear cloth. Techiman people used to wear ornaments made of gold. The Asante used pieces of iron from the blacksmith's shop and they called it gold. Techiman Queenmother Dwamenawaa taught the Asante what gold was. Techiman knew pure gold and it was only pure gold that they used. . . . The culture of Asante came from Techiman. Ohene Ameyaw was a great king. His treasury was different from that of Asante. Techiman had a gold treasury, but Asante had pieces of iron. Asante had no gold. How could they make gold ornaments? The Asante did not know anything like gold state swords. Everything they had was made of iron, the same as is used for making hoes, but they called it gold. Kente weaving came from Techiman. Even the ancestors of the present Bonwire Chief came from Techiman. When the Asante conquered Techiman, they picked some of the people who knew handiwork and took them to Asante. They selected goldsmiths and men who knew other crafts.

The beating of the talking drums came from Techiman. It is the responsibility of every chief to know the first words of the talking drums. The words go like this: "Odomankoma boa adee obɔɔ Bono ansa na abɔɔ adee biara." This means: "When [the Creator] created things, he created Bono before any other thing." There are many people who do not understand these words. The Asante had similar sayings [but in] their [own] words. Instead of "Odomankoma boo adee obɔɔ Bono," they play "Odomankoma boo adee Boreofo boo ada." They do not want to play "obɔɔ Bono," "it created Bono." The Bono are proud to say that they are the firstborn people, the first people to come to this land. Techiman has a golden stool still on Techiman land. The Asante took another of the Techiman golden stools away to Asanteland. [For instance,] the Buoyam Stool is pure gold. No one is allowed to see it. It is not in the village, and no one knows where it is kept. People are afraid that if the golden stool were shown to the public it would be stolen.

THE IMPORTANCE OF THE YAM FESTIVAL

The yam festival is celebrated every year. During yam festivals the chiefs remember their ancestors. They prepare mashed yam, sometimes mixed with palm oil, call the ancestors, and give the food to them. That particular day is a meeting day. The entire family congregates to pay homage to its chiefs. The most important thing about the yam festival is the family reunion. They meet the members who are sick. They ask what has happened to those who could not come. They pray to the ancestors to help them and guide them through another year.

KRA DWADEE ("WASHING THE SOUL—PURIFICATION OF THE KRA [(SOUL)]")

Kra dwadee is the purification of the *sunsum*, "spirit." The elders say that a man's life and his capacity for hard work depend on his *sunsum*. During the *kra* purification, they call on their *sunsum* to give them long life. They include the names of Onyankopon and the earth, [Asase] Yaa. It is a blessing and they beg to meet another year. When they pour a libation, they first call Onyankopon [Creator], followed by Asase Yaa and the ancestors, asking them to come and drink wine. The new year has emerged. They beg for long life, for success and for children. They also beg for the protection of the farmer against cutlass wounds, the protection of hunters against gun wounds, and the protection of travelers. They beg for children for women who are not productive and beg that women regain those of their children who died after birth. They also ask help for the building of the family. Finally, they promise to give Onyankopon, Asase Yaa, and the ancestors another sheep next year if they still have life. Libation is prayer. The chiefs' yam festivals and the *musuo yi* [removal of misfortune] are the same as those of the *abosomfo*.

THE FANTE AT TANO ANAFO

The grandparents of the Fanti migrated from Techiman to the coast about seven hundred years ago. Fanti Abakrampa people are called Aborafou meaning Bonofoɔ, Bono people. Brobro Fanti means Bono Bono Fanti. Bono Bono has been changed to Brobro. The Abakrampa asked that Nana Akumfi Ameyaw stay with them when he was young. He stayed with them for some years before he became a chief. He was a chief when the Anomabohene died. He buried the Anomabohene. As Techiman's chief, he used to go to Abakrampa, Mankesim, and other Fanti towns on occasions such as funerals. He encouraged most of those people to come to Techiman. Later, some of them came and Nana sent them to Tano Anafo via Nsuta. They settled there and started cocoa farms. Nana knew this would encourage other Fanti to come back to Techiman, their place of origin. During Nana's reign, the Fanti at Tano Anafo used to come to greet him every year during festivals. They sent him gifts of wine and money. They know they are part of Techiman.

Oral Traditions of Adanse and Denkyira

Kwame Y. Daaku

In the 1960s the Ghanaian historian Kwame Daaku (1933–74) pioneered an approach to the collection and analyzing of oral-historical data in Ghana, leading an invaluable effort to record and translate (from indigenous languages into English) a vast set of oral data from southern and northern Ghana. This data set incorporated the self-representations of many societies throughout the new nation. The result was a far-reaching collection of oral historical materials, providing insights into how the various peoples of Ghana view(ed) the movement of their societies through history, ecologies, and foreign encounters. Representing two early and principal societies of the forest—one south of Lake Bosomtwe, the other to the west—the story of Adanse and Denkyira, respectively, is revealed through Daaku's reading of the oral and documentary evidence. Unfortunately, Daaku passed away in 1974, only a few years after the project on Adanse and Denkyira was published.

Oral Tradition of Adanse

Adanse, a small traditional state in southern Asante with a population of about 94,000 [in 1960], has a rich and varied history. Lying south of Bekwai, with the [River] Pra to the south, Banka and Asante Akyem to the east, and Denkyira to the west, Adanse was once the home of most of the Akan clans. Indeed, it is traditionally known in Akan cosmogony as the place where God started the creation of the world. In the area bounded by the Pra, [Ofin], and Oda Rivers, the Akan first developed virtually all their political and social institutions. It was here that the Akan ideas of kingship, personified in the activities of Awurade Basa, first took shape. In traditional history Adanse was the first of the five principal Akan states, "the Akanman Piesie Anum," [and] the rest were Akyem Abuakwa, Assen, Denkyira, and Asante, in order of seniority, although not of power and resources.

Most of the ruling clans of the Akan forest states trace their origins to Adanse. Beyond Adanse all stories of migrations and modes of travel tend to be ill-supported, hazy, and, more often than not, unintelligible. Akyem

Abuakwa, Edweso, and Offinso or the Asona clan, trace their origins to Kokobiante, near Sodua, a small village on the Akorokyere-Dompoase road. The Assen, both the Asenee of Attandasu (Fante Nyankomase), the Asona of Apemanim, the Afutuakwa of Fosu, and the Aboabo of Assin Nyankomase trace their original homes to that stretch of territory between the Pra River and the Kwisa range, their most renowned former sites being Nimiaso and Apagya for the Attandasu and Ansa for the Apemanim. The Denkyira people or the Agona clan were once known to have occupied the land stretching from Asokwa westward to the neighborhood of Obuase and Akrofo to the confluence of the Oda and Ofin Rivers. Whilst most of the Bretuo of Mampong, and Kwahu trace their home to Ayaase and Ahensan, Abadweem and Edubiase are known to be the early homes of the Oyoko clan. Adanse then could be said to have nurtured most of the important Akan clans. The Asakyire of Akrokeri and Odumase, however, trace their home to places in the north, while the Asenee of Dompoase trace their origins to the neighborhood of their present town. The Ekona of Fomena also claims to have originated from Adanse.

There appear to have been two main reasons why most of the people moved from the Adanse area. Whereas in the early days scarcity of land resulting from overpopulation caused many people to move out in search of land, at a later date, especially from the middle of the seventeenth century, it was the rise of the empire states of Denkyira and Asante which forced out many people to emigrate to avoid being brought under the rule of members of different clans.

A significant and much more interesting factor in the rise of Adanse is the rule of its traditional deity, Bona. Unlike the successor states of Denkyira and Asante, which became important on account of the striking force that enabled them to bring different clans under their control, in Adanse it was the deity sited in the neighborhood of Patakoro which wielded much power and influence. At the height of its power and prestige in the pre-Denkyira period, Adanse was merely a loose confederation of clans or city-states that only came together under one leader to defend themselves in times of war. There never developed anything near the Denkyira and Asante systems in which one stool managed to impose itself on the others and got itself accepted as the paramount ruler. The degree of autonomy that prevailed is epitomized in the popular Adanse saying "Adanse nkotowa nkotowa obiara da ne ben!" Freely rendered, it means the various towns were like little crabs each of which controlled its hole, thus showing that each clan was completely autonomous and could do as it pleased in its sphere of influence. In spite of the tendency to remain independent, sometime in the sixteenth century Awurade Basa, the most renowned of the leaders of Adansemanso, attempted to unite all the clans under his leadership. This was done by creating a mystical sword known as the Afenakwa. Although it was generally accepted that whoever had custody of the sword should lead the Adanse in time of war, in peacetime the leader was never accorded any special privileges.

Unlike the Sasatia of Denkyira, which enhanced the power and prestige of the Agona clan, or the Golden Stool of Asante, the custody of which was permanently vested in the Oyoko clan of Kumase, the Afenakwa used to be passed on from father to son. It therefore never remained with one clan for a long time. First associated with Awurade Basa of the Asenee clan, the Afenakwa was inherited by his son, Apeanim Kwafromoa of the Bretuo clan in Ayaase. After Apeanim it went to Akora Foripa of the Asenee clan in Dompoaso, and from there Bonsra Afriyie of the Ekona clan in Fomena was given the sword sometime at the beginning of the eighteenth century.

It was Bonsra Afriyie who wisely kept the Afenekwa at Fomena with the Ekona clan. This was partly because he did not marry from another royal clan outside Fomena itself, and principally on account of the fact that the Ekona were blessed with a long line of brave and active leaders who never became too old on the stool to be forced to hand over the Afenakwa to their sons in times of national crisis. In spite of the leadership that had been offered by the Ekona since the beginning of the eighteenth century, the tendency for the other rulers to harp on their autonomy still continued. It was the introduction of British rule in Asante at the beginning of the twentieth century that crystallized Fomena's political leadership by raising it to the status of paramount stool over and above the other stools. From that period the Fomena chief was accorded the title of Adansehene.

On the other hand, from very early times people came to accept the power of Adanse Bona (Adanse Kunturapaa), the tutelary deity over all the state. At times referred to in the oral traditions as the creator, not much is known about the origins of Bona. Sited somewhere in a cave in the grove between Akakyere and Patakoro, it was the only regular connecting link between the various rulers. Patakoro, where the Priest of Bonsam, the God spokesman of Bona, stays, has been the scene of regular resort of people of all walks of life wanting to consult the deity on all sorts of things. At the annual yam festival for Bona, which falls at the end of August or the beginning of September, not only the Bonsam priest and the Bonahene, but also people from all parts of the state come to take part of it. In every December a much grander festival known as the annual dance is also celebrated. It is during this time that the priest, the keeper of the national annual calendar sends

Bonasuo (water from the Bona cave) to all the stool occupants to be used in the general purification of the state. And in times of danger or national calamity there is the "carrying of the Deity" or the divination ceremony for the whole state. It is during this ceremony that the subservience of the chiefs to the Bona deity is clearly seen. The Deity has allotted specific functions to be performed by each chief. The Akokyerehene is the Akradwarefohene (chief soul washer), the Adansehene head of the hammock bearers, Ayaasehene, the chief executioner, Akrofuomhene the treasurer, Edubiasehene the spokesman, and Dompoasehene the Gyaasehene. As a tutelar deity, not only is Bona expected to purify the state every year with the Bonasuo, but also each town is given a Bonsambɔɔ (Bonsam stone), on which sacrifices are made to appease the God when people go against his injunctions in the town. Thus people are spared the necessity of having to travel all the way to Patakoro when the deity is offended. It is interesting to note that virtually in front of the palaces of all the principal Akan chiefs who trace their original homes to Adanse are to be found Bonsambɔɔ, which in all instances is considered sacred—visible relic of their Adanse origins.

Within easy reach of the European trading centers at the coast and not far from the sources of kola from eastern and western Asante, and the area itself rich in gold deposits, Adanse stood to gain from the long-distance trade to the north and to the coast. Adanse traders were known to have traveled to both the northern and coastal markets to seek their fortune. In Adanse itself there developed an important market center at Edubiase, where people from far and near came to trade. Athwart the important trade route between Kumase and Cape Coast, the people benefited from the constant flow of traders moving up and down. Even those who could not go to the centers of trade profited from it by issuing their local foodstuffs and by providing accommodation to strangers. The desire to derive maximum benefits from trade accounts for the fact that most of the townships moved their settlements as and when the trade route was diverted.

It was its favorable economic position that always drew her into the power struggles of the later states. From about 1696, when their refusal to help Asante against Denkyira forced them to cross the Pra to seek refuge in Akyem, some or all of the Adanses have suffered from constant emigrations across the Pra to the south. Whereas most of them had always returned to their former homes after such flights, the beginning of the [nineteenth] century saw a large part of Asante, the Apemanim, Afutuakwa, Aboabo, Attendansu, all now known as Assen, moving to settle permanently south of the Pra. The last wave of migration took place in the later part of the [nineteenth] century, when the Bekwai-Adanse War forced them once again to move across the Pra.

Oral Traditions of Denkyira

Adawu, Adawu Denkyira, that devours elephants,
Whenever we kneel down, we call on the name of Denkyira,
Whenever we rise up we look to Denkyira,
The mighty one,
Let one hasten to look at Denkyira,
The great one,
That swallows elephants,
If Denkyira went to sleep
It is now arisen, it is arisen indeed!
The Porcupine [i.e., Asante] is subject to Amponsem
Boa Amponsem, who uses only the freshly mined gold.

These and several other praises were always called out on festive occasions by the creator's drummer (Odomankoma Kyerema) of Denkyira to tell the story of the heroic past of the state, which, between 1650 and 1700, was without doubt the most powerful and certainly the most wealthy [of] all the Akan forest states of modern Ghana. Now divided into Upper and Lower Denkyira, which are separated by Twifo, it was once a vast empire stretching as far west as the Tano.

The people were formerly known as the Adawufo, but during their very long stay at Nkyiraa in the Brong Ahafo region they became known as the Denkyiras. Before the 1650s, Denkyira formed part of a loose confederation of states known as Akani, which were found in the area washed by the Oda, Ofin, and Pra Rivers. Throughout the first half of the seventeenth century the most important of these states was Adanse, which was being centralized by Ewurade Basa of the Asenee clan. Although all the states of the confederacy were grouped around their clan leaders, they had a common bond of unity in their worship of their traditional deity—Bona.

By the beginning of the seventeenth century, however, the long trading contacts with the north and with the coastal states were creating many difficulties and problems which could not be easily solved by the traditional consultation of tutelary deities. This was because trading, especially the coastal trading with the Europeans, brought in prosperity, with its attendant problems such as population growth and new economic demands.

When in 1482 the Portuguese erected their castle at Elmina, they brought the sources of supply of foreign manufactured goods closer to the states of the Akani Confederation. The problem of population growth is evidenced by the frequent reports of wars in the interior. But it was the period after 1650 which was to intensify the struggle to assert one's power over one's neighbors. Several factors made possible the increased rivalry in the inland states. Firstly, there was the rush for footholds by virtually the whole of the Western and Northern European nations. The defeat of the Portuguese by the Dutch in 1637, and their eventual expulsion in 1642, was the beginning of a long period of keen and bitter European rivalry on the coast of Ghana. Between 1650 and 1701, the Brandenburgers, Danes, Dutch, English, French, and Swedes established their forts and castles along the coast. The period of European concentration witnessed a great proliferation of firearms on the Gold Coast (Southern Ghana). These firearms helped in intensifying the interethnic wars, which produced countless slaves for the trans-Atlantic trade. It is interesting to note that it was not the coastal states which first came into possession of firearms which led in the building of empire states on the Gold Coast. This was primarily due to the dependence of these states on the European trading nations, which overtly and covertly interfered in local politics for their own benefit.

The rise of Denkyira in 1659 is closely associated with the spread of firearms. Lying farther away from the area of direct interference of the Europeans, Denkyira was able to concentrate its efforts in subjugating all the neighboring states. By the end of the 1680s, when it directed its attention to the southern and southwestern states, it had already laid a good foundation of the state. By the end of the seventeenth century Denkyira had subjugated Adanse, Asante, Assin, Sefwi, Wassa, and Aowin. To the east, Denkyira had entered into an alliance with Akyem Abuakwa, one of the important Akan forest states.

Like Asante after it, Denkyira had a common bond of unity in the sacred objects which its rulers succeeded in introducing to the state. The most celebrated of these are the *Abankamdwa* (made of beads), the *Sasatia*, and the Executioner's Sword. These objects are said to have come together during the reign of the founding ancestress Adekra Adebo. The foundations of a politically strong state were said to have been laid by the fourth ruler, Wirempe Ampim, who in 1659 rid Denkyira of Adanse rule. A strong ruler, Wirempe Ampim was perhaps the most fearful of the Denkyira rulers. In his drive towards national unity he caused the court and all the institutions of kingship to be well regarded. Those who disregarded his instructions were severely punished, hence the saying "Wirempe Ampim a owo ntam nso yenka," i.e., Wirempe Ampim whose oath is not to be sworn.

It was, however, Boa Amponsem I whose name is closely associated with the stool. In spite of the fact that he was the fifth king, the Denkyira Stool is known as "Amponsem Stool"—a testimony to his enlightened leadership. Coming to the stool in about 1662, at the tender age of eight, he ruled until 1692. In his eventful reign, he extended the borders of his empire to reach the Tano in the west and the Birim in the east. It was he who brought virtually all the gold mining areas under Denkyira rule. Gold from the tributary states poured into the coffers of Denkyira at Abankeseso, hence the popular epithet "Boa Amponsem a odi sika atomprada," i.e., "Boa Amponsem who uses only the freshly mined gold."

At the height of its power, Denkyira, under Boa Amponsem, controlled not only the sources of gold, but [also] all the trade paths that led to the European establishments dotted between Half Assine and Anomabo. All the European companies endeavored to attract traders from Denkyira to transact business with them to the exclusion of their rivals. It was with this in view that between 1680 and 1694, Abankeseso, the Denkyira capital, became the resort of messengers from the European companies. Nor did the king remain an inactive participant in the trade. To safeguard his interests and those of his nationals, he appointed his trade consul to the coast. Tributary states [that] disrupted the free flow of trade were sure to incur the displeasure of Denkyira. In 1697, for instance, Assin was punished for interfering with the coastal trade.

Between 1670 and 1700, it was Denkyira which dictated the terms of trade because of its control over the sources of supply. Since Denkyira was the most powerful Akan State on the Gold Coast, it was to be expected that the Dutch, which was also the most powerful European trading nation in the area, would seek understanding and friendship with it. It is not certain when Dutch-Denkyira relations were first forged. But it is most uncertain that the Elmina Note, which formed the basis of the relationship between the two, did not come into Denkyira possession by a mere accident of war. It is believed that at a certain point in its history, Denkyira took the Note from Eguafo, to whom the ground rent of the Elmina Castle was being paid. The evidence in support of this contention is hard to come by. It is true that the Dutch were on friendly terms with Denkyira, and that Denkyira might have received some payments from the Dutch. But the origin of the agreement is more likely to have been a commercial agreement to induce the Denkyira traders to come to the Elmina Castle to trade with the Dutch. The haste with which the Dutch dispatched an emissary to Kumasi after the Asante defeat of Denkyira to induce the Asante traders to come down to their forts confirms one in this belief.

By 1670, Denkyira had evolved an administrative machinery to suit its ever advancing empire. The whole state was divided into three fighting forces—the Akumatire (Right Wings), the Kyeremfem (Left Wing), and the Agona Adontendom (Advance Guard). Each of these divisions was under an Osafohene or war leader who exercised political control over his division in time of peace. Under the Osafohene were some chiefs and village heads. Under some of these major divisions were such officials as the Gyasehene, Tumantuhene, Dwanetoafohene, Kronkohene, etc. These divisions were later to be perfected by the Asante, who introduced such titles as Kronti and Akwamu, etc. With its wealth, fame, and strong government, the court of Denkyira was filled with royal hostages from the various tributary states who[se] continuous safety depended on the good behavior of their states. Here the young royals were educated in the intricacies of the Akan system of government. One of the most renowned of such hostages was Osei Tutu, who served his royal apprenticeship under the famous Boa Amponsem. This event, above all else, may have given rise to the popular saying "Kotoko som Amponsem," i.e., The Porcupine (Asante) is subject to Amponsem (Denkyira).

Power and wealth seem to have blinded Denkyira to the plight of its subject states. Bosman and other contemporary observers described Denkyira as "haughty and overbearing." It did not hesitate to punish tributary states which defaulted in the payments of their yearly tributes. Tradition has it that it was because of such excessive demands that the Asante under Osei Tutu rebelled and fought its successful war of independence between 1699 and 1701. His policy of extortion did not endear Denkyira to its tributary states, which patiently awaited an opportunity to rebel against their overlord. Contrary to the popular assertion that it was the overconfidence and thoughtlessness of Ntim Gyakari which brought about the defeat, the evidence seems to suggest that it was the desertion of the subject states which played a decisive [role] in the defeat of Denkyira. Of all the many states it was only its ally, Akyem Abuakwa, which was known to have fought for Denkyira at this crucial moment. This fact explains the presence of the Abuakwahene of Denkyira, who is now the Nifahene of the Denkyira State.

The defeat of [the] Denkyira state was one of the most significant events, and certainly the most remembered event, in the traditions of the Akan people. This event is well-remembered by the famous dirge, which shows when and where the Denkyira nation fell; it runs:

Ntim Gyakari,
Obrempon honyani a,

Osoa ne man kobaa no Feyiase,
Ntim Gyakari Nana firi Feyiase akoem

Ntim Gyakari,
The wealthy noble
Who led its nation to its doom at Feyiase,
Grandchild of Ntim Gyakari hails from Feyiase

An Account of Early Asante

Agyeman Prempeh I

In 1907 Asantehene Agyeman Prempeh I (1870–1931) wrote The History of Ashanti Kings and the Whole Country Itself, *a detailed account of the Oyoko ruling dynasty of Asante from the seventeenth to the nineteenth centuries that was eventually published in 2003. This important text by Prempeh I, the thirteenth ruler of imperial Asante, is the only surviving record of its kind for a Ghanaian state and perhaps the earliest of such histories written in English by an African ruler. Though the transcribed text is not grammatically correct, the use of brackets, asterisks, and question marks makes it intelligible enough for the reader to follow. Included in Prempeh's account is a seminal but mythic narrative of that dynasty, featuring the arrival of the foundational ancestress of the royal Oyoko, Ankyewa Nyame, and the emergence of her people from "holes in the ground": that is, the Asante are an indigenous rather than an immigrant people. The following excerpts focus on Nyame's arrival and the origins of the Oyoko and other clans.*

[The Arrival of Ankyewa Nyame at Asantemanso]

After the beginning of the world at an Ashanti town called Akim Asiakwa there was a hunter. [Then the thing to do was hunting.] Once he said he was going to the forest and then he saw a Bear in a hole, but this hunter [who knows all] had recognized the speaking of every creature, and this Bear told him that after a certain Ashanti feast, the son of God will come on earth. And a week after the feast the hunter went to the forest and hid himself in some [bush and] place. Then a great thunder bust 3 times and then a long gold chain descend from heaven to the earth and Essen came down carrying a bell & a stool called *Dufua* [early form of a stool consisting of solid block of wood with a handle] and wearing a fur [hunter] hat made of animal skin and then an immense copper dish ornamented by statues of beasts and inside a [*man sitting on*] woman carrying a stool and then another woman called Anchōyami [Ankyewa Nyame] [*came*] by the chain and sat on the stool and the former gave her the stool and sit behind her and this woman saw the hunter and called out for him with her hand because she was [*something . . . *]. Ohemah and that woman made a press gesture with his hands and sat (?) in a little circle and then pointed his hand to his mouth but that man (?) was unable to understand it. And in a minute after the woman and the copper dish together flew and came right to in the [middle] midst of the city and all the citizens gather near [him] her and did the same press gestures as before and the people killed a hen and made a soup for [him] her when she had tasted it then she was able to speak. The only [thing] word she said was "I only mistakenly come here. Here is not the place I mean to come."

So saying she disappeared and went to a district called Asumyia Santimansū [Asantemanso]. And there certain [people?] from the ground appeared near her and the 10 family Royal [all] also appeared from the ground in different parts. The first came, and she was nearly bear a child and at that time people can go to heaven, and return afterwards. When that woman enter (?) he said: I am the son of God and my mother is called [Afua (?)] Insua and there it was sent to him from God 2 Sūman [any protecting power, including the *abosom*] one called Kwābinăh & the other [one Kotuo (?)] Kūntror and a medicine called damtua [came] with (?) together. That's why when any Ashanti woman is nearly to bear her son, they put (cloth?), but Kwabinah is only worn by all the royal persons.

*[Ankyewa Nyame and the Gathering of the Clans (*mmusua*)]*

When Anchioyami came upon a place called Asumyia Ashantimansu a family called Oyuku sprang from the ground and sat at her right hand. Then another family called Dākū sprang from the ground and sat on her left hand. Then another family called Oyuku sprang and sat on her right hand. Then seven other different families came altogether, but they were not her families.—(Marginalia: from a place called Adansi Ahinsan [Adansimansu]. When they heard of Anchoyami they flocked to her).

Biletuo [Biretuo]
Atnah (?)
Agonah [Agona] [or] and Assokole
Jume [or] and Assunnāh [Asona]
Ekuonah [Ɛkoɔna]
Assachily [Asakyiri]
Adduanah [Aduana] [or] and Achua

But there are some more Ayuku which are not families of Anchiayami. At that time when Anchiayami came to Assumi Asantimanso but it has been further explained that Yuku were the first people to come to her. There are three kinds of Oyuku. When these Yukun came near to her she asked one "Who are you?" and they said we are [part] member of your Yukun: and she told them "if you are Yukus, then I am Yuku-Kor-Kor-Kon, i.e. I am more Yuku than you." She also asked them what was the name of their Yukus and they said "we are Oyuku Abohen." To the second Yukun she asked them what was the name of their Yuku, they said "we are Yuku Atutuō." To the third she asked the name of their Yuku and they said [that] "we are Yuku [Bléman] Blaémam." There are three kinds of Oyukun Abohen

1st are called Asarman (The [*chief*] head of all Yuku)
2nd are called Kenassie
3rd are called Manpontin

There are three kinds of Atutuo

1st are called Adenchimansu
2nd are called [*Papasu*] Panpasoo
3rd are called Ayuomu

Fante Oral Traditions: Kwamankɛse and Komenda

John K. Fynn

We do not know much about the earliest peoples who occupied the coastline of the Gold Coast. Certainly, there were some, such as the Etsi, who settled along the coastal region; the Fante peoples encountered them on their arrival. But is it the Fante who came to dominate the coast perhaps as early as the fourteenth century, and even though Fante accounts of early migration and settlement include something about the Etsi, there is very little about the latter and their history before the newcomers. In the following two excerpts, the late Ghanaian historian John Kofi Fynn (1935–2005) utilizes both oral and documentary evidence to explore the origins and organization of two early and important Fante states—Kwamankɛse and Komenda—that were among the first to trade with European merchants on the Gold Coast. Fynn's work among the Fante follows closely the approach developed by Kwame Daaku, a pioneer in oral-historical research among Ghanaian societies.

Kwamankɛse

Kwamankɛse state shares borders with Assen Attandanso in the north, Abeadze in the east, and Abora in the south and west. Apart from Ayeldo, the capital, the Kwamankɛse state consists of Kwaman, ɔbosome, ɔsɛkyerew, Tekyiman, Nyamebekyerɛ, Brenyi, ɔdɔmpɔ, Katakyiase and a number of villages. Kwamankɛse literally means "Great Kwaman" and derives its name from Kwaman, the ancient settlement of the Bɔrbɔr Fante. The people of Kwamankɛse claim that they did not join the other Bɔrbɔr Fante who settled at Mankessim and that their chief, Idan I, organized the state out of the remnants of the Akans who stayed behind at Kwaman. Hence Kwaman was traditionally called "Akan nkaase," "remnant Akans."

The earliest mention of Kwaman known to the writer is contained in a Dutch report of 1653. In that year, Louys Dammaert noted in his *Journal* that as a result of civil war in "Fantyn" (i.e., Mankessim), the Braffo of

Fante "with the most part of the Caboseros (chiefs)" had departed to *Quaman* (Kwaman) and that Adonnie (Adonu), the leader of the faction opposed to the Braffo, had fled with his followers who were too few to Anianj (Eyan). Some versions of Bɔrbɔr Fante tradition assert that the Kwaman formerly formed part of the Abora traditional area and that the chief of Kwaman was the *ɔbaatan* or mother of the Aboras.

The Kwaman people, however, say that their state had always been independent and that it was the Aborahin Samuel Gardiner (Otu V) who made unsuccessful attempts to incorporate Kwamankɛse within the Abora state. They admit that in the olden days they closely cooperated with all the Bɔrbɔr Fante, including the Aboras, for the defense of Fanteland against the incursion of their common enemy—the Asante. But they deny that they had ever been subordinate to Abora. The Abora-Kwamankese dispute was the subject of a judicial enquiry by a commission appointed by the British colonial administration in the early years of this century. In spite of the evidence of the Amanhin of Mankessim and Anomabu, or J. B. Brown and of John Mensah Sarbah, to the effect that Kwaman had always formed part of the Abora division of the Bɔrbɔr Fante, C. H. Harper, chief assistant colonial secretary, ruled that:

1. Kwaman and Dominase are not subordinate in their ordinary jurisdiction to Omanhene Otu Ababio of Abra.
2. Omanhene Otu Ababio of Abra has no control over Dominase and Kwaman lands.
3. On ceremonial occasions, the Omanhene of Abra takes precedence of the chiefs of Kwaman and Dominase and the tie between Abra, Kwaman and Dominase is [a] sentimental and ceremonial one in that they have at different times been in alliance in time[s] of war and have consulted together in times of peace, but that the Omahene of Abra has claim of right to the assistance in war and in council the chiefs of Kwaman and Dominase. As a result of this, the British colonial government recognized both Abeadze and Kwamankese as independent states and their chiefs Amanhin.

It seems to me, however, that it was the policies pursued by Otu V, Aborahin, which brought about dissensions in the Abora division of the Bɔrbɔr Fante, which eventually led to the breakup of the division. Samuel Gardiner was enstooled Aborahin in 1900 but was deposed four years later. The available evidence indicates that the chiefs who engineered his deposition included Ewusi Tsenase, chief of Dominase, Idan I, chief of Kwaman, Kwesi Abawa, chief of Mpeseduadze and Adontsihin of Abora, and Kwaa Yeboa, chief of Odonase and Tufohin of Abora. For instance, Ewusi Tsenase played a major role in the enstoolment of Kwame Tawia of Bondze as successor to Gardiner. In a letter dated 10 November 1906, Ewusi Tsenase informed the provisional commissioner, Central Province, that "I have completed the installation of Kwamin Tawia as the Omanhene of Abra pending a reasonable explanation which I shall give at the next proposed meeting on hearing from you after the agricultural show; as the people do not think fit that the district should remain without one who owns the head on account of those who refuse to join it."

Kwame Tawia or Otu VI, however, abdicated in 1906 and Samuel Gardiner was brought back to the stool as Otu VI Ababio. Samuel Gardiner, of course, could not have as his principal advisers those who had been the cause of this removal from office in 1904 and so he initiated moves to punish the chiefs whom he regarded as ringleaders. It was against this background of uncertainty and confusion that some of the chiefs decided upon noncooperation with the Aborahin. As Kwesi Abowa, the Adontsihin of Abora, told Commissioner Atterbury, "It is a fact that Abura, Abiadzi and Kwaman were united together. One is not above the other but we should be strong in order to fight against the Ashantis. If the three chiefs meet together they call each other brother. I heard from ancestors that they make one up to Kwesi Brebo's (Otu IV's) time. The Omanhene called Gardiner has brought a dispute amongst the division. He stopped the supply of gunpowder being given to Abeadze and Kwaman unless the applications are sent through him. This brought the dispute." He noted further that Gardiner laid claims to Abeadze lands and requested that if anything was to be done in Abeadze and Kwaman he should be informed. He added that Gardiner was "fond of litigation so everybody must be independent of him."

Komenda

The Komenda state is bounded on the west by Shama, on the east by Elmina, on the north by Wassa, and on the northeast by Eguafo and Abrem. The capital of the state is Akatakyi, known in European records as Little Commando, Aitaco, Akitakij, or Ekke Tokki. Apart from Akatakyi, the state of Komenda consists of Aboransa, Antardo, Bisease, Dominase, Dompoase, Kissi, Kwarhinkrom, Kyiasi, Kokwaado, Kafodzidzi and a number of villages. . . .

According to their traditional accounts, the founder of the Komenda state was one Kɔme, who migrated with his people from Takyiman in the present day Brong-Ahafo Region of Ghana. It is said that, in the remote past, the Takyiman area was constantly in great turmoil; there were wars and rumors of war. In this general state of insecurity, it became necessary for a number of families to leave their homeland in search of peace and security. It was in a moment of such crisis that Nana Kɔme, a warlord, and his sub-chiefs and people left Takyiman and began the long march southward to the coast. They fought on their way until they reached Mankesim where they stayed for some time. From Mankesim they moved to Kromantse, Yamoransa, Eguafo and finally to Akatakyi. It was here that the peoples dispersed to found settlements which later on constituted the Komenda state.

Eguafo tradition, however, states that the Komenda people were originally part of the Eguafo kingdom and that, in the olden days, Eguafo stretched from the Benya river in the east to the mouth of the river Pra in the west. They add that Akatakyi itself was formerly a small fishing village peopled by immigrants from the Nkusukum area.

Some twenty years ago, Nana Kofi Asefua, chief of Kankan (Dutch-Komenda), and his elders told Mrs. Eva L. R. Meyerowitz that Akatakyi was founded by Akyene Takyi, a grandson of the first Eguafo king, and that it was referred to in the early European records as "Little Eguafo." The Komenda people admit that the lands they now occupy formerly belonged to the Eguafo but they insist that the founder of their state was Kɔme and that they had never been subjects of Eguafo kings. Their story is that when Kɔme and his people arrived in Eguafo, they appealed to Abo Takyi, the king of Eguafo, to give them a place to settle. Abo Takyi told the Nkusukum immigrants that all his lands had been taken up and settled except the area between Kankan and the estuary of the river Pra which was inhabited by a man-eating monster. The Eguafo king further told Kɔme and his followers that if they could capture and kill the monster, he would give the land to them as a present. Kɔme, being an old warrior, accepted the challenge. He attacked, captured and killed the monster which he found to be half-human and half-animal. After completing this assignment, Abo Takyi and Kɔme "drank [*ɔbosom*]" to be friends. The king of Eguafo not only honored his promise by giving the land between the Benya and the Pra rivers to Kɔme and his people but also he brought a young girl who had just reached her puberty age to be sacrificed to the gods to mark the occasion.

There is documentary evidence, however, to show that up to the early years of the eighteenth century, the kings of Eguafo controlled the land area now occupied by the Komenda people. A "Dutch Map of the Gold Coast of Guinea" drawn at Moure in 1629 shows that (a) the Eguafo kingdom stretched from the east bank of the Benya river to the Pra river and (b) that Akatakyi was a small fishing and salt making village on that coast.

Secondly, in 1687, the English reported that the French were attempting to settle at Komenda with the assistance of the king of Eguafo. The following year, Amoasi Esilfi, king of Eguafo, on behalf of himself, his chiefs, and their descendants, signed a treaty with N. Sweerts, the Dutch director-general at Elmina, which, among other things, ceded the beach "beginning from the river of Shama (Bosompra) as far as to the river of del Mina named Banja (Benya) on which beach are situated the small villages Cottebre, Obriebie, Akitakij or Commany and Ampenyi." The chief of Eguafo also agreed not to permit any foreign nation to settle on the said beach except the English, who should be allowed to keep their lodge at "Akitakij or small Commany." And in the early 1690s, king Abo Takyi of Eguafo invited the English at Cape Coast to build a fort at Akatakyi.

In 1695 it was reported that the Dutch were angry that the Eguafo had invited the English to settle in their country so they solicited the help of the Twifo and the people [of] Cabes Terra to fight the Eguafo. The English added that they assisted the Eguafo in raising a large army which defeated the Dutch and their allies.

Nevertheless, by the middle of 1696, the English had not completed the building of their fort and they had no goods to sell. In January of that year, the Council at Cape Coast Castle noted that "Aguaffo is dissatisfied that Commeda is neglected which cannot be done without supplies . . ." Since the Eguafo people wanted trade badly, especially guns and gunpowder, king Abo Takyi signed a humiliating treaty with the Dutch in October, 1696. Among the clauses was one which stipulated that nobody should be allowed to build a fort or lodge "between river Banja and Bosompra."

Finally, in 1700, Takyi Adico who had become king of Eguafo with the support of the English, exempted the latter from paying ground rent whenever there was not enough trade at the English fort at Akatakyi. It is clear from these accounts that by the second decade of the eighteenth century at least the people of Komenda formed an integral part of the Eguafo kingdom. The political growth of Akatakyi from a dependent market center into an autonomous city-state was largely the outcome of the perpetual tension between rival European trading companies which competed among themselves for commercial supremacy on the Eguafo coast. The servants of the European trading houses wanted to ensure that the reigning king in Eguafo was in their respective company's interests. Thus, from the second half of the seventeenth century, the European traders actively interfered in the politics of Eguafo. During this period, kings of Eguafo were enstooled and destooled in rapid succession, largely as a result of troubles fomented by the Dutch and the English. In 1698, for instance, Nicholas Buckeridge, the English governor, lured king Abo Takyi into Cape Coast Castle and murdered him. Buckeridge, who believed the king of Eguafo was too independent to be trusted, had helped to replace him with Takyi Ankan, the king's younger brother who had been for long on English pay. Also, between 1714 [and] 1716, the Dutch were known to have enlisted the support of the Fante to reinstate Takyi Kuma, who had been deposed at the instance of the English.

Thus, in Eguafo, as in neighboring Efutu, one of the results of European contact was the subversion of the traditional power structure. Akatakyi, in which stood the English fort, became a fast-growing town and the town's prosperity and wealth from the increased volume of trade enabled the Akatakyi chiefs to rival the Eguafo kings in importance and power. It seems to me therefore that the political instability in Eguafo during the second half of the seventeenth and the early years of the eighteenth century largely as a result of the European contact partly explains the emergence of Akatakyi as a new center of political power.

Archaeological Reflections on Ghanaian Traditions of Origin

Kwaku Effah-Gyamfi

Much of the oral tradition presented thus far has been of great use not only to historians but also to archaeologists. In fact, many of the traditions of origin from holes and caves do point to real ancient settlement sites that have been investigated by archaeologists, though more still needs to be done. Discoveries from some of these sacred sites have expanded our understanding of earlier societies and have also been part and parcel of debates about the origins of the peoples who came to or originated in the region that became Ghana. In the following excerpt, the late Ghanaian archaeologist Kwaku Effah-Gyamfi, who died prematurely in 1983, provides a very helpful way to organize the various oral traditions associated with migration and settlement. It should be noted that most traditions of origins make vertical claims—descending from the sky or arising from holes in the ground—that, conceptually, make it impossible for their bearers to be migrants and mark them, rather, as indigenes.

Traditions which explain how and why the Akan came to occupy their present localities are many and diverse, and at the outset the writer wishes to admit that he does not claim to know all of these traditions in view of the large size of this ethnic group. However, a fairly representative number of these traditions of origin are known and they seem to fall into broad categories:

(a) Traditions of migration.
(b) Traditions of origin from the sky.
(c) Traditions of origin from holes in the ground or caves.

Traditions of Migration

Migration stories are the commonest of the Akan traditions of origin. Two sub-types are distinguishable. The first type involves long-distance migration from beyond the present borders of Ghana. Daaku (1969) recorded traditions from Adanse Akrokerri which claim that the ancestors of that town migrated from Egypt with intermittent stops until they reached their present locality. [Eva] Meyerowitz (1950) also recorded traditions from Takyiman which say that the founders of Bono migrated to where they are from as far as Mossiland, even beyond. Many of these long-distance migration stories are garbled and it is not certain where exactly to pinpoint the source of the migration. In many cases the route is not known. Many of such traditions also gained currency surprisingly in the early [1950s] and have since been refuted, in some cases, by the very oral informants who are claimed to have provided the information. For example, of the seventeen oral historians whom the writer interviewed on the origins of the Bono, many of whom had previously been interviewed by Meyerowitz, only two (both of whom, incidentally, happened to be Muslims) mentioned ancient Ghana as the original home of the Bono; the rest were unanimous in claiming a local ancestry of the Bono. In fact recent research is increasingly indicating that Meyerowitz's informants either deceived her or that she herself grossly exaggerated or totally misunderstood the meaning of some of the traditions she collected not only in the Brong-Ahafo region but also at the coast. Although the present writer strongly doubts the authenticity of such traditions, it is possible to argue that such traditions involve only a few groups of people who ultimately became absorbed into a larger indigenous population, but who through rise in political power, maintained their identity and, therefore, tradition. In this case such a tradition may not be dealing directly with the bulk of the population but of the minority group. This view may be strengthened by the fact that in almost all the states where long-distance origin is claimed, there is another version, which is in most cases more popular and which claims to have originated either in the locality or somewhere within the confines of modern Ghana.

Migrations from areas within modern Ghana form the bulk of the migration traditions. Indeed it may not be wrong to estimate that over half of the Akan states have come to their present localities through migrations. At the coast many of the Fante states such as Kommenda, Efutu, Edina and Mankesim claim to have migrated from the Bono state located at the northern forest margin of Ghana. Indeed, this Bono-Fante relationship is not only shown in language similarity, but also certain similarities occur in festivals and stool names. In addition, the story of this Fante migration and the mention of the leaders involved are told, quite independently, in the two now widely separated areas. The Denkyira are also claimed to have migrated from settlement in the Bono state. In the forest proper several states such

Exposure of a fourteenth- and fifteenth-century metallurgical workshop in the Banda region of Ghana. In the foreground, burned basins associated with the processing of copper alloys have been bisected to determine their shape in profile. To the right rear, anvil stones associated with a series of forges occur near the original ground surface. To the left, a sharpening stone and two intact clay pots surround another forge. Photograph by Ann B. Stahl, 2009. Courtesy of the photographer.

as Akim Kotoku, Akim Bosome, Assin Atandansu, Assin Apimenin, Mampong, Dwaben, Kokofu etc. claim to have migrated at various times from the Adanse area of the Asante Region.

Many of these migration stories of the second sub-type involve conquest or peaceful [incorporation] of the original inhabitants who themselves were either Akan or Guan but whose populations were relatively small. The many reasons for such migrations include secession from the parent state due to quarrels, most often between two royals over a stool succession, deliberate search for better agricultural lands, greater economic gain and less populous land, war and famine. From the available archaeological, oral traditional and historical evidence, these migrations took place at various time[s] between the fourteenth and eighteenth centuries CE. It seems to the writer that the migrations from the Bono state would have taken place slightly earlier than any of those from the Adanse area. For at the time of European contact many of the Fante states had been established at the coast, whereas during this time many of the states mentioned were still in the present Asante area. However, it is also most likely that some of the Fante states migrated much later and that the Bono-Fante movement probably involved a steady trickle of kindred groups which would have covered the whole of the above time bracket.

Traditions concerning Origin from the Sky

These traditions are not unique to the Akan. Even in Ghana there are a number of non-Akan groups such as the Ndumpo of Bofie in Brong-Ahafo Region who claim to have descended from the sky. In Nigeria the Yoruba creation myth mentions the founders of Yorubaland as having descended from the sky. These traditions are indeed difficult to interpret. How, in reality, can people descend from the sky? No wonder many scholars have considered these traditions as myths which merely symbolize the autochthonous standing of the groups in possession of such traditions. While this interpretation is logical, an alternative must also be allowed: perhaps such traditions are a clothed language to refer to people who originated north of the present Akan land. In the Twi language the word *soro,* which means "the sky," may often be used to mean "the north." Thus to descend from the sky may mean that the founders of the particular state or settlement came from the north. This view may be strengthened by the fact that even though the traditions are widespread in Ghana, the mechanism of descent seems to be generally the same: The founders either came down in a large brass bowl (*ayaa*) or along a metal chain (*nkonsonkonson*). It must be noted that until the arrival of the Europeans, brass and other trade items were obtained largely from the trade between modern Ghana and the Middle Niger area. Thus it is possible that between the thirteenth and fifteenth centuries CE brass bowls and other brass objects would have been one of the most valuable belongings of a migrant group, and that these would have been fundamental regalia to the descendants of such a group. It must be mentioned here also that, although not directly associated with the origin of any founders, there are three main ancient brass bowls located in the Brong-Ahafo Region of Ghana which are all claimed to have descended from the sky on the same day. These brass bowls are said to have been located (1) at Nsoko in the former Begho area which is claimed to have been one of the earliest international commercial centers in Ghana, (2) at Kagbrema and Bono state, and (3) at Bono Manso, the capital of the former Bono state. (The original brass bowl from Bono Manso is said to have been seized during the Asante invasion of the Bono state in 1723 CE and sent to the Asantehene's court. It was later replaced, most probably by a European import.) All three brass bowls are as highly venerated and ritualized as those associated with founders. The two brass bowls from Nsoko and Kagbrema have been identified as of

North African manufacture which would have been traded into the area around the fourteenth century CE.

We may not have a straightforward interpretation to this category of traditions of origin among the Akan. In any case what seems intriguing to the writer is the fact that almost all the Akan traditions from the sky make mention of metal, particularly of brass. In Ghana, the earliest available evidence for ironworking is not earlier than the first half of the first millennium CE. Brass crucibles have been excavated within contexts dating to the sixteenth century CE at the artisan quarter of Begho and to the same period at Bono Manso. One would suggest that at least the founder of those possessing such traditions had then known the use of brass, and from the archaeological evidence above, this would most probably be between the fourteenth and sixteenth centuries CE. Considering the fact that most of the migrations discussed above were later than this period, the areas where the founders of the groups possessing these traditions settled would still have been sufficiently unoccupied to allow the founders to claim an autochthonous stand.

Traditions concerning Origin from Holes and Caves

Like traditions [involving a] sky origin, these traditions are also widespread, though not as widely as those of migration. They are also considered by many writers to be myths. To emerge from the ground, it has been interpreted symbolically that founders were the autochthones, and, by implication, the unchallenged able owners of the lands around. This interpretation as it stands is plausible, but the recent archaeological discoveries made at the spots of some of the sacred sites of the so-called origin have led the writer to go beyond mere symbolic interpretation. I have suggested elsewhere that many of the traditions which involved people emerging from the ground may be related to the founders living in caves or rock shelters or artificial holes made for some specific purpose.

The sacred hole associated with the founders of Bono state, Amuowi I, was, upon inspection by the writer, found to be adjoining a large rock shelter, which when excavated showed far more occupation, dating to the fifth century CE. Interestingly, the pottery from the rock shelter was much akin to that from the earliest deposit at Bono Manso, the capital of the state. Similarly the elders of Gyamma village, about two kilometers north of Takyiman town, claim their ancestors, who preceded the founders of Bono state, lived in caves nearby. It was later that the Bono absorbed them into their political structure. All the spots shown to the writer by the elders of Gyamma as the sacred sites inhabited by their ancestors, were found to contain tools typical of the Kintampo Industrial Tradition which is regarded as the earliest evidence for settled farming communities in Ghana dating back between 3,500 and 3,000 years. These two sites have been discussed in some detail elsewhere. Two similar sites in the same Bono Manso area have been reported through oral traditions. These are Nkyiral/Anyiman and Kokuman, and they are also claimed to be sacred sites related to some of the early groups who formed the nucleus of Bono state. These have not been visited yet but they have similar stories to the one at Amuowi I and it is not unlikely that similar archaeological discoveries may be made there.

Away from the Bono Manso area, just about thirty kilometers northwest of it, Boachie-Ansah has excavated around the sacred hole known as Bonso, claimed to have been inhabited by the earliest ancestors of the present Wankyi (Wenchi) state. The excavation shows that the site was indeed inhabited and two dates falling in the second half of the [first] millennium CE have been obtained for the site. Still in the Brong-Ahafo Region, and farther (northwest of Wankyi) (Wenchi) in the Begho area, the Hani people who are also Bono (Brong) speaking claim their ancestors emerged from two holes at a place called *Nseserekeseso* (a large area of mainly boval vegetation) where they lived before they moved to their present area. An excavation by Agorsah (1973) showed that the so-called sacred holes were for storing water in an environment where water is relatively scarce. All around the holes were pitted with grinding hollows which tradition associates with the grinding of *ayuo* (sorghum). This latter tradition is, incidentally, related to the Amuowi I sacred hole in the Bono Manso area, where a similar feature is also clearly represented. It must be pointed out that though traditions do not directly refer to it, a Neolithic village site has also been discovered close by the sacred hole of the Hani people.

Further south in the forest proper a large number of the states forming the Asante nation . . . claim that their ancestors emerged from a hole at Asantemanso. Indeed, as early as 1923, Rattray, who visited this sacred hole, observed:

> Myths and traditions are strongly substantiated some respects by visible proofs, in the vicinity of this spot is an area of dense primeval forest and the keen observer will note there are no clearings and no cocoa trees, and if the mounds, through which every now and then the motor road cuts, are minutely examined, they will be found not to be ant-hills but "kitchen middens" from which project Neolithic instruments.

It is a pity that archaeologists have not as yet had the opportunity to visit this site, let alone to excavate it as has been done for the sacred sites in the northern forest margins. Therefore it is not known what type of artifacts Rattray discovered. In fact many of the artifacts he described as "Neolithic" have been found to be Iron Age artifacts. This site, together with the Bugyekrom cave in the general area first occupied by the ancestors of the Ekoona clan of Adanse Akrokerri, needs urgent archaeological exploration. At least in the case of Asantemanso, archaeological objects and features have been reported suggesting former habitation of the area where this sacred hole is located.

From the above examples, the writer does not think that the archaeological finds associated with these sacred spots are coincidental. Indeed, the observations above suggest that many (though not all since some may have been diffused to other traditional states) of the sacred sites are ancient archaeological sites which have been inhabited or used, most probably by the ancestors of the people who hold the said places sacred. Rather than merely considering such traditions as outright myths, archaeologists should first visit these sites. This finding is also important because it contradicts [an] earlier notion about the Akan, that [is,] "the local people have no tradition of their origin, but they only settled in the district three hundred years or so ago." Indeed, of much more importance is the fact that it shows the potential wealth and the greater time depth of oral traditions of some African societies than has hitherto been considered. Perhaps this observation also lends support to the view that the Akan people . . . may have been in the confines of modern Ghana for the last three thousand years or more.

There are other isolated traditions of some of the Akan-speaking peoples which do not fall under the above three categories. One of such isolated traditions is that associated with people who emerged from streams and rivers. There is also no doubt that some of the traditions are merely mythical. The above examples should certainly caution archaeologists to visit the sites concerned with such "myths." May these traditions not be pointing to the same time period as those of holes in the ground and caves, especially when one considers that during the Neolithic and Early Iron Age, societies would be more attached to their natural environment than later when states became crystallized? Perhaps a systematic collection of all these traditions, followed by archaeological explorations could yield useful information on the whole question of Akan prehistory.

Prelude to the Atlantic Slave Trade

Gérard L. Chouin and Christopher R. DeCorse

Gérard L. Chouin served for six years as a lecturer at the Universities of Ghana and Cape Coast before completing his doctorate on the history and archaeology of Southern Ghana, where he worked under Christopher DeCorse, who is professor of anthropology in the Maxwell School of Citizenship and Public Affairs at Syracuse University. In the excerpt to follow, Chouin and DeCorse reconsider previous archaeological data in light of their research and in light of proposals about the early history and societies of the Ghanaian forest. They provide an alternative hypothesis to the model proposed by Ivor Wilks, placing that history in a much broader and deeper context. But this alternative hypothesis extends the work of other scholars, such as A. Norman Klein and Kwasi Konadu, who have argued for a deeper chronology for the Akan peoples who came to dominate much of the region, other polities, and the Atlantic trade with various Europeans along the coast.

The most comprehensive model of the pre- and early Atlantic history of the region has been proposed by Ivor Wilks. According to this "big bang" model of Akan origins, the history of agriculture in the Ghanaian forest and Akan sociopolitical development were the result of a series of transformations that occurred after the advent of European trade at the end of the fifteenth century. These observations and the conclusions they entail have important implications for the understanding of both the Atlantic and the pre-Atlantic past of West Africa, as well as how that past is conceptualized. Current research, including a growing amount of archaeological data from southern Ghana, suggests a substantial settlement of the forest by agricultural populations well before the beginning of European trade. . . .

Archaeological evidence from earthworks, as well as from other sites in southern Ghana, establishes the existence of a sedentary agrarian society well adapted to the forest environment long before the opening of the Atlantic trade. This is in contradistinction to Ivor Wilks's "big bang" model of the emergence of sociopolitical complexity in southern Ghana in the fifteenth and sixteenth centuries. This theory has remained largely accepted and unchallenged, with the exception of a few archaeologists who have found it difficult to reconcile such a presentation of the past with emerging archaeological data. . . .

A Revised Chronology: A Pre-Atlantic Agrarian Society

Archaeological data has provided increasing evidence that the Ghanaian forest was well occupied by settled agricultural communities prior to the advent of the Atlantic trade. In particular, Brian Vivian's and Peter Shinnie's data from Asante indicate the existence of stable village communities as early as 800 CE. Additional data emerging from the Central Region suggests a pre-Atlantic settlement density greater than the post-1500 period. These settlements include hilltop and lowland sites of various sizes as well as entrenchments, all with substantial evidence for iron production. Sites with entrenchments are the most visible of these pre-Atlantic settlements. Their chronology is therefore of particular significance.

The main challenge is to determine whether earthworks belong to the pre- or post-Atlantic period; if they were built before or after the opening of the Atlantic trade. The amount of work involved in their construction suggests a social organization capable of mobilizing, controlling, and co-coordinating labor, and relatively sedentary settlement over long periods of time.

Unfortunately, sites excavated before the 1970s were poorly dated, mainly because radiometric dating was not yet available. Chronologies were posited on the basis of the relative depth of the archaeological deposits, the weathered nature of some of the ceramics, and the presence/absence of European trade materials. Prior to Kiyaga-Mulindwa's excavations in the Birim valley, most authors agreed—not without some doubt—that earthworks were ancient but belonged to the Atlantic period or to the immediate pre-Atlantic period. . . .

New Chronological Evidence from the Akrokrowa Earthworks

Archaeological research undertaken as part of the Central Region Project was specifically aimed at evaluating the age of the earthworks. Although some sites, such as the Monsa earthwork excavated by Kiyaga-Mulindwa, were reoccupied during historic times, others are only associated with early ceramics and, therefore, appear not to have been reoccupied after their abandonment. To avoid archaeological disturbances associated with settlement reoccupations, entrenchment sites only showing evidence of a single occupation were considered to be the best sites from which to obtain radiocarbon chronologies. The Akrokrowa earthworks site, identified near Abrem Berase by Gérard Chouin in 2002, produced only early ceramics and no evidence of reoccupation after its abandonment. It was therefore an ideal site from which to collect samples for radiocarbon dating and to compare results with Kiyaga-Mulindwa's. . . .

The Akrokrowa radiocarbon dates point to the construction of the entrenchment system in the second half of the first millennium CE, most likely during the eighth century, long before the arrival of the first Europeans on the Costa da Mina. Notably, these results coincide nicely with SI-2718 collected by Kiyaga-Mulindwa in the ditch at Monsa. The radiocarbon results from the Akrokrowa earthworks provide the first series of radiocarbon dates undoubtedly entirely related to the construction and occupation of earthworks by the makers of the Atetefo pottery. The fact that the site is located far away from the Birim valley, but seems to belong to the same historical period, radically changes our perception of sociopolitical and economic life in the forests of southern Ghana before the opening of the Atlantic trade. In the forest area that Wilks envisioned as being sparsely populated by bands of hunter-gatherers, a network of fully formed agrarian settlements now comes to light. . . .

Abandonment of the Earthworks

Excavations at Akrokrowa and associated sites afford a glimpse of a well-settled landscape predating initial European contact in the fifteenth century. The chronology of Akrokrowa is in agreement with an abandonment of the site by the mid-fourteenth century. This in turn is amplified by data coming from other earthworks in southern Ghana suggesting a major change in settlement pattern before the opening of the Atlantic trade, characterized by the abandonment of earthworks. This remains a working hypothesis that needs to be tested on a larger number of entrenchment sites. If the hypothesis is confirmed, why were they abandoned? Whatever happened must have been quite sudden, able to affect a vast area, and traumatic enough to dramatically alter people's way of life within a generation, wiping out the structures of a centuries-old agrarian order.

Looking at world history during this period, it seems that only one event can possibly explain such a large-scale phenomenon: the occurrence of the Black Death or Great Plague. Well documented in Europe, as well as in North Africa, where it may have killed a third or more of the total population between 1346 and 1352, for lack of direct evidence, the Great Plague is often believed to have spared sub-Saharan Africa. Looking at the highly

A view of the Ghanaian coastline, facing the Atlantic Ocean, from Cape Coast Castle. This structure served as a "slave fortress" during transatlantic slaving and later as the capital of the Gold Coast Colony. Photograph by Kwasi Konadu, 2005.

infectious nature of this disease and the dense network of links between West Africa and North Africa, as well as between eastern Africa and the Arab world and Asia during this period, this seems highly improbable. The Plague reached the Maghrib in 1348 and it is plausible that it reached the forests of West Africa in the mid-fourteenth century. In affecting societies living in forest areas of southern Ghana, the Plague would have had exactly the same effect as in other parts of the world: it would have destroyed a large portion of the population living in densely populated settlements, resulting in their abandonment—a well-documented phenomenon in many other contexts.

Here it is useful to quote Merrick Posnansky, one of the few researchers to have considered the Plague as an unknown component of West African history: "We have no idea if the plague spread across the Sahara in the 14th century but we should not discount its possibility." We believe the widespread abandonment of earthworks in the fourteenth century is an indirect indication that Posnansky might have been right. While the only consideration here is the abandonment of the earthworks of southern Ghana, it may be more than coincidental that other abandonments and transformations in settlement organization appear to have occurred in other parts of sub-Saharan Africa during the same period.

II

Between the Sea and the Savanna, 1500–1700

Around the late fifteenth or early sixteenth century, the Atlantic littoral and savanna regions that would form the Ghanaian landscape received three sets of relatively new arrivals. By then, Mande migrants or warriors had entered the savanna region and established the polity of Gonja near the Black and White Volta Rivers, while other Mande merchants settled in trading communities along the northwest corridor, among Bono/Akan peoples in commercial centers such as Begho and Bono-Manso. On the coast, the Gã and Ewe peoples had more or less completed their migrations from the east, across the Volta River basin from an area between present-day Togo and Nigeria. The Portuguese became the first Europeans to come upon the region and some of its hinterland; they were awed by the civilizations and commerce they encountered and, owing to their primary interest in the region's gold deposits, called it Costa da Mina ("Coast of the Mine"). Eventually, the Portuguese and other Europeans would erect more than forty trading fortifications along the coast to facilitate the first European "scramble for Africa" (where no less than eight European nations vied for commercial dominance on the coast between the fifteenth and eighteenth centuries), attracting Mande, Akan, and other African traders to the coastal region and making this region the center of African-European transactions in gold, beads, metals, cloth, and captive peoples.

By the late fifteenth century, the Portuguese encountered indigenous (and primarily Akan) societies with sophisticated cultural and commercial knowledge after centuries of experience, and the latter approached these and other Europeans with tact, though the phenomenon of transatlantic slaving—which exported approximately 1.2 or 1.3 million peoples from the Gold Coast between 1514 and 1866—was rarely anticipated. Between 1480 and 1530, gold from the Gold Coast financed much of Portugal's brief global dominance, but once attention shifted from gold to commodified African bodies that would labor in overseas European colonies, the competition between Gold Coast Africans and Europeans and among Europeans increased dramatically. Guns and gold were used for procuring and exchanged against captive peoples, and the flow of these commodities paralleled the rise and disappearance of inland and local polities; the more predatory ones excelled in this environment. Though warfare and raiding increased, so did pawning, debt leading to bondage, and other consequences associated with transatlantic slaving for African societies and their members. Beyond the Gold Coast littoral, inland polities and peoples were not immune to the effects of transatlantic slaving: peoples from northern Ghana, such as those in Dagomba and Salaga, were a major source of captive peoples for the more powerful forest-based polities, and quite a few of them would join those procured along the coast and its hinterlands for a one-way voyage across the Atlantic. The sea that had been a meeting point for new arrivals became an exit for undesirables, those used for collateral against debt incurred for European trade goods, and the raided.

Encounter with Europe

Kwesi Brew

The Portuguese were the first Europeans to establish a presence on the Gold Coast. Through relationships with indigenous polities, both contentious and cooperative, the Portuguese laid claim to what became their West African base of operations at the São Jorge da Mina fortress (Elmina), rather than the adjacent, indigenous town of Edina. In "Don Diego at Edina (Elmina)" and "Don Diego at Edina (Elmina)—'The Great Rebuff,'" poet Kwesi Brew paints a picture of the encounter between the Portuguese admiral Diogo de Azambuja (1432–1518) and the peoples of Edina as represented by its ruler, Caramança or Kwamina Ansa (whose name is still in some debate). Since the two poems are best read in sequential order, we have provided both.

Don Diego at Edina (Elmina)

At the confluence of tempers, the sweet, slow, the Surowi quick,
To serve the majesty of the sea
The Surowi joins allegiance with the Sweet River at Ituri.
Here once a goblet of cut crystal
From which the fierce sun drew beams of white light,

Blue light, red, and gold, scintillating like unsheathed rapiers,
The imperial servant of Prince Henry the Navigator,
Don Diego D'Azambuja slaked his thirst
After his long and salty voyage from Portugal.
While his tongue savored these strange sweet waters
The questing wisdom of Kwamina Ansa, Edina's King
Pondered his fear of strangers with swords
Bedecked with emeralds, diamonds, sapphires, and gold,
Gold, gold, and gold worked by master gold-smiths.
The sea was quiescent like a face concentrated in thought.

And the brown in the King's eyes thickened darkly over
The presage of gold on hands of iron, gold, gold, gold.

Will there be enough gold to dampen these fierce appetites,
Will there be enough gold, Kyeame [*ɔkyeame*, "speech intermediary"]?

There is nothing of pageants about this river:
Quiet, unassuming, and inward-looking,
King Ansa, thought of its waters. But these waters,
These waters will one day refresh friends gold has turned into enemies

If there was no room at the inn for Him, Nana thought,
There should be no place on these shores for Diego!
A rumble of thunder passed unheard
Across the sky: No rain, Oh no, no rain.
A cloud passed and threw a comforting shadow
Between us and the blaze of the sun.

The eyes of Don Diego were of the black of unfired coal
With the tinder buried in their smoldering depths.
In their dark, dark shadows
Where the sun is dark and silent
(As it was to the blind bard of Paradise)
The King discerned a pile of gold on a cask of rum.
Against the walls leaned slim and elegant dane guns [i.e., guns
introduced by Danish merchants]
With the shine of newness glowing ominously through the gloaming;
Short, rotund kegs of gun-powder and pellets
Stood sentry round the musketry
Weighing their burden of destruction against the evil day
When brother shall fight against brother
And breaking through the engulfing darkness
With the light of searching torches
Recognize each other only as merchandise for bauble.
But the chains that were to bind body and soul
Of his scions across the foaming breakers to painful diaspora
Were kept in the darkest corners
Out of range of mind and inner eye,
So that it might come to pass the evil thoughts of their hearts
And the lies of those hypocrites
Impaled on a crucifix of smiles.

Don Diego at Edina (Elmina)—"The Great Rebuff"

The King's eye turned to look across the sea
Searching the purple distance marking out the horizon,
Where the waters of sea brought these men
From a dim kingdom who are now suppliants
Seeking land for settlement,
Only a small corner of the tertiary rock
Where the sea-weeds grew and no hoe can till.
In a land where trees grow and springs flow.

They sat motionless waiting for an answer.

The sea was quiescent like a face concentrated in thought
And the sea-gulls screamed like demented children burning in a fire.

When the king's gaze returned to land they sat there
As trees planted in the soil of the land and
Sprouting roots with the glide of the sun.

Again he looked upon the sea, and the sea told nothing;
The sea that had borne them to these shores knew nothing.
For all was there to say in the noble spirit of the people.

His eyes fell on the sea
And he saw as for the first time a flotilla of ships
Anchored in the road and being nuzzled by trusty dug-outs;
Saw the waves churned to white fury
Breaking upon a rock barring their path.
Relentless beating, brutal savagery
Had split the rock now worn and pock-marked.

Like the green breezes that temper the heat of the sun
The spirits of our ancestors came to him.
And Kwamina Ansa saw his Kyeame, his spokesman,
The wrinkles on his lips have notched
The passage of wise counsel over the years
That have poured blessings on a head
Now white as a field of ripened sugar grass.
With hands lying secure in the calm of his laps
He inclines his head in gentle courtesy to whisper.

Remember, Nana, temptation's honor is disgrace.
The stranger seeks the nether edge of your bed

To snatch your pillow for his head
when sleep overtakes your wakeful care.

Azambuja looked on.

Tell them, Kyeame tell them,
Friends who met but seldom,
Til death parts them.
Savored the sweetness of untroubled friendship.
The nature of human heart wreaks its mischief
Upon close neighbors each smoldering with his own craving
From unfulfilled desires burst forth consuming anger

Many years passed into centuries
And as part of our flesh to part of Africa's soil
Wherever we go, far or near,
The soul still yearns for the places
Where the umbilical cords of our forebears
Were buried by their mothers:
Nostalgia is the umbilical cord stretched
To painful lengths.

The Voyage of Eustache de la Fosse

Eustache de la Fosse

The Flemish-speaking merchant and sailor Eustache de la Fosse (1451–1523) traveled with Spanish sailors from Palos (Spain) to West Africa and was captured by the Portuguese while on the West African coast. He would end up working for the Portuguese and eventually obtain his freedom, though he sold enslaved Africans between Benin and the Gold Coast (then called the "Mina" coast) during his short stay. It is assumed he wrote his account while back in Europe in the 1480s. The following excerpt from de la Fosse's account of 1479–80 provides early evidence, possibly the earliest, for the Akan language as spoken in the late fifteenth century and something about the indigenous peoples he observed and the commerce in which he participated.

And after we had for long frequented the aforesaid coast, we [two vessels] made toward the Mine of Gold [São Jorge da Mina] and arrived on [Friday] 17 December 1479, the Saturday following being Christmas Day, and we left the other caravel at the Malagueta Coast [present-day Liberia] since they wanted to obtain more pepper and some slaves to bring to the Mine to sell there. And before departing one behind the other we drew lots for which of us should go further forward six leagues, because there are two harbors at this Mine of Gold, the first of which has the name Shama and the other, which is six leagues further on, Village of Two Parts, so called because there are two villages a bowshot apart, and it fell to my lot to go the six leagues further on. And for this reason I left the day after I arrived at the aforesaid Mine in order to go to my agreed locality, this being the Sunday before Christmas, and then we put ourselves under the protection of the *manse* and the *caremanse*, who are the king and the viceroy, and the next day which was Monday we set about to begin our sales, but we did little the first four or five days until the merchants in this country were alerted to our arrival, and then we saw the Berrenbucs who made their way down from the hills and came to buy our goods. In this land "merchants" are called *berenbues*, "gold" *chocqua*; "water" *enchou*; for "you are welcome" you say *berre bene*, and for "love-play" *chocque chocque*; *barbero* means "a child," *baa*, "white," *barbero baa*, "a white child"; "cloth" is *fouffe*, *concque roncq* means "a chicken," *concque ronconcq agnio* "eggs," *bora* a ring to wear on the arm made of brass, *dede* "good," *fanionna* "bad," etc.

And on Twelfth Night, which was a Wednesday, early in the morning when there was a heavy drizzle / thick mist, there appeared four Portuguese ships which fired their guns at me in such a way that they overcame us and we were left at their mercy. And the previous day they had taken the other ship that came with us, and on their way by sea they met another one which they brought back with them to the Mine, and we were all pillaged. And then since we leading men were prisoners they handed over one of our caravels to the sailors and poor members of our company, with water, biscuit, a sail, and an anchor, and sent them off [to take their chance], and thus they returned to Spain, and the Portuguese kept back us, the leading men, in order to take us to the king and daily we helped to sell our own goods which they had seized from us, but those of us who were kept there were divided among several ships, four to one and six to another. I was placed with a fine knight called Fernand de les Vaux who treated me very honorably, but since he was charged to go 200 leagues further, I asked to be placed in one of the ships remaining at the Mine and this was granted, and I was placed in the ship of a man called Diogo Can [Cão], who was a thoroughly awkward creature, and I was no longer as well treated as I had been before, which I had to put up with. This Diogo Can bought my caravel out of the booty and, as said earlier, I daily helped to sell my goods and daily accounted for them.

And once as I was going through the streets and carrying two basins to sell I was called into one of their houses hoping that I would sell my basins, and when I went in I saw there several women, standing up and talking together, some five or six of them nattering together while I held my basins in each hand. I cannot explain how these women so bewitched me that I left my basins behind and went out of that house. And when I was two or three houses away in the street it came to my mind what I had done with my basins, and I instantly returned to that house and went in and found no one there, and there was a young lass who came to attend on me by asking if I wanted *chocque chocque*, and she began to take off my breeches, thinking that I wanted to dally with her, which I had no will for, being vexed by the loss of my basins, which remained lost.

And so we stayed there, selling until Shrove Tuesday itself, and just as we were ready to depart, there then arrived the two caravels which had gone

200 leagues further on to the River of Slaves, bringing back a large number of slaves, a good 200 each, and they sold most of them at the Mine of Gold, but despite this we left in the evening of Shrove Tuesday in order to return to Portugal and I was placed back in my own caravel which Diogo Can had bought as booty and it was named *La Mondadine*.

Translated by Kwasi Konadu

A View of the Gold Coast from the *Esmeraldo de Situ Orbis*

Duarte Pacheco Pereira

Duarte Pacheco Pereira (1460–1533) was a late fifteenth-century Portuguese navigator and then governor of the São Jorge da Mina fortress on the Gold Coast. By the sixteenth century, the term "Mina" was shorthand for the São Jorge da Mina fortress, through which Portuguese trade flowed, but the "coast of Mina" also referred to a wider region beginning with Axem (Axim) in the east and terminating with Accra in the west. Pereira wrote his account between 1505 and 1508, and although he knew Diogo de Azambuja's lieutenant, he was not present during the construction of the São Jorge da Mina fortress. Between 1520 and 1522, Pereira was governor of the São Jorge da Mina fortress, the primary base of the Portuguese in West Africa until the Dutch captured the fort in 1637. The following excerpts include his descriptions of various localities, forms of commerce, and some of the indigenous peoples along the "coast of Mina."

From Cabo das Tres Pontas [Cape Three Points] to the islets of Anda [Hanta] is four leagues. . . . The region of Anda extends for seven or eight leagues; it contains a gold mine, which although not very large yields 20,000 doubloons or more; the gold is taken to be bartered at the Castle of São Jorge da Mina and at the fortress of Axem. . . . The blacks of this country live on millet, fish, and yams, together with a little meat; they are naked from the waist up, are uncircumcised and heathen, but, God willing, they will soon become Christians.

The islet of Anda lies [northeast] and [southwest] from St. John River [Pra River], eight leagues [farther] along the route, a very small and narrow river, at high tide only a fathom and a half at its mouth, and this mouth can only be seen when very close to it. Here is a place called Sama [Shama], with 500 households, the first place in this land where trading in gold was done, and at that time it was called the Mine. This trading place and its commerce were discovered, on the orders of King Afonso V, by João de Santarem and

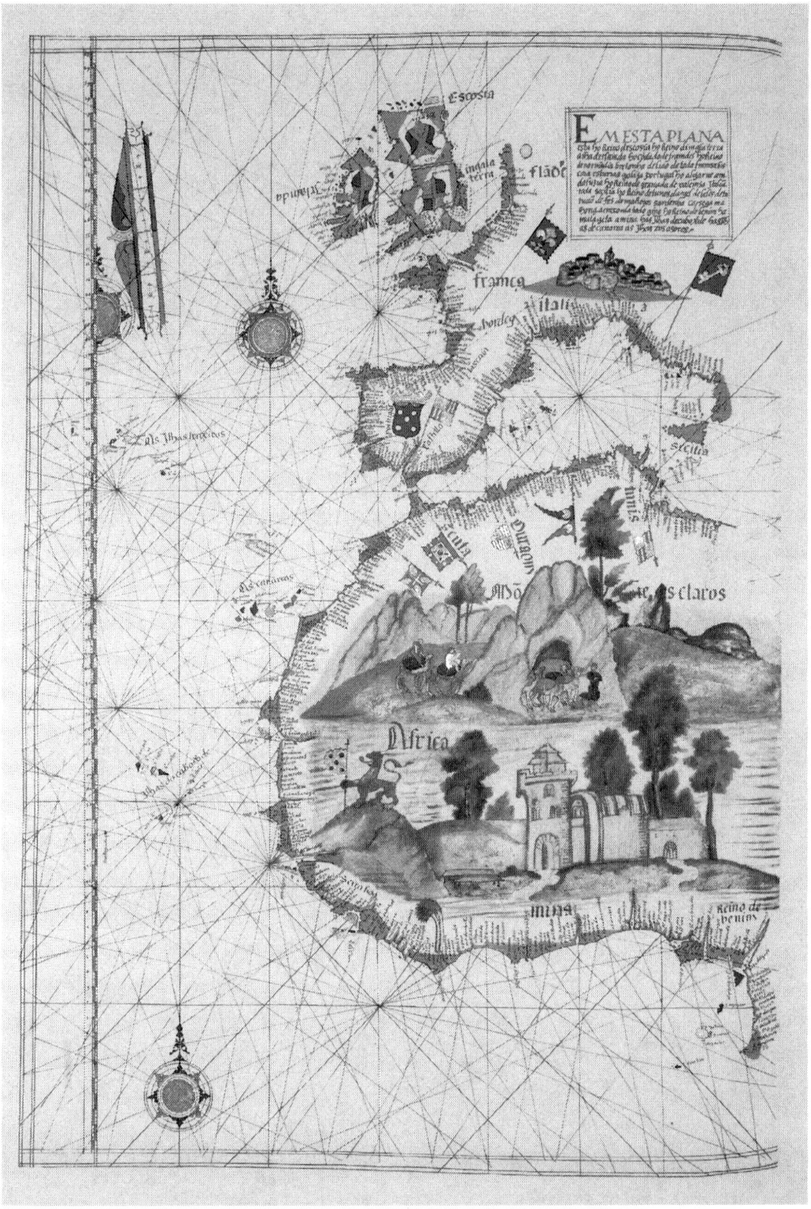

Portuguese map of West Africa from Lázaro Luís's 1563 atlas. "Mina" refers to the São Jorge da Mina fortress, which was an integral site for the fifteenth- and sixteenth-century commerce in gold and enslaved Africans. "Nautical Chart of Portuguese Cartographer Lázaro Luís, 1563," archived at the Academia das Ciências de Lisboa. Photograph by Joaquim Alves Gaspar, March 2008.

Pedro d'Escobar, his knights and servants, on a certain day in January 1471. These two captains carried as pilots Alvaro Esteves, citizen of Lagos, and Martin Esteves, citizen of Lisbon, the former being the most competent man of his profession in Spain [i.e., Iberia] at that time. . . . From the Bay of Sama to the village of the Crooked Man is three leagues. . . . From there to the Castle of São Jorge da Mina is three leagues. . . .

Since in the paragraph before the last . . . we have previously spoken of how the excellent prince, King Afonso V of Portugal, had the Mine [Mina] discovered, and of the captains and pilots who for this purpose were sent, it is now fitting that we should tell how his son, the most serene prince, King João of Portugal, after the death of his father, ordered the first work in founding the castle of São Jorge da Mina to be done. On the command of this magnanimous prince it was built by Diogo de Azambuja, knight of his household and high commander of the Order of St. Benedict. On the first day of January 1482, having taken out and being accompanied on nine caravels by as many other captains, most honorable men, Diogo de Azambuja being commander, he took out two *urcas*, ships of 400 tons each, with lime, worked stone, and enough other material to construct this fort. And although there was much disagreement between the blacks of this land and our people about the building of this fort, for they did not wish to agree to it, finally it was done despite them, so that, with great service and diligence, there was completed what was then necessary for the lodging and defense of all our men. Afterward, as time moved on, the same King João II accepted as necessary that it was appropriate to construct much more. We know that in all Ethiopian Guinea, this was the first solid (stone) building to be constructed in this region since the creation of the world. Through this fortress trade so greatly increased [in] good fine gold. . . . It is bartered from the black merchants who bring gold from distant lands. These merchants belong to various nations: the Bremus, Atis, Hacanys, Boroes, Mandinguas, Cacres, Andeses or Souzos, and many others. . . . These people have hitherto been heathen, but some of them have now become Christians. I speak of those who live near the fortress, for the merchants come from far and have not the same interaction with us as these neighbors and accordingly continue in their false idolatry. . . .

Three leagues beyond the castle of São Jorge da Mina . . . there is a cape which we call Cabo do Corço [(Cape Coast)]. . . . Twenty leagues beyond Cabo do Corço is a[nother] cape which we call Cabo das Redes [Fetu], because of the many nets that were found here when this land was discovered. . . . All the country between these two capes is fairly high and mountainous, halfway along there are three fishing villages, Great Fante, Little Fante, and

Little Sabuu [Sebu]. . . . The blacks of this country speak the same language as those of Mina, and their word for gold is *vyqua* [Akan: *sika*, "gold"]. . . . Twenty leagues beyond this mountain[ous area] is the Rio da Volta [Volta River], which is fairly large.

Translated by Kwasi Konadu

Letter from Mina Governor to the Queen [Catarina]

Afonso Gonçalves Botafogo

In a letter addressed to Queen Catarina (1507–78) of Portugal, wife of King João III (1502–57), the governor of Mina, Afonso Gonçalves Botafogo, writes to her about a wide range of topics surrounding Portuguese commerce on the Gold Coast between the coastal settlements of Axim and Accra, respectively, telling us something about Portuguese commercial and social relations with local African politics and political leaders as well as the trade which brought the former there. Excerpts from this letter, dated April 18, 1557, appear below.

[Defining the Gold Coast]

The whole coast from one end to the other . . . namely one part from Axim to this port, and the other from here to Cara [Accra]. . . .

[Relations with Rulers of Accra and "Great" and "Small" Akani]

It seemed good to Cristovão d'Oliveira, before leaving for Portugal, to send Pero da Costa to Cara with gifts for the king and his brothers, gifts which, at his request, I gave the latter from this trading post. With him he sent his ship's master [?], and I sent the pilot of the *caravellão*, and the master mason who was here, to investigate and observe where it will be best to build the fortress, and in what way the coast can be approached, and whatever else they can find out. . . . The gifts which the King our Lord sent from Portugal for this King of Cara it did not seem right to give at present, since the fortress is not built. I sent other gifts, as I now inform Your Highness, and the former ones will be kept until the King our Lord and Your Highness order what is to be done with them.

I wrote to Your Highness by the previous fleet about how I had to [send] a man to the kings of *Acanes Grandes* and the *Acanes Pequenos* to get them to mend relations and open up their roads to this fortress. This man spent more than eight months there and reconciled these kings and made them friends, and he opened roads that had been blocked for many years. As a sign of reconciliation and friendship he brought to this fortress a son of each of the kings. The son of the King of the *Acanes Grandes* is his oldest son and heir, and is called António de Brito, the António de Brito who used to be [a] captain here having once visited him. These hostages I received at this fortress very warmly and I ordered them to be given their customary food.

After these roads had been opened up and all was completed, there happened to come here a brother of the King of the *Acanes Pequenos,* and over a black whom he killed in this town a great fight broke out. I and some men hurried there, but the black came out of it dead, without my being able to intervene. To have this set right also cost me afterwards a great deal of trouble, and in bringing the matter to a peaceful conclusion some expense. Dom João [ruler of Fetu] also helped in this, and now I have everything settled and all runs well.

After these ships came to port, the wife of António de Brito came here to be with him. I warmly welcomed her and soon made her a Christian, and she took the name Dona Catarina, in recollection of Your Highness, and I and Cristovão d'Oliveira were her godparents. Opening up these roads, like opening the others I have cleared from restrictions, has cost me a great deal of trouble and I have spent on this activity some of the property of this establishment and also some of my own salary. Since all is for the service of the King Our Lord and of Your Highness, it must be counted well-spent.

[Trade between Africans and Europeans]

So that the King our Lord and Your Highness may not blame me for not making approaches to the kings of the surrounding districts, to persuade them not to trade [with the enemy], as I did last year, [let me explain]. I was very ill when the pirates [i.e., competing European nations] began to arrive, despite which I did not fail to approach the kings, through men I sent to the kings of Afuto [Fetu] and Comane [Komenda], for these are the leading kings in terms of wealth and power, and if they withdrew from trade what was left would be little. I ordered the men to offer them gifts and other things if the kings desired them, just as was done successfully by me the previous year. Notwithstanding all this, I was quite unable to bring the kings to agree to renounce trading. Dom João, in which I most trusted, gave as an excuse that it was only because his people were compelling him to [permit] this against his own wishes. If last year they had not traded it was because they were bribed and given more than 500 *pesos,* but now he did not dare to quarrel with them. Nevertheless neither he nor his son-in-law was trading. But all this was mere words, an evasive reply from blacks who do not recognize or keep to the truth, especially when self-interest is involved. I have found out through spies that Dom João and his son-in-law, and the people of the king of Comane, traded more than 30,000 *pesos*. Whenever pirates come they will do this and will not forbid trading, because self-interest and the profit they gain count for more than whatever this fortress can give them in bribes.

A Report on Mina

Anonymous

Almost a century after the Portuguese landed on the Gold Coast, an anonymous Portuguese report dated September 29, 1572, provides us with a rare and detailed glimpse into a range of matters relevant to the Portuguese presence. This report also offers an insightful window into a grand strategy that included Portuguese settlement in the Mina region, the hopes invested in Christianization, and the gold trade that brought these Europeans to the Mina coast.

[*Four Strategies for Mina*]

Profit can be gained from Mina in any one of four ways. Things can be left much as they are, but in certain aspects reformed as much as possible. Or things can be changed so that as much profit as possible can be made at less expense. Or Mina can be rented out, which should not be considered, as I will argue later. Or it can be developed so that it can be settled, which I believe to be the strategy most fitting for the service of God and the service of the King our Lord.

[*Christian Teaching*]

I rejoice that they [the *padres*] have put into effect the saying of mass at a certain hour, and have taught the blacks the stations of the cross; and I believe that eventually there will be a roll-call, as is done in many parts, including Spain, which seems to me very necessary because the blacks are an indolent and careless people; and also so that they can hear their Christian names repeated, because I understand that all the other [converts] after leaving the company of Christians and returning to their village, call themselves by heathen names, [for instance,] the man named Joanne being known as Tabo and the woman Maria as Adua [Adwoa].

Gold Coast Fetish Object. Illustration of brass-pan shrine (left) and an Akan *kuduo* (brass vessel) used for divination (right) by French merchant and slaver Jean Barbot, ca. 1679, from *Barbot on Guinea: The Writings of Jean Barbot on West Africa, 1698–1712*, edited by P. E. H. Hair, Adam Jones, and Robin Law (London: Hakluyt Society, 1992), vol. 2, plate 74. Used by permission of Hakluyt Society.

[Portuguese Settlement Recommended]

This land should be given out for settlement and should become a new Portugal or a new Indies, richer than the Indies of Castile [Spain]. Those who follow [in this settlement], as they overcome the difficulties they will find in settling it, will more reasonably boast about their land than complain about their predecessors and ancestors who let the opportunity pass by. . . . For if matters proceed as now, I believe that these blacks will make an effort to discover . . . how to protect themselves against us, and how to throw us out of their lands, rather than to discover how they should become Christians and how they should receive us into the lands. . . .

[Foods and Domestic Animals]

The blacks sow *milho grande* [large *milho* or maize] which they call *Bruy* [*aburo*; Akan: maize] and which in Castile is called "Indies corn," and *milho meudo* [small *milho*] which I think is the same as the small *milho* there [in Castile]. They sow yams, which in this land provide a very good staple food, and another sort which they call *cocos* [? coco-yams], which is really *rumilho* [?], food for pigs in Castile, but the blacks, especially those at Axim, eat a large quantity of them. They also plant bananas, which in the Spanish Indies they call *platanos* [plantains]. . . . Very good cotton is produced in this land, and a great deal of profit could be made from it.

The only domestic animals I know about are goats, sheep and cows. The goats are very small. The sheep are the size of those there [in Castile]. . . . The cows are very small and the same color as those over there. The pigs, which are brought here, adapt well in this place but badly at Axim, where the governor's horses and an ass also died. Dogs are found in this land, and the Alandes bring them here to sell. . . .

[Gold Mining and Gold in the Interior]

They do not open mines or seek gold anywhere that is at all far from the water [required] to wash the earth from which they remove the gold. Even if they find gold elsewhere they do not dig for it, because of the difficulty in carrying the earth to where there is water. . . .

There has now come here a black, a son of the King of the *Asaees Grandes* as they say, who was baptized in the time of António de Brito, then a Captain here, and took his name. He is a respected black, of good bearing, and he brought with him a son, a youth of about twenty years of age. When asked about that land, in the presence of the Vicar and in his own house, he [the son] replied—for he speaks Portuguese reasonably well through having been here with his father—that it was very rich, but that the gold which came from there was not extracted from the lands of his grandfather, who is still alive, but from further on, in another kingdom, which he says he has visited, by making a five days' journey. The kingdom or lands where the mines are to be found is called Taafó [an area north of Asante]. He stated that he saw the mines, and also lumps of gold, just taken from the earth, some as big as his head or his fist, some large and some small, but even when only the size of hazelnuts, still worth a lot. As far as I could judge from his manner, it seemed to me that the black was telling the truth. He also told me that when a black man or woman went to extract gold, normally twelve *pesos* would be extracted in one day. I asked him if the ground where the gold was found was loose earth or rock; and he replied that the land had all types of ground, but that I would only be able to collect gold from ground which was like [sticky clay], and fairly compact, some lumps emerging from it almost like stones, and he added that these lumps were white.

The Gold Kingdom of Guinea

Pieter de Marees

By the late sixteenth century, the Portuguese commercial presence on the Gold Coast was occasionally threatened and later seriously challenged by incursions from English, Dutch, and French merchants. All sought control over the lucrative trade in gold and then in other commodities, such as ivory and enslaved individuals. Written in Dutch and first published in 1602, Dutch merchant Pieter de Marees's Beschryvinge ende historische verhael vant Gout Koninchrijck van Gunea *(*Description and Historical Account of the Gold Kingdom of Guinea*) provides one of the earliest and most detailed descriptions of a West African society, focusing primarily on the Gold Coast and informed in part by his observations and in part by his use of published sources. The following excerpts from de Marees's account focus on commerce between indigenous peoples and the Dutch for whom he worked, and on social and cultural uses of the latter's trade goods by the former.*

[Dutch Trade and Earning a Living among the Local Population]

As far as I have been able to gather from the Inhabitants of these Countries, before the Portuguese came here to trade with them, they had only a few goods with which to meet their needs, and they merely made do with what they produced locally, which was nothing very notable, especially with regard to anything to clothe themselves with; for in the olden days they used to go around naked, as we have related in greater detail above. Similarly, they had also far less victuals or Livestock to live on than has since been brought there by the Portuguese. Today the Country is filled with various animals and grains, and there is hardly any shortage of things for the upkeep and needs of the people. There is enough of everything, as we shall later describe in detail; and since the Portuguese began to trade here and traffic with the Savages of these Lands, they [the natives] have become acquainted with all kinds of things.

I shall now drop this matter . . . and turn to the real subject of this Chapter. In the early days the natives came to the Portuguese with their Gold and bought what they needed—Linen, woollen Cloth etc.—from them. Since the Peasants of the Interior did not at first dare to come to the Portuguese to trade with them, because they were unacquainted with other nations and it was something frightful for them to see white people, who, moreover, were clothed (and they all black and naked), they did not dare to come near them. And so it also happens to many of our nation: they too are at first frightened when they see Moors or Black people for the first time. So they brought their money to the Inhabitants of the coastal towns (where the Portuguese were trading), telling them what goods and Wares they wanted for their money. The latter went to the Castles and bought what they [people from the interior] needed, such as Iron, Pewter, brass Basins, Knives, woollen Cloth, Linen, Kettles, Beads and similar Wares; and to the Trader who had despatched them for these [goods] they paid so-and-so-much gold out of every Peso; if he bartered many Pesos, he also received much Gold as his reward, and in this way they earned a living.

But later on, we got to know this coast and Ships from Holland began to navigate here. (The first [Dutchman] to trade with the Blacks was a man called Barent Ericksen, from Medemblick.) Seeing what profits the Portuguese were making there, we ventured to sail thither, and sent someone with a Ship, namely the aforementioned Barent, as he had been there with the Portuguese and knew the situation well. But not having (like the Portuguese) any stronghold on the Coast, where we might take goods and merchandize ashore to be stored in Warehouses till the time was ripe to sell them, and being on very inimical terms with the Portuguese, our people were not allowed and did not dare to go ashore anywhere on the Coast. Instead, they were obliged to stay out at Sea on their Ships and anchor off the Towns, waiting for the traders to come in their Canoes and trade with them. The Savages or Blacks, seeing that the Dutch had merchandize, ventured to trade with them, bringing with them their Wares (namely gold).

As they now do little trade with the Portuguese, but [instead trade] only with our Dutch nation, I shall first of all describe how they trade with us. Early in the morning they come from the Shore with their Canoes or small Boats, heading for the ships in the Roadstead of their town in order to trade. The reason why the traders come aboard to trade early in the morning is this: in the morning the wind from the Land, which they call *Bofone*, blows, and then there is a lull and bad water; for towards noon the wind begins to come from the sea and they call it *Agom Brettou* [Akan: *ahum beretu*, "storm or sea breeze"]. They make sure that they are back on Shore by the time the

Akan gold weights (*mmrammuo*). The Akan peoples in Ghana and Ivory Coast have produced these weights since the thirteenth century. The weights, in brass and silver, were used for measuring gold dust, their currency. The geometric weights were inscribed with glyphs or characters that suggest a writing system. Photograph by Kwasi Bempong, 2010. Courtesy of the photographer.

wind comes from the sea; for the Peasants who come from the Interior cannot stand the sea; and when they come aboard they can neither stand nor walk, but lie down like Dogs, vomit and are very sea-sick. But their Rowers or Pilots who take them to the Ships are sea-hardened and do not feel sick, because they are accustomed to go to the Ships every day. Some Traders are so sea-sick when they come on board that they throw up nearly all they have in their bodies; and being so sick even when the weather is good, they are so afraid of the wind (and of the sea when it is a little choppy) that they return ashore in time.

Indeed, some Peasants and Traders dare not go out to the Ships at all, but give their Gold to those Pilots and tell them what goods they want them to buy. These Pilots or Interpreters come on board the Ships with this Gold, having it in a little Purse hanging on their body. They keep the money or Gold of each party in a separate little piece of Cloth or Paper, keeping in their memory: This money comes from the Man, who wants such-and-such goods to be bought for it; and that little Bag of gold comes from or belongs to that Trader, who wants such-and-such Wares to be bought for it. Thus they have commissions of many kinds to buy goods; it happens, indeed, that they have ten or twelve commissions at the same time, one worth 1 *Engels* of gold, others 3, 4 or 5. If the weight of a particular amount is not sufficient, they put it back in its little Bag and take it back to the Man; for if the Pilots were to add some of their own gold in order to make up the full weight, the Trader might not give it back to him; for, since they do not trust each other, they first weigh their Gold on Shore and know how much money there is before sending it to the Ships. Then, when they have spent their money, one has to give them a tip, which they call *Dache* [small gift offered before an agreement or transaction]. . . .

Thus factors competed with each other, drawing one another's Customers away through these gifts; and this giving of presents has become so ingrained that nowadays these *Daches* amount to 6 or 7 per cent. Through the rivalry of the Factors (or their failure to reach a trading agreement), this *Dache* has come to stay and has turned into a *rente* [interest rate], so that one now knows how much of a *Dache* or gift should be given them when they buy a given quantity of Linen, cloth, Iron, Basins or Kettles; according to the size or weight, one gives a certain amount for the trader and a certain amount for the Rowers who bring him on board. It is an unheard-of outrage that one must give one's goods as a *Dache* in this way. And even though they have already finished buying, one still has the greatest headache in the giving of the *Dache*. . . .

[Merchandise and Goods Brought by the Dutch and Sold on the Gold Coast]

In the first place, we bring them [the Blacks] large amounts of Silesian Linen, which sells there in great quantities, because they clothe themselves with it and it is the most popular cloth which they use to wear.

In the second place, all sorts of basins are brought there, such as small and large Neptunes, Barbers' Basins, cooking Basins, *fater*-Basins, chased basins, big Scottish Pans, not less than 2 fathoms in circumference, and small rimless Cups. These Basins they use for various purposes: they use the small Neptunes to store Oil with which they rub themselves; the big Neptunes to immure in Tombs on the graves of the dead, and also to carry something or other in. They use Barbers' basins to wash and shave; *fater*-Basins as lids, to cover other basins, so that no dirt may fall into them; on chased Basins they put their ornaments and trinkets; those big Scottish pans they use for slaughtering a Goat or Pig and cleaning it in, instead of a tub; small rimless cups to cook in; for them, these are quite convenient and they do not want handles on them, like those we use in our Country. Such Brass Basins, which the Ships bring there in large quantities, have become so common in the Country that people often sell brass-ware as cheaply (to the Negroes or their Landsmen) as it is bought in Amsterdam. Although these Basins are brought there in such quantities and are not as perishable a commodity as Linen, one does not see much old brass-ware there; so there must be a huge population in the Interior which uses and employs such quantities of imperishable goods. Furthermore, great heaps of Cauldrons are brought there, which they use a lot for fetching water from Wells and Valleys, as well as red copper stewing pots, coated with tin on the inside, which they use to store water, instead of putting a beer Barrel in their house. They also use earthenware Pots to drink from.

They use the Iron to make their weapons, namely Assegais, Machetes, Daggers etc. They use the Assegais and Daggers as weapons with which to go to war. The Machetes they use in Agriculture to dig the earth with, instead of spades; on the other hand, they also use them to cut wood in the Forest and for carpentry, for they have no other tools.

They also buy many red, blue, yellow and green *rupinsche* Cloths, which they tie around their bodies as Belts in order to hang their things on them, such as Knives, Purses, Daggers and so on. They use the white Spanish Serges to hang over their bodies instead of Cloaks; and red and yellow copper Bangles, which they usually wear around their arms and ankles, as a great ornament. In addition they use Pewter articles, such as Pewter Bracelets, but not in great quantities. They take many Knives which we make in our Lands, of the type we call *Dock-messen*.

Furthermore, they take a great quantity of Venetian Beads of all sorts of colors, but prefer one colour to another. They break them into four or five little pieces, polish them on a stone in the way children polish cherry-stones, string them on Tree-bark in bunches of ten, and trade extensively in this commodity. These polished Beads they wear around their necks, hands and ankles. They also use round Paternoster-beads, especially big, round *Contoirteeckens* [large rosary beads] which they hang and plait in their hair, letting them thus dangle along their ears.

They buy Pins, which they use to make Fish-hooks when they go out fishing. They use stuffed Horse-tails for dancing and also when they are sitting around doing nothing, to keep the Flies off their bodies. Mirrors, small copper Milk-Jugs and many such knick-knacks are bought. But the commodities which are most popular there and are used and traded in great quantities are Linen, woollen Cloth, Copperware such as Basins, Cauldrons, Knives and Beads. Other goods are traded only in small quantities.

Furthermore, one still learns every day which of the goods one brings are useful to them; this applies even to some goods which are brought [merely] in the good hope of selling them there and gaining a little profit on them, for everything is done for that purpose. For instance, people brought them as a sample a number of blown Crumpets of earth: at first it was a great novelty to blow them; but seeing that they broke when they fell on the ground, they would not buy them again. Secondly, they were brought stirrups for Horses, and on first seeing them they asked the Factors whether women wore those stirrups in their ears; but then they said, "Don't bring them again, because our women's ears are too small to hang these big Rings in."

Letter 17

Jean Barbot

French merchant Jean Barbot (1655–1712) traveled to West Africa in 1678–79 and 1681–82 as a commercial agent on French slaving voyages. His account is a series of letters based partly on personal observations and partly on published European sources, often confirming earlier European observations and their biases. In letter 17 below, presumably written in 1679, Barbot describes the body types, character, and dress of Gold Coast peoples.

I treat the Gold Coast as extending from the Rio da Sueiro d'a Costa [Tano River] to River Volta, although the Dutch regard it as beginning at Axim and ending at Acra [Accra]. I think this extension fully justified, since more gold can be found [in the additional localities] than other communities, it only being between Lay and River Volta that the trade is limited to slaves. . . .

You discover daily that the natives have a splendid mental capacity (*génie*), with much judgment and a sharp and ready apprehension, which immediately understands whatever you suggest. They have so good a memory that it is beyond comprehension, and although they cannot read or write, they are admirably well-organized in their trading and never get mixed up. I have seen one of the brokers on board trading four ounces of gold with 15 different persons and making each a different bargain, without making any mistakes or appearing the least harassed. . . .

Although their forms of dress are completely different from ours, they are nevertheless of interest, and they make a display in them. However, there is one kind of dress which is very common among both the great and the small, the rich and the poor, and this is always to wear a cloth (*pagne*) (from Holland, Cape Verde or elsewhere) around the waist, a cloth which passes between the thighs and whose ends hang down to the ground, behind and before, or in some instances only to the knees. This is worn in the house or when travelling. But when they go through the streets, they take a length of Leyden serge or *perpetuana*, 2–3 ells in length, which they pass around their neck, above and below the shoulders, like a mantle, and they take a spear (*assegaye*) or a stick in their hand, for the look of things. They go about this way in the village, carrying themselves with gravity and deliberation, and followed by a slave with a little seat. Nobles and merchants distinguish themselves from the common people by wearing larger and richer material, China satin, or colored Indian cloth, worn as a mantle.

They wear their hair in various fashions. Some shave it all off except for a cross the size of a thumb, others leave a crescent shape, others again a circle or several circles. Others again put their hair into plaits and put these in curl-papers. However they do it, each man seeks to arrange it some new way. Plaiting of hair is the duty of wives. Most of them have hats bought from the whites, but others have hats made of straw or of goatskin or the hide of dogs, these skins having been stretched on wooden blocks to dry. Others again have caps of the same materials, and in various shapes for different hair-styles. They attach to them fetish-objects, glass trinkets, goat's horns, or bark of the fetish tree, and some enrich them with small pieces of worked gold, or with monkey's tails. Slaves go bareheaded.

They adorn their necks, arms, legs and even feet with many strings of glass beads, coral and Venetian *rassade* [colored glass beads]. I have seen some who had whole bunches of 4 ct. [carat] of this *rassade* hanging aslant from their necks, intermixed with an abundance of their small gold ornaments and bark from the fetish tree, over which they mutter their frequent prayers. They have also on their arms and legs ivory bracelets they call manilas, often three or four on each arm. They make these themselves, from elephant tusks brought from Ivory Coast or from the interior. I have specifically prepared for you an illustration showing these little trinkets, so that you may more easily visualize them. Almost all are of gold or of *Conta de Terre*, which is a bluestone [called *akori* beads] from Benin, as costly as gold itself.

Liking display, they achieve it. They also take care of their clothes, changing them when they return home or storing them carefully in little deal chests we sell them. They like to have plenty of clothes, and they want the fabrics we sell them to be sound and well conditioned. That, Sir, is all I have to say to complete the portrait of these African men. I will now labor on that of the women, after drawing for you some of these Moors, to satisfy you.

The women/wives of these blacks are in general of a lithe, relaxed and upright build, tending to average size, and decidedly plump, with a fine head, sparkling eyes, an aquiline nose mostly, long hair, a small mouth, beautiful teeth, and a well-turned neck. They are lively in spirit, lascivious and covetous, attached to their house-keeping, great talkers, haughty to

Noble Women. Jean Barbot's depiction of three Gold Coast women of noble stature, ca. 1688, from *Description des Côte d'Afrique*, vol. 2, United Kingdom National Archives: PRO, ADM 7/830B, p. 43. Used by permission of the Image Library, United Kingdom National Archives.

their inferiors, fond of eye-catching dress and of their wardrobe, and eager to steal when they can. They take great care of their house and their children, and make their daughters help in house-keeping and cooking as soon as they begin to grow up. They are sparing in their eating, and very clean, inasmuch as they wash themselves daily in the sea or a stream. They keep their heads very tidy. . . . They anoint their hair with palm oil, and decorate it with gold ornaments or red sea-shells and with *rassade*. They often put red or white coloring on their faces, on the brow and eyebrows, and on the cheeks, and they make little cuts on each side of the face. Others have raised marks (*tumeurs*) and pinking (*découpures*) done on their shoulders, breast, belly, and thighs, so that from a distance one might think that they were dressed in pinked material (the men do much the same). They load their neck, arms and legs with bracelets or ribbons when a ceremony is being held. I saw some at Acra so attired, and they seemed very pretty, their complexion apart, which nevertheless was fine and smooth. . . . But although some of these African women were very pleasing, among them are some called *etiguafou* [Akan: *aguamamm[fo]*, "prostitute"], who have made themselves public prostitutes, and who are distinguished from the others by their fine appearance and their clothing. . . . They dance very well in the fashion of the blacks, and have dancing schools for the young people.

Treaties between Gold Coast Polities and the King of Denmark and the Danish Africa Company

Ole Justesen

The relations between Gold Coast polities and the representatives of the Danish trading companies and the Danish government in Copenhagen were regulated by treaties and agreements, reflecting over time changing balances of power and views between the parties. The Danish trading companies represented a small European nation among the many European companies and nations trading on the Gold Coast in the seventeenth and eighteenth centuries. In 1658, the Kingdom of Fetu provided soldiers to help the first Danish representative, Heinrich Carloff (1621–94), and his soldiers conquer the main Swedish fort (Carolusborg) at Cape Coast. Fetu was the first Akan polity to enter into a 1659 treaty—and Accra was perhaps the first Gã polity to do the same in 1661—with the new representatives sent out by the Danish Africa Company. In this, against payment, the company was permitted among other things to build a new fort, Frederiksborg, in the Fetu territories. Thereby Fetu secured the establishment of a new European trading company as competitor to whoever occupied the fort in Cape Coast. The following excerpts lay out the terms of both the Fetu and Accra treaties, which themselves are "representative" in the sense that other treaties between Gold Coast polities and European trading companies or nations would more or less conform to the structure and tenor of the ones below.

Treaty between the Kingdom of Fetu, the King of Denmark, and the Danish Africa Company, December 20, 1659

We, *Adu Afu, Ree; Adiu Macu, Fetero; Acroissen, Tay; Aheno, Braffo;* and *Cobre,* Captain, do rule over the Kingdom of Fetu and its lands and coasts.

We hereby confirm for ourselves, our heirs and successors in government, and proclaim by these presents that we have entered into a treaty with the honorable Joost Crahmer, Governor in the name and on behalf of Your Royal Majesty of Denmark and your Noble Chartered Danish Africa Company, with respect to the following articles, which we and our successors shall observe and fulfill in perpetuity, which we have also confirmed in our own manner by swearing an oath and eating fetish [i.e., indigenous ritual for consummating an agreement or transaction].

1. First, we have, for the sum of 50 *benda* of gold, perpetually sold and transferred to the said Cramer, on behalf of his principals and their successors, the hill of *Amanfro* [just east of Cape Coast] (which the Germans call Friedrichsburg) with its coasts and harbors, so that this shall henceforth belong to the Chartered Danish Africa Company as free property; and we the above-mentioned and undersigned have received full payment from Joost Cramer, each his part in our own hands, and are thus satisfied.

2. Secondly, we do grant the said Danish Africa Company a free lodge at *Cabo Cors* [Cape Coast] with our consent that a stone house may be built there at any time, for better protection against fire and other mishaps. . . .

In order that each and every thing thus agreed shall be observed loyally and inviolately by us and our successors in perpetuity with respect to the said praiseworthy Danish Africa Company and its officers, and shall be fulfilled in all respects, we have eaten the fetish called *Coassy* [or "Quassi"] to this effect, and have confirmed the three [copies] of this contract with our own marks and signatures, such that one copy shall be sent to the Noble Company in Denmark, the second [shall remain] in the keeping of Governor Cramer, and the third shall be given into the hand of our *Tay, Acroissen*, called *Jan Claessen*.

Treaty between King Okai Koy, Great Accra, the King of Denmark, and the Danish Africa Company, August 18, 1661

I, *Kanckoy* [Okai Kwei] King of Great *Acra* [Accra/Nkran] do hereby proclaim with this document, three (copies) of which, identical in content, have been drawn up and signed by my own hand, for myself and all my successors, caboceers ["headmen"], and whosoever may head the government of Great *Acra* and serve as its leaders, whether on land or along the coast, that from this date on I do make settlement, and once more for the present and in perpetuity, have sold *Ozzou*'s [Osu] lands and coasts for a sum of 50 *benda* [unit of weight for quantity of gold] in kind to the noble Mr. Jost Cramer, Governor at Friedrichsborg in Guinea, in the name and on behalf of HRM of Denmark and his Noble Chartered Danish Africa Company, with which I am also sufficiently satisfied, subject to the following conditions: that the said Governor Cramer shall build for his King and his Noble Chartered Danish Africa Company a fortress and stone house at *Ozzou* at the first possible opportunity, and [when] this becomes possible. I further undertake to grant him all possible assistance, and there *bonebons* [?] also to help and protect the said Danish Company in *Ozzou* and in all other lands and coasts belonging to me by birth against all hostile attacks and nuisances, whether committed by the inhabitants and natives or other white nations, whosoever they might be. Thus do I hereby transfer and surrender once again, free and without encumbrance, to the said Cramer for his principals, the right to use and employ as their property, at their will and pleasure, the whole area and rights in *Ozzou* in all perpetuity. And as further affirmation I have eaten the fetish called *aquandoe* to this effect in the presence of *Ahen*, son of the late King *Hennequa* [Ahenekwa] of *Fetu*, who has been sent here to this end from Futu [Fetu], and *Jaan Claesen* [Acrosan] of Friedrichsborg, and in proof of this have signed three documents with my own hand and impressed them with my ring "K" below. Given in Great Accra, the 18th of August, anno 1661

Kanckoy

The Dutch and the Gold Coast

Albert van Dantzig

By the latter seventeenth century and into the eighteenth, the British had interrupted a Dutch monopoly on the Gold Coast. The intense rivalry between the British and Dutch over the control of transatlantic slaving reached its pinnacle in the infamous Komenda Wars (ca. 1695–1700) fought between the parties and their respective African allies. Once the Dutch monopoly was broken, their commercial interests shifted more intensely from the procurement of gold to enslaved individuals in the eighteenth century through the second incarnation of the Dutch West India Company (WIC). In the late 1970s, Albert van Dantzig (1937–2000), a Dutch historian who taught at the University of Ghana (Legon), compiled and translated a range of Dutch sources from the WIC. The resultant publication, The Dutch and the Guinea Coast, 1674–1742: A Collection of Documents from the General State Archive at The Hague, *remains a veritable gold mine that covers the seventeenth- and eighteenth-century history and politics of the Gold Coast from Dutch perspectives. The following excerpts were drawn from this collection.*

[Plantations on the Gold Coast, March 14, 1707]

Concerning the sugar, cotton, and indigo plantations [on the Gold Coast], that we would be quite able to continue that work, if only the required tools, slaves, and other materials were sent, and especially if we were to be allowed to buy as many slaves as President Nuyts proposed in his letter of 24th April 1706. It should however be added that one difficulty in the cultivation of sugar is that much of it is stolen by the Negroes themselves, as they have a very great liking for it. . . .

[Dutch Slaving on the Gold Coast and in Its American Colonies, September 17, 1710]

Agreed, after deliberation that since the slaves being bought for the slave ships at the various factories on the Gold Coast are very costly to the Com-

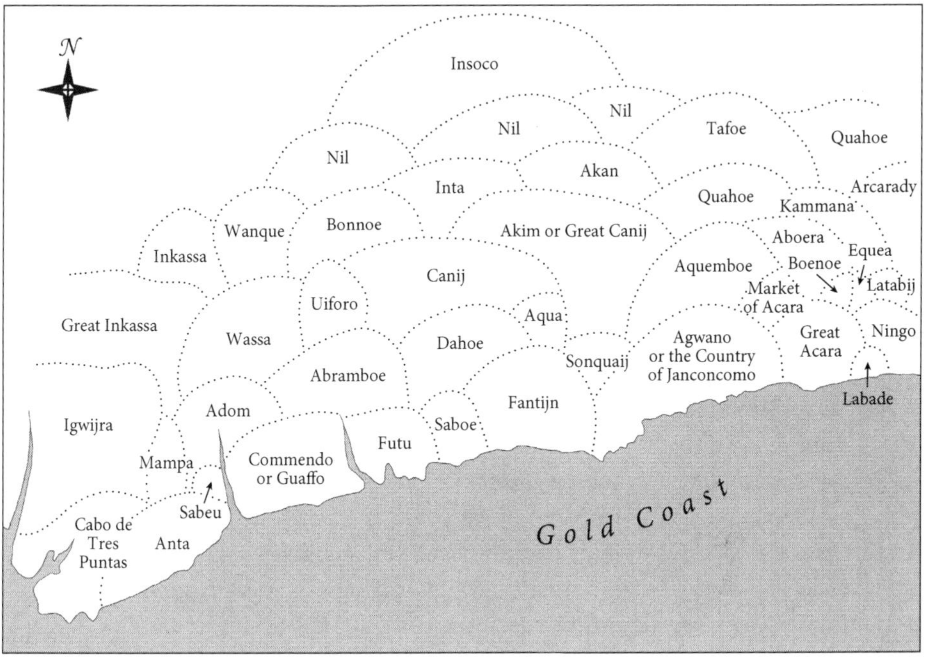

Dutch Map of the Gold Coast by Hans Propheet, ca. 1629. Redrawn by Rebecca Wrenn.

pany because of the many expenses for their maintenance, their long voyage, and the great mortality among them, and that they are therefore more expensive than those bought in Ardra and Angola, to write to the D-G [Director-General] and Members of the Council that after receiving this letter they should desist from further purchases of slaves on the Gold Coast, and rather barter the cargoes which arrive for gold and other current trade goods. If for some very important reason the slave trade were yet to be continued and could not be totally abolished, they should explain to us on the first occasion which presents itself the reason for it. As we presume that on receiving this letter there will be some slaves present on the Gold Coast, it will be recommended to send them to Curaçao on board of the yacht "Elmina."

Denkyira in the Making of Asante

T. C. McCaskie

By the early eighteenth century, the title of "most powerful" polity on the Gold Coast had shifted from Denkyira to Asante; likewise, the Dutch shifted their alliance from the former to the latter around 1701. In the following selection, historian T. C. McCaskie examines the relationship between Denkyira and Asante in the late seventeenth century, when the former was supplanted by the latter as the leading power among the Akan peoples of the southern Gold Coast. McCaskie emphasizes the well-developed military and sociopolitical structure of these indigenous polities before their eventual capitulation to European incursion.

Between the 1660s and 1690s Denkyira was the dominant power among the Twi-speaking forest Akan of the Ofin-Pra river basin. It was the most important inland supplier of gold and slaves to the Dutch at Elmina and the English at Cape Coast, and the wealthiest importer of European guns and munitions. Denkyira and the Europeans had a mutual interest in keeping open the 130-mile trading corridor between them. In 1692 Dutch, English, and Brandenburgher emissaries travelled to Abankeseso, the Denkyira capital, to hold talks with Denkyirahene Boamponsem (ca. 1650s–1694) about trade. Boamponsem sent a resident to act as his representative on the coast. In 1698 this man died. His remains were sent back to Denkyira by the English with a gift of rum, cloth, and gunpowder to celebrate his funeral.

In the 1690s Denkyira fought wars with Asen and Twifo to its south to keep the trade route open. Akan and European sources make it clear that the task of controlling the corridor to the coast stretched Denkyira's gold and manpower resources to the limit. This made its rulers more demanding and predatory towards their own people as well as their tributaries. Two developments tipped the scales against Abankeseso's struggle to maintain its authority. First, in or about 1694, Boamponsem died after a reign of some 40 years. Admired by Europeans for his valor, he was memorialized in Denkyira traditions as a successful if autocratic ruler. His successor was Ntim Gyakari (c. 1694–1701), a capricious young man of uncertain judgment according to the same traditions and European observers. Second, in the mid- to late 1690s Denkyirahene Ntim Gyakari's increased demands provoked resistance from a coalition of his northern tributaries, famously led by Osei Tutu of Kwaman (Kumase) and, so traditions recount, Komfo Anokye. In essence, this insurgency committed Denkyira to conducting military operations in the north while holding down the south. This placed a great strain on its resources. Abankeseso used exaction and force within Denkyira itself to sustain its military posture. This led to a growing rejection of its authority among its own people. At the end of the 1690s, when Abankeseso faced the Kwaman coalition that was to become Asante, it had many enemies and few friends.

The Dutch left the best chronological account of what happened. In August 1699 they reported that trade had dwindled away because "the peoples in the interior" had "war on their minds." By June 1700 there were "no goods more current than fire-arms." Denkyira, whose plans were "difficult to predict," was rumored to be about to go to fight with "the Asjantese" (Asante) or with Twifo, Wassa, Fante, or others in the south. In May 1701 there was "heavy warfare" reported between Denkyira and the Kwaman coalition ("Assjantee"). All the peoples along the trade corridor from the coast to Abankeseso interdicted Ntim Gyakari's supply of munitions, for the Denkyira "have for long been very bellicose and proud of their victories, and so they have become insufferable to their neighbors." The Dutch surmised that "the Assjanteese" might gain the upper hand, because they were "much stronger in men and well provided with everything." If that happened then all of Denkyira's neighbors would join in to attack it for being "such a fearsome and warmongering state." In November 1701 it was reported that the Kwaman insurgents had won "a complete victory" over the Denkyira. The "towering pride" of Denkyira was "in ashes," and its people were in flight from enslavement. Trade remained moribund, because the victors were engaged for "fifteen days" in sacking Abankeseso and "lustily" plundering Denkyira. They had too much "rich loot" to be bothered with trade. The Dutch immediately sent an emissary to the victorious "Zay" (Asantehene Osei Tutu). He saw the Asante ruler's "personal booty," worth "some several thousand marks of gold," displayed in his war camp in Denkyira.

Denkyira and Asante traditions tell more or less the same story in exhaustive detail. The Denkyira forces advanced from Abankeseso northeast through Gyakobu, and in fierce fighting drove Asante forces north out of Adunku, Aboatem, and Aputuogya. Ntim Gyakari set off in pursuit. A mile north of Aputuogya he encountered Osei Tutu's main force deployed at Feyiase. The battle that ensued was epochal, for it gave the nascent Asante polity (the Kwaman coalition) the beginnings of control over the Ofin-Pra river basin and so opened the way for it to become the dominant power in the precolonial Gold Coast. Ntim Gyakari was killed, and Denkyira traditions report that "the remnants of Ntim's army" streamed south to seek refuge "in their territory over the Ofin River on the south bank." Osei Tutu directed his attention to Abankeseso, "a large city with seventy-seven streets watered by seven streams, which was now undefended." It was sacked of its gold, accumulated by Boamponsem "and stored there against an evil day that had now, alas, arrived. The Ashantis took all this huge wealth in gold from its storage jars and strewed it all through the streets until calming down they recollected themselves and gathered it all up again and bore it off to Kumasi." After Osei Tutu's return home the Denkyira crossed back over the Ofin and reoccupied the ruins of Abankeseso. In 1706–7 they rose up in revolt but were suppressed. Thereafter, they were truculent and intermittently rebellious Asante subjects until they joined the insurgency against Kumase that engulfed the Gold Coast between the 1800s and the 1820s. In the course of this war their position became untenable and they emigrated south of the Ofin-Pra Rivers to establish a new homeland around Jukwa in the southern Gold Coast.

Today old Denkyira—the place ruled over by Boamponsem and Ntim Gyakari—has disappeared from historical view. The now long-abandoned site of Abankeseso is unknown to geography and archaeology, and the ancient Denkyira settlements that served it are erased, subsumed or supplanted by the palimpsest of occupation first imposed by precolonial Kumase and then revised by migrant colonial cocoa farmers. . . .

Asante was created out of and thereafter enlarged through the incorporation of men and women from many localities with different histories. It was not in the interests of Kumase to countenance discussion of earlier identities and older allegiances. Nkawie, with its origins in Denkyira royalty, was supremely a case in point. Yet memories of the pre-Asante past did survive in Nkawie as elsewhere. They resurfaced from time to time, most pointedly in the late nineteenth and early twentieth centuries, when Asante suffered civil wars, the exile of its ruler, and the loss of its independence to British colonial rule. These shocks occurred in rapid succession (1883–1901). By the 1900s the order created at Feyiase was fractured and many in Asante looked for ways and means to negotiate an adjusted identity within the new colonial dispensation. One such was the Nkawiehene Kwabena Kufuor.

In 1896 Nkawiehene Antwi Agyei was exiled with Asantehene Agyeman Prempeh, and died in colonial captivity in 1908. In 1901 the British appointed Kwabena Kufuor to the stool. He was an Nkawie royal who had made a great deal of money from the rubber trade. He spent the 1890s in the Gold Coast, for he disapproved of Antwi Agyei and his lending of Nkawie resources to support Agyeman Prempeh. In the Gold Coast, Kwabena Kufuor learned of the importance of colonial legal documentation. As Nkawiehene he made great use of the courts to defend his and his stool's interests. In 1906 he went to law in Cape Coast to secure title to the gold-mining concession on his land held by the Bibiani Company. From this he was paid an annual concession rent of £600, supplemented by discretionary payments that sometimes raised this figure to over £1,000 a year. He invested these monies and his income from other businesses in Kumase property. Kwabena Kufuor was probably the richest person in early colonial Asante.

Kwabena Kufuor was increasingly troubled as the twentieth century advanced. His problem was his wealth, for he spent much of his time defending his lands, businesses, and properties from predatory fellow-chiefs (notably including Bantamahene). He was prominent among those who saw the 1924 repatriation of Agyeman Prempeh as presaging a return to the royal loans extracted from Antwi Agyei. Kwabena Kufuor's opposition to any restoration of the precolonial order led him to resurrect his historic Denkyira identity. In 1926 he astonished the British by declaring, "I am not a real Ashanti man," adding that he declined to contribute to the making of new ornaments for the Golden Stool because "I am a stranger in Ashanti." In any case, he continued, the Golden Stool was junior to and less distinguished than "my own Stool of Denkyira." When it became evident that the British did intend to restore the Asante kingship, Kwabena Kufuor abdicated from the Nkawie stool. Instead, he made much of his historic connection with the ancient Denkyira royal family—so much so, in fact, that he was offered the *abankamdwa* as Denkyirahene. The affairs of Nkawie had come full circle. In the seventeenth century, Asensu Kufuor repudiated Ntim Gyakari, Abankeseso, and his Denkyira identity. In the twentieth century, Kwabena Kufuor rejected Agyeman Prempeh, Kumase, and his Asante identity.

Ta'rīkh Ghunjā

Ivor Wilks, Nehemia Levtzion, and Bruce M. Haight

By all accounts, the Gonja state was established by migrant Mande warriors following the ancient trade routes between the middle Niger River valley and the forest-savanna ecologies of the former Gold Coast. Gonja came into existence in the late sixteenth and seventeenth centuries and was located in the north of present-day Ghana, around the confluence of the White and the Black Volta and north of the Asante heartland. A century after its existence, Gonja first appeared on European maps in the early eighteenth century. The Ta'rīkh Ghunjā *(*History of Gonja*), which appears below in English translation from the Arabic original, is an oral narrative (reduced to writing) of the exploits of Gonja's founding ruler, Jakpa. The narrative follows Jakpa from his and his followers' departure from their Mande homeland to his death in the Gonja division of Kpembe. The text has been divided into paragraphs by the editors, and since more than one manuscript version exists for this account, we have chosen manuscript 1 (Ms/1). We have used Ms/263 only where necessary.*

In the name of Allāh the Merciful, the Compassionate; Allāh whose help is called for.

1. This is the Story of Salgha [Salaga] and the History of Ghunjā [Gonja] as narrated to me by Gharba Baghunjā, the brother of Limām Alfā, a very old man (*shaykh kabīr*) who is lame and lives on alms. Actually, when you ask the Ghunjā to tell you their history, they do not do so. As for me, what I have been told by Gharba, I am going to tell you. Gharba said:

2. A notable (*kabīr*) called Jakpa (he had a name but none is known except this) set out with his people from Mande land since he had made an oath never to come back until, Allāh willing, he had fought, conquered the land up to the ocean, and divided it among his descendants.

3. [Ms/1] Jakpa told the 'ālim, Fāti Morukpe, of his intentions. Actually, if you want to wage war and you don't find an 'ālim, then it is impossible for you to do so. So he asked Fāti Morukpe to join him in his campaign, to

pray to Allāh on his behalf, saying: "I shall give you one hundred horses, one hundred young slaves (male and female), one hundred sheep, one hundred gowns, and one hundred [pairs] of trousers with their ropes. If you died, your people and your children would take [all these], and if I died, my people would be kind to you and to your people. . . ."

4. The 'ālim accepted and accompanied Jakpa, who fought and was victorious everywhere, until he arrived at a town called Buwāde [Bole] and conquered it, and there he let the 'ālim dwell. The 'ālim built a big house and appointed one of his followers *imām* there because his followers were many. Jakpa made his grandson the *amīr* of Buwāde and the surrounding area, that is, the province of Buwāde. He instructed him to fight and conquer more lands. He ordered him never to conceal anything from him, that is, "Do not deceive me, and never resort to highway robbery. Do not be a tyrant, nor a stupid person. Be kind to the vanquished and do not do wrong to anyone, otherwise your land and army would be spoiled."

5. Jakpa heard that one of the notables (*kubarā'*) had left the Land of the Arabs and was coming to him. He set out and met him at a place that was a march of three days away. When he arrived [Jakpa] greeted the notable, who returned his greetings. Jakpa let him live in the house of the first 'ālim [Fāti Morukpe]. This is why it has become the custom of the Ghunjā, that when a guest comes to them they lodge him in the house of the 'ālim. The notable and the 'ālim used to talk and converse. The 'ālim treated that notable reverentially. The notable told Jakpa, "Your 'ālim is a learned *shaykh*." Therefore Jakpa honored him, even more than he had at first.

6. Jakpa asked that notable to live with him, saying, "I will give you land to live on because I do not see the end of my march." The Arab agreed and Jakpa gave him land so that he might build on it. Jakpa ordered his people that none of them should treat the Arab unjustly; rather they should be kind to him. That Arab built the town called Larabanga, that is, "The Arabs," which is still there. Nobody treats [the people of Larabanga] unjustly; rather they are treated with deference by everyone who meets them. If fighting takes place on that land, they are left alone.

7. That Arab copied the Book, that is, the Qur'ān. It was a great book, and therefore he bound it in two volumes, each containing thirty *hizbs*. He embellished it with different colors of ink: black, red, green and saffron. When the Arab died, the Qur'ān remained with his descendants until there was no 'ālim left in their family. Whenever a calamity befalls them or when they want anything, they implored [Allāh] through [the Qur'ān]. They made supplications, saying, "Lord, in honor of our grandfathers who brought us this Book. We do not know anything. It is your Book that knows. In honor

of your Book we direct ourselves to your benefaction, asking you, being omnipotent, to grant us everything we ask." Then they all say, "Amen," and wipe the palms of their hands on their faces. If a cow is brought, they slaughter it. Then they fold the Qur'ān and return it to its container, that is, to its skin. They still do this until now. Others treat this Qur'ān as if it were an idol. Everybody knows this. The town and the Qur'ān are still there until now.

8. Then Jakpa set out for Ghūfi and made it a great market for people, so that the Hausa might come there and buy kola nuts. Kola is of two kinds, white and red. The white comes from Bītughu [Bonduku], the red from Asantī [Asante], to Ghūfi [Gbuipe]. When the Hausa came, they used to say, "We want *ghun jan ghūru*," and [since] they called the object of their travel and trade *ghunjā*, they call the land "Ghunjā" and its people "Ghunjāwa."

9. Jakpa went on fighting until he arrived at another place. He said, "I shall live here." He built a big house, one [story] rising above the other. It was called Buti, that is, the residence of the *sultān*. It is still there. The Hausa call it Garin Bisa, which means "the town on top." Its reputation has now diminished because its inhabitants are few. Yet whoever sees it now knows that in the past it was a big town.

10. Nowadays it is at Salgha that the people of Ghūfi and the surrounding area, and even the Asantī, gather for trade.

11. [Ms/1] Then Jakpa went on fighting and came to a river where salt was found. He built a town which he called Dabūyā [Daboya] and made his grandson an *amīr* there. He told him: "Do right to the town, that Allāh might cause it to prosper. If you extract [salt], treat it well and do not mix it with anything else." Dabūyā became a prosperous town. The extraction of salt was the task of their women because they were experts in the craft.

12. Its people and the people of Ghrunsi [Grusi] bought this salt, as did the Daghunba [Dagomba], Kunkunba [Konkomba], Bāsārī and Kabari [Kabre]. They all bought this salt except the people of Asantī who did not like it and preferred the salt of Ada [i.e., lagoons at the mouth of the Volta River], which was expensive. If the people of Asantī saw salt from Dabūyā with someone, they levied a tax. As for the salt of Dabūyā, its trade reached the utmost horizons.

13. Then Jakpa went on until he came to another place where he built a town called Yāghun. He wanted to make it the [seat of the] paramount *sultān*, and [therefore] made his eldest son an *amīr* there. The people of Ghunjā do not call [their ruler] *amīr*; they call him Yarīman Ghunjāwa.

14. Then Jakpa set out, and in every town taken over Fāti Morukpe left people to live with them [for one of them] to be their *imām*.

A view of the Black Volta River in northern Ghana. Photograph by Kwasi Konadu, 2007.

15. Between Buwāde [Bole] and Salafī [Seripe] he [Jakpa] built a house for himself, but he did not live there. It is still there, the palace, until now and no one lives there. It is said that he kneaded oil and mud and built it.

16. [Ms/263] Then he left with his army for the town of Qawsaw [Kawsawgu] and conquered it. He built a house there and made his son to sit [on the skin] there. Then he said to his son, "O my son, take good care of these people." Then he said to the people, "Be friendly to my son."

17. [Ms/1] Then Jakpa went on fighting until he arrived at a town called Dibr [Deber], conquered it, and appointed an *amīr* over them. Then he arrived at another place. Then he set out also for Tuluway [Tuluwe] and made his son an *amīr* there.

18. Now his authority became overwhelming, and he was feared everywhere. Then he was told, "In front of you are many people. Do not go [there] lest they ambush you in the bush." He said, "There is no one who can ambush me, and whoever intends that [are] like mice and their bush is the Bush of the Mice." He set out, reached them, and routed them in all directions. He then built a town called Zughunkulu [Sugu Kolo], which means in the Dhanghuy language, "Bush of the Mice." The town is still there until now.

19. Other people gathered on a waterless highland. They had stored water so that they might fight Jakpa until noon, drink their water, and then fight again. They said that Jakpa, and his men and horses, would die of thirst, and they believed that they would be victorious. Jakpa and his soldiers came and they tried to block his way. The two parties met and fought fiercely. Jakpa rose and said, "*iburmāsi*," that is, "beat them," and they were defeated. Jakpa and his people found the water that they had stored, and drank it. He built there a town called Burmāsi [Brumase].

20. [Ms/1] Nearby there was a town on the river where all sorts of people had gathered. They met him with food, seeking protection (*amān*). He laughed and asked them, "What is this?" Their head, a man from Barnū [Borno], said, "It is *kafa-kafa*." [Jakpa] said, "Stay where you are, and I will bring you a *sultān* of my own." The name of the town is now Kafāba.

21. Then Jakpa crossed the river and halted at another place. He met some people and told them, "I am going forward." They said, "There is a place in front of you that is not good, because your horses and cattle will die if they drink its water. [This is] because there is a snake called Yaghi [Yeji] which vomits poison in it." Jakpa called the water and the town Yaghi.

22. He went [back] across the river and sought a place to pass the night. In the morning he said, "Let me rest today." He rested, and called it Kulfī [Kulepe], which means "the day of rest." It is still there. Because of this the Ghunjā do not work there, and call it Kulfī.

23. Then Jakpa set out for a town called Kunbi [Kpembe], raided it, and took it over together with the surrounding area. There is a small land called Nanunba [Nanumba]. They were pagan. He invaded them, defeated them, and took possession of their land. He built Kunbi . . .

24. Then Jakpa set out through the country of the Nanunba and Kunkunba until he reached Bāsārī and Kabari. He took [land] there and let his people dwell there, that is, in the town of Alfāyi [Alfaye]. Their *amīr* is Kanankulāyī [Kanankulaiwura].

25. He felt at home there after he had made his eldest and strongest son its *amīr*. He built in that town a house for himself, lived and died there. He called it Ghindinfī. His tomb is still there. If one breaks [the wall of] his house, he will see the honey, oil and mud which he kneaded during its construction.

26. The Ghunjā revere his tomb. Anyone who sought refuge at it for protection would have been left alone. I even saw one of his descendants who killed someone flee there and he was left alone. But as a punishment they denied him [any claim to] chieftaincy (*wilāya*). . . .

29. The people of Ghunjā profoundly revere Ghindinfī where Jakpa died. When one who stands wants to mention its name, he sits down, takes off his cap, and then mentions the name. One who sits lies down and takes off his cap. Both men and women do so. They swear by its name, and this is their most solemn oath. [The formula of] their swearing by Ghindinfī is "If I did such-and-such."

III

Commerce and the Scrambles for Africa, 1700–1900

By 1701, Asante had emerged as the most powerful polity in the forest interior, occupying the once dominant position of another polity, Denkyira, but expanding its rule to an area the size of present-day Ghana (known as "Greater Asante"). Meanwhile, the Fante peoples dominated the coastal trade, functioning sometimes as intermediaries between, and sometimes as rivals of, Europeans (e.g., British, Dutch, and Danish) and the Asante Empire. Indeed, the Fante competed as well as cooperated with the Asante until the latter and then the former were effectively brought under British colonial rule by the end of the nineteenth century. For much of the forested interior and the savanna ecology of northern Ghana, British imperialism in the late nineteenth century would serve as the primary occasion for any significant European commercial or missionary presence on the coast, in the forest, and to a lesser extent in the savanna zone. This uneven pace of European penetration—owing in large part to the internal workings of local societies and the geography and disease environs they occupied—would shape the contours of present-day Ghana, as well as one of the most powerful historic polities, Asante, who dominated the region between the eighteenth and nineteenth centuries.

This section includes the perspectives of merchants, slavers, combatants, local informants, chroniclers, physicians, pastors, colonial officials, and scholars. These perspectives graphically illustrate how the encounters and sociopolitical transformations caused by transatlantic slaving created the climate for so-called legitimate trade, localized forms of enslavement, and the Gold Coast Colony by the end of the nineteenth century. Those perspectives also show a number of critical paradoxes: as international slaving was gradually abolished and such human trafficking declined, local forms of enslavement and mechanisms of servitude increased; as the British, Dutch, and Danish attempted to bring the plantation scheme from the

Americas to the Gold Coast to be worked by Gold Coast laborers—rather than export them to the Americas—these Europeans, especially the British, also tried to convince African holders of captive peoples to relinquish their ownership in return for protection from local rivals and access to European imported goods, schooling, and religion. The role of African merchants in Euro-African commerce and African converts who become proselytizing missionaries were crucial to the success of British imperialism on the Gold Coast, since the success of African(-descended) converts hinged on their linguistic and cultural competency in local settings, and, in some cases, their genetic or phenotypical qualification. The common denominator in the persistent internal revolts over the control of trade, tensions around servitude and domestic enslavement, and the consumption of European goods and (religious) ideas and their effects were Gold Coast Africans who converted to Christianity and the gospel of capitalism. In effect, those minimally seduced by Christianization and Westernization had the least successful African converts and the greatest allegiance to a spiritual culture that rationalized their society, whereas Christian orthodoxy and British commerce among coastal Fante peoples, for instance, caused the deepest ruptures in culture, society, and the ideological constitution of self vis-à-vis its once spiritual culture.

The Various Nations of Blacks in Guinea

Christian G. A. Oldendorp

Christian George Andreas Oldendorp (1721–87), a Moravian clergyman, maintained that the "Amina" (Akan) were the most numerous in the Danish colonies of St. Croix and St. John in the late eighteenth century. If his observation is accurate, the Akan accounted for a sizable share of St. Croix's enslaved population. Oldendorp's account is significant, since he interviewed a number of peoples ("baptized slaves," predominantly Akan) from the Gold Coast and thus provides an invaluable window into their late eighteenth-century world in West Africa and in the Danish Caribbean. Most of Oldendorp's Gold Coast informants were multilingual: they understood Twi (Akan), Gã, and Ewe.

The greatest number of slaves brought to the West Indies are from the Gold Coast and its region. They consist of many nations. The most noble, belligerent nation, which also most often practices the capture of persons, even among itself, is the nation Amina [Akan peoples].

I have talked to five respectable and intelligent blacks of this nation. One was a noble and rich merchant and slave capturer, who had also been traveling far and near, another the king's brother, another a cousin of a "subking," who had had a large army of blacks—3,000 men of it had been under his command. They had on each side of their heads three incisions, one beneath the other, from the ear to the eye. They said that they had these because they considered it beautiful and also to distinguish themselves from other nations. These had already been made when they were children, by their mothers. The skin is cut with a knife and palm oil mixed with coal is rubbed into it, so that it cannot grow shut again, and several times more palm oil is brushed over it. One had lived a day's journey, another a fourteen days' journey away from the ocean, one a day's journey from a British fort [Cape Coast Castle?].

They have a belligerent spirit and great courage and there are brave people among them. They do not like to work in Guinea but rob, if they can, the neighboring nations and capture people from them, sometimes also among

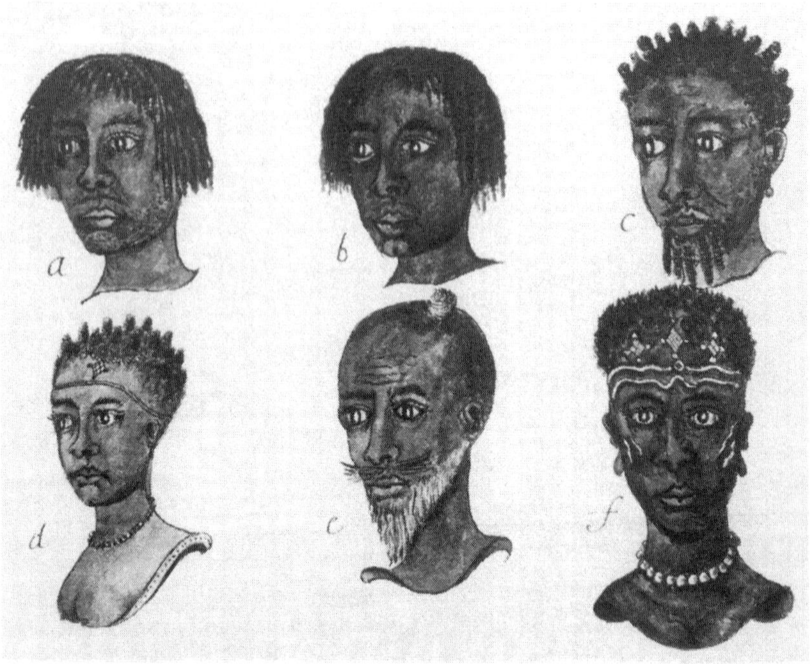

"The Various Nations of Blacks" on the Gold Coast, as represented by Jean Barbot during the late seventeenth century, from *Barbot on Guinea: The Writings of Jean Barbot on West Africa, 1698–1712*, edited by P. E. H. Hair, Adam Jones, and Robin Law (London: Hakluyt Society, 1992), vol. 2, plate 74. Used by permission of Hakluyt Society.

their own countrymen. They have only one king and "subkings," or governors, in every district. In these lands such blacks are called Caboseer. They are feared by their neighbors because of their power and cruelty. They (the people telling the stories) named many nations with which they are at war: the Fante, Akkim [Akyem], Akkran [Nkran/Gã], Bemang [Aboraman], Asseni [Asen], Kifferu [Twifoɔ], Atti [Ati/Etsi], Okkau [Kwawu], Adansi [Adanse]. . . .

They named as cause of these wars, that thereby they were able to capture people and sell them. They have firearms, which they obtain from Europeans; their enemies, for the most part, have only bows and arrows. The occasions for internal wars are often given by the many heirs of the king and the subkings, who also would like to become persons of importance and are trying to oust others or start a fight for succession among themselves.

Their land is very large and full of villages, some of which could be called cities because of their size. They have plenty of gold, but no iron. The former merchant had traded in the country with gold, which he had obtained from the whites (as payment) for slaves and he got for a piece that was about as big as half a hand, 10 pieces of Achten, if one counts it in the currency of the West Indies. For a knife, such as is used to cut sugar cane, they would, he said, give about 10 pieces and for an axe 20. There they pay in gold, partly in grains (of gold), partly in whole pieces, or with shells or slaves, whatever they have and are able to do it with. Five shells, which are called *bujis* or cowries, amount to approximately one West Indian stueber or half a penny (groschen). He also traded with gold, ivory, and slaves. One Amina nation, which he called Quahu [Kwahu], kills many elephants. From these he bought a tooth for about four pieces of West Indian money and sold it again to another nation for ten pieces, and took those elephant teeth also often to British or Dutch manufacturers. If a nation owed him something, he gave them three months to pay. If they did not pay, he waited another month. If after that nothing was done, he sent people out to waylay them and capture whoever they could. He let them prey especially on the children of his debtors and he sold whoever he got, to the whites as slave. He said that life in Guinea was good; one did not have to work as hard as in the West Indies, but one's plight there was insecurity, because people tried to catch and sell one another. . . .

The general name of the god of the Amina, whom they evoke in Guinea, is Jankombum [Onyankopɔn]. He is also the sky. But some say that god in the sky, who made the world and their nation, is called Borriborri [Bɔrebɔre; an appellation for the Akan Creator]. This one has a wife, Jankomaago, and a son, Jankombum, who is the intercessor with the great god and to whom they pray in all their concerns. Another one also told me that they have three gods, but that in his region the father is called Quereampum [Tweadeampɔn], the mother Kieampum, and the son Jankombum. They are close to the son and call him too father. During war they sing in the midst of shooting to Jankombum: He should help us, he is the father, we are his children and cannot help ourselves. Every morning after they have washed themselves they call to him that he should protect them, give them good nourishment and let them be happy. Many blacks, especially on the Gold Coast, have learned from the whites the division of time into weeks. The Amina celebrate every week the day on which they are born, for instance Monday. On that day in the morning before washing themselves, they grind up portulak—*aggra* in their language—or another weed which they call sombee, in water and take a mouthful of the water three times and every time they spit out the water they pray to Jankombum. They do not know why they are doing this or where they acquired this custom. They simply do it as an old habit. Someone who owes another person something also pleads with Jankombum to pay for him. They especially call to him or one of the other gods in time of disease for recovery. . . .

They have certain holy places, where they pray. Most of the time these are very round hills, which are always kept clean. They believe that god had emerged from those. And when they pass such a hill, they pray to god and put a stone or twigs on it in his honor. In one place is water and a square near it. They go there when they are asking for rain and sacrifice sheep and poultry, so that blood is flowing, they eat and drink and ask Jankombum to let rain flow as abundantly as they are now spilling blood. One man told that it often started to rain before they arrived home. On their New Year's Day and at the time when they are planting corn (maize) and other foods, they meet under a tree and erect many stones. They thank Jankombum for food throughout the past year and ask him for blessing in the coming year. They dine together and drink a type of beer after a black priest has given a speech. First the children eat. The firstborn have an advantage here. Each of them receives a gourd of corn (maize). They pour some beer into it and the children eat and drink from it. When they are finished the priest gives a speech to the elders and these eat and drink the same meal. Some perform their worship under a tree, which they revere as divine. They believe that it is bending its branches downward. Then they climb it, and remain sitting on it for eight to ten days, without eating or drinking, except for a little bit of chalk that they take along.

Translated by Kwasi Konadu

An ɔpanin (elder) performing libation with palm wine in a calabash. Almost all formal, and some informal, occasions are opened with libation. Photograph by Clifford Campbell, Techiman, July 2009.

Greetings are central to being human in African cultures, and this ritual occurs in both formal and informal settings in Ghana. Photograph by Clifford Campbell, Techiman, July 2009.

Schoolgirls in uniform. Photograph by Msia Kibona Clark, Volta Region, Ghana, 2011. Courtesy of the photographer.

Two boys at play in the Volta region. Photograph by Msia Kibona Clark, 2013. Courtesy of the photographer.

Ghana plays England in a friendly football match at Wembley Stadium in London, March 29, 2011. Photograph by Akira Suemori, 2011. Courtesy of the FIA Foundation.

A popular Ghanaian dish commonly referred to as "red red"—a rough translation of the Akan/Twi term *kɔkɔɔ*. The dish consists of fried ripe plantains and stewed beans. Photograph by Ọbádélé Kambon, 2014.

Ghanaian women dominate the commerce at the Techiman Market, the largest outdoor market in West Africa. Photograph by Clifford Campbell, Techiman, July 2009.

Asantehene Otumfuo Nana Osei Tutu II rides in a palanquin in royal regalia during Akwasiadae celebration in Kumase, October 2009. Photograph by Kwasi Bempong, 2009. Courtesy of the photographer.

Ghanaian health care volunteers distribute medication as part of a nationwide deworming program at the Kuntanase Presbyterian School, in Asikuma-Odoben-Brakwa, Ghana, 2012. Photograph by Marcus Perkins, 2012. Courtesy of GlaxoSmithKline Services Unlimited.

(*facing*) Ghanaian lawmakers meet during a session of Parliament in Accra, Ghana, June 16, 2006. Inside the *adinkra* symbols and "parliament of Ghana" phrase on the parliament floor and within the coat of arms behind the speaker lies the "black star" of Ghana—a pan-African symbol adopted by Ghana's first prime minister and president, Kwame Nkrumah, from Jamaica-born nationalist Marcus Garvey. The speaker seated below the coat of arms is assisted by two deputy speakers from two different political parties, whereas the speaker is chosen by the majority party. The first incarnation of the Ghanaian Parliament dates to the late nineteenth century and the first half of the twentieth, when the Gold Coast Colony, out of which the republic of Ghana was born, had a legislative council that functioned in a purely advisory and later auxiliary capacity. Upon achieving political independence, the Ghanaian parliament followed the British Westminster model of governance with its own national assembly and elected officials, including a few women. But the fluctuations between military and civilian rule from 1966 to 1996 meant that Parliament was either dissolved or dwarfed, only to emerge again during the current Fourth Republic of Ghana. Photograph by Jonathan Ernst. Flickr.

Performers at the Accra Carnival, 2013. Carnival is one of many imports from the Caribbean and the broader African diaspora in the Americas. Photograph by Clifford Campbell, Legon, April 2009.

A performance by Adzewa, a Fante women's group whose music tackles topical social issues. Photograph by Clifford Campbell, Accra, September 2009.

Revolt on a Danish Slaving Voyage

Paul Erdmann Isert

Chief surgeon and merchant at the Danish headquarters (Christiansborg) on the Gold Coast, German botanist Paul Erdmann Isert (1756–89) arrived in November 1783 at a time when the Danish forts at Ada, Keta, and at Teshi were being built. Isert stayed on the Gold Coast for three years, leaving in October 1786 by way of a slave ship bound eventually for Copenhagen. After two days at sea the enslaved captives from the Gold Coast revolted, and Isert was attacked and seriously injured, though he would recover two months later. The following account describes this event. Isert reached home in Denmark in the summer of 1787, but the enslaved would never see their homeland again.

It was on 7 October last year that I left Africa and boarded the ship "Christiansburg" which sailed that very evening. Picture the tumult in front of a ship of black slaves, a ship which when used in the King's service would hold no more than 200 people, now holding more than 452 slaves, who have to be kept in check by 36 Europeans. Imagine the sight of such a multitude of miserable people—some who were by chance born to slave parents; some who were captured in war; some who were stolen and innocent of any crime; some who, for other casual reasons, were sold to the Europeans—all of them now about to be transported in heavy chains from their fatherland to another country which they do not know. Their future cannot possibly hold anything good in store for them when the Europeans use such violent means to secure them. In their own country they have themselves heard such dreadful tales of how the slaves are treated in Columbia [i.e., the Americas] that one is appalled when one hears them. I was once asked by a slave, in complete earnest, if the shoes I was wearing had been made of Black skin, since he had observed that they were the same colour as his skin. Others say that we eat the Blacks and make gunpowder of their bones. They cannot imagine that they will be used only for the cultivation of fields and other manual labor, since, in order to sustain themselves here, this kind of work requires so few hands and demands so little time that it would be absolutely superfluous to bring strangers into the land to do it. Furthermore, they give no credence to all the assurances from the Europeans that they are going to be taken to a beautiful country, and other similar cajolery. On the contrary, whenever the opportunity presents itself they take flight or kill themselves, since they fear death far less than slavery in West India. Indeed, all precautions must be taken to prevent their having the opportunity of committing suicide. For this reason on the French ships they are not even allowed a narrow strip of loincloth for fear they will hang themselves by it, which has in fact happened.

This prejudice, and the too strict treatment these unfortunates not infrequently are forced to suffer at the hands of barbaric captains, often results in a conspiracy among them. They conspire at night that, notwithstanding their chains, they will kill the Europeans whom they so greatly outnumber and let the ship drift in to land. Usually this kind of mutiny occurs either while the ship is in the roadstead or during the first day, when the ship is sailing away from the coast. During my stay on the Guinea Coast I have heard of a number of sad examples. In the year 1785 the slaves on a Dutch ship revolted on the very day that the ship was to sail to West India. The Europeans were overpowered and beaten to death, except for a young cabin-boy who had climbed to the top of the main mast. Before the Whites had been completely overpowered, they had shot off several alarm signals which had been heard on land, and a number of canoes manned with armed, free Blacks had been sent out to help. As soon as these approached the ship and the rebellious slaves saw that they had to become the losers, they decided to do away with themselves. With this in mind, one of them ran with a firebrand to the powder magazine and blew it up. The canoes did not fish up more than some thirty Blacks, and the cabin boy as well. The rest, more than 500 in number, fell victim to the waves.

Less lucky were the Blacks on an English ship, who also rebelled on the Gold Coast that same year. They had killed all the Europeans, cut the anchor rope, and let the ship drift to land. When it reached the breakers, all the Blacks jumped overboard and swam to shore. But, to their great sorrow, the free Blacks standing along the shore fished them all up and sold them once again to the Europeans. The ship and its cargo were good spoils for the Blacks at the point where it drifted into land.

I report these two examples only from hearsay, but now a word about an uprising of slaves on a ship on which I found myself. A slave ship is equipped amidships with a strong, high, [transverse] wooden partition called the bulwark whose side facing forward must be extremely smooth, without any open grooves in which the slaves might get a fingerhold. On top of this wall

Bondage. Painting by Martin Numadzi, 2009. Courtesy of the artist.

there are as many small cannons and guns as there is room for, and these are kept loaded at all times and are shot off every evening in order to keep the slaves in a state of fear. There is always a man on watch near these, who must pay meticulous attention to the movements of the Blacks. In the stern section on the other side of the bulwark, all the women and children are kept, while the men are kept on the forward side of the bulwark where they can neither see the women nor join them. The men are alway[s] chained together, hand and foot, in pairs. Moreover, along the row in which they sit on the deck, a strong chain is drawn between their feet so that they cannot stand up without permission, nor can they move from the spot, except when they come up on deck in the mornings and are locked in the hold in the evenings. But, since their number is so great, they can only enjoy this exercise every second day, having on the other days to stay below, where they are packed together like herrings.

It was on the second day of our sailing, when most of the Krepees [Ewe] were on deck, that they started to rebel. At that moment I found myself alone among the Blacks, and since I understand the language of the Akras

[Gã] I was exchanging pleasantries with some of them and with some Dunkos [peoples from present-day northern Ghana] (a most well-mannered nation). Because there is always a great tumult with such a number of people, I noticed that it had suddenly become extremely quiet. Since most of the crew were below, eating, I decided to go to the bow of the ship to see if everyone was at his post, in case the Blacks had some kind of rebellion in mind. When I had reached about midships the door of the bulwark was opened, because the first mate intended to come out to join me. But at that same moment there arose from all the male slaves a shriek of the most horrifying tone that one can imagine. It resembled the one I had heard, at an earlier time, when they were going to attack in battle. Hearing this cry, all the men, who were usually seated, stood up. Some of them hit me on the head with the hand-irons with which they were chained together, so that I immediately fell to the deck. But since they were also chained at the feet I was able to crawl away from them, and I reached the bulwark door. Here I now battered in vain, because, when the crew tried to let me in, such a number of Blacks seized the door that the crew had great difficulty in closing it. Furthermore, it is established policy that it is better to let a European be killed than to allow the Blacks to gain control of that door, since they could then make their way to the stern of the ship, which is full of weapons hanging there. It would then be a simple task for them to become masters of the ship. Meanwhile I was not left idle at the door for long, but was immediately forced to seek the deck as before. When the Europeans in the stern of the ship realized what was happening on the other side, they tried to keep the bulwark free from attack, by stabbing with bayonets from above. In order to be able to kill me more easily, the slaves pulled me by the foot to the bow of the ship, where one of them, using a razor he had seized from another who was in the process of shaving him when the rebellion began, made a slash across my forehead and temple, through my ear to deep down as far as my neck. But while he was working on my neck, not being able immediately to achieve his purpose due to the thick silk scarf I was wearing, I was delivered by a shot from the bulwark which went through his chest. This made him fall backwards and the other slaves who were holding me released me. Thus I was free again. More musket shots were fired, and there was also firing from two three-pound cannons loaded with grape-shot, so that the Blacks withdrew as far as possible towards the bow to avoid the shots. As a result, the door of the bulwark was left free and I had just enough strength to crawl to it, leaving a trail of blood marking my path, since my right temple artery had been severed. The mate, too, had a number of wounds, but not as serious as mine, and since he was a better sailor than I was, he had saved himself by leaving the deck through the cannon port and then climbing up again on the other side of the bulwark. From the bulwark an attempt was now made, using either kindness or force, to bring the Blacks to their quarters below. Some of them had, in the meanwhile, hammered off their irons, but when prodded by guns, those who had not been party to the conspiracy went to their quarters without any further resistance. The others, however, when they saw that they could not succeed all sprang overboard into the sea. Some boys from the same nation as the rebels but lacking the courage to take such a drastic step were deliberately pushed over by the older ones. The slaves below deck were secured, and with great haste small boats were launched. As many slaves as possible were fished up, some living, some dead. It was astounding how some pairs, although they each had only one hand and one foot free (because they were chained together by the other hand and foot), were very adept at staying above water. Some were stubborn even in the face of death, defiantly casting away the rope which had been thrown around their bodies from the ship in order to draw them up, and diving under with force. Among the others there was a pair who had a difference of opinion, the one demanding that he be saved, the other, on the contrary, so desirous of drowning that he pulled the first one under water with him, with great force. The first one cried piteously and was pulled up with his comrade who, however, had already given up the ghost.

The uprising, before it could be completely quelled, lasted for two hours. Upon counting our men, we found that we had lost 34 Blacks in the action, all of whom had drowned. None of the Europeans, however, had died, but two, as mentioned before, had been wounded.

As for me, I was only in a very moderate condition. Since I had lost so much blood my strength ebbed away so quickly that I could not even bandage myself, but could only wrap some handkerchiefs around my head to try, if possible, to prevent further loss of blood. Because of this effort the weakness got the upper hand and I fell full length to the deck in a faint, from which I recovered only after a few hours. By the Captain's orders I had been taken immediately to a proper bed and my head moistened with warm wine. When I awoke the whole episode seemed to me to have happened in a dream. I was surprised to find where I was lying and to see the Black women who were sitting around me, crying tears of sympathy. I tried to get up but then I received the message. My head, which was as heavy as a hundredweight, partly because of the fomentation, partly because of the blood seeping through which had soaked all the cloths, reminded me of the cause. Due to the many blows from hand-irons, some of which had fractured my skull, my head was violently inflamed, so that when I awoke after 24 hours the wounds gaped to a width of two fingers, and since my temple muscle was completely severed I could not get my teeth apart but was forced to live on purely fluid nourishment. As serious as this condition seemed at first, still I recovered from it, happily enough, so that on the day we arrived in West India the wounds were healed, a process which had taken precisely two months.

Are you asking why the Blacks were so inflamed precisely against me since in those few days I could not have done them any harm? I found out later that since I boarded the ship so late they had concluded that I was the owner of all the slaves, and that it would be best to send me into the other world first, after which the Europeans, like mercenaries, would surrender all the sooner. After this, however, they treated me very well during the rest of the voyage, so that when I went down to them in the morning they received me with loud applause, which to the unpolished nations is as much a sign of approval as it is in our theatres.

One of the ringleaders of the conspiracy was a Black who had already been in West India and in England, and had come back to the Coast from there—I know not why—as boatswain in the service of our establishment. He had fallen deeply into debt, so in order to get rid of him they had sent him on our ship to West India. This villain had persuaded the Krepees that they should beat the Whites to death, then he would bring the ship back to land, since they were fairly far out to sea. Moreover he told them much of both truth and falsehood about West India: that it is a land of torment where they would be given little to eat but much work and many beatings. This was indeed a dangerous man, and it was certainly necessary, after the uprising, to isolate him completely from the others. Therefore he was given residence in the pigsty where, neither by his tongue nor any other parts of his body, could he be dangerous any longer.

Had it not been for that unhappy uprising, we would have made a very favorable journey, since we had no more than seven dead on the crossing, which, for such a great multitude of people, and in such conditions, is a very small number. There are examples of ships having brought to the West Indies not more than half of the slaves they had bought on the African coast. The length of the journey and especially the treatment of the Blacks are to a great extent the factors which give rise to the high mortality so common on slave ships. On this ship the greatest care was taken to maintain cleanliness, and the slaves had to exercise on deck every second day, as well as they could in the space they had. They were provided with as much fresh air as possible by means of ventilators which were, admittedly, not of the best sort—being made only of sacks of sailcloth whose upper ends were positioned above deck with open wings to catch the wind, and whose lower ends were placed below deck in the hold. In the evenings, before the slaves were allowed to go down again, all the chambers were well fumigated with dampened gunpowder. Their food consisted for the most part of products from their own land, such as maize, rice and yams. They seemed to find our pearl barley very tasty. On the other hand, the so-called "horse beans" which are the usual provision on slave ships were not at all to their taste. We were lucky enough to catch great numbers of dorado [dolphinfish or mahi-mahi] every day, so that not only was our entire ship's company well provided, but a considerable amount was dried for future use. Some of these fish weigh 150 pounds. When they are fully grown, they are called *halbe Kurte*. It is common knowledge that this variety is more numerous the closer one is to the equator.

Water, on the other hand, is a very precious item. A man is given not more than three quarters of a *kanne*, or 24 ounces, daily. This is very little considering that according to medical dietary rules one's intake should be four pounds of fluid every 24 hours, and that here in this torrid area it is so much more imperative to pay attention to this. The slaves' food is always cooked dry, so they cannot relieve their thirst in this way. Therefore it is not strange that one hears of the high mortality which often occurs on slave ships. On the other hand, it is incomprehensible when one hears of the great number of sailors who die on warships after a short cruise. They have been provided with all the necessities in abundance; their number does not begin to approach the number on a slave ship; their spirit is not tormented with fears of the future, as are the slaves. Would not the cause of the high mortality, then, lie in incidental things? How much would it not be to the benefit of mankind to find the causes and prevent them! Then one would not see the unwillingness and the desertion which are now so usual when the sailor has been drafted into military service!

A few days after our arrival here the fate of our Blacks was decided. They had been brought ashore, adorned according to the best of their country's custom, allowed great freedom of movement, treated with the delicacies of their own land, so that they were convinced that they had come to a paradise. But appearances were deceptive. The day of their sale had come. They were arranged in rank and file and none of the buyers was allowed to see them on that day until the predetermined moment. Then the door was opened. An army of buyers stormed in and like madmen grabbed the particular Black men and women they had decided upon the day before when the Blacks had been exhibited for inspection, and they took them to the seller to agree on a price. Since the entire business was conducted in such a frenzy that I myself soon became alarmed, one can easily imagine what the Blacks' reaction must have been. Before four hours had passed most of them had been sold. The rest, numbering 48, were for the most part frail or ageing Blacks who were sold wholesale the next day, through the bank, for 200 *thalers* apiece. The sum for all the Blacks sold came to 97,000 and a couple of hundred *thalers*.

Journal and Correspondences of H. W. Daendels

Herman Willem Daendels

Herman Willem Daendels (1762–1818) was governor-general of the Dutch forts on the Gold Coast between 1815 and 1818. Because of Britain's abolition of international slaving in 1807, and its efforts to compel other European slaving nations to follow suit, the Dutch banned slaving in 1814 (and an 1824 treaty between Britain and the Netherlands would seek to strengthen the 1814 ban). Against this changing economic backdrop, Daendels sought to create a plantation colony—with ample agrarian land and with commercial relations with inland polities—in place of the former Dutch slaving posts on the Gold Coast. But amid mismanagement, corruption, illegal commerce, and misconceptions about African polities, his attempts to implement this imperialistic policy failed. The following two excerpts from Daendels's journal focus on the foregoing matters.

Report to the Department of Trade and Colonies regarding the State of Trade on This Coast, 1816

The slave trade has caused the trafficking of goods for gold and ivory to be very greatly diminished. It has extinguished industry, and not only caused a reduction in the number of gold diggers, but also the regular work in the mines to cease in the dry season: so that now digging for gold is practically only done by the slaves of kings and caboceers, who win a very small amount compared with former times. It has also so much lessened the desire for agriculture that one finds periodical famines in many places where formerly abundance prevailed, the supply of one year then being first consumed in the one following. The uncertainty of not any day being seized and sold to the ships extinguished the courage for all peaceful labor, and made the negro into an armed and restless robber who laid snares for his fellowman to catch and sell him, as he feared and expected for himself and his.

Report to the Department of Trade and Colonies on the Cultivation of Colonial Products in the Dutch Settlements on the Coast of Guinea

The slave trade, which although (it is) [what] little one ever hears of murders and house breakings [i.e., robberies], had brought the wild-tempered negro to (such) a state that he lived in a continual quarrel with his neighbors, so that soon there existed no Krom [town] which had no palaver [lengthy debate], claim, or dispute with its nearest neighbor from which resulted the panyarring [illegal seizure of someone for sale], capturing, and carrying off of men, women and children, who thus neglected all regular work in the field and limited it to the most necessary of foodstuffs—has not only depopulated the countries along the Coast of Guinea, but has caused such a decline in cultivation and increase in the forests that on the one hand it will cost a great deal of trouble to reclaim this country afresh, while on the other hand no doubt remains that the present circumstances inspire infinitely more security not only to the Negro, but also the European who desires to commence the cultivation of colonial products.

The "Bowdich" Treaty with Asante and the Oath at Nyankumasi

Anonymous

The first decades of the nineteenth century were filled with a series of conflicts between the dominant African polity on the Gold Coast—Asante—and the dominant European actor in the region, Britain. Relations between Asante and Britain were strained, and both the British and the Dutch vied for the good favor of Asante in order to benefit from the trade that came through Asante's wide geographical rule. In fact, at its height, Asante controlled an area the size of present-day Ghana. Thus after invading Asante, the British renewed negotiations with its people through the African Company and the governor of Cape Coast Castle, whose nephew, Thomas Bowdich (1791–1824), was dispatched to sign a treaty with the Asantehene (the ruler of Asante). The Asantehene saw this treaty and the payments of "notes" (fees) as a reopening of transatlantic slaving and as an affirmation of his authority over the Fante peoples of Cape Coast and Anomabu. As Asante sought to maintain its hegemony, the Fante and other anti-Asante groups allied with the British. The following two excerpts include the above-mentioned British-Asante treaty and an oath-taking ritual for war involving the British, the Fante, and their allies against the Asante.

The "Bowdich" Treaty with Ashanti, September 7, 1817

Treaty made and entered into by Thomas Edward Bowdich, Esquire, in the name of Governor and Council at Cape Coast Castle, on the Gold Coast of Africa, and on behalf of the British Government, with Sai Tootoo Quamina [Osei Tutu Kwamina], King of Ashantee [Asante] and its Dependencies, and Boitinnee Quama [Kofi Boaten], King of Dwabin [Juaben] and its Dependencies.

1st. There shall be perpetual peace and harmony between the British subjects in country and the subjects of the Kings of Ashantee and Dwabin.

2nd. The same shall exist between the subjects of the Kings of Ashantee and Dwabin, and all nations of Africa residing under the protection of

Akwasi Boakye ("Aquasi Boachi") with two of his children, ca. 1898. Asante royal Akwasi Boakye was educated by the Dutch in Europe as part of efforts to foster good relations with Asante and to recruit Asante soldiers for the Dutch colonial army in the Dutch East Indies (Indonesia). The Dutch were commercial rivals on the Gold Coast with the British, who also sought good relations with Asante. Akwasi Boakye became a mining engineer and lived out the rest of his life on the Indonesian island of Java. Photograph by P. Herrmann, Buitenzorg, Dutch East Indies.

the Company's Forts and Settlements on the Gold Coast, and, it is hereby agreed, that there are no palavers now existing, and that neither party has any claim upon the other.

3rd. The King of Ashantee guarantees the security of the people of Cape Coast from the hostilities threatened by the people of Elmina.

4th. In order to avert the horrors of war, it is agreed that in any case of aggression on the part of the natives under British protection, the Kings shall complain thereof to the Governor-in-Chief to obtain redress, and that they will in no instance resort to hostilities, even against the other towns of the Fantee territory, without endeavoring as much as possible to effect an amicable arrangement, affording the Governor the opportunity of propitiating it, as far as he may with discretion.

5th. The King of Ashantee agrees to permit a British officer to reside constantly at his capital, for the purpose of instituting and preserving a regular communication with the Governor-in-Chief at Cape Coast Castle.

6th. The Kings of Ashantee and Dwabin pledge themselves to countenance, promote and encourage the trade of their subjects with Cape Coast Castle and its dependencies to the extent of their power.

7th. The Governors of the respective Forts shall at all times afford every protection in their power to the persons and property of the people of Ashantee and Dwabin who may resort to the water-side.

8th. The Governor-in-Chief reserves to himself the right of punishing any subject of Ashantee or Dwabin guilty of secondary offences, but in case of any crime of magnitude, he will send the offender to the Kings, to be dealt with according to the laws of his country.

9th. The Kings agree to commit their children to the care of the Governor-in-Chief, for education, at Cape Coast Castle, in full confidence of the good intentions of the British Government and of the benefits to be derived therefrom.

10th. The Kings promise to direct diligent inquiries to be made respecting the officers attached to the Mission of Major John Peddie and Captain Thomas Campbell and to influence and oblige the neighboring kingdoms and their tributaries, to befriend them as the subjects of the British Government.

Signed and sealed at Coomassie [Kumase], this seventh day of September, in the year of our Lord, one thousand eight hundred and seventeen.

The mark of Sai Tootoo Quamina X (L.S.)
The mark of Boitinnee Quama X (L.S.)
Thomas Edward Bowdich.
In the presence of William Hutchison, Resident.
Henry Tedlie, Assistant Surgeon [et al.]

The Oath-Taking at Nyankumasi, December 20, 1823

The whole of the native chiefs who joined . . . against the Ashantees [Asante] were not satisfied until they had evinced their sincerity by swearing allegiance in their fashion, as follows. The person about to swear took a sword in his right hand and with great animation, whilst expressing his determination, called heaven to witness that he would be faithful to the cause, continually putting the sword upwards at the Governor's head, and flourishing it round his own, so near at times that His Excellency's eyes were frequently in imminent danger. They would also swear on the bible (white man's fetish as they term it), but before any of them would consent to join in the war against the Ashantees, Sir Charles was obliged to assure them that he would never make peace with that tribe without acquainting with his intentions, and that their interest would ever be considered.

The reason which they gave for this stipulation was that . . . in 1807 . . . [the Asin fugitives] arrived at Cape Coast, expecting to find protection, but on the contrary the governor, colonel Torrane, seized Chebboo their king, an old, infirm blind man, and delivered him over to the Ashantees . . . at Annamaboe [Anomabu], where he was put to death with the most excruciating torture. Those of his people who remained at Cape Coast . . . were taken prisoner [and] lingered out a painful existence in the dungeons of the castle, many of them died, and the few that remained were brought to the hammer and sold as slaves to the best bidder. At Annamaboe, the treatment of the natives was equally dreadful. Even those who found protection in the fort were led by Colonel Torrane, on the pretense that the king of Ashantee had made a present of them to him, and many of them were actually sold and put on board of slave vessels.

She Who Blazed a Trail: Akyaawa Yikwan of Asante

Ivor Wilks

In 1821 the British settlements on the Gold Coast were placed under the responsibility of Governor Charles MacCarthy (1764–1824), who shortly thereafter pursued a policy of invading Asante. MacCarthy's armed forces, however, were resoundingly defeated by Asante troops in January 1824, and MacCarthy was beheaded in the process. Other British-Asante battles would occur—such as the battle at Katamanso, where Asante troops suffered a major defeat—until a peace treaty between the two parties was negotiated and ratified in 1831 by George Maclean (1801–47) on the British side and Akyaawa Yikwan (ca. 1770–ca. 1840), the principal negotiator, on the Asante side. In the selection below, Professor Emeritus Ivor Wilks of Northwestern University tells the extraordinary story of Akyaawa Yikwan.

To the best of our knowledge, Akyaawa was born in Akorase [between 1764 and 1777]. Her full name was Yaa Kyaa, of which Akyaawa is an affectionate diminutive. Akorase lay about six miles northeast of the Asante capital, Kumase. It was on an old road plied by many of the travelers making their way to and from Salaga and other distant markets where the produce of Asante was traded for that of Hausaland and beyond. Few of the travelers, however, would have found reason to stop in Akorase. In 1960 it comprised only 23 houses with a population of less than two hundred, and there is no reason to believe that it was ever larger. It was, however, a village of considerable importance, for it belonged to the Asantehene and the Taa Dwemo shrine was located there. . . .

Akyaawa's mother was named Ampomhemaa. She was certainly an Akorase royal. Indeed, her very name acknowledges her kinship with Kra Amponsem, both being variants on the name "Ampon." The precise relationship is not known, but it is highly likely that Ampomhemaa was a daughter of Kra Amponsem's sister, Tamra. . . .

In Asante it is women who are the knowledgeable genealogists, doubtless because it is through them that descent is reckoned. In 1965 I was able to talk with the elderly Nana Yaa Kyaa of Akorase, a great-great-granddaughter of Akyaawa. True to form, she was able to narrate the intricate ramifications of her family history. Ampomhemaa of Akorase, she related, was one of those whom Asantehene Osei Kwadwo (1764–77) chose to take into the *hiaa* or royal harem as a true wife. Two daughters were born to Ampomhemaa and Osei Kwadwo, the one Yaa Kyaa or Akyaawa, and the other Akua Afiriye. . . . Yaa Kyaa was . . . able to narrate without hesitation the names of Akyaawa's children by her unidentified husband: "Nana Yaa Kyaa [i.e., Akyaawa] married someone, and there were two daughters, Nana Abena Konadu and Nana Bago, and one son, Kyeame Kofi Nti." That Akyaawa was indeed the mother of at least Kofi Nti is verifiable from a strictly contemporary Dutch source.

Akyaawa's three children must have been born in the 1790s. The two daughters, Abena Konadu and Bago (or, more fully, Birago), attained marriageable age, therefore, in the early part of the reign of Asantehene Osei Tutu Kwame (1804–23). Again, the Asantehene himself chose not to take either as wife. The elder daughter, Abena Konadu, was married to a young royal of the Golden Stool, Kwaku Dua. He was a son of Osei Tutu Kwame's sister Amma Sewaa. As Kwaku Dua was still in his early teens in 1810, the marriage (though not necessarily the betrothal) probably did not take place until the middle years of the decade. The younger daughter, Birago, appears to have married earlier. She became the wife of Oti Panin, who succeeded his wealthy father, Boakye Yam Panin, as *okyeame* or counselor to the Asantehene in or about 1815. Their first son, Boakye Tenten, was born around the mid-1810s. Akyaawa's son, Kofi Nti, was to marry only some two decades later. . . .

[In 1820, Akyaawa] was probably in her late forties and presumably approaching, if not already past, the menopause. She had seen many of her brothers of the *Osei Kwadwo ahenemma* [i.e., sons and daughters of Osei Kwadwo] enter into public office of one sort or another. Owusu Bannahene, for example, had held a number of positions under successive Asantehenes and in 1818 had become Kumase Kyidomhene, a position of much responsibility in both civil and military spheres. Owusu Afiriye had risen to become Kumase Apagyahene, responsible for the organization of transport in times of war and for the collection of tributes in times of peace. Others of her brothers inherited high office by reason of their maternal affiliations, such as Owusu Sekyere Panin, Owusu Tia, and Owusu Ansa, who became Mamponhene, Boamanhene, and Asakore-Mamponhene, respectively. . . . In 1820, then, Akyaawa might well have derived some satisfaction from the successes of her brothers. She perhaps also felt reasonably sanguine about the future of her own children. . . . In 1820 Akyaawa could not, in her wildest flights of imagination, have foreseen what the future in fact held in store for herself. . . .

In 1825 Asantehene Osei Yaw devoted himself to preparations for a renewed offensive against those provincial rulers who had been persuaded to transfer their allegiance from the Golden Stool to the British. The campaign plan was to march first upon Accra on the southeastern Gold Coast, there to reestablish the Asantehene's authority, and then with Gã and other local reinforcements to attack Cape Coast once again. The omens, tradition has it, were not auspicious. The various gods consulted included those of Tano, and they and the Muslims in Kumase all counseled prudence. Asantehene Osei Yaw nevertheless mustered his forces and took the field. He established camp some twenty miles northeast of Accra in late July 1826, and on 7 August he engaged the British and their local levies, supported by the Danes, in battle at Katamanso. The Asante suffered a catastrophic defeat. Casualties were heavy, and the booty taken from them was computed at half a million pounds sterling in value. Among the slain were at least two of Akyaawa's brothers, Kyidomhene Owusu Bannahene and Apagyahene Owusu Afiriye, and her son-in-law Oti Panin was captured and subsequently executed. Akyaawa, too, became a prisoner.

Akyaawa was among a group of women, including Osei Yaw's wife Akua Pusuwa, his daughter Yaa Horn, and Dwabenhene's wife Kokowaa, who were seized when the Ada and other levies recruited by the Danes penetrated the Asante ranks to where the king was positioned. The Danish governor, Niels Broch, took immediate steps to procure these women from their captors and to ensconce them near his headquarters at Christiansborg. The British governor, Sir Neil Campbell, somewhat ruefully informed London that Broch and others, "Europeans as well as native headmen," were treating their prisoners very well, reckoning that if, on the one hand, peace was made with Asante, they would be able to use them to obtain preferential conditions of trade but that if, on the other hand, the Asante took the offensive again, they might equally be used to conciliate the king. Campbell's commandant on the Gold Coast, Captain H. J. Ricketts, compiled a rather garbled list of prisoners from the best information available to him. On it was "the king of Ashantee's Crabah, a female dedicated to the sooman, fetish." "Crabah" is *ɔkrawa*; this term described a class of female servants of the Asantehene having to do with his spiritual well-being. "Sooman" is *suman*, a term strictly describing a charm but often loosely applied to the shrines of such gods as the *atano*. As none of the sources assigns a religious role to any other of the female captives, we may be reasonably sure that the "Crabah" was Akyaawa, and the "sooman" Taa Dwemo. . . .

[After Akyaawa played a significant part in the peace negotiations process with the Council of Merchants' new president, G. Maclean, the] Council approved Maclean's policy, and resolved ["]that every effort should continue to be made to keep open our communication with Coomassie [Kumase], and by means of the woman Atianah [Akyaawa] to induce the king to come into our arrangements for peace[."] In the event it was not until 8 November 1830 that Maclean was able to report success. Addressing the Council, Maclean announced ["]that at length he had procured the attendance of the kings of Assin, Dinkera and the Fantee chiefs, and that after some difficulty they had acceded to the measures proposed. It was then agreed that arrangements should be made for escorting Atianvah to Ashantee and the President authorized to pay the necessary expenses[."] Akyaawa arrived in the Asante capital presumably in late November or early December, after an absence of some four and a half years.

It is unfortunate that no account of the discussions of the proposed treaty by the Asantehene and his council is on record. On 13 January 1831, however, messengers from Osei Yaw arrived in Cape Coast to announce that the terms of the treaty were acceptable, that 600 ounces of gold and two hostages would be sent to the British as a guarantee of Asante good faith, and that trade would be resumed. Maclean wrote to the Committee of Merchants in London to express his satisfaction that events had "in a great measure justified the hopes we entertained from the alleged influence of the Princess 'Atiawah' over the King of Ashantee." What Maclean could not have known at the time of writing was that the Asantehene himself was so impressed by Akyaawa's conduct of affairs that he had chosen her to be head of the next mission to the Gold Coast. It was an appointment for which no precedent is known. . . .

In Cape Coast the talks between Akyaawa and the members of her mission, on the one hand, and Maclean and the members of his council, on the other, proceeded apparently without a hitch. On 15 April Maclean felt able to assure his superiors in London "that Peace with Ashantee is no longer doubtful"; Akyaawa, he added, had entered Cape Coast "in triumph with the Gold and the Hostages." The expression "in triumph" is curiously revealing, for certainly the Asante negotiators did not see themselves as in any way supplicating for peace but, if anything, as conceding it. Indeed, on 15 April Akyaawa decided that the time was appropriate to have the Asantehene's message formally delivered to the Dutch in Elmina. Her envoy arrived there that day and met with the Dutch and Elminan authorities the next. [After having all major business concluded, Akyaawa would finally reach Kumase in early November 1831 and the treaties would be approved in the Asante capital.] . . .

Her conduct of the mission approved and all honors awarded, Akyaawa appears to have settled into retirement. Certainly her involvement in high affairs of state was at an end, as well it might be, granted that she must have been somewhere around sixty years of age. . . . We do not know how long Akyaawa lived to enjoy her retirement, but the absence of any references to her in the journals of the missionaries who visited Kumase in the late 1830s and early 1840s suggests that she did not survive the decade. Throughout the greater part of the long reign of Asantehene Kwaku Dua, however, from 1834 to 1867, relations with the British continued to be determined by reference to the treaty of 27 April 1831. Indeed, Ɛkyeame "Kwakwa," who had served as Akyaawa's lieutenant in the negotiations, became after her death the major authority on matters relating to the treaty, for not all that had been agreed between Maclean and Akyaawa was embodied in the written text. In 1844, for example, he proceeded to Cape Coast to discuss matters of jurisdiction over a prisoner convicted of a murder in Assin, and in 1863 his presence was required in Cape Coast to explain Akyaawa's understanding with Maclean in the matter of the return of runaway slaves and other refugees. . . .

With the conclusion of the treaties of 1831, Akyaawa's public career was virtually ended. It was an extraordinary invasion of a sphere that was, in Asante, all but totally male dominated. Yet the fundamental role of the Asante woman was to see to the reproduction, not only in a biological but also in a social and economic sense, of her lineage. Akyaawa's descendants commemorate her for this rather than for her brief intrusion into public affairs. It was, after all, the former rather than the latter that ensured their very existence. . . . Akyaawa Yikwan's children made all the necessary funeral customs to ensure her a place in the Asaman, that Asante Valhalla where both the ancestors and the ancestresses reside.

Plantations and Labor in the Southeast Gold Coast

Ray Kea

Scholars often overlook the fact that after Britain abolished international slave trading, they, other Europeans, and some Africans used enslaved labor in the production and transport of agricultural exports (cash crops) through plantations established on African soil. In the selection here, Ray Kea, a professor of history at the University of California at Riverside, examines the Danish efforts in establishing commercial agriculture in the Gold Coast using slave labor before the Danish withdrew from the Gold Coast in 1850. Kea notes that since this kind of agriculture was geared toward the local markets, it was not much affected by the abolition of transatlantic slaving.

Covering the period from the late 1780s to the 1840s, the present essay offers an initial interpretation of the "transition" from the export of slaves to the export of produce by considering certain aspects of the material and social organization of commercial agriculture in southeastern Ghana, specifically the inland Akuapem polity and the hinterland of the coastal Accra and Adanme towns. Until 1826 these places were political dependencies of the Asante state. . . . During the period under investigation there were two identifiable forms of commercial agricultural production in the southeast Gold Coast: food production for local urban markets (including the European coastal trading establishments and shipping); and cash crop production for overseas markets (principally European and West Indian). This production engaged various forms of social labor: slaves purchased in local markets; pawns; debtors; slaves hired out by their owners; and free wage labourers.

Denmark was the first European state to prohibit its subjects from participating in the transatlantic slave trade. In 1792 a royal edict decreed that the Danish slave trade was to be abolished in 1803. Great Britain and the Netherlands abolished the slave trade for their subjects in 1807 and 1814, respectively. To replace the slave trade and to place its West African trading stations on a firm economic basis, the Danish government made a strong commitment to the establishment of plantations in the hinterlands of these stations during the first four decades of the nineteenth century. The plantations were to produce tropical plants (indigo, coffee, sugar cane, cotton, and tobacco) for the Danish market. In 1850 the Danish government sold its Gold Coast possessions to the British government.

In the course of the first half of the nineteenth century British and Dutch authorities, too, envisioned the Gold Coast as an exporter of cash crops, and the Basel and Wesleyan Methodist mission organizations were also strongly supportive of plantation development and the export of agricultural commodities. However, it was Denmark which took the lead in promoting a commercial agricultural sector organized for export. The main Danish trading stations on the Guinea Coast included the following forts: Christiansborg, the headquarters and administrative seat, at Osu; Fredensborg at Great Ningo; Kongensten at Ada; and Prinsensten at Keta. These were the nodal points in what the Danish authorities called "Danish Guinea," a territory comprising eleven "provinces" according to an early nineteenth-century Danish report. The move from a trade in slaves to a trade to agricultural commodities signaled a shift in Danish state interests in "Danish Guinea," a shift from mercantile—the administration of trade—to the administration of export production; a shift from the operations of a chartered company which managed the external trade in slaves to the operations of royal administrative department (the General Customs Chambers) which was responsible for plantation development and management. The profits derived from the sale of agricultural commodities were to be used, in part, to maintain the Danish Guinea establishments.

For a period of more than fifty years, from the 1780s through the 1830s, the Danish government sought to establish a plantation complex in the southeast Gold Coast, either directly with state subsidies and under state management (thus, the royal or state plantations) or indirectly by supporting and encouraging Danish and Afro-Danish merchants to engage in cash crop production (thus, private plantations). One can identify three phases in the plantation project: (1) from the late 1780s until about 1811 the plantations were organized primarily for export production to Denmark; (2) from the early 1820s to the 1830s the Danish West Indies was the market for the plantations; (3) from the late 1830s to 1850 (the year Denmark gave up its West African possessions) plantation production was geared solely to local urban and rural markets. Employing a dependent labor force of men, women, and children, both non-waged and waged labourers, the Danish plantation project was a labor-intensive, capitalist agrarian enterprise.

If the Danish and Afro-Danish planters represented one "direction" or "component" in the agricultural history of the southeast Gold Coast, the Accra, Adanme (namely Krobo and Shai), and Akuapem landed proprietors (pl. *awuranom* in Akuapem-Twi; sing. *nyontsho* or *owulali* in Ga) represented another. The term "plantation" (*Plantage* in Danish; *Pflanzung* in German) was used by Europeans to refer to the farms, "planted fields," or "cultivated places" (*Rosahr-pladser/Rosarre Plads* in Danish) in the rural hinterlands. The proprietors pursued three different production (and wealth accumulation) strategies: (1) producing subsistence for their own labourers and urban households; (2) producing provisions and supplies for local urban markets; and (3) producing cash crops for overseas markets. Various kinds of dependent labor, including dispossessed sectors of the social order, were employed. The proprietors included merchants and/or brokers, officeholders, and "gentry" (i.e., "those of the middle class who . . . own a certain amount of estate, money, [and slaves], and through their affluence are themselves above the rank of slaves"), many of whom had been directly involved in the selling of slaves to the Danish and other European factors. The agricultural strategies of these dominant strata were oriented around their conditions of consumption and their "regimes" of wealth accumulation.

From the 1790s to the mid-1810s the plantations of the Accra proprietors followed, in the main, strategies (1) and (2); from the mid-1810s through the 1830s the third production strategy assumed considerable importance; in the 1840s and thereafter there was an almost exclusive reliance on the first two production strategies. From the 1790s until the 1830s the plantations of Akuapem and Adanme (i.e., Shai and Krobo) proprietors followed the first and second production strategies almost exclusively; from the 1830s export production for European markets assumed overwhelming importance. For the period under study agricultural practices in the area can be characterized as heterogeneous and multileveled, and thus not reducible to a single, linear development.

Export-oriented agriculture and legitimate trade demonstrated a particular set of patterns and variations of economic, social, and cultural activity, changing power relations, and new authority structures; they generated, too, new contradictions, conflicts, and struggles. The establishment of new organizational forms in the political and commercial centers during the course of the first half of the nineteenth century was no chance event. New technologies of power and new disciplinary apparatuses with their specific organizing and socializing practices framed the development of legitimate trade. Schools, churches, prisons, hospitals, and police-militia barracks were set up in various towns, where they functioned as "organs" of control and surveillance; schooling, medicalization, missionary evangelizing, and judicial incarceration emerged as normative procedures in the new social and moral economy. Like the plantation projects, such phenomena can be interpreted as the effects and the conditions of the complex repositioning of the Gold Coast's political economy within the world economy's elaborate system of functional relations and division of labor. . . .

Private Danish and Afro-Danish traders resident in Osu, Labade, and other coastal towns assumed the mercantile role formerly enjoyed by salaried agents of the Danish chartered companies of earlier years. From about 1794 onwards they set up warehouses and "shops" and/or factories in different towns. Salaried state administrators at Christiansborg and other forts provided the traders with legal and military protection as well as, on occasion, credit and warehousing facilities.

The Danish government, however, wished to expand the economic role of private traders living in the vicinity of the Danish forts and factories and, at the same time, to encourage Accra, Adanme, and Akuapem notables to actively support export agricultural production. . . . Setting up plantations presupposes access to land and labor. In the first decade of the nineteenth century the Danish priest H. C. Monrad (who was on the Gold Coast from 1805 to 1809) remarked that nothing was easier than to purchase a sizable stretch of land in the hinterlands of the Accra towns and in the foothills of the Akuapem mountains. He indicates that a person with the means could purchase a substantial quantity of land for several ankers of spirits. Presumably, he meant the usufruct could be bought and absolute ownership of the land itself. A Danish report of 1803 suggests that this was, in fact, the case, for, it relates, "The Blacks will not sell the land, but will allow the Danes to live on it, lay out plantations, and build fortifications against the payment of gratuities and regular stipend." In other words, continued use of the land necessitated the regular payment of "rent."

In the first decade of the century there were evidently many residents in the Accra towns who were acquiring farming rights and, perhaps in some instances, land as well. . . . Monrad noted that Danes and "many Mulattoes and Blacks" had begun to lay out plantations, or "cultivation-places," beginning about two miles from the littoral and extending up to the Akuapem foothills. The plantations were, generally, worked by servile labourers. The Danes were primarily engaged in export production; the others, for the most part, in market-oriented food production. Interestingly, Monrad wrote that an Accra man who owned a "palm-forest," in whose shadow cottages are raised for his laborers, is esteemed "a rich man." Evidently, large-scale farming efforts carried social prestige. One supposes that wealthy traders and brokers in various Accra towns were purchasing land or the rights to it in the Akuapem foothills for the purpose of producing palm oil and other palm products, not, at this time, for export but for local consumption. . . . Danish state funds and Danish merchant capital were responsible for the development of an export-oriented agricultural sector, just as Accra merchant capital was responsible for the parallel extension of commercial food production. . . .

Writing in 1831, the Danish official B. Christensen stated that there were only about twelve plantations which formed the basis of the Danish state's plantation endeavor. Two belonged to Danes, the rest to Afro-Danes. In addition to yams, maize, millet, plantains, "baco," palm(-oil) trees and other crops, the plantation owners had begun to cultivate coffee. Christensen commented that in 1828 there was hardly a total of 4,000 coffee trees on all of the plantations combined. By 1831 there were as many as 20,000 young trees, and the expectation was that shortly they would produce enough coffee for export. There were also plans to raise sugarcane, indigo, cotton, and rice. He goes on to say that in the vicinity of the Danish/Afro-Danish agricultural establishments there were "many, in some cases considerable, plantations belonging to several of the more high standing free mulattoe families in Danish Akkra [Accra], however, just as in the single, neighboring Blacks' plantation, they only cultivate the common cereals of the land." Some plantations cultivated food crops for local markets and shipping and cash crops for export; other plantations produced for local markets. According to the Danish historian O. Justesen, Danish and Afro-Danish merchants were "disinclined to put their own money into the production of [export cash crops]." It was more profitable for them to "invest their capital in trading in other locally-produced commodities [such as gold and palm-oil] and in the production of the established provisions which could be sold locally. . . ."

Bulk export trade was labor-intensive, and as this trade began to take off in the 1830s there was a rapidly growing demand for slave labor in areas of expanding agricultural production, whether for local or overseas markets. Christensen stated that without slaves plantation agriculture in the Akuapem foothills was virtually impossible, and in 1848 a Danish official stated that all work in the houses and in the fields was carried out by slaves.

According to Monrad, the greatest number of slaves sold on the coast, for example at Osu, came from Asante, Fante, Agotime ("Acotim"), Krepe ("Crepee"), and Donko ("Duncan" [i.e., peoples from northern Ghana]). The three Accra towns (Kinka, Ga, and Osu) formed together a major trade center for slaves throughout the first half of the century. In 1819 it was said of this centre that "from its extensive trade with the interior [it] is of considerable commercial importance"; in the 1830s and [18]40s it was a leading slave market for the internal slave trade.

Christensen offers one account of how a merchant or official becomes a plantation owner:

> One buys from some Black, who because of a "palaver" or gambling has fallen into debt, which regrettably happens all too often, a piece of land, whose price up till now . . . has been 50–60 *pjastre* for 20–25 *toender* [27–35 acres] of land, and whose quality is excellent, for without manure and only a short fallow it can be harvested twice a year and, yet, yield maize 7–900 fold. Now one acquires a couple of slaves or more . . . and sends them into the interior, and there in a twinkling they build for themselves, without a whit of expense to the owner, their cottages of clay, battened in wood and thatched with grass.

The owner provides his slave with a wife as well as tools, household goods, a flintlock musket, etc. Christensen continues: "The slave works a lot and certainly mostly for himself; indeed, he works at the most only four days a week for his owner, and, besides that, he shall pay a predetermined rent [*Afgifter*] in kind." With respect to the Bikube plantation he relates that its thirty unfree workers had to smoke-dry the plantation's coffee beans and hand over to the owner a "rent" of yam, maize, and other produce. In the early 1830s an adult male slave bought at Accra cost 150 *rigsdaler* and his annual subsistence amounted to 30 *rigsdaler*. . . .

In the late eighteenth and early nineteenth century only a very few persons were brought from the Caribbean to manage the plantations. This idea was again put forward in 1828, but was deemed unsuitable. Instead, there were proposals that youths from Osu be sent to Denmark to be trained as millers or artisans, or to the West Indies to be instructed in plantation cultivation. In 1828 another submission advised that four sons of the richest Osu families be sent to St. Croix, where they could learn plantation management, after which they could return to the Gold Coast to manage the Danish plantations. Of these proposals the only one implemented was to send youths to Denmark. Still another plan was presented in 1829: "One should let the school children from the mulatto school cultivate the land on the Frederiksborg [cotton] plantation: the boys plant and the girls clean and spin; this is to be done in order to make this useful plant better known." However, this project was never seriously carried out.

Petition of the Principal Mulatto Females of the Gold Coast

Multiple Signatories

The following petition involves claims made by wealthy and self-described "mulatto females" (that is, the offspring of European merchants or missionaries and African women) for their enslaved workers. When Commissioner Dr. Robert R. Madden (1798–1886), an antislavery advocate, was sent to the Gold Coast, much of the coastal region was under nominal British control or protectorate status. But the Gold Coast was also a region where "British subjects" (a vague group and a status that local elites rejected) were in possession of enslaved individuals in what was viewed as British territory. In fact, the women in the petition attempt to make the case that "slavery" in other British territories was "still recognized by the British Government."

Petition of the Principal Mulatto Females of the Gold Coast to the Right Honorable Lord John Russell, Cape Coast Castle, March 29, 1841

The humble Petition of the undersigned natives of the Gold Coast residing under the protection of the British settlements, showeth,

That your petitioners, natives of Africa, are the proprietors of a number of slaves, agreeably to the laws and customs of this country, established from time immemorial, and which they learn are in many respects similar to those in the East Indies where slavery to a certain extent is still recognized by the British Government, and the same having been invariably acknowledged, countenanced and protected by all the European governments established upon the Gold Coast, British, Dutch and Danes.

Your petitioners have been surprised to find, by a proclamation issued by His Excellency Sir John Jeremie . . . dated the 4th March, 1841 and made known and promulgated here by the government of this settlement and by Her Majesty's Commissioner, Dr. Madden, on the March [23], 1841, that they were without the least warning to be deprived of their rights and property,

Hand-colored illustration of "A Mulatto Woman of the Gold Coast," ca. 1820, from *A Voyage to Africa*, by William Hutton (London: Longman, Hurst, Rees, Orme, and Brown, 1821), facing p. 93.

and in one moment to lose the services of the whole of their slaves: but having been given to understand that the British Government, desirous of granting to all slaves their freedom, wherever they have influence, power or authority, have, in equity and justice to the proprietors, in all cases hitherto, awarded compensation for the slaves so liberated:

Your petitioners therefore humbly pray that in submitting to the will and wishes of the British Government, their cases may meet with like consideration, and that compensation be awarded them as in every other instance.

And your petitioners will ever pray.

Grievances of the Gold Coast Chiefs

Richard Pine

On the Gold Coast, the majority of the so-called chiefs (i.e., rulers of coastal polities) presented their grievances about domestic enslavement, like the "principal mulatto females" before them. In early 1864, these grievances reached Governor Richard Pine as a protest against what they saw as encroachments on their rights to hold captive individuals. On the one hand, these local political leaders had no real desire to stand in opposition to British antislavery efforts and thus risk losing British protection, but on the other hand, there were local tensions between colonial officials and their implementation policy, the interests of slaveholders, and the emancipatory strategies of captive individuals themselves. It is therefore not surprising to find in the grievances below an argument for the continuance of domestic slaveholding.

Grievances of the Gold Coast Chiefs, August 9, 1864

First. That they are as it were deprived of the power of holding domestic slavery, which has greatly reduced their power and dignity as kings and chiefs, their influence destroyed and then rendered them helpless. They agree to follow agricultural pursuit if they will be permitted to hold domestic slavery for reasons assigned by them. . . .

Second. That they are for very trifling cause now and then cast into prison by the officials, which insures to them great disgrace, and places them upon the same par with their subjects.

Third. That it had been the custom of the former officials to create a court consisting of native kings and chiefs, to sit and adjudicate cases in which kings and chiefs are involved. But this is not the case now. Therefore they want his Excellency to remedy that. They observed also that the country in sixty or seventy years past was in a thriving position when domestic slavery was prevalent, but now since the great alteration that has taken place with reference to the slave holding, the country is totally deprived of its wealth.

That the kings and chiefs are not to convert themselves to shepherds, farmers and such like. They further remarked that if they had been allowed to hold domestic slavery, they would have given the Government for the transport corps, at least each fifty men, without any expense to the Government but that of subsistence alone. They lastly, in an urgent manner, begged of the Governor not to tender the method of peacemaking to the enemies until they (the enemies) asked for it, because it will add more shame to the British flag.

Proclamation of George Cumine Strahan

George Cumine Strahan

The 1874 proclamation of Governor George Strahan (1838–87) legally abolished domestic forms of captivity on the Gold Coast, but this imposed legislation on slaveholding segments of the local population met with some resistance, and rather than resolving the issues involved, it facilitated huge struggles over what would come of this law. Because the 1874 law abolished domestic slavery and offered emancipation only within the Gold Coast colony and protectorate as well as Christian missionary stations in the interior, slaveholding remained legal until 1908. The postproclamation era, however, was not simply a continuance of slave- and pawn-holding, but also the desertion of such individuals, the use of self-redemption and kin-based redemption, and other African initiatives, including those of the enslaved, in the emancipatory process. The imposition of the 1874 law, which appears here, meant that local slaveholders would not be compensated—as in the case of abolition in the British Caribbean—which led them to protest in various ways.

Proclamation

By his Excellency George Cumine Strahan, Captain Royal Artillery, Governor and Commander-in-Chief of the Gold Coast Colony

Whereas the Queen's Most Excellent Majesty has resolved to abolish slave-dealing in Her Protectorate of the Gold Coast and the importation thereinto of slaves and persons intended to be dealt with as slaves, and also to provide for the emancipation of persons holden as slaves within the said Protectorate:

And whereas the Governor and Legislative Council of the Gold Coast Colony have by Her Majesty's command, enacted an Ordinance bearing date 17th December 1874, by which all selling, buying, or dealing in slaves is declared unlawful, and is absolutely and forever abolished, prohibited and made penal, and another Ordinance also bearing date 17th December 1874, providing for the emancipation of persons holden in slavery.

Now I do hereby proclaim, publish and make known the said Ordinances to all persons whom it may concern.

And further, in order and to the intent that all the Kings, Chiefs, Headmen and other persons throughout the aforesaid Protectorate and elsewhere may the more readily understand and obey the laws now made and enacted, I hereby require every person to take notice and observe that now and from henceforth:

It is unlawful to sell or purchase or transfer or take any person as a slave.

It is unlawful to sell or purchase or transfer or take any person so as to make such a person a slave.

It is unlawful to put or take any person in pawn for or on account of any debt.

It is unlawful to bring any person, whether slave or free, into the Protected Territory from Ashantee [Asante] or elsewhere in order that such person should be sold or dealt with as a slave or pawn.

It is unlawful to take or send any person out of the Protected Territories in order that such person should be sold or dealt with as a slave or pawn.

It is unlawful to make any contract or agreement for buying, selling, or pawning any person, or for bringing any person into or out of the protected Territories to be sold or dealt with as a slave or pawn.

It is unlawful that any King, Chief, Headman, or other person should, in any palaver, or by any means whatsoever, force or constrain any person for the purpose of compelling him to remain at any place or serve any master contrary to the will of such person.

Whosoever offends against these laws shall be punished with imprisonment and hard labor and may also be fined.

If in any contracts hereafter made, it should be agreed that any person shall be put in pawn, or bought or sold or transferred, the whole contract shall be null and void.

And further, let all persons whom it may concern, take notice that all children whom after the 5th day of November 1874, have been or shall be born in the Protectorate, have been declared free. But it is not intended by any of the aforesaid laws, or otherwise, to offer inducement to any persons to leave any master in whose service they may be desirous of remaining, or to forsake the krooms [i.e., towns] where they have been accustomed to inhabit, and that it is intended to permit the family and tribal relations to continue in all respects according as used and wont, except only that of slavery and such customs as arise therefrom and are thereon necessarily dependent.

Given at Government House, Cape Coast Castle, this 17th day of December in the year of Our Lord, 1874, and of Her Majesty's Reign the 38th.

Gold-Mining and Colonial Capitalism in the Gold Coast

Raymond E. Dumett

The enduring importance of gold in the economies of Gold Coast societies remained central before, during, and after transatlantic slaving and its nineteenth-century domestic forms in the region. The modern rush for gold on the Gold Coast—specifically, the 1875 gold-mining boom in southwestern Gold Coast / Ghana—occurred in the late nineteenth century among African women, rulers of polities, "chiefs," farmers, and miners, as well as colonial engineers and speculators. Against this dynamic of indigenous and expatriate mining industries, historian Raymond Dumett, professor emeritus of history at Purdue University, argues that families rather than enslaved workers formed the primary unit that engaged in indigenous gold mining in the southwestern region of Wassa, and although some captive peoples worked in the mines, most of the gold was mined by families and free individuals. The following excerpts from Dumett's larger study focus on the roles of African women and men (of elite status) in the gold rush of 1877–85.

The Roles of Women

For centuries female winners of gold aroused the curiosity and respect of foreign travelers to the Akan region. I have noted that women virtually monopolized panning operations at seashore washing sites; and, aided by young boys, they also dominated placer mining in small holes alongside or near the riverbanks known as "women's washings." But these brief descriptions scarcely do justice to their overall contributions. A close study of the available literary evidence combined with field data indicates that, if anything, we have greatly underestimated both the numbers of women and female adolescents involved, and the functional tasks they performed, in gold production. One extremely important yet neglected point is that women served as the major transport carriers for the gold trade, lugging sacks of earth or huge chunks of unmilled ore from the mines to the crushing and separation sites. This tradition of women serving as porters was not overlooked when the first European mechanized companies tried to recruit transport labor in Wassa and Asante. . . .

Women also participated with men in prospecting—both as a regular occupation and indirectly in the course of other tasks. This was particularly true in the discovery of new river panning sites; but they might also direct their husbands to promising outcrops or topographic features that suggested the existence of rich underlying reef gold. Of course, the whole question of Akan gold discovery methods is one that deserves far greater attention. Over the centuries the reputation of the people of the Gold Coast and its hinterlands as "born gold finders" grew in the literature. Whether this was traceable, as some supposed, to special psychic powers of certain individuals in detecting gold through the presence of a mysterious "mist" above auriferous ground, or, more scientifically, to perceptions about the chemical content of soils passed down through the generations, British geologists who toured Wassa and Asante in the early twentieth century did not doubt that many rural Akan people possessed an extraordinary talent for discerning the presence of underlying gold from innocuous signs in the surface topography. One method was to locate the presence of gold in the yellow or pink siliceous streaks in the weathered outcrops of oxidized ores. Much more ingenious was "loaming"—Akan miners' ability to locate the presence of deeper underlying gold from ordinary samples of surface soils.

Finally, I must repeat that the presumably rigid division of labor between men (digging) and women (washing and pulverizing) stressed in most early written accounts of Akan gold mining did not always hold. As we shall see in the next chapter, we have examples of open cast mines—literally "gold fields"—where very large numbers of women, men, and children labored side by side to carve out long trenches, which could sometimes reach a quarter mile in length. In such instances eyewitnesses reported that females outnumbered the males two to one.

In terms of the numbers who participated at all stages of the extractive process, then, it is possible to argue that in a given year more women than men participated in mining operations. Let us take hard-rock gold extraction first. When we consider the fact that both a part of the pulverization (at least one day's work per cubic foot of quartz), practically all washing and separation (another day or sometimes two) of reef gold, plus carrying sacks of ore, tended to be women's work, it is not unreasonable to suggest that female labor accounted for at least one-half of all the labor inputs in Akan reef gold mining—considered to be mainly men's work. In addition, their traditional supporting roles in collecting firewood (for both the men's fire setting and for cooking) plus gathering food and water and preparing meals for their husbands and work crews during the mining season would have to be factored into any calculation. And yet this estimate does not even include traditional alluvial mining for river and seacoast gold, which was, as we have seen, almost entirely the work of females. Of course, we can never know the proportions of exported African trade gold derived from hard-rock versus alluvial sources. All factors considered, it does not seem an exaggeration to guess that women contributed anywhere from two-thirds to three-fourths of all labor inputs connected with traditional gold mining in the Akan region.

Another issue on which we need much more historical data concerns the degree of women's independence from, or subordination to, male supervision on mining projects in the nineteenth-century context. One interpretation is that their leeway was considerable, demonstrated in the fact that a wife or mother could take her children and female servants to pan for river gold whenever and wherever she chose. The question of the distribution of earnings also reenters our discussion here. Informants from Ghana say that given the patriarchal structure of the Akan household, it was highly unlikely that women of one hundred or more years ago, particularly rural women, would have retained any of their earnings in a personal savings box in the manner of market women today. Rather, the earnings from deep-level gold mining and pulverization by the nuclear family probably would have been kept by the head of the family under one account. . . .

[The Wassa "Gold Rush" of 1877–1885]

From the 1860s through the mid-1880s the most vociferous spokesman for capitalistic gold mining as the key to general economic development in the Gold Coast was Ferdinand Fitzgerald, editor of the London-based *African Times*. A Liberian by nationality, Fitzgerald (ca. 1807–84) had launched his career in the West African palm oil trade in the 1830s and, as a result of numerous contacts built up in produce brokerage, had moved to Great Britain, where he earned a living as the London agent for a variety of commercial and political organizations, including British export-import houses, African traders, the Kingdom of Bonny (east of the River Niger), and numerous other groups. Fitzgerald began his newspaper in 1861 as a vehicle for the African Aid Society, an association devoted to promoting representative government and economic self-sufficiency for African peoples everywhere; and this body subsequently became the mouthpiece for the Fante Confederation in the United Kingdom. Almost from its inception the *African Times* took up the call for industrialized gold mining in the Gold Coast as one of the cardinal themes in its editorials. Thus in 1863 we find Fitzgerald exhorting his fellow West Africans to emulate the example of the Americans in the Great West by discovering undreamed-of El Dorados of mineral wealth. "Whenever the day for extracting their precious stores may arrive, we feel convinced that they will prove to be among the greatest gold deposits of our globe." What made Fitzgerald's appeal doubly provocative was his belief that mineral development was inseparable from African economic "self-help" and the drive to modernization and political independence. For if ["]the natives did not take the mining industry in their own hands, armies of English, French and American miners will rush in and dispossess, if not exterminate the populations that have been left from the ravages of the slave-traders and the constant butcheries of a relentless and most bloody superstition[."]

During the 1860s and first half of the 1870s, Fitzgerald had written on a wide range of political, social, and administrative issues, such as the suppression of slavery in West Africa, new educational opportunities for indigenous peoples, increased expenditure on public health, and most important, a greater say for Africans in the colonial government. But in 1879, as the concessions boom gathered force, he focused increasingly on West African economic issues—the call for imperial government-assisted transportation projects (roads and harbors), the promotion of an indigenous Black capitalism and, especially, the development of the gold-mining industry. Indeed, the determined and articulate Liberian did more than perhaps any other person to popularize the notion that there was indeed a West African Gold Rush. As time wore on, Fitzgerald became less blatantly anticolonialist. Though he never forsook his call for African nationalism and self-government, his earlier idealism merged with the understandable practical search for business deals and earning a living; and he himself became an investor, director, and promoter of six to eight different London-centered mining and concessions companies. Again, these separate goals were not necessarily incompatible. Fitzgerald and his colleagues saw no contradictions between their long-term hopes for African self-determination, the concomitant need for powerful doses of both private and public investment as a base for general economic development, and the natural desire to earn a personal profit from within the capitalist system.

James Africanus Horton

Probably the most famous African involved in the gold rush of the later 1870s and 1880s was Dr. James Africanus Beales Horton. A Nigerian Saro (descendant of freed slaves), raised and educated by missionaries in Sierra

Leone, Horton had attended what became Fourah Bay College, Freetown, and later studied medicine at Kings College, London, and the University of Edinburgh before taking up practice as assistant surgeon in the Army Medical Service of the Gold Coast. As a medical practitioner of great intellectual breadth, he had conducted research on the disease of guinea worm and had written four books on various aspects of tropical medicine. But in the latter part of his career he turned away from medicine toward educating both his fellow West Africans and the colonial authorities about the necessary strategies for West African political liberation, economic development, and social change. His name, like that of a number of other Africans in this story, was closely linked with the Fante Confederation. While his mining projects are the focus of attention here, one should not forget that Horton's career spanned an impressively broad spectrum of service to public health and medicine, political activism, and scientific and professional activities quite apart from his forays into private business.

Some may ponder why a man of Horton's stature became deeply involved in so many mineral development schemes of a risky and dubious nature. There is no doubt that Fitzgerald, Horton, and their colleagues engaged in some promotional practices and deals for the sublease of mining lands from chiefs to gullible foreign buyers that cut a fine line between acceptable "sharp dealing" and outright misrepresentation. At the same time, exaggerated stories and rumors played into the hands of biased British journalists and colonial officials, who frequently criticized the actions of educated coastal Africans by the most hypocritical double standards. On the one hand Horton and Fitzgerald had talked of—and continued to truly believe in—the highest civic ideals and national political and economic goals. On the other, these two leaders, and many of their colleagues from the business and professional elite of the coast, desperately needed money—especially after they had expended so much of their time and personal fortunes in the failed Fante Confederation over the preceding years. Besides, this group had observed and borne the brunt of sharp practices by European "old coasters" and wholesale suppliers of manufactured goods for decades. Why should they have felt any compunction about trying to attract as much European capital as possible, whether from London, Paris, or Liverpool? All gold mining was uncertain, dangerous, and to a great degree speculative. Who expected any guarantees? As emphasized throughout this study, respectable bourgeois nearly everywhere (Europe, North America, South Africa), viewed mining speculation as a special kind of game—with no holds barred—almost totally divorced from the canons of ordinary business enterprise. Horton's diverse interests included not only West African medicine and the Fante Confederation, but ventures in Sierra Leone such as the first African-owned commercial bank—an enterprise he hoped would provide low-interest loans for hard-pressed indigenous businessmen in the Gold Coast, Lagos, and Sierra Leone.

During 1880 and 1881, amid rapidly spreading news about the gold rush, Horton urged his deputy, Swanzy Essien, another prominent coastal African entrepreneur and a former employee of the F. and A. Swanzy Trading Firm, to buy up as many concessions as possible from Wassa rulers, such as Kwamena Enemil and Chief Ango of Apinto. Horton then resold these leases to the directors of London-based companies, who paid him partly in cash and partly in paid-up shares. All told, between May 1878 and June 1882 the government noted that 109 different mining concessions for the western districts (Wassa, Nzema, Ahanta, etc.) were registered at Cape Coast. And of these the largest number, about thirty-one, were owned by Horton. Not all were underground blanket mining tracts; many were river washing sites of the sort purchased by Bonnat and others. By the mid-1880s Horton had overextended himself and was deeply in debt. Nevertheless, a number of Horton's concessions *were* turned to productive account after he sold them to London-based operating companies.

Joseph Dawson

Horton's leading associate and main up-country agent at the mines was Joseph Dawson, another well-known alumnus of local Wesleyan missionary schools and representative of the African middle class of Cape Coast. Along with Horton, John Sarbah, F. C. Grant, Jacob W. Sey, and George Blankson, Dawson too had played an active role in framing the constitution of the Fante Confederation and had served as a roving ambassador between its leaders and the rulers of interior states like Wassa Fiase and Asante. After appointment as official emissary to Kumasi by the Gold Coast government before the 1873–74 war, Dawson was taken prisoner by the Asantehene, along with Bonnat and the missionaries F. A. Ramseyer and J. Kuhn. According to more than one account it was Dawson, rather than the Asantehene or his advisers, who first drew Bonnat's attention to the wealth of the Tarkwa district. After the war, through prior contacts and familiarity with Akan customs and society, he played a central major role in negotiating mineral leases from the chiefs and subchiefs of Wassa. Dawson wore several different hats and he moved freely between the European, Eurafrican, and traditional African communities. It was not long before officials at Accra became apprehensive about what they termed his extraordinary political and personal influence with Chief Ango of Apinto. British traveling commissioners who toured Tarkwa spoke of him disparagingly (and probably excessively) as a gray eminence, a so-called bush magistrate, whose political and judicial advisory power "rivaled that of the king himself." Future critics of the gold rush would trace this as one more example of the causal connections between an advancing capitalism, excessive Westernization, and the deterioration of traditional African political structures.

Grant, Sarbah, Amissah, and Brew

This did not exhaust the record of African middle-class participation in the first gold rush. It also included the formation of the first fully African-owned mining syndicate. In the spring of 1882 four members of the Cape Coast business community—F. C. Grant, a leading exporter, shipowner, and member of the Gold Coast Legislative Council (who was elected chairman); James Amissah, his brother-in-law, also a trader (elected vice-chairman); James Hutton Brew, lawyer and editor of the *Gold Coast Times* (elected secretary); and John Sarbah, prosperous merchant (elected managing director), formed the Gold Coast Native Concessions Purchasing Company. This was the first of at least three examples . . . of mineral lands and mining companies with headquarters in the Gold Coast, boasting wholly African managing directorates. Though it was primarily a real estate venture, established to purchase and sell mining lands in Wassa, the directors intended eventually to undertake mining operations. The company started with a nominal capital of £25,000 in twenty-one shares, with the promoters taking up 10,000 shares and advertising the remainder to the general public. The company stands as an interesting might-have-been of Gold Coast mining history. Sarbah, Amissah, and Sey hoped that it might serve as a forerunner for "developing industrial tendencies among our peoples." Its failure underscores the formidable obstacles that any African-owned company had to face in the harshly competitive world of late nineteenth-century Atlantic capitalism. In the 1970s two of the latter-day heirs of this enterprising group of Cape Coast African entrepreneurs, S. Sey and W. S. Kwesi Johnson, explained to me the limited entrepreneurial success of their forefathers in terms of lack of access to European capital markets, lack of local banking facilities, and lack of experience in the tough-minded ways of the European corporate world. The downturn in the fortunes of the G. C. Native Concessions Purchasing Company was traced at the time to the inability of the promoters to secure the service of a professional mining engineer (which they knew was essential), and to the unwillingness of the colonial government to acquiesce to their application for local incorporation under the English Companies Acts of the 1850s and 1860s—which were in fact applicable to the Gold Coast.

Swanzy Essien and the Essaman Gold Mining Company of Heman-Prestea

The hypersuspicious Colonial Office view that practically all the African-owned and most of the European concessions syndicates of the 1880s were purely speculative real estate ventures, devoid of serious productive intent, was far from accurate. It was common practice for most of the concessionaire directors to maintain their hold over at least one bona fide producing mine, while floating simultaneously a host of less secure speculative ventures. One of Horton's best-known companies, the Wassa and Ahanta Syndicate, formed in 1882 with a capital of £10,000, controlled some of the most valuable riverbank and hinterland concessions of the Heman-Prestea region, twenty-three miles northwest of Tarkwa. Another member of the embryonic African "middle class" who played a more than passive role in the development of operational mining as well as promotion was Horton's close associate Swanzy Essien. He knew the western region well, having served as a trader for the Swanzy interest at Sekondi, Axim, Beyin, and at Assini on the French Ivory Coast. More important, Essien, who had negotiated the original lease with Chief Kofi Kyei for the valuable two-thousand-square-yard block of territory at Heman-Prestea, was the first man to transport machinery to this subdistrict with the serious purpose of developing its rich lode in 1885.

Essien was practical and energetic. Thus, contrary to official opinion, not all the early indigenous mining entrepreneurs were mere real estate promoters. Essien single-handedly tried to bridge the gap from land acquisition and prospecting to mechanized plant installation and ore production. Working from old African diggings at the Essaman or "Arsarman" mine, he drove 180 feet straight into the side of the hill, along what came to be known as Essien's Adit, until he had reached the paying lode. Unfortunately, rapid depletion of its small working capital forced the Wassa and Ahanta Syndicate to liquidate without retrieving much gold. Access to European capital markets remained the bugbear for pioneering African and Eurafrican mining capitalists. As a last resort the firm sold its various properties to an offshoot, the new Essaman Mining Company, in which Essien, Horton, and Fitzgerald retained an interest.

The Essaman Company was capitalized in 1885 at £50,000, of which about £15,000 was paid up by the end of the first year. . . . Its properties were valuable enough: in addition to its main leases at Prestea, it also gained control of the nearby Brumasi mines, later developed into a major producing lode by a separate company. Ultimately the mines of the Heman-Prestea and Brumasi zone, which stood northwest of Tarkwa, proved to be among the most valuable in Ghana. . . . But, in a pattern characteristic of the first wave of active companies, the Essaman enterprise was plagued by a lack of capital, transportation problems, underground flooding, and the constant breakdown of machines, which were hard to fix owing to lack of skilled mechanics and spare parts. A small number of primitive "elephant"-type stamping machines were carried in, none of which functioned properly when emplaced. . . .

The Sam Family of Cape Coast and Tarkwa

Of all the African mining pathbreakers of the Gold Coast, the most redoubtable were the members of the Sam family—William Edward Sam and his two sons, Thomas Birch Freeman Sam and William Edward Sam Junior. The Sams were the descendants of an eastern Akan family who traced their roots back to one of the chiefdoms of Akyem. Educated at Christian mission schools, they were by midcentury recognized leaders among the middle class of Cape Coast and points west. This trio of father and two sons reflected many of the dynamic traits and attitudes noted elsewhere as part of the tradition of indigenous entrepreneurship in the Gold Coast. Inspired by the teachings of the distinguished Eurafrican pastor Thomas Birch Freeman in the 1840s, the elder Sam began his adult life as a teacher in the local Methodist schools, but later shifted to trade and commerce. . . . During the 1860s William Sam worked as an agent for a number of European and African merchants on the coast, including J. A. B. Horton and the Swanzy firm, where he gained a solid reputation not only as a businessman but as a skilled negotiator and arbiter. So considerable were the elder Sam's linguistic and diplomatic skills that the colonial government employed him off and on in settling disputes between the Dutch, English, and African rulers on the coast. Partly because of Britain's traditional support for the Fante (central coastal) states against the expansionistic power of Asante, the Sams (father and sons), like most of their friends in the coastal African community, tended to identify with the aims and policies of the colonial occupying power.

Between the Sea and the Lagoon: The Anlo-Ewe of Southeastern Ghana

Emmanuel Akyeampong

The Anlo-Ewe of southeastern Ghana went from a nonmaritime people and became, to many, the quintessential mariners of the Gold Coast / Ghana. In the selection below, historian Emmanuel Akyeampong, professor of history and African and African American studies at Harvard University, explores the migrations of the Anlo-Ewe, their settlement, and their struggles to effectively master a new environment by developing skills and technologies suited for life by the Keta Lagoon and the Atlantic Ocean. Inevitably, their role as mariners brought them into commercial relations with Europeans engaged in transatlantic slaving. Though the Anlo-Ewe still have a strong attachment to land and the sea, persistent coastal erosion and increased marginalization in colonial and postcolonial Ghana have ruptured the balance between nature and tradition.

The Ewe ancestors who founded the settlements that fringed the Keta Lagoon basin in what is now Anlo in southeastern Ghana migrated from Notsie in central Togoland around the mid-seventeenth century. Political dissension and, most probably, land pressure were key motives in this migration. The Ewe migrants moved into the aquatic and marine environment east of the Volta River's estuary. This was a landscape littered with bodies of water. The river Volta served as the western boundary; the Atlantic Ocean bordered the south; and the large inland Angaw, Avu, and Keta Lagoons, fed by the Volta and Todzie Rivers through a system of channels and smaller lagoons, dominated the Anlo interior. The hydrology of the area was dynamic, and the sea, rivers, and lagoons were interconnected through a complex network. Although Notsie was located between the Haho and Shio Rivers, nothing in the experience of the Ewe migrants seemed to have prepared them adequately for the aquatic ecosystem in southeastern Ghana. Nevertheless, J. M. Grove has commented on how the Ewe migrants "adapted themselves to their new, and apparently rather unfavorable environment with remarkable skill and completeness. . . ." Anlo oral traditions on migration provide a charter for kingship and the alternating succession between Adzovia and Bate clans. These traditions also shed light on the religious nature of kingship and the importance of the *awọamefia* (the Anlo paramount chief) as priest-king in the domestication of nature. From an initial foraging of nature in an unfamiliar environment, Anlo's economy and society developed a more systematized structure based on agriculture, fishing, salt making, and trade. . . .

Though several versions of the Anlo-Ewe migration tradition exist, they seem to agree in substance on the centrality of Ketu, Tado, and Notsie as important points in migration and on the political insecurity caused by wars and oppressive overrule as the major factor in this constant movement. However, there are still problems of interpretation in assessing the exact nature of the Anlo-Ewe links to Tado and Ketu—in particular, the scale of migration into southeastern Ghana and the dating of this last movement. The Anlo-Ewe oral traditions cite Ketu, an ancient Yoruba town now in the Republic of Benin, as the original home of the Ewe. . . .

In this series of migrations, the component that became the Anlo was led successively by Togbui Gbe, his son Gemedra, and his grandson Wenya. Wenya's sister married the chief of Tado, Adza Ashimadi, and the marriage produced Kpone, later installed as Sri I. Wenya notified King Agokoli of Notsie of the arrival of his nephew with Ashimadi's stool. The aging Wenya appointed Kpone leader of the Dogbo, and Agokoli installed Kpone as chief of the Dogbo under the name Sri (from the Ewe word *srô da*, "to respect").

Tensions emerged between the Dogbo and their Notsie hosts. Charles Mamattah informs us that this was because Sri believed that Agokoli had unduly delayed his installation as chief after his nomination by Wenya. A dispute erupted between the Notsie and the Dogbo during a drumming session in the Dogbo quarter of Notsie. . . . The Ewe law of vengeance demanded that Agokoli hand over his relative for execution in compensation for the Dogbo loss. This was accordingly carried out, but Agokoli later discovered the Dogbo ruse: the Dogbo deceased was not the injured Aga.

A new phase opened in Notsie-Dogbo relations, marked by the harsh rule of Agokoli. Anlo traditions vividly recount this experience. . . . In Anlo today, this flight is commemorated in the annual festival of *hogbetsotso*. Anlo traditions recount that a small group of famous Dogbo hunters at Notsie—Tsatsu Adeladza, Amesimeku Atogolo, Akplomada, Sri, Etse Tsadia Tsali—had often gone hunting west of Notsie and had discovered the region of southeastern Ghana. They had informed Wenya of this sparsely populated and yet attractive region. The distance between Notsie and Anlo makes it unlikely that hunters from Notsie ranged that far. The emphasis here is on the fact that these named hunters played a pivotal role in the successful establishment of settlements in early Anlo. As hunters they were comfortable both in nature and culture and served as frontiersmen. The Dogbo who fled Notsie split into three groups. One group went northwest and founded settlements such as Hohoe, Peki, Awudome, and Alavanyo in the northern Volta Region of present-day Ghana. The second group fled west and founded Ho, Klevi, Abutia, Adaklu, and other polities in the central section of the Volta Region. The third group, led by Wenya and Sri, headed southwest to the coast and set up settlements such as Keta, Tegbi, Woe, Anloga, and Kodzi, which formed the core of *Anlo akuaku* (Anlo proper). . . .

The Dogbo migrants to southeastern Ghana moved in two parties headed by Wenya and Sri and founded the early Anlo settlements through a series of stops and splits from the main parties. Oral traditions have it that the aged Wenya was carried by two famous hunters, Atsu Etso and Etse Gbadze (twins), as they headed southwest from Notsie. They hit the northern shore of the Keta Lagoon at Ewetoko (present-day Atititi near Afife), and the group proceeded through a narrow creek to Kedzi on the coast. After negotiating the vast watery expanse of the Keta Lagoon, a relieved Wenya is reported to have exclaimed: "Mie do eke dzi azo" ("We have at last arrived on sand"). The place was named "Kedzi" from Wenya's exclamation. The group now moved west along the narrow sand bar sandwiched between the Keta Lagoon and the Atlantic Ocean. The migrants were impressed by the unique physical features of the landscape. Further west of Kedzi, Wenya reached another spot and was struck by the shape of the coastline. He remarked: "Mekpo ke fe ta" ("I have at last seen the head of the sand"), and the name "Keta" was given to this location. Keta literally means "on top of the sand." Wenya's party continued westwards, founding Tegbi, Woe, and Anloga. At Anloga, the tired Wenya protested: "Menlo!" ("I can go no further"; "I have coiled"). Anlo oral traditions see "Anlo" as derived from Wenya's "Menlo," and "Anloga" ("big" or "great" Anlo) became the political capital of Anlo. Sri's party moved southwest along the northern shore of the Keta Lagoon, and members from this group hived off to establish settlements such as Wheta, Dzodze, and Afife. Sri and his followers founded Kodzi and later settled on the lagoon island of Fiahor (literally, "chief's hut"). Wenya sent for his nephew to join him at Anloga. Through the process of naming, the new Anlo landscape was made recognizable and invested with meaning. Settlements and their names constituted signposts in the Anlo historical experience.

Bodies of water dominated the land the Anlo ancestors moved into, and the surface area of Anloland offered little arable or solid land for settlement. This explains the concentration of settlements along the narrow coastal strip and the northern shore of the Keta Lagoon. The geographical features of Anloland from south to north are: a narrow coastal sand bar from the Volta River east to Aflao; the Keta, Avu, and Angaw Lagoons, with their associated islands, creeks, and marshland; and plains extending north of the Keta Lagoon to the southern border of Togo. A series of depressions marked the coastal strip between Whuti and Tegbi, perceived as the former basins of dried-up lagoons. Anlo soil is sandy and infertile, and these depressions constituted an important part of the scarce arable land. Anloland is situated in the Benin (Dahomey) Gap, the natural extension of savannah land that interrupts the West African forest belt and extends to the coast between the Volta River and the Lagos Channel. This open land facilitated commercial and cultural exchanges among the Ewe-speaking peoples and sustained the political ambitions of Aja states such as Allada, Whydah, and Dahomey. . . .

In [the twentieth] century the Anlo can be described as "people of the sea." However, as late as the end of the eighteenth century, the historical record noted an Anlo shyness of the sea. The absence of natural harbors, the rough surf and a parallel sand bar that rendered launching and landing boats a perilous experience partly explain the Anlo cautiousness. The Anlo preferred the safe and calm waters of the lagoon system that united the area between the Volta River and the Lagos Channel or what was referred to as the Slave Coast. . . . The Anlo were originally "land" people, who migrated from Notsie to the southeastern Gold Coast in the mid-seventeenth century. They were neither aquatic nor maritime people, and their land-bound orientation explains the continuing salience of land in Anlo history and the fierce attachment to land. This is in sharp contrast to maritime peoples, who often held land ownership in disdain and eschewed rootedness.

The influx of war refugees shortly after Anlo settlement in the Gold Coast intensified competition for scarce land in Anlo, but these strangers also brought relevant technical knowledge in boat construction, salt making, and fishing methods. The Anlo actively entered the coasting and lagoon trade along the Slave Coast, supplying the important items of fish and salt. Anlo coastal towns, such as Keta and Woe, also served as provisioning stops for European ships in the era of the Atlantic slave trade. The Anlo entered the slave trade and constituted the last region in what became colonial Gold Coast to give up the slave trade, reluctantly, in the mid-nineteenth century. In their evasion of European attempts to impose abolition, the Anlo environment with its interconnected lagoons and creeks proved to be the ideal smuggler's paradise. Abolition caused an upheaval in Anlo economy and society and generated a desperate search for economic alternatives. The introduction of the beach-seine net or *yevudor* in the mid-nineteenth century was timely and underpinned the successful Anlo transition to maritime fishing. Largely operated from the beach, this net enabled the Anlo to avoid lengthy sea-fishing expeditions or offshore fishing; they maximized marine catches without necessarily becoming seafaring. An important dimension to the effective Anlo transition to maritime fishing was the transfer of relevant marine and sky deities from related peoples along the Slave Coast. Becoming people of the sea involved both technological and cognitive adaptations.

Lagoons and the sea dominated the Anlo environment and loomed large in the daily lives of littoral dwellers. Anlo's littoral communities were located on a thin sand spit sandwiched between the sea and the large Keta Lagoon. But even farming communities in inland Anlo depended on the lagoon for water transport, and all came to the important coastal market of Keta, a trading emporium on the upper Slave Coast. The Keta Lagoon and the sea were, perhaps, the most important economic resources in Anlo. The narrowness of the sand spit east of Tegbi made fishing and salt making the major economic pursuits in this part of Anlo. The availability of land—albeit limited—made farming a viable option west of Tegbi, and the traditional Anlo capital of Anloga was the center of farming along the coast. Limited land is reflected in the small sizes of farms, the current average farm size being 0.5 hectares, compared with the national average of 3.7 hectares. Communities north of the Keta Lagoon also farmed, and foodstuffs were exchanged in a north–south direction. In Anlo today, almost everyone has knowledge of fishing, and the communally owned Keta Lagoon ensures a basic livelihood for men, women, and children. Multiple fishing techniques, some of which required little or no real capital investment, made the lagoon a democratic economic resource. *Tekali* was particularly useful when the lagoon became shallow. This involved two people drawing a long rope across the surface of the lagoon, while others formed a line behind the rope. Fish ducked the rope and got stuck in the mud of the lagoon bed because of the shallow water. A silvery reflection indicated the location of the trapped fish, and those behind the rope picked up the fish and deposited them in baskets. Women especially favored the use of bottles in fishing. Commonly, an empty beer bottle would be perforated in the middle, maize dough placed in it and the top sealed. This constitutes a fish trap, and it is set at the edges of the lagoon, while the owner keeps watch over the bottle. As soon as a fish enters to eat the maize dough, the incision is covered with the palm and the bottle quickly removed. The trap is reset. Angling, basket traps, nets, and dams are also deployed in lagoon fishing.

Maritime fishing was another matter and required heavy investment. Sea-fishing nets were mostly made from imported European manufactured materials, and the size of these nets made them costly. But the sea also served as an important highway, which brought European missionaries and traders, who transformed Anlo society and economy. They brought the education and commerce that opened up new socioeconomic opportunities and cemented Keta's emergence as a cosmopolitan center and the economic jewel of Anlo. Behind the missionaries and the European traders came colonial rule, attracted by the revenue prospects of the booming commerce generated by the activities of the former. Keta became the colonial administrative headquarters for the Keta District, and later of the Keta-Ada District. . . .

The sea could also become a means of destruction, and acute coastal erosion from the early twentieth century devastated the Keta area and initiated the long-term causes of socioeconomic decline. The Anlo turned to the colonial government for a solution to their environmental hazard, but the colonial government ruled that it was not responsible for uneconomic environmental programs. Shoreline stabilization and marine fisheries were not central to a colonial environmental policy, which focused largely on the conservation of forests and the regulation of timber felling and mineral extraction. A disappointed Anlo resorted to their knowledge of the past and a belief system that hinted at ancestral ability to manipulate the sea. The Anlo perceived a breach in their moral ecology, the equilibrium of the social, cosmological, and natural worlds that facilitated a successful pursuit of life and underpinned the Anlo understanding of their landscape. The futility of a "moral" solution provided a backdrop for an Anlo critique of colonial rule and the "modernity" that had encouraged the dismissal of custom and the loss of valuable knowledge about the sea. As Keta lost its little land and suffered urban decline, the commercial firms and the government departments that had underpinned the town's cosmopolitan status relocated and took away the "white-collar" jobs.

One Hundred and Fifty Years of Christianity in a Ghanaian Town

John Middleton

The city of Akuropon, capital of the Akan state of Akuapem, became the headquarters for the Basel Mission in the first half of the nineteenth century. The mission would become the Presbyterian Church of Ghana. In the essay that follows, the late John Middleton (1921–2009), former professor emeritus of anthropology at Yale University, focuses on the development of a Presbyterian congregation over a century and a half. He shows that although most of the townspeople are Presbyterians (or at least claim to be), they also consult the indigenous spiritualists as well as Christian and Pentecostal movements in order to find remedies to combat diseases or increase their chances of success in the world. Rather than replacing the previous spirituality of the Akan peoples, Christian missions, once they were established and their management moved into African hands, became simply another pragmatic option for individuals seeking help for life's challenges.

This [essay] deals with certain aspects of a Christian congregation in a kingdom of southern Ghana, in particular its growth over the past 150 years and the part it plays in the lives of the people of the capital town of the state. . . . I am concerned with the development of a Christian congregation that is neither syncretist nor separatist and with its place as one element of a total local religious system which includes other faiths. It is the local congregation of the Presbyterian Church of Ghana in the town of Akuropon, the capital of the eastern Akan kingdom of Akuapem, in the Akuapem Hills that lie some twenty-five miles north of Accra, the national capital. The state has a resident population of about seventy thousand and the town one of some six thousand. However, the number of people who, wherever they live, regard themselves as *Akuroponfo*, "people of Akuropon," probably amounts to some twenty thousand. Those who live elsewhere return to the town when they can at weekends, Christmas, Easter, and the great annual purificatory festival of Odwira, held in September or October; and most hope finally to return to their "hometown" (as it is known in Ghana) to be buried. Although not a large town, it is known widely as the seat of the main educational facilities of the Presbyterian Church since the arrival of the Basel Mission in the then Gold Coast in 1828. Due largely to this fact it has provided more than its share of political, educational, and other leaders of Gold Coast and Ghanaian society.

The State of Akuapem (Okuapeman) was founded in 1733 at the Concord of Abotakyi, when representatives of the local population formally accepted as their rulers a group from the state of Akyem, to the immediate west, who had driven out the former overlords, the Akwamu. The dynasty has been in power ever since, its king, *Okuapehene* or *Omanhene* ("state ruler") living in the town of Akuropon. The kingdom comprises seventeen traditional towns set along the Akuapem Hills, with many lesser settlements in the valleys below. Each town is the seat of a chief and the centre of its own "custom" (*amanne*) that marks its identity and distinguishes it from other towns. Here I discuss only the capital town, to which the Basel Mission came in 1835, seven years after having started work on the coast. The town is about a mile across and has some seven hundred houses, of varying sizes, ages, and conditions. In the centre is the royal palace, in which is the royal stool-house where are kept the stools (the carved seats in which the souls of the ancestors are believed to reside) of previous kings. It is a place of great sanctity and the traditional ritual centre of both town and state.

The basic principles of local organization are those of descent and rank. The relationship between them is too complex to be discussed fully in this paper, and in this context a brief outline is sufficient. The people of Akuropon are Twi-speaking Akan and are members of the several matrilineal clans (*abusua*, pl. *mmusua*) that are found throughout the Akan areas of Ghana and the Ivory Coast. The localized branches of clan that live in the town itself may be called "subclans," each consisting usually of several "houses" (*ofi*, pl. *efi*), each based on a matrilineal lineage (*yafunu*). The "house" head has responsibility for the stools of the ancestors. Some heads have "black" stools, awarded by past kings for loyal service: these stools, like those of the palace, are traditionally "fed" with blood—in the past human blood but today sheep's blood. At the top of the traditional system of ranking was the king, elected from one of the three kingly lineages of the royal subclan, Asona, in rotation (the subclan also has nonkingly lineages). Below the king came the heads of "houses" who had "black" stools, and then the ordinary citizens, followed by pawns and slaves of various kinds. High rank depends on closeness to a past or present king, either by kinship or by being granted a "black" stool, and within this framework personal qualities count for much as far as the exercise of actual power and influence is concerned. This is still considered to be the ideal system according to "custom," except that today there are no slaves, slavery having been formally abolished in 1875.

When the Akyem came to Akuapem they found the majority of the local population were Guan, whose form of government was by priests of traditional deities, mystical forces found also among the Akan. The Twi word for these deities is *obosom* (pl. *abosom*), usually translated in the literature as "fetish." They may be seen as representing powers from "outside" society, in contrast to the ancestors who may be seen as representing its "inside" life and the perpetuity of subclan and "house." Above the deities in traditional Akan religion is God, Onyame or Onyankopon (and there are other terms), and Asase Yaa, the goddess of the earth. This religious system has never been totally static but has continually accommodated new religious movements brought by prophetic leaders from both other Akan and non-Akan areas. It is likely that several nonindigenous cults appeared in Akuropon before the nineteenth century and over time were amalgamated into the so-called "traditional" religion; but we know nothing of them in detail. We may assume that they were associated with the appearance of new forms of external power originating largely in the Sahel region, which was the source of most social innovations until the coming of the Europeans along the coast. These influences took religious form as cults of new deities, a phenomenon that has continued until the present day.

The Growth of the Christian Congregation in Akuropon

The Presbyterian congregation in Akuropon was founded by the Basel Mission, which from 1835 until the First World War built up a formidably efficient organization for its work, based partly on its famed linguistic achievements and its emphasis on vocational education. During the First World War the field was given to the United Free Church of Scotland, and in 1926 the church became the Presbyterian Church of Ghana, independent of, although still closely linked to, its parent missionary bodies in Basel, Stuttgart, and Edinburgh. In Akuropon most supervisory posts were held by Europeans until the 1950s.

The history of the Akuropon congregation has largely been determined by its relationship to the changing local society of which it has been part. We may distinguish three main phases: the first, from the beginnings in 1835 until about the 1860s, was one of opposition of interests, if not antagonism, and frequently open hostility on both sides. This was followed by a period of ambivalence and compromise until about the Second World War,

The Wesley Methodist Church (now the Wesley Cathedral) of Cape Coast is the oldest Methodist church in Ghana and where Methodism began in the 1830s. Photograph by Kwasi Konadu, 2005.

since when we may discern a period in which the congregation has increasingly become an integral part of local society. During this century and a half its role in the town has changed radically, from that of a new religious movement akin to other prophetic cults of the time to that of being the local "establishment" church with an essentially conservative role.

It is still told in Akuropon that when the missionary Andreas Riis first came to the town on 25 January 1835 to ask the then *Omanhene* Nana Addo Dankwa I for permission to establish a new church, he was taken as one of a series of new prophets, although perhaps an unusual one. His request was granted but he had little immediate success, due mainly to dynastic wars that ravaged the town and its people, most of whom left it for their villages. Riis withdrew from the town in 1838. However, he built houses and opened gardens, and is remembered as *osiadan*, "builder of houses," some of which still stand. After a few years it was decided to make a second attempt. A group of West Indian artisans was recruited from the West Indies who, it was thought, might better adapt to the climate, help with building and farming, and show that black men could become Christians. Three missionaries, including Riis, and the new recruits arrived at Akuropon in 1843.

The first local converts appear to have comprised three main social categories. The most important, although few in number, were princes, the sons of kings and chiefs who in this matrilineal system could not themselves become rulers. It is traditionally the responsibility of the father to provide for his children's upbringing; the rulers wished the princes to receive the new European education, which they did not care to give their sisters' sons until several decades later. The missionaries on their side were enthusiastic to recruit these young men, gave them a good education, and appointed many of them to become pastors and evangelists. However, they never ranked as high in the church organization as did the Swiss and German missionaries themselves. In the very early days the majority of converts were ex-slaves, who became free if they could escape to the mission and who were trained as artisans and married other ex-slaves. Then there were free members of the town's population. At first these appear to have been mostly widows (especially those without children able to help them), divorced and deserted women, orphans, and various kinds of people who had wittingly or unwittingly broken taboos; early reports mention those born with six fingers being saved by the missionaries from starvation or abandonment. Adult male free converts seem to have been few until the later years of the century. However, for the first few years most converts were children, both free and ex-slaves, who were taken into the missionaries' houses as servants and protégés, educated, and baptized. After midcentury the number of free adults who joined the mission increased, but it seems that many of these came as runaways of various kinds from Akuapem towns other than Akuropon, and so had no kin in the town itself. Of those who did come from Akuropon many in fact were allowed to keep their own slaves until this practice was stopped on orders from Basel.

It is significant that princes, slaves, widows, and other categories mentioned were persons of ambiguous social status. The situations of ambiguity in Akuropon society, as in all Akan societies, are defined mainly in terms of descent, rank, and moral and physical characteristics. A person's relationship to his or her father is ambiguous in that they belong to different clans and the father's duties to his children are never very clearly defined; but there is a closer personal, spiritual, and mystical link between them than between a child and its mother. The traditional position of a slave was also ambiguous in the sense that he was attached to and part of a "house" but not of its core descent line. And there were many situations of what local people saw as "moral" ambiguity, such as being parentless, childless, divorced and unable to remarry, even being very poor or shiftless, or possessing physical features considered only semihuman, such as having six fingers or severe mutilations. Oral tradition holds that such people in pre-Christian times would have had recourse to cults of deities; in this respect, at least in the early years, there were similarities between these cults and Christianity.

The internal organization of the mission was in some ways a replica of that of the indigenous town, which we may assume the missionaries accepted as being "normal." The European missionaries were in the highest rank, as "rulers"; then the princes (and some others) as indigenous pastors and evangelists; then ordinary "commoners," and then the artisans and servants of slave origin. We might hazard that this strongly hierarchical organization appealed to the king and his free subjects, who would not have relished egalitarianism.

At this period there was marked differentiation between Christian and non-Christian. The Christians lived in their own part of the town, which had been offered to them by Nana Addo Dankwa I and was known as Salem, in their new-style dwellings designed by Andreas Riis. This separation was deliberate mission policy, to remove Christians from what the missionaries saw as immoral and "heathen" townspeople. Converts did not enter the palace, and many did not like to walk in the streets of the town outside Salem for fear of ridicule or even attack; they wore European clothing as much as possible in place of indigenous cloth; they did not marry with non-Christians; and the religious distinction was rigidly maintained.

An important question is that of which parts of the traditional religious system the missionaries could accept and which they could not. They found the Akan notion of the High God acceptable: at least they saw no reason not to use the same term, Onyame, for the Christian God, and so whatever differences there were were presumably not important enough to matter. They seem never to have worried very much about the ancestral cult, presumably because the king was at the centre of the royal cult and possibly because they understood little of it since ancestor sacrifices were normally made in private; but they did try strenuously to prevent human sacrifice as part of that cult. What they considered abhorrent was the cult of the deities: their reports of the entire period stress their utter condemnation of these practices.

On the other side there were several reasons for local fear and distrust of the missionaries. Since the king was both the political and religious head of state, the establishment of a church whose members could no longer accept his religious position would thereby affect his political status. Religious and political affiliation were traditionally inseparable, and the welfare and indeed the continuity of the state depended largely on the proper performance of their religious obligations by both king and subjects. Moreover, subjects who chose another religious affiliation would thereby come under the everyday jurisdiction of the new church and might refuse both the king's authority in jural matters and that of "house" heads in domestic ones. The mission's attacks on slavery were taken as attacks on local "custom" and the kingship itself, as was the opposition of the mission to the practices of human sacrifice and coffin-carrying. Any abolition of these institutions was seen by the mass of the people as striking at the very base of their religious and jural systems.

Towards the end of the nineteenth century this mutual opposition began to crumble. The last king to own slaves was Nana Kwame Fori I (1880–95), and his successor, Nana F. W. K. Akuffo, had been educated at the mission schools. By this time also the mission's earlier attacks on human sacrifice and coffin-carrying were no longer necessary since both had been forbidden —not always successfully but fairly effectively—by the British colonial government. Thus the missionaries no longer aroused such dislike over their attitudes as they had done originally. We come here to the second phase in the development of the local congregation, one of somewhat uneasy mutual accommodation between church and state. The isolation of the Christians was breaking down, with an increasing number of free adherents, men as well as women and children, so that henceforth local families comprised both Christian and non-Christian members and there was no longer such a gap between educated and uneducated. The intricate network of kinship and residential links between the families of the town cannot be described here, but ties of marriage, friendship, and alliance connected to the histories of individual conversion and baptism are clearly traceable in mission records and oral tradition. Influential factors in this regard included the opportunities for social mobility and for new wealth from cocoa and trade. These were closely linked to the development of the new educational and mercantile systems by the Basel Mission. A boys' school was opened in 1843 and one for girls in 1847, both boarding institutions that removed the pupils from the influence of home and family; teaching was in the vernacular for younger children. The seminary for the training of ministers and evangelists was opened in 1848. The mission's educational achievements helped its converts enter trade, acquire capital, and so purchase new lands in the centre and west of the Gold Coast for cocoa growing. Cocoa was introduced into the Gold Coast in 1858 by the Basel Mission and it was Akuapem farmers who created the cocoa industry. These events were followed by the abolition of slavery, and so mission-trained ex-slaves as well as those of free ancestry could participate in the expanding economy.

The period of the United Free Church of Scotland, between the two world wars, was marked by a widening of the educational facilities, an increased emphasis on literary as distinct from the vocational and industrial training that had been so important in the Basel Mission's program, and a lessening of the earlier missionaries' sense of opposition to local society.

During the second and third quarters of this century there has developed an increasingly organic relationship between church and state. The local congregation is now a major institution in Akuropon, with perhaps three-quarters of the population being baptized Presbyterians, although not all are paid-up members. It is controlled by Ghanaian presbyters and ministers, and its sense of exclusiveness is today less than it has ever been. Since the 1960s the Europeans have gone and all offices are held by Ghanaians, although not all are from the town itself or even from the state. This period has seen the appearance of new Christian sects in the town, largely in opposition to the central position of the Presbyterian church. There are now Pentecostalist and many other separatist groups in Akuropon, and many loosely organized and often ephemeral prayer groups. It is perhaps they, rather than the mass of the Presbyterian congregation, who feel themselves obliged to maintain a sense of purity and exclusiveness, although there remains a significant number of Presbyterians who continue to emphasize their distinctiveness from, and superiority to, other Christians. In a sense the wheel has come full circle.

The Multitude of Faiths and Their Beliefs

Many of the townspeople are practicing and devout Christians of the local congregation of the Presbyterian Church, paying their dues, attending services, and wishing to see their faith spread to all other members of the town. Others are devout non-Christians, many associated with the palace and regularly attending the rites held there to do with the royal ancestors. Many young men and women are adherents of new sects that have appeared, from Pentecostalist churches and Christian prayer groups that are concerned especially with the healing of sickness, to cults of newly "imported" deities, whose main aim is to combat witchcraft. The present king, Nana Addo Dankwa III, was educated at the Presbyterian Training College in the town; on his accession he was required to adopt the religious practices of his predecessors as an essential part of his royal role. During my stay there were two former kings still alive who had abdicated and converted to Christianity. The queen-mother is a practicing Christian, although not a Presbyterian; in this respect she is a rare exception, as she is traditionally at the centre of palace ritual. An elder who formerly held important religious posts in the palace, and now is chronically ill, intends to become a Presbyterian so that he may be buried in the Presbyterian cemetery. Many members of the palace singing groups of women are Christians, and some of these groups have even sung in the Presbyterian church (a matter for some disagreement in both palace and church). Many Christians go to deity shrines to be cleansed from pollution after deaths in their families: I should add that these visits are usually made surreptitiously, at night. I could list many other situations of what at first sight might be thought self-contradictory religious behavior. Christians and non-Christians are kin, often brothers and sisters and even husbands and wives. Although many on both "sides" have objections to this accommodation of faith, and presbyters argue among themselves about doctrinal matters and about which palace rites they may attend, there is no doubt that the townspeople include adherents of many faiths who manage to live side by side. In addition, many follow more than one faith in different situations, without feeling any too great inconsistency. This religious system, which I suggest should be regarded as a single religious complex comprising many faiths, merits some discussion. The point that I wish to demonstrate is that there is a complex relationship between the kinds of affliction people consider important enough to be treated by religious means, the means that they use to remove these afflictions, and their social standing in the town. . . .

Far more men than women are at any time absent from the town as cocoa farmers and urban workers. Those women who attend the church tend to be the older women, or younger ones visiting their families in Akuropon from their husbands' places of residence elsewhere. It is said that in the first quarter of this century the church was filled to overflowing, but that since then the exodus of younger married couples has severely lessened the size of the regular congregation. I think that another factor here is the changing roles of the ministers, whose message has become stale: I return to this point below. Men tend to spend Sundays, when many people return to Akuropon, discussing "house" affairs at "house" meetings, whereas women do not do so to the same extent. Men are considered to be more concerned with their ambitions and business successes, which are not seen as concerning the church. On the other hand, women are thought rather to be concerned with the status of their families, so that they are expected to attend the prestigious Presbyterian church to show their meritorious behavior and to represent their families. Men in Akuropon are ideally or traditionally polygynous, and those who are so are less likely to attend church; they may do so but may not attend communion or hold church office, and only their first wives may attend. Attendance shows that a person is a member of the town recognized to be of good social and moral standing, of a fair or good standard of education, and generally of a family of reasonable wealth, social responsibility, and reputation.

On another level to attend church is to feel oneself a member of a congregation and community, and to acquire the sense of personal security brought by it. To this end the symbols of church attendance are important: the regular and carefully organized ritual of the service, beginning with the slow entry of ministers and choir to the processional hymn, which is the same week in and week out, continuing with sermon, prayers, hymns, and collection with an ever-heightening emotional atmosphere that is usually expressed during the collection (when people move up the aisle to the collection table, often exhorted to compete in generosity) by women dancing up the centre aisle. The sense of community and of a shared power—that of a congregation rather than of a mere gathering of people—is then very high.

If people on other occasions appeal also to non-Christian mystical forces, this is seen more as their own personal concern and is normally made at shrines in the villages below the hills, that is, in places that are socially "invisible." Those who do not attend the Presbyterian church but go to others and to deity shrines, even if they have been educated at Presbyterian schools, mostly include those who cannot afford dues, fees, and the required standards of clothing, or who are illiterate and generally of low social position (I refer here to the newer churches, rather than to the handful of other long-established ones such as the Methodist or Anglican, both of which have churches in Akuropon but very small congregations). With ever-increasing differences of wealth and social standing between top and bottom of the local social hierarchy attendance at the Presbyterian church has become an increasingly important criterion for measurement of class differences. In addition to church attendance, burial in one of the Presbyterian cemeteries, following a funeral service in the church, is greatly looked forward to by those who have increased their standing in the community, and their worldly success while alive is then reflected in the prestige that this will bring to their kin. With ever-increasing social mobility this is an important reason for conversion to Presbyterianism in later life. This is not an egalitarian church but, as might be expected, one that reflects the society in which it is placed. Today many younger and poorer men and women tend to go to Pentecostalist churches and to prayer groups, perhaps as a sign of rebellion against their elders. These churches may also be visited by non-Christians if they think attendance at them may help solve their difficulties.

The Christian Congregation in the Changing Town

I mentioned above the final phase in the growth of the Christian congregation in Akuropon as that of an organic relationship with the remainder of town society. I now return to this point.

The church plays many roles in the town that are not formally religious in the sense of being directly part of worship. One of these is educational. Akuropon is a famed educational centre, with schools run by the Presbyterian Church from primary to college levels, and it has been so since the middle of the nineteenth century. Education is one of the keys to social mobility in Ghana, as elsewhere, and the church in Akuropon has long provided education necessary for those who wish to increase their social status. Citizens of the town who live elsewhere are proud to send their children back to it for education, to live in the care of grandparents or other kin.

The roles played by the church are also associated with central jural functions of Akuropon as a "hometown," the town that is regarded as home and the seat of traditional custom by the many thousands of "people of Akuropon," Akuroponfo. As I have mentioned, people living elsewhere return to it as often as they can. Their visits include taking part in family discussions on property, succession, and inheritance, the stewardship of "house" affairs by the elders, and the like. This factor makes Akuropon the "hometown" of the many widespread networks of members dispersed across southern Ghana and beyond. Discussions about succession to family office and inheritance of family property also take place, publicly, a few days after the funeral of a family member. At these meetings the heirs are named, the children (who are not of the same lineage as their father) are formally recognized to receive a portion of the inheritance, and witnesses and executors are appointed to ensure that all will be carried out properly and justly. Although this is a traditional pattern, when the deceased has been a church adherent, these meetings are supervised by the presbyters, who attend and control the formal proceedings, which are recorded by the presbyters' clerk. Over time the presbyters have succeeded in modifying traditional rules so that today widows' and children's interests are cared for to a greater extent than they were a century ago. In this way one of the "dilemmas" of matriliny is at least partially resolved and the pattern of succession and inheritance, as a central "custom" of the town, maintained in a world of change. The presbyters also play an important although more informal role in the settlement of disputes over use, sales, and inheritance of land within and between Presbyterian families. Land disputes are perennial, drawn-out, and expensive, and the presbyters have here also succeeded in making precedents for their settlement when the parties are so disposed. The church thus plays an important jural role in the central issues to do with relations between and within constituent "houses" of the town, and with their perpetuation as effective groups. There are only a few families that are not affected to some degree by the church in these ways.

For several years now the Odwira festival, the annual non-Christian cycle of royal purification centered on the cult of the royal ancestors, has ended with the king taking part in a special harvest thanksgiving in Christ Church. This would have been unthinkable only a few decades ago. Even though conservatives on both sides have misgivings, this meeting of church and state has become a regular part of Odwira, a sign of the near-complete acceptance of the church as an organic part of town society. Christians also observe essential parts of Odwira, such as the ban on eating new yam until after the proper rites and attending the public parts of the festival.

The Peoples of the Gold Coast Hinterland

George Ekem Ferguson

The end of the nineteenth century signaled the effective end of African sovereignty on the Gold Coast and the installation of British rule. A consolidation of the Gold Coast colony followed, which, by then, came to include essentially all the peoples and territories that would constitute the republic of Ghana half a century later. The writings of George Ferguson (1864–97) explore matters of culture, commerce, and colonial subjectivity, for he worked as an official of the British colonial government and in that capacity shaped the structure of modern Ghana by bringing the northern parts of the country into the colony through a set of treaties he negotiated on behalf of the British government. Ferguson's reports are also important because they provide detailed accounts of these northern peoples and territories and the movements of other colonial powers on the eve of the Berlin conference (ca. 1884–85), which effectively divided much of Africa among the various European imperialists. The following excerpt from Ferguson is a summary of his observations on the peoples of the Gold Coast hinterland.

The King of Kumassi [Kumase], having determined upon subjugating certain revolted provinces of Ashanti, continued a series of wars against them till at last turning his attention to the North in 1893 he scattered the Nkoranzas and their allies and made King Kofi Fa flee with them, for refuge into the British Protectorate of Atabubu and into the surrounding Brong [Bono] countries; Prempeh then threatened to invade Atabubu itself, and it was in connection with this menacing attitude of Ashanti that I left Accra on the 23rd September 1893 (under instructions No. 151 of 22nd September 1893) to obtain information respecting Ashanti and its army prior to the dispatch of the Expedition under Colonel Sir Francis Scott to Atabubu. While at Atabubu I received instructions to make treaties with the Brong tribes and afterwards to make a survey for the proposed Cis Volta Road, but I had only partly carried out the first of these two instructions by treating with Amanting on 21st December 1893, with Nkoranza on 25th January 1894 and with Abease on 8th February 1894 when Your Excellency's instructions dated at

Accra on 9th January 1894 arrived at Atabubu for me to proceed on the mission to the Hinterland, Colonel Sir Francis Scott having afforded me every facility required by Your Excellency. I handed over my first instructions to Captain Lang and then left Atabubu on the 24th February for the Hinterland to take part in what is described by Ravengstein as "a race for African territory which has been nowhere more active than in the region which lies between the Gold Coast and the lower Niger."

The instructions of 9th January and 9th March 1894 relating to my operations exterior to the Zone had been carried out upon my arrival at Sansani-Mungo from Mossi, and with Yendi commenced the negotiations in the Neutral Zone. In the course of my operations the Government has been acquainted with the equipment and organization of the mission, its progress and general results etc. as stated in varying letters. I beg now to submit to Your Excellency the following report containing (1) a summary of my observations on the Physical and Political Geography of the Hinterland, and (2) memorandum of the political proceedings of the mission.

There are certain points of strategic importance, commercially, in connection with existing arrangements with Germany and France which are suggested by the Map, such, for instance as (I) the neighborhood of the Volta-Daka junction. For some ten miles between Akanem and an island up its course the River still remains in British territory and ferries might be established there in connection with the new Cis Volta Road. (II) Sansani-Mungo, at the Northeastern corner and exterior of the Zone on the Road leading to the caravan producing countries of the North has its importance manifest connecting us as it does with the Niger territories. (III) The principal caravan routes nearly all fall into the Neutral Zone. (IV) The Western exterior of the Zone has no important caravan routes so that this makes it all the more desirable to secure the industrious and populous district of Bona and its dependencies. (V) Oti and Komoe Rivers: Advantageous as natural boundaries which could be understood by the natives and economical in the future defense of the frontier.

The *itinerary* accounts for the days I was on the move and includes details which are for the most part required by the Intelligence Department of the War Office in the Colonial Secretary's Circular of the 29th July 1892 and in the Memorandum of the War Office dated 28th August 1893 with regard to my traverse, topography, positions of towns, routes, bearings, astronomical observations &c., a few examples of numerals as distinguishing one tribe from another are also included.

Tribes. The people of the Hinterland were classified in my report of 18th August 1894 according to their various degrees of capacity for political nego-

The scenic Tamale road is the main artery through northern Ghana. Tamale is the capital city of Ghana's Northern Region. Photograph by Kwasi Konadu, 2007.

tiations. Parts of my investigations with regard to tribal affinities and inheritance formed the subject of the reply to the Colonial Secretary's Circular of 22nd May, 1895 copy attached. To trace to their origin the stock from which the present tribes occupying the Hinterland have been derived would require not only an analysis of their diverse dialects but also a comparative study of their customs, manners, history, migrations, wars, and in short all the physical and political influences, internal as well as external, by which the divergence of each, tribe from the original to the present condition has been developed. If the original Wangaras [long-distance traders of Malian origins] who founded the inland states were Mohamedans [Muslims] their descendants are not: the Government is now in the hands of Fetish Worshippers. Colour and physique by which race types could be recognized have been obscured by marriage with slaves and foreign tribes, so that what the prevailing ethnological and anthropological influences have been it is difficult to decide from the scanty materials collected during the short time comprised in my tour. The object of my mission being also political I acted on the experience of not arousing the suspicions of a superstitious people by too many enquiries relating to a matter which might mar the success of my negotiations.

Nevertheless I collected native traditions, examples of vocabulary and observed the system of Tattoos a consideration of which has conveyed to me certain impressions on the subject of race which I submit in later paragraphs. They are at present used for the purpose of explaining the distinctions among the present tribes. Near the Coast Ashanti speaking tribes prevail: the Ashanti and Fanti States, Adansi, Denkera [Denkyira], Akim [Akyem], Kwahu, Akwamu, Akwapim, Assin, Chuful (Tufel [Twifo]) &c., amongst whom there is a common relationship in clans (exact number in dispute among historical writers) named after buffalo, fox, tiger and other animals. Of Ashanti proper Mampong and Kumau alone fall within the range of the present map of the Hinterland. Between these tribes and the bend of the Volta there is a district occupied by tribes known to the Ashantis as Brong or Abronu. This term appears however to be generic, and used in the same form as the Romans did "barbarians." Thus Nkoranza Kwahu, Atabubu, Amanting, Abease, Jwan, Basa, Prang, though speaking dialects but little different from Ashanti are classified as Brong. Likewise Ahafu [Ahafo] and even Wam. Countries which speak the Nchumuru language diverging very far from Ashanti dialect are also politically included under the Brong tribes. Late and Kyiripong are Nchumuru dialects.

Accra or Ga claims to have no connection with the Ashanti speaking tribe. The dialect resembles a mixture of Gonja and Lobi with Ashanti infused, but it is also stated that the Ga and Adangbe dialects bear some similarity to the language of Bonny and Benin and that the Accra people migrated to the Coast from a country to the North West of Dahomey.

Northward of the bend of the Volta between the Western or main branch and the Oti River are: Gonja, a Mendi [Mande] (Wangara, Bambara, Njira or Jila) tribe by tradition. Gonja tradition says that the first settlers met the Dagombas in their present habitat. The Gonja dialect has some 15 to 20 per cent of Ashanti words in it and appears like the language of the Nchumurus to be compromised between Adangbe and Ashanti.

By the three parallel knife marks drawn downwards from the temples and to the cheeks and/or on the arms, abdomen and different parts of the body, Dagombas, Mamprusi, Mossi and Dagarti appear to be all referable to the Wangara family, while the aboriginal Grunshi, Pampamba, Lobi and Mo appear to be those whom these tribes have displaced. Three curvilinear slanting marks converging from the cheeks to the corners of the mouth distinguish the Jila family: the Bandas, the Mendes of Kong and most Mahomedans of Bona and Bawle conform to this Tattoo. Mamprusi and Dagomba are anthropologically related and have five to eight fine parallel lines from the temples to the cheeks.

Grunshi marks are more complex including fine lines and broad strokes (combined or not). The sub-tribes are Talensi, Kpau, Tiansi or Bulsi, Nakaransi, Isale or Nagruma, Achilon, Kanjaga, Yulsi or Tiole, Nunuma, Lama and Nohkodosi. Dagarti, Nienege and Kiprisi are sometimes reckoned genetically under Grunshi. Among the Grunshis the sub-tribes sometimes distinguish themselves by their dialect rendering for the sentence "I say that"; "Misiha" is spoken by Isale sub-tribes; "Misiblawa" by Achilon sub-tribes. This distinction may even be applied to the Chi tribes on the Coast where "Misi" or "Misise" is spoken by Ashanti and Akan tribes and "Miside" by Fantis. Interesting as this appears it nevertheless illustrates the difficulty of race investigations already pointed out. The Dafina system of Tattoos appears to be between those of Grunshi and Mendi.

The Pakhalla [Mfantera/Nafana] tribes inhabit the Bona and Gaman [Gyaman] region, stretching North West and South East and between the Volta and Komoe Rivers. In their gable roofed buildings they conform to Ashanti style, but the dialect is different from either Ashanti or Kong. The Mendi style of building is flat[-]roofed buildings and circular huts with conical roofs. Ashanti supremacy extended in the Pakhalla region northward as far as Bona and eastward to Mangotu (Anno [Agni]) and Bandohlo on the other side of River Komoe. The Mangos speak a dialect similar to that of Sefwi. A portion of this tribe having formed an alliance with Mamprusi in a war against Dagomba not more than two or three hundred years ago eventually settled on the Oti River and called their capital Nsraanu or "the Camp": this is known in Hausa as Sansani-Mungo [Sansanne Mango]. But the territory is called Chakosi and Male.

The "Broad arrow" distinguishing the Awuna tribe from others on the Coast is peculiar. Nevertheless, Tattoo is an uncertain basis for race investigations as some belonging to one tribe have been adopted by another as fashions. Thus Tattoos (more especially regular geometrical figures) with which the women of Dagomba adorn themselves are to be seen on the Coast at Accra, Fanti and elsewhere on the bodies of both men and women. In some instances where a woman has lost her issues consecutively a disfigurement by Tattoo is practiced to "prevent the child returning to the land of spirits." Jimini lies between Mango and Kong.

On the West of the Hinterland the Kong states (Komono, Karaboro, Dokhosie, Tiefo and Bobo) extend roughly from the 9th to the 11th parallel. Beyond Mossi, Fula settlements in Gando [Gwandu] territory which extends to the Niger are met with at Jelgohi, Arabinda, Libtaku, Yagha &c. As the language of the Hausa is different so is the system of Tattoo distinct from Mossi or Dagomba.

A mountainous region lying to the East of the River Oti and known as Bawsu is occupied by Adele, Ajuti, Timu and Kotokori, tribes which speak a language different from Ashanti but allied to Pampamba and Kiripong. Chief Kojo of Tetepene in this region paid tribute to Ashanti.

The principal tribes of the Hinterland have now been enumerated, some of their migrations noticed and their probable geographical distribution in the past suggested. The aggrey beads valued so much on the Coast did not seem to be much known by tribes outside the former dominions of Ashanti; they appear to be the reminiscences of former commercial connection by the Coast tribes with ancient foreign nations probably Carthagenians as tradition does not say that they were manufactured by the ancestors of the present Coast tribes. In connection with the past geographical distribution of man in this region I believe however that some of the tribes of the Coast and Hinterland have become extinct. Besides the evidence afforded by slave-raiding, marriage customs, lessened fertility of the women from anxiety, tribal wars and struggles together with other influences tending to extinction which are still found (e.g. Grunshi) among the aboriginal savages and which influences must have acted more strongly in times past, I may also state that the stone implements found at Akim and other places, respecting which no tradition is extant accounting satisfactorily for their existence point to this direction. . . .

When we reflect that a thousand years ago resemblances amounting to mutual intelligibility existed among the languages of Anglo-Saxon England, of Upper and Lower Germany and of Holland but that now, whatever radical affinity scientific dissection may reveal among English, German or Dutch, it is well known that a person speaking only one of these needs an interpreter for the other two, it is not difficult to conceive that all the aborigines of the Colony and its Hinterland are of one stock. For a confirmation of this impression we naturally turn to the traditions relating to the origin of the various tribes. It is said that the ancestors of Late, Obutu, Gomua, Ga, Akim and even Ashanti are distinct tribes which migrated from various regions beyond the sea; but in the same breath it is also said that the various tribes classify themselves according to the clans in which they first migrated to their present habitat from a far interior. The traditions are seemingly inconsistent, and even sometimes disfigured with a cloud of fables and exaggerations springing from tribal vanity; nevertheless the impression which I have formed upon examining these various accounts is, that, pressed by the advances of Islamisin, the Ashanti or Tchi [Twi] tribes migrated from the Northwest of Kong and settled in family communities in the region between Kong and Abora at which time they displaced the aboriginal Kiripong and Nchumuru tribes. Some time anterior to this the Mo and Dagomba tribes were already in occupation of the region between the Black and White Volta from which they were expelled by Gonja.

Ashanti is said to have derived much of its imposing Court Ceremony from the Court at Yendi. Nevertheless it soon developed to be the most powerful kingdom of the Hinterland; it subdued Gonja, the Brong tribes, and Dagomba itself; Komoe and Oti Rivers were not the confines of its conquests, Mangotu and Kotokori were both under its sway; it was feared by the King of Bona, whose Head Priest was also Chief Priest of Kumasi; it was respected by Mossi, to whom a deputation was sent to court its friendship. Its subjects raided Grunshi to supply the King of Kumasi with slaves. The King of Kumasi distributed honours and Court decorations to the various Kings of his Kingdom. For full 300 years persons were collected from all parts of its vast dominions, who having been instructed in the barbarous customs and manners practised at Kumasi including extortion and execution were distributed as residents, royal executioners, tax collectors and other official agents in every part of his dominion. Its merchants met the caravans from the North at Salaga. Thus its language became widely diffused and with Hausa and Mossi became the language of Commerce. It was only in 1873 when Kumasi fell to the prowess of British Arms that this vast dominion of Ashanti became disintegrated and its members formed various minor confederations.

Under these circumstances it is found that the manners and customs practised by those tribes which possess a Government are either those of Ashanti or Mossi or else in a transition stage between their aboriginal customs and that of Ashanti. Thus (1) the society of Nkoranza, Kwahu, the Brong tribes, Abrong, Gaman, Mangotu are examples of the first type, (2) that of Mossi second type, (3) that of Mo, Gonja, Wa, Dagomba, a third type. To complete the enumeration I may mention (4) the savage tribes of Lobi, Pampamba, Kusasi, Busansi and Grunshi which are without organized Governments; and (5) the little colonies of Mohammedan settlers found in the larger [centers] of population. A few of the priests there write in Arabic characters, but do not understand Arabic language. With the exception of Kong there are no states governed entirely by the Codes of Islamism. . . .

Organized Government. Mossi Type. The Government is administered by a Council of Chiefs or Nabas; there are Chiefs of Provinces and Districts, each with its own Council to administer its affairs, but subordinate to the King. The Council and King constitute the Lawgiver and Judge. Political transactions are usually conducted through the Housemaster. The King has his harem of a thousand wives with a crowd of intriguing eunuchs.

Succession is always open to dispute and rival mothers usually seek to poison each other's son. The King's wives are not to be seen by his subjects; they are, therefore, always accompanied by eunuchs who drive the crowd away. He keeps about 100 horses always in his stable and his saddlery is mounted with silver. In the Courts there are young men usually good looking wearing brass anklets and armlets constituting the officers of the Court. When the King enters, the assembly rises and sits down and similar ceremony performed when he retires. The state umbrellas of Ashanti Custom are conspicuously absent. In saluting they either . . . prostrate or else bend the knee to the ground and with the elbow a little raised snap the fingers repeatedly. The population is mostly fetish the national fetish of Mossi being called Tiebo; but there are few Mahommedans. Some wear large trousers with cloth thrown round the shoulders, others dress like Mahommedans. They are industrious and courageous. People of humbler rank travel on foot, those of higher station on horseback. Their principal pursuits are pasture and agriculture. During the sowing season sheep are muzzled and for injury committed by a stray cattle the animal may be slain but the [carcass] must be given to its owner. Labour is performed by slaves. In preparing their food the cereals are beaten with pestles, but deformity of the knee is often to be seen among the women from their repeatedly kneeling to grind food stuffs on stone. After harvest season the caravans start with horse, donkey, country cloth and cotton webs as well as a few saddlery and trinkets for the South all to be exchanged for Kola nuts. Cowries are the medium of exchange. Polygamy is practised and sons usually succeed. They use bows, arrows and spears but a few dane [Danish] guns are to be seen here and there. The majority of the buildings are round huts with grass roofs but the King's palace is flat-roofed, oriental in style with a court-yard beautifully leveled. . . .

In the *memorandum* of my *political proceedings* attached there will be found declarations with regard to the external relations of the authorities as well as the extent of their territories. Supplementary information as to my proceedings will be found in my letter of 21st December 1895. . . .

With regard to all these treaties I may state that to the native mind the friendly alliance of a powerful country with a weaker tribe implied a protection of some kind or other to be given by the former to the latter. Hence the import of their accepting a British Flag and signing the treaties of friendship and freedom of trade would, from the ideas suggested by the nature of their society or by that of their external relations, not be easily distinguishable by them from the import of a Treaty of Protection. Thus I have an idea that an expectation of our alliance with them in defense of their territories might be retained in the Hinterland.

I was the first official of a European Power to visit Bona, Lobi, Wa and Sansani-Mungo, and I had accomplished in 1894 the object of my mission to the Hinterland including Mamprusi and Moshi when, in 1895, some of the places which came within my sphere of operations were, as Your Excellency is aware, visited by Foreign Missions. These Missions proceeded there not with the object of compelling the Natives to conform to a previously existing arrangement with any of them; they went to negotiate treaties of alliance, so that the declarations of the native authorities at the time of their negotiations with me, that they were free from engagements with other Foreign Powers, were reliable.

The Foreign Missions referred to were thus anticipated by that upon which Your Excellency instructed me. By the treaties signed with the Mission, the British Sphere of influence on the East extends northward along longitude 3° 30' W. On the West our Hinterland becomes conterminous with Gruma and Borgu. . . .

In submitting this report political reflections and moral inferences with regard to interior policy have generally been omitted. The condition of the people of the hinterland had been described. . . . I trust my proceedings connected with the object of securing the hinterland, by treaties, against the encroachments of Foreign Powers may merit Your Excellency's approval.

For the Safety of the Public, and the Welfare of the Race

Gold Coast Aborigines

Published in 1822, the Gold Coast Gazette and Commercial Intelligencer *was the first newspaper of the region, albeit for the colonial government. Though handwritten and designed for European merchants and civil servants, the newspaper also promoted literacy among the Africans schooled at the various Christian missions but sought to do so by repressing their political aspirations and by supporting loyalty to the colonial regime. But such "native" elites would in fact appropriate the technology of print media and English literary attitudes, and a number of African-owned newspapers were created by the late nineteenth century. The* Gold Coast Aborigines *was one of those newspapers, and though it was based in Cape Coast like the* Gold Coast Gazette and Commercial Intelligencer, *its aims were radically different. The excerpt here comes from its first issue (Saturday, January 1, 1898), where the editors lay out their hopes for the paper—which shared much in common with other newspapers of its kind—and in so doing reveal the tensions in colonial society and why the language of race, nation, and literacy mattered.*

For some time, it has been the wish, of the members of the Gold Coast Aborigines Rights Protection Society, to have an organ of their own and the appearance of this paper before the public today is nothing else, but that wish, after all taking a practical shape. For this appearance of the GOLD COAST ABORIGINES we do not think there is any necessity to make [an] apology.

We have in the Colony two or three newspapers, and how faithfully, devotedly and fearlessly these have been doing their work, their readers will judge for themselves, we earnestly hope they will live to continue their noble work. When might would beat right, these speak out, perhaps in some instances, bluffly and boldly, but certainly, justly and fairly; and sticking to their remarks they gain their end: when certain reforms considered necessary by the powers that be in the laws of the country are enacted and are ruthlessly enforced, the journals being more in contact with the people and consequently finding them unworkable put in their veto and the desired effect sooner or later realized; by their endeavors, in a country like ours, where almost all our laws are passed in the Gazette scarcely any effort being put forth by the authorities for the information of the general public concerning them, they have tried that with these laws there be no corners and no night, so that of a few, it may be said, as it was said of the celebrated Lord Somers that they knew of no good law proposed and passed in their time to which these papers did not direct their attention. Theirs has been a considerably arduous task. Nor has the disturber of the peace and quietness of our social world escaped their notice: where necessary, they have instituted a relentless inquisition, exposing every secret to the light of day: they have turned the glare of their solar microscope in every malfeasance thus making the public a more terrible spy, than any private detective; by their efforts no undue advantage has been taken of our weakness, for we have our weaknesses. Thus in a measure we have been rid of those incrustations which might have been our ruin before we knew where we were; we do not forget, that it is usually said, that in spite of all that these journals say, things go on as if nothing has been said; how far this is true, those only know concerning whom those things are said.

Perhaps it would be idle and gratuitous for us to say, that we do not intend to compete with any of these admirable organs: we come forward however to join their ranks, trusting that in some resemblance however distant, we too may endeavor to serve our fatherland. One has only to see the keen interest which recent events have made people to take in politics, and it will be allowed that there is room enough for us, and to spare. The GOLD COAST ABORIGINES has worthy and noble predecessors—these have their own history and trophies; we do not go into any of them here, and to speak from a local point of view, it may be said, that we consider it not a little pride and honor to be able today, to designate ourselves the contemporary of the *Gold Coast Methodist Times*: we may perhaps be reminded by a critic, that this is primarily a religious organ: and so it is, nor has it lost sight of this fact in her short but brilliant career: whatever may be said against it, we know what it has done for us in conjunction with the other organs in other parts of the Colony. We make special mention of the *Times*, because in the eyes of our people her peculiar position as a religious paper, is considered a justifiable reason for it to shut its eyes to the troubles in the land and for this we know it has been its privilege to pass through troubles, apart from those attendant on all such undertakings. Whether the theory, that religious papers on the Gold Coast should take no interest in passing events and all that materially affect the weal or woe of the country but confine themselves to the chronicling of sermonettes, and the reporting of the news of the Churches be right or wrong, we are not prepared to say: we only desire as a people to thank this religious organ in going out of its way to play such a noble part in our political arena: that step might have been wrong—it might have been right—let the results decide.

We trust the GOLD COAST ABORIGINES will honestly undertake to do what the *Times* is requested from certain quarters to leave undone.

Of the many difficulties and drawbacks that usually attend journalism on the coast we are fully aware and enough has been said of these things so that we have no need to repeat them here.

Whilst we are encouraged by the many successes and warned by the failures of some of our predecessors, our hands are also very much strengthened by the fact that comparatively speaking no paper has been started under better auspices, and with such widespread interest in politics (thanks to the Land Bill) as the GOLD COAST ABORIGINES: but we sincerely hope that such enthusiasm as one is forced to see displayed around him, may not die out as days increase: and of ourselves, it is perhaps unnecessary to remind our readers we are but young, with no experience whatever in journalism, quite a novice, but we shall endeavor to do our duty according to our ability, honestly and faithfully without any fear or favor, racial or tribal prejudice: we would seek to pluck the crow with no one. To be brief, we shall only seek to follow, in the wake of our predecessors: and inexperienced as we are, we are emboldened to assume this responsibility, when we glance at our constituency, the Protectorate, to wit. How enthusiastic and full of zeal we all seem to be—may these sweet virtue continue to live amongst us! From Assinee right down to Togoland we may have a few, manly, clever, well-bred men who possess the talent of writing off-hand pungent paragraphs expressing with clearness and courage their opinion on any person or performance: for the good of dear fatherland, we hope these may not hide their talents, but laying aside all selfishness and prejudices where these may exist, they would speak to the country through the GOLD COAST ABORIGINES.

We do not forget that most of our people do not contribute to the papers, simply because, as they say, they [cannot] write: these think, until they are able to make free use of high-sounding, thundering words, to put in here and there some choice, neat phrases and sentences they should make no attempt to write to newspapers. In this they err: such a style is good and does its work in its own way: we do not condemn it, but even those who are able to write like this, are educated to it: in civilized countries for instance, this comes out of the crowded state of the professions, and the interest which all men take in politics &c. Such a state of things is quite an accidental and arbitrary direction or their general ability: we would not be discouraged by this. Academic elegance is good, classic allusions are fine, but to so write as to be easily understood, by the educated and the uneducated is better and finer: indeed in these days it is safer to be as plain and simple in one['s] writing (and speaking for the matter of that) as one possibly can. No one need be discouraged to write. To the young we would mostly appeal, and where is much heat of gallantry shown in the onset, we trust the steadiness of the aim of this paper may be sustained by this fire being directed tempered and fed by older and more experienced hands.

To the Educated Community in the Gold Coast Colony

Carl C. Reindorf

At the end of the nineteenth century, a group of elite intellectuals—nationalists, lawyers, pastors—were emerging as both voices for the aspirations of their segment of Gold Coast society and as intermediates between the indigenous populations and the British colonial government. Self-publishing his History of the Gold Coast and Asante *in 1889 (with a revised English version in 1895), Basel Mission pastor and historian Carl Christian Reindorf (1834–1917) produced the first general history of the Gold Coast peoples written by an African and using a judicious selection of published and oral sources from "more than two hundred persons of both sexes." Reindorf's protracted struggle to publish this work on his own terms and at his own expense, however, testifies to the colonial and even racist context of his times as well as the audience for whom his* History *was written—his contemporaries, the "educated community" of the Gold Coast colony. We have chosen to reproduce Reindorf's preface; in it, we find his message to that audience and through the audience we discover more about the Westernized, Christianized, and "educated" population that would shape the late nineteenth-century and early twentieth-century history of the Gold Coast / Ghana.*

Dear Friends,

The sole object of this publication [i.e., *History of the Gold Coast and Asante*] is, to call the attention of all you my friends and countrymen, to the study and collection of our history, and to create a basis for a future more complete history of the Gold Coast. A history is the methodical narration of events in the order in which they successively occurred, exhibiting the origin and progress, the causes and effects, and the auxiliaries and tendencies of that which has occurred in connection with a nation. It is, as it were, the speculum and measure-tape of that nation, showing its true shape and stature. Hence a nation not possessing a history has no true representation of all the stages of its development, whether it is in a state of progress or in a state of retrogression. In the place of a written history, tradition, which from antiquity was a natural source of history, was kept and transmitted regularly by our ancestors to their children in their days. It was not, of course, in uniform theory, but existed and exercised its influence in the physical and mental powers of our people. This important custom of a nation—which our forefathers felt obliged to preserve and transmit from one generation to another, so as to enable us to compare our times with theirs—has, since the dawn of education, been gradually neglected and forgotten. Since then it has been the good fortune of the Gold Coast to possess educated men of powerful mind, who I am sure were well qualified to collect the traditions of their forefathers as a basis for a future history of the Gold Coast. But unfortunately such collections have not been preserved by their successors, but have been left to the memories of the uneducated community. Such a work as writing a history of the Gold Coast would not have been difficult for such of our brethren as the late lamented Rev. William Hansen, and Charles Bannerman, and some others in Fante; they possessed the mental powers which would have enabled them to do it successfully. Unfortunately, however, these lights on the Gold Coast were carried away by death in the prime of life.

A history of the Gold Coast written by a foreigner would most probably not be correct in its statements, he not having the means of acquiring the different traditions in the country and of comparing them with those which he may have gathered from a single individual. Unless a foreigner writes what he witnesses personally, his statements will be comparatively worthless, as it is the case with several accounts of the Gold Coast already published. Hence it is most desirable that a history of the Gold Coast and its people should be written by one who has not only studied, but has had the privilege of initiation into the history of its former inhabitants and writes with true native patriotism.

It is no egotism when I say I have had the privilege of being initiated into, and also possessing a love for, the history of my country. My ancestors on the father's and mother's side belonged to the families of national officiating high priests in Akra [Nkran/Accra] and Christiansborg. And I should have become a priest either of Nai at Akra or Klote at Christiansborg, if I had not been born a mulatto and become a Christian. My worthy grandmother Okako Asase, as in duty bound to her children and grandchildren, used to relate the traditions of the country to her people when they sat around her in the evenings. My education and calling separated me from home, and prevented me from completing the series of these lessons in native tradition. However, in 1860 I felt a craving to spend some days with her, so as to complete it; but she died whilst I was absent from home in Krobo as a catechist. Four years later Rev. Fr. Aldinger asked me to collect traditions for him; but the old lady was dead, and the old people, though possessing a vast store of tradition, refrained from imparting it; so I obtained very little for him. This treatment of the then old people stirred up a greater desire in me to use all available means in my power to collect traditions. From more than two hundred persons of both sexes I obtained what knowledge of the subject I now possess. These traditions I have carefully compared in order to arrive at the truth. The result I now humbly present to the public, to whom I have to suggest a few remarks. If a nation's history is the nation's speculum and measure-tape, then it brings the past of that nation to its own view, so that the past may be compared with the present to see whether progress or retrogression is in operation; and also as a means of judging our nation by others, so that we may gather instruction for our future guidance. When such is not the case with a nation, no hope can be entertained for better prospects. Keeping this in mind, we shall more clearly understand the necessity of collecting materials for a complete history of the Gold Coast from every source within our reach.

The title chosen for this publication, "History of the Gold Coast and Asante," may be deemed to promise more than I was actually able to give. For, from want of reliable information, the principal and important portion of the Gold Coast, Fante, the land of history, the land of poetry and enlightenment and semi-civilization, could not be treated from its origin. Still I venture to have the book so named in the hope that our brethren and friends on the Gold Coast, both native and European, may possess better sources of information for a history of the Gold Coast, and may, laying aside all prejudice, be induced to unite to bring the history of the Gold Coast to perfection; I deem it impossible for one man unaided to carry out such an important work to perfection. Having described the principal object I have in view in writing this work as a desire to produce a complete history of the Gold Coast, I trust, my friends in Fante, or elsewhere, will cooperate with me in revising, if need be, what I have written, and in assisting me by furnishing additional information, in order that a subsequent edition may be more complete.

Another important subject, besides that of Fante, &c., which ought to be more fully investigated before the work would be complete, is the different conditions and concerns of various European nations on the Gold Coast and their connections with the people there since their establishment in this country. I may also state briefly my object in connecting the history of Asante with that of the Gold Coast. There must be a starting point in writing a history of a nation. If the kingdom of Akra, which appears to have been the first established on the Gold Coast, could have continued and absorbed that of Fante, or been absorbed by the latter, I might have easily obtained the starting point. But both kingdoms having failed and the kingdom of Asante having become the leading and ruling power, a Gold Coast history would not be complete without the history of Asante, as the histories of both countries are so interwoven. Thus my present work carries us from the origin of the different [groups] to the year 1856, i.e. the rebuilding of the town of Osu or Christiansborg, a period of at least three centuries. If, in conjunction with the united efforts of all the educated community of the country and those foreigners who take a special interest in us, we could collect materials of those dark days to complete this pioneer work, that from 1857 up to the present time, some thirty years only, could be easily obtained, as there is sufficient matter already in store for us.

Regarding dates and historical facts, I have made references to such works as I could lay hand upon. The records of the Colonial Government would have furnished me with correct dates and substantial informations [*sic*], but I was unable to obtain access to them. I am, however, highly thankful to the Rev. P. Steiner for the translation of some pages from the following work into German, viz.: W. J. Muller, Danish chaplain in Frederiksborg (now Fort Victoria) near Cape Coast Castle from 1662 to 1670, published in Hamburg, 1673, and in Nürnberg, 1675; Fr. Romer, a Danish merchant in Christiansborg from 1735 to 1743, published at Copenhagen 1769; Dr. P. E. Isert, Copenhagen, 1788; H. C. Monrad, a Danish Chaplain in Christiansborg from 1805 to 1809, Weimar, 1824; Dr. O. Dapper's *Africa*. The short history of the Bremen Mission was kindly given me by the Rev. G. Binetsch, of the North German or Bremen Mission on the Slave Coast. Besides those, I have got the following works in English: William Bosman, *A new and accurate Description of the Coast of Guinea, [divided] into the Gold, the Slave, and the Ivory Coasts*, 1705; Bowdich, *Mission to Ashantee*; Cruickshank, *Eighteen Years on the Gold Coast*; Sir [John] Dal[rymple] Hay, *Ashanti and the Gold Coast*; *The British Battles*; *A brief history of the Wesleyan Missions on the Western Coasts of Africa* by William Fox, 1851; the *Report of the Basel Mission for 1879, or a Retrospect on fifty years Mission Work*; and the *Gold Coast Almanack* for 1842 and 1843, with some few manuscripts of the late Old James Bannerman and Charles Bannerman, which were kindly communicated to me by Edmund Bannerman and from which I obtained some information about Sir Charles McCarthy's war with Asante. And lastly, I am thankful to the Rev. A. W. Parker and the Rev. John H. Davies M.A., the Colonial Chaplain, for their information.

And in conclusion I must beg you, my native friends, not to despise this work coming from one of your own brethren, but let it rather encourage you to assist me by your kind information and co-operation, so as to get our own history complete. To interest you chiefly I collected so many names of our forefathers, who defended our country from the yoke of Asante, trusting that every one of you will be pleased to find his grandfather's name in the lists. May our dear Lord bless this poor means I now offer to the public for the improvement of ourselves as well as our country!

IV

Colonial Rule and Political Independence, 1900–1957

In its transition from "model colony" to "model democracy," Ghana's official colonial past was rather brief in terms of foreign rule, but quite influential, as evidenced in the myriad ways British colonialism still affects Ghana's present. Colonialism was not simply territorial occupation and an exploitation of valued human and material resources, but also an ideological occupation of the subjugated psyche. Consequently, this period is characterized by a constant negotiation between so-called traditional values and its colonial counterparts. Viewed from this perspective, Ghana could not (and did not) begin its life as an independent republic with peace and equanimity. Political elites, conditioned by colonial schooling and cultural values, differed profoundly in their vision of what the nation's identity and destiny should be. This section provides readers with a sense of the tremendous difficulties inherent in forming a nation while Ghana's structural position remained that of a colony and, later, postcolony.[1] This section will also recognize Ghana's role as a center of pan-Africanism long before the Nkrumah era, by looking at protonationalist movements that advocated nationalist as well as pan-African aspirations.

The physical geography of the colony that later became Ghana was formed by 1901, after the Yaa Asantewaa War of 1900. The victorious British sought to consolidate their martial dominance of the region by incorporating the Northern Territories and the Asante heartland into protectorates that became part of the Gold Coast Colony proper. From the early 1900s to political independence in 1957, the British colonial enterprise was mostly concerned with the extraction of resources. Ghana, which had a long history of producing gold, also experienced a "gold rush" at the turn of the twentieth century. In addition, there was a marked increase in the demand for cocoa, and Ghana, where the value of women's labor on cocoa farms became increasingly important, was poised to be a major supplier in that market. These factors combined to make the Gold Coast an important economic colony for the British. Some Gold Coasters who benefited from this economic upturn invested monies in procuring Western schooling for their children, resulting in unintended consequences for Britain. The same British schooling that is often touted as a benefit of colonialism soon served to provide Ghanaians with means to effectively claim the moral high ground in their relationship with the colonizer, based on principles of liberty and equality. Building on the precedent of local agitations against British rule, set in motion through the efforts of people such as King Aggrey and movements such as the Fante Confederation and the Aborigines Rights Protection Society, British-schooled Ghanaians were able to mold themselves into a unit that would demand political independence not only for the Gold Coast but for all of British West Africa. The National Congress of British West Africa, for example, was perhaps the first truly pan-African organization in the region. Formed in 1920, its founding members included many who are now considered among the pantheon of Ghanaian nationalists. This organization's formation, while not successful in its ultimate aim, signaled a clear indication that the colony wanted to be free from colonial rule.

By the middle of the century, Ghanaians were effectively challenging the status quo vis-à-vis Britain's relationship with the colony. Lessons learned by those who had to endure certain aspects of the colonial experience further informed this challenge. For instance, soldiers sent to fight for freedom and justice abroad returned to the Gold Coast imbued with a strong sense of accomplishment and the conviction that humans should not live in servitude of other humans. More importantly, the "myth" of European (male) superiority was debunked on the battlefields of the two world wars. Clashes in Accra between local ex-service men and the colonial government over unpaid benefits brought this into sharp relief in 1948.

Adding to the country's birthing pains, specific cultural, geographic, and religious affiliations came to characterize the new political parties that competed for stewardship of the colony as the Gold Coast grappled with whether or not to adopt a federal system of government as it moved toward political independence. The 1954 election, not surprisingly, was contested by a number of these ethnic or religion-based parties: the Togoland Congress, formed in 1951, agitated for the unification and independence of Togoland (present-day Togo and the Volta Region in Ghana); the Muslim Association Party, formed in 1953, was religion-based and as such opposed forging a new and united nation out of the multicultural colony; and the Northern People's Party, formed in 1954, promoted the interest of the marginalized peoples of the northern parts of the colony.

All this was further complicated by the Asante-based National Liberation Movement, which was formed in 1954 and argued for a federal constitution that would give the region control over its vast cocoa wealth. This position stood in stark contrast to the agenda of the ruling Convention People's Party (CPP) and, along with the anti-Asante Bonokyempem movement based in Techiman (Takyiman), was one of the factors behind the 1959 legislation that created a new administrative region—Brong-Ahafo—out of the Ashanti Region, effectively weakening the Asante position. Finally, there was the question of Togoland. Since the First World War, German Togoland had been divided and assigned to the British and French for administration. With independence approaching, the section of Togoland under British administration grappled with whether they should opt to be part of an independent Ghana or unite with the French-controlled portion of Togoland. In a context of growing internal resentment and of a global decolonization movement, those who became Ghanaians were able to effectively negotiate their political independence in a process that culminated in 1957, when the world experienced the "Birth of Ghana."

Note

1. For more on the notion of a postcolony, see Achille Mbembe, "Provisional Notes on the Postcolony," *Africa: Journal of the International African Institute* 62, no. 1 (1992): 3–37, and *On the Postcolony* (Berkeley: University of California Press, 2001).

The Petition of 1913

Agyeman Prempeh I

The British defeat of Asante after years of civil war and internal political strife within the latter half of the nineteenth century culminated with the exile of its leader, Asantehene Agyeman Prempeh I (1870–1931), to the Seychelles Islands in 1900. While a political prisoner in the Seychelles, Agyeman Prempeh composed or had committed to writing a number of historical and ethnographic pieces. Among them, a petition written in 1913 is instructive because it details the events leading up to the 1896 Anglo-Asante War and his deportation, with the conviction that remorse or apology was the best way to convince the British to repatriate him. In the petition addressed to Governor Charles R. M. O'Brien (1859–1935) of the Seychelles Islands, which appears here, Prempeh wrote, "We now take the opportunity in submitting this petition to confess our sin and fault which has led us to this fate, and to humble ourselves lowly and reverently for your Excellency's kind consideration." Gold Coast governor Hugh Clifford (1866–1941) opposed Prempeh's repatriation, and the petition was dismissed.

Our ancient King Kofi Karkari in his time raised up a large army against the Fantis who were close to the Coast without any cause or reason of attacking them. A great battle was fought in which the Fantis were defeated and driven as far as to a district known as Afoutou Manpon. Where Amanquatchia, the commander-in-chief of the Ashanti received a message from the English Governor on the coast that His Excellency congratulates the Ashantis for their bravery in expelling the Fantis to such an extent and requested the Ashanti troops to retire from Afoutou Manpon where they had reached and to give up the fight and fail to do so, the English Government will interfere in the fight and take up the part of the Fantis for the said place where they had reached is a British town.

The Ashanti's army neglected the advice given to them by the Governor and continued to fight and persued [*sic*] the enemy as far as to a district known as Bankranpan where the Ashanti army met with the English army under the command of Lord Wolseley; the Ashanti army was defeated and Lord Wolseley entered the capital Kumasi.

But Lord Wolseley remained three days at Kumasi and was so good towards us that he did not devastate our town but only laid a fine on us which we were allowed to pay by instalments [*sic*] to the English Government to recover the cost of Lord Wolseley's expenses in the war; and before Lord Wolseley set off from Kumasi, he gave the following orders to the Ashantis that:

1st. Not to kill people.

2nd. Not to block the route of traders to prevent communication from the coast to the main-land.

3rd. To have a new route be made from Kumasi to a district known as Fominah.

4th. The Ashantis from the date have not to go to war without the permission of the English who are from the date bind themselves to protect them.

Only a minimum part of the fine laid upon them was paid; the King and the chiefs did not carry out the orders given to them; and the result was that King Karkari was dethroned and his Younger brother Bonsu was crowned; the latter also did not carry out the orders and raised up an army against the King of Juabin without the knowledge of the Governor. After the war the Governor sent ambassadors to Kumasi to claim for the fine laid upon them by Lord Wolseley. The reason for having gone against the 4th rule of Lord Wolseley; but King Bonsu only paid £2400._. _. out of the rest of the fine.

The Governor sent another ambassador to King Bonsu asking him to accept the institutions of school buildings for training at Kumasi; the King and the chiefs refused to accept same; and the end was that King Bonsu was dethroned by his own people.

After the dethroning of King Bonsu, there was a great rebellion in the country which lasted about ten years and all the time the chiefs in the town were trying to put a King on the throne to obtain peace, but their trials were in vain. Then the chiefs sent ambassadors on the Coast to the Governor to ask for assistance; the Governor acted very kindly and sent two English officers to Kumasi to help the chiefs and about four months the officers had completed the task which had lasted the Ashantis ten years and even had not been able to find an end of it.—and I Prempeh was proclaimed the King of Ashanti under an age of about 16 years.

A couple of months after I was proclaimed, the Governor sent another officer to Kumasi to announce that as his Excellency himself has set a King on the throne, he will make the King as a planted tree which is being watered and had grown up favorably; and to be able to do so, there must be Education Buildings for training;—and if we do accept this term, the officer to remain 40 days at Kumasi to put everything in proper order. But I the King and all the inhabitants not knowing that it was for our own good, refused to accept same.—

In the last rebellion most of the Ashantis went and served under the Government on the coast and when through the help of the English I was made a King, I sent ambassadors to the Governor and begged to send back my men who were under him. The Governor in reply sent an English officer named Captain Stewart and an interpreter Froem and announced that if education is accepted in Kumasi, all my men under the Government shall be sent back to me.—

2nd. The Government will not interfere in the exercising of my power against my people.—

3rd. The Government will also pay to me, the Queen and each regiment each a certain amount per year.

4th. The Government will also hold responsible to protect Ashanti against her foes.

These were the 4 messages sent to us by the Governor and to this excellent bargain, we allowed ourselves to be deceived by our own mischievousness and refused to accept same.—

Besides these few instances we have procured, there are many other faults which we had done to Government and which we confess they are too numerous to procure; we always under the persuasions that ours were the best.—

After refusing several advices, the Government at last set on to exercise its power over us by taking us prisoners; and when I the time that we should be captured was nigh, I reflected over the past good deeds of the English Government towards me by putting me on the throne and moreover promised to make the best of me which we refused, we made up our minds to surrender than to resist to make matters worst.—

About 4 or 5 years after I and some of my chiefs were captured, the few remaining chiefs at Kumasi instead of submitting themselves loyally and reverently under the supervision of the English Government and followed my step of not to resist, they misbehaved and after resisting against the Government, they were also captured and sent to meet me. And since we are here, we sympathize greatly for our misdeeds; but we blessed our Sovereign King George V for the kind treatment and Supervision we still receiving in His Majesty's hands.

Fathering, Mothering, and Making Sense of *Ntamoba* in Colonial Asante

Jean Allman

The literature on Ghana is saturated with a number of ethnographic and historical studies on Asante. Jean Allman, a professor of history at Washington University in St. Louis, departs significantly from the master narrative of Asante history—which focuses on the Asante empire at its peak—by exploring changes in the social structure of Asante during the colonial era. In Asante, ntamoba *was understood as a form of payment given to the father of a young woman by a prospective husband. The payment can be explained as compensation to the father for losing the services of his daughter. In this excerpt from a scholarly article, Allman offers a detailed explanation of the concept and practice of* ntamoba, *and its connection to the father, the larger matrikin, and the responsibilities of children. The author also examines the disappearance of this practice from "traditional" Asante notions of fathering and mothering in the colonial era, which she connects with broader changes within the colonial economy in Asante as a whole.*

Some Contradictory Pieces of the Puzzle

Fortunately, among the few written sources there is some consensus on meaning. The second edition of Christaller's *Dictionary of the Asante and Fante Language* defines *tammoba* as "indemnification to parents for a child that refuses to stay with them and runs away to the relations, *to be paid by the latter.*" . . . Danquah (1928) provides a more elaborate but similar definition. It warrants fuller quotation:

> A father has right of use over his children, but the true ownership is vested in their maternal family. The tie between mother and child can scarcely be broken; but the relationship between father and child can be destroyed by a customary process. This is the process involved in "Tamboba." It not infrequently happens that a father has to part with

Mother and Son. Mosaic by Martin Numadzi, 2009. Courtesy of the artist.

> his "right of use" over his children in favour of their maternal relations. This demand is generally made by the wife's family. . . . For the father to part with his life interest in the children our customary law provides that a sum of money fixed by law and called Tamboba should be paid to him in respect of each child so taken away by its maternal relations.

So far, so good. But what of the oral sources?

Of those older Asantes with whom I have spoken in recent years, a majority did not recognize the term at all. Of those who recognized *ntamoba* and spoke with some confidence as they defined it, most remembered it as a marriage payment of one sort or another. . . . It is a response I found to be particularly common in Kumasi, especially around the *ahemfie* (palace) at Manhyia. . . . Nana Baffuor Osei Akoto, another of the Asantehene's senior linguists and, at age ninety-two, widely regarded as a leading authority on custom and tradition, also associates *ntamoba* with marriage and the payment of a fee by the husband-to-be to his future father-in-law (Akoto interview).

But other older Asantes, many of them outside of Kumasi proper, connect *ntamoba* not with rites of marriage but with rites of birth. Yaa Dufie of Effiduasi explains that "when you give birth to a child and you are going to name the child, the things that the father brings to the child after the naming are called *ntamoba*" (Dufie interview). Efua Tebiaa of Agogo provides a similar definition, along with some etymological detail. She suggests that the term comes from the phrase *tan a wo ba* (the father who has given birth to a child) and that, in order for a man to be recognised as *tan a wo ba,* he must meet certain financial obligations: "If the father gives birth to a child and he doesn't look after the child, and the child grows, and he wants to go for the child, he will be asked to pay all the expenses that the woman incurred in looking after the child."

Thomas E. Kyei, an Asante educator who worked with Meyer Fortes on the Ashanti Social Survey, remembers *ntamoba* . . . as a sum "paid by the family to the father to signify that the father has been relieved of all the fatherhood responsibilities." Kyei recalls only one such case from his childhood in Agogo. "There have to be extraordinary circumstances," he explains, "for a father's rights in his children to be totally severed."

Kwame Nkansah, a ninety-year-old man living in Agogo, explained: "You have given birth to a son. You have raised him and then he says he will not serve you. Then you have to get *ntamoba*. You will get it from his family."

Aberration or Artifact: Historicizing the Conflicting Fragments

So what is one to make of these conflicting and contradictory definitions—*ntamoba* as any number of marriage payments, *ntamoba* as a rite connected with birthing and naming, and *ntamoba* as marking the termination of a father's rights in his offspring? That the definition of *ntamoba* as a marriage payment to the wife's father was widespread in Kumasi, especially around the Asantehene's court, and that the definitions closest to the Bompata case seem to derive, like the Bompata material, either from Asante Akyem or from Akyem itself, may suggest that the inconsistencies here are simply geographical. This simple formulation, however, would not explain why many older, longtime inhabitants of Agogo (Asante Akyem) unequivocally define *ntamoba* as a marriage payment, or why the informants in M. J. Field's 1938 study in Akyem offered similar testimony. The problem may, indeed, be one not simply of location but of time and of social rank. . . .

First of all, we should recognise that the multiple definitions emerging in both oral and written sources are not entirely disconnected. They all seem to share an underlying concern for a husband/father's reciprocal obligations and rights *vis-à-vis* his wife's and/or his children's family, or *abusua*. All these definitions situate *ntamoba* as a mechanism through which an *abusua*'s relationship with the husbands/fathers of its members is mediated. . . .

The Disappearance of Ntamoba *and Transformations in the Family Economy of Child-Rearing*

And so what happened? How and why may this notion of *ntamoba* have disappeared from the historical record?

I would like to propose here a two-stage hypothesis that attempts to foreground time and social place/status as key variables in explaining the disappearance of *ntamoba*. The first stage is based on the postulation that *ntamoba* is of great antiquity, that as a mechanism for mediating the relationship between a man and his wife/children's *abusua* it may very well date back to the creation, in the fifteenth and sixteenth centuries, of the great Akan matriclans. . . . But does *ntamoba* continue to make sense, as we move from Asante's immediate protohistorical period *(firi tetemu)* to the historical? The answer is—for some, yes, but for others, no. The emergence of the Akan state *(oman)* coincided with the emergence of specific social groups or classes for whom *ntamoba* would have made little sense. Again, Wilks's work on Asante's early history provides some important clues. In "Founding the Political Kingdom" he argues for the critical role of entrepreneurs ("big men" or *aberempɔn*) in the founding of the early Akan state. . . . The descendants of these early developers became the nobility, the *adehyeɛ,* of the state and were distinguished from both free settlers (*ɔmanmufo*) and from the unfree. Many from among this latter group, Wilks hypothesises, were incorporated into Akan society as members of the *gyaasefo* (the people of the hearth), who were the servants of the nobility. Certainly, for the nobility and for the unfree, *ntamoba* could not mediate transactions surrounding marriage and child-rearing in the same way it did for free-born commoners. For example, the slave wives of an *ɔberempɔn* gave birth to children who were incorporated into their father's lineage, not into the lineage of their mother, who was considered kinless. While *ntamoba* as a marriage payment to the *ɔberempɔn* father may make sense here, little else does, for the father and his royal lineage quite clearly owned such children and had rights over them that a male commoner married to a female commoner simply did not. The meaning of patrilineality, in other words, had to become class/rank-specific. I would like to suggest, therefore, that the first stage in *ntamoba*'s fracturing and eventual disappearance coincided with the emergence of the state in the Akan forest. While *ntamoba* could continue to articulate the ongoing exchange between a common man and the *abusua* of his free wives and children, it was obsolete in the realm of power, wealth, and privilege in which both *ɔberempɔn* and *gyaasefo* operated. In that world, trees might stand in the street but—the Akan proverb notwithstanding—the roots of some of them could be found there, as well. . . .

By the time we reach the restoration of the Asante Confederacy Council in 1935, if not decades before, *ntamoba* clearly exists only in a rare, vestigial form and primarily as a type of marriage payment. Even among commoners we have only scant evidence of its existence. Why? It is my speculation that *ntamoba* vanishes among commoners in the late nineteenth and early twentieth centuries for the same reason it was reconfigured among Asante's ruling classes hundreds of years before. To put it quite simply, *ntamoba* no longer made sense for anyone—rulers or ruled, noble or commoner. And it no longer made sense because a commoner father's rights in his children, like an *ɔberempɔn*'s rights over his non-free children, had become inalienable. . . .

After 1924 and the implementation of the Native Jurisdiction Ordinance in Asante, colonial administrators empowered chiefs and their councilors to rule on "custom," so it is after 1924 with the establishment of native tribunals throughout the region that we encounter a wide range of customary court documentation that allows us to chart changes in so-called "customary law." Certainly, from the very beginning of this period, we see numerous cases in which native tribunals rule on inheritance cases in favor, at least partially, of a wife's and/or children's claim on a husband's/father's estate. These cases reflect a growing social tendency, I would argue, to recognize an inalienable connection between fathers and children. In child custody/child maintenance cases, however, a noticeable change in judgments occurs more slowly and less dramatically. Many of the judgments from cases of the late 1920s and early 1930s seem to echo what we know of rights in and obligations toward children in the precolonial period. In these cases reciprocity was upheld. For example, in *Kwadjo Safo v. Kwame Antwi et al.* (Native Tribunal of the Kumasihene, 1929b), the plaintiff claimed £100 in damages from his wife's family because, as he testified, "they had deprived me of my children." When subsequent testimony proved that the father had not supported his children over the years, the plaintiff was nonsuited with costs "in that his action is inconsistent with Native Customary Law."

In cases like this, and countless others, *ntamoba* makes absolutely no sense, because paternal rights were, at once, severed from paternal duties and transformed from rights of use to inalienable rights of ownership. Indeed, a father's relation to his child and to his wife's children's *abusua* resembled nothing less than the relations which prevailed in precolonial and early colonial times, when a father held his child as a pawn—a practice technically outlawed by the British in 1908. . . .

As pawnage was collapsed into the categories of son, daughter, and wife, rights, duties, and obligations in Asante were broadly recast. The rights of the colonial father/husband became the rights of the nineteenth-century pawn-holder. And those rights, in turn, became increasingly detached from reciprocal obligations and duties. We need to connect the final disappearance of *ntamoba* in Asante, therefore, with the conflation of subordinant categories or, more specifically, with wife/pawn, daughter/pawn, son/pawn. That *ntamoba* survived in Asante only in a vestigial form, as a marriage payment from son-in-law to father-in-law, makes sense in this context. Only in this form did *ntamoba* not challenge or undercut the inalienable rights of ownership of the colonial Asante father. As a one-way marriage payment from son-in-law to father-in-law, it was given in recognition of all that the father had endured in raising the child and marked the moment wherein (certainly not the *process* whereby) the daughter/pawn became wife/pawn, as well.

The Blinkards

Kobina Sekyi

Born in 1892 in Cape Coast, Kobina Sekyi pursued higher education at the University of London and the Inns of Court, where he studied law. In 1918, he began practicing law in Cape Coast and was active in politics until his death in 1956. Despite the opportunity to accept the status quo and enjoy a life of relative ease, Sekyi chose to champion the cause of African freedom by involving himself in the two most prominent protonationalist movements in Ghana: the Aborigines Rights Protection Society and the National Congress of British West Africa. Challenging British overlordship in the Gold Coast through his acumen, Sekyi became one of the foremost intellectual nationalists of Ghana. The Blinkards, *written in 1915, is set in that same period in Cape Coast and lampoons how Gold Coasters imitate British culture often at the cost of their own, regardless how ludicrous it made them appear. The following excerpt from this satire underscores the depth of cultural imperialism that afflicted the affluent on the Gold Coast—poorer Gold Coasters simply could not afford the material trappings required to "be British." In the satire, Sekyi calls into question the commitment of well-to-do Fante peoples toward their own culture.*

Scene One

Mrs Borɔfosɛm's Drawing-room. Doors R. & L.
Enter Nyamikyɛ, in short knickers and singlet, with dust-pan and brush, L.

NYAM *(sweeping)* I wonder why I always find cigar-ashes here, when I come to dust this room always. I shall sweep them up once more and see if there will be any more tomorrow. I should like to know what is the use of sweeping a room which is never clean. *(Sees a nicely-bound book)* What a pretty book this is! *(Places brush and pan on floor, and takes up book)* I'll open it. *(Opens book. Some dried leaves fall out)* O! What are these dried leaves in the book for? I suppose they are to be swept away—I'll pick them up.

Enter Mrs Borɔfosɛm, in a loose European undress gown, lorgnette on nose. L.

Group portrait of three Fanti women, Ghana. The two seated women hold umbrellas. Unidentified photographer, ca. 1910. EEPA 1995-018-0067. Ghana Photographs [between 1885 and 1910], Eliot Elisofon Photographic Archives, National Museum of African Art, Smithsonian Institution.

MRS BORƆFO Look here, you idiot, what are you up to? Give me those leaves *(Takes leaves from Nyamikyɛ)*. You are too much of a bushman. Haven't I told you that, in England, leaves are placed in books to dry, the books when the leaves are dry, being placed in the drawing rooms? *(Replaces leaves in book, shuts it with a snap and thumps it back to its place. Sees ashes in dust-pan, takes up pan and thrusts it in Nyamikyɛ's face.)* And what have you swept up those ashes for? How often do you want me to tell you that cigar-ashes are good for carpets? Do you not know that, in England, cigar-ashes are used to kill the moths in the carpets? *(. . .)* You are a great nuisance. Get out of this room. *(Exit Nyamikyɛ, L.)* How sweet this room looks *(Looks round admiringly)*. When I reflect that our forefathers had only *ntwoma* to scour their floors with, and had no pretty washes for their walls. I feel glad that I was not born in their days, when they lived their lives in darkness. I am particularly glad to have been born in the period when Religion had brought us refinement. *(Sits in an easy chair)* Consider this chair, for instance. You sink into it when you sit in it, it is so pleasantly soft. It is not like the native stool, which gives you a pain in the loins when you sit on it. *(Looks perplexedly at ceiling)* What I cannot understand is that, in spite of all which makes our lives so enjoyable, our ancestors, whose lives seem so hard to us, lived longer and were happier than we can live or be. *(Jumps up suddenly)* Just fancy! I do not now practise the songs I was told to sing, when I was in England. *(Sings falsetto)*

Snowdrops, lift your bell-like petals,
Ding! Ring! Ni—ng!

I have forgotten the pronunciation of the word: is it *peetal* or *pettal*? I'll consult my dictionary. *(Exit. L.)*

Enter Mr Borɔfosɛm L. in pyjamas and slippers. Smoking a cigar, with newspaper in his hand.

MR BORƆFO I heartily curse the day my wife decided to go to England. Ever since then, I have had nothing but we *must* do this, because it is done in England, we *mustn't* do that, because it is not done by English people and so on *ad nauseam*. *(Sits down, and spreads out newspaper)* It serves us jolly well right for allowing ourselves to be dazzled by all this flimsy foreign frippery. (*Throws away newspaper, gets up, and walks up and down*) The worst of it is that some of us got into these foreign ways through no fault of our own. We were born into a world of imitators, worse luck . . . and blind imitators, at that. They could not and cannot, distinguish cause from effect, so they have not been able to trace effect to cause, as yet. They see a thing done in England, or by somebody white; then they say we must do the same thing in Africa. It is that confounded *must* that annoys me. Why *must*? Dash it all! It becomes deuced unpleasant when it involves the sacrifice of one's comfort during the daylight hours, at least. *(Winks at the audience and laughs)* Ha! Ha! If I had not been 'cute enough to make a bargain with my wife—By the way, you know my wife don't you? You've seen her here. You simply couldn't help seeing her, I'll wager. She jumps to the eyes, as, I think, the French say. Well, as I was saying, if I had not been 'cute enough to make a bargain with my wife, my life would be perfectly miserable. You see, she says she heard in England that cigar-ashes were good for carpets. So she allows me to wear pajamas and slippers in the house, when we have no visitors, on condition that I smoke cigars, and spread the ashes about. *(Knocks on to floor the lump of ash at end of cigar)* Rather a good idea, that, don't you think so? Fact is I like cigars. That's one of my weaknesses. You say cigars are European? Of course they are. *(Walks to extreme edge of stage)* But then, my parents set out deliberately to make me as much like a European as possible, before they sent me to England. They would have bleached my skin, if they could. I am rather glad that idiotic American hair-straightening thing did not come out in their time. I am sure they would have got me one: and I should have looked like a mad golliwog. *(Cigar goes out. He finds matches on the floor. Relights cigar, and takes a few appreciative puffs.)* I remember I was often caned for not wanting to wear boots and thick stockings, I always used to take them off when I was beyond view of the parental eye. Ha! Ha! But I must confess to my shame, that I feel hampered when I put on the native dress, because I do not know how to wear it properly: it is always slipping from my shoulder. That is why I wear pajamas in the house: they are the freest clothing my wife will permit. Just fancy that I, a Fanti, should be able to express my thoughts better in English, because I evolved from youthhood into manhood in England: Then, when I want now to speak my own language as much as possible, my wife compels me to speak to her always in English, since otherwise the sulks.

The Trial of Akrofi

R. E. Obeng

Richard Emmanuel Obeng (1868–1951) was born in Akropong and worked as a teacher/headmaster before serving as treasurer to the Kwahu State Council. After retirement, he began writing his first novel. Published in 1943 and considered the seminal novel from the Gold Coast, Eighteen Pence *traces the fortunes of its protagonist, Akrofi, from a state of impoverishment to wealth and success. Forced to pawn himself as labor to pay for a cutlass that cost eighteen pence (hence the book's title), Akrofi embraces the latest agricultural techniques of his day and is able to amass a sizable fortune through assiduousness. Set in the Kwahu Mountains, Akrofi's story extols the values of hard work, honesty, and rural life against a backdrop of encroaching colonial influences in agriculture, education, and jurisprudence and how these different factors confront their counterparts in Kwahu society. The excerpt below looks at how Akrofi, within this context, negotiated an encounter with the local ruler in a colonial court.*

Akrofi was arraigned before the District Commissioner on a charge of having dug up a jar of treasure which was the property of the Kwahu Stool, and of having kept it for himself instead of taking it to the Omanhene and claiming his share.

When the charge was laid before the District Commissioner and the Registrar asked Akrofi how he pleaded, the Commissioner stated that a case involving the sum of a hundred thousand pounds could not be tried by his Court; therefore it was transferred to the High Court, to be tried by his Lordship the Chief Justice of the Gold Coast Colony and its Dependencies.

There were already many cases on the Chief Registrar's list, and as Akrofi's charge was not heinous according to British Law, he was allowed to remain at large. When some of the other cases had been disposed of, he was called before the judge. As the local lawyers usually demanded exorbitant fees, especially in cases involving such large sums as this one, Akrofi did not retain a lawyer.

Akrofi stated that he bought a piece of land which he farmed, and, while digging on a part of the farm, he dug up a jar. According to custom, he sprinkled blood on it and took it home. Before he had time to report this discovery in the proper quarter, he was arrested, and, without any investigation being made, was sent for trial. At the Native Tribunal he declared that that Tribunal had no jurisdiction in a case involving a sum of a hundred thousand pounds, and so it was transferred to the British Court.

His Lordship said that if Akrofi bought the land on which the treasure was found, then, in the sight of the British law, there was no reason to bring him to trial. A letter was sent to the Omanhene to inquire whether the land was really sold to Akrofi or not. Very soon a reply arrived, declaring that Akrofi had not bought the land, for it had been given to him freely as a citizen of the State; and in these circumstances, any citizen discovering treasure was bound to present that treasure intact, to the Ohene of the State.

Akrofi was again called and charged with having made a false statement. It now appeared that the first case had been put aside, for he had to prove to the satisfaction of the Court that he bought the land. He therefore asked the permission of the Judge to retain the services of a barrister, and this request was granted. He also wished his son Sam to come to help him. But as Sam was a Government Official, filling the post of a District Magistrate, the Colonial Secretary decreed that he could not take any professional part in this case. This perturbed Akrofi not a little, for though Sam could give him advice, he could not render assistance in a professional capacity. However, a newly-arrived barrister having been consulted, Akrofi decided to retain him. His name was William James Akotua, M.A., LL.B., Ph.D. He asked Akrofi for a retaining fee of two hundred and fifty pounds, which was paid at once. . . .

The Omanhene's representatives arrived in Accra and retained the services of a barrister from Lagos, named Okulola. He too was a well-qualified lawyer, holding the same degrees as Akotua.

When the day came for the hearing of the case both lawyers appeared in Court to display their ability and eloquence. Okulola opened the case for the prosecution and addressed the Judge and the Court as follows:

"Your Lordship, and you, gentlemen of the jury! It is well known in every corner of this Colony that in the days of yore, the Ashantis were very aggressive, waging unlawful wars against peaceful people and States, such as the Kwahu State. Because of their strength and power, they carried all before them. This continued until the year 1826, when all the Amanhene and principal Chiefs along the Coast combined in resistance, aided by the British Government. During the month of August, King Osei Yaw was defeated at Akantamansu. His gold stool was almost captured by the enemy, but the brave King of Juaben, Nana Boaten Akuamoa, fought with the fury of a lion and recaptured it for him. As it is, there is no person in this Court who has not had an ancestor killed in one of these bloodthirsty Ashanti wars. It would annoy and [antagonize] the Ashantis, who believe that they always had a reason and gave a warning if need be. Because of this, well-to-do persons used to bury their treasure to prevent it from falling into the hands of the invading armies. In those days, if a person were gentle and taciturn, he was proverbially spoken of as being 'tame and simple as a Kwahu man'!

"Since time immemorial, the people of this State have been enterprising. . . . In short, the inhabitants of this State were so thrifty and industrious that their Kings, naturally, became very rich.

"The ancient Amanhene were indubitably wealthy. They possessed many gold trinkets, heavy bangles, headdresses with gold amulets and gilded gourds, gold sandals and rings, wrist and leg amulets, and above all a large Gold Stool, every part of which was of solid gold. Now when a rumour of war arose, the wise Omanhene of that time, fearing that the Ashantis might make a sudden attack and despoil the royal treasury, took four large jars and filled them with all the wealth of the Palace, including gold-dust and nuggets, all the regalia, the Court-Criers' caps, Soul-washers' breastplates, Linguists' sticks, and so forth. Deep holes were then dug, and these jars with their valuable contents were buried. To mark the places where they were hidden, thick chains were passed through the handles of each jar and fastened to trees. . . .

"One of these jars, your Lordship, is said to have been dug up by the accused. According to custom, anyone who discovers such a treasure has to sprinkle blood upon it before recovering it, after which it is sent to the Omanhene through the Ohene. In the present case it should have been sent through the Adontenhene. Akrofi knows this custom very well, your Lordship, and his failure to follow it is a very heinous offence.

"These, your Lordship, are the facts of the case, and I feel that your Lordship's experience and ability will lead to a prompt decision against the accused, whose offence in endeavouring to steal from the Omanhene this jar and its precious contents is without precedent in the annals of the Kwahu State."

He sat down amidst great applause, for the people in Court were much impressed by his eloquence and his knowledge of Gold Coast history.

Barrister Akotua rose to his feet.

"Your Lordship and gentlemen of the Jury, I must crave your patience. I am not here to relate fairy stories and waste your valuable time, as my learned friend has done. From what he said I gather that he has laid all his facts before you. It still remains to prove those facts by the testimony of witnesses.

"There are only two points which I wish to bring to your Lordship's attention. To begin with, my client informs me that he bought the land from the stool, so that it is his by right of purchase, together with all it may contain.

"To continue, my learned friend has told the Court that the jar in question contains gold-dust, nuggets, regalia, bangles, head-dresses, sandals, amulets, gilded gourds, Court-Criers' caps, Soul-washers' breastplates, Linguists' sticks, and above all a large Stool, made entirely of massive gold. These facts must be supported by evidence, personal or documentary, in order that your Lordship may arrive at a decision.

"These two points which I labour are these. First, if the land was legally sold and Akrofi bought it legally, then that land and all it contains is his by right of purchase. Secondly, the jar in question is to be brought to this Court as an exhibit. If your Lordship opens it and it is found to contain all the articles which my learned friend enumerated so eloquently, then there can be no doubt that it belongs to the stool, and must be given to the Paramount Chief, together with its contents. If it does not contain these articles, then the jar and contents are the property of Akrofi."

Barrister Okulola consulted the Omanhene's representatives, and readily gave his full assent to these terms.

His Lordship then ordered that evidence in support of the legal sale and purchase of the land in which the jar was buried should be produced, as he held that the whole case hinged on this point.

Barrister Okulola then stated that Akrofi applied to the Omanhene for permission to farm the land, but it was never sold to him.

Akrofi was asked if he had any evidence to prove the legal sale and purchase of the land, and, when he replied in the affirmative, was asked to produce it. He said that the evidence was documentary and was in the hands of his lawyer.

At this point the case was adjourned until the following day.

When the court resumed its sitting, the witnesses for the prosecution were called in support of Barrister Okulola's statement. Akotua then cross-examined the principal witness as follows:

"Do you know the person to whom all land in this State belongs?"

"Yes."

"Tell the Court his name and title."

"Akaumoa, the Omanhene of Kwahu."

"Do you know how long it is since Akrofi applied for permission from the Omanhene to farm this land?"

"Yes."

"In what year was it?"

"I am not an educated man, so I cannot tell you the year, but according to the amount of land Akrofi has brought under cultivation, I should say it was ten or eleven years ago."

"Very good. Do you know if there has been any change of rulers during that time?"

"Yes."

"What change?"

"The Omanhene who granted the land to Akrofi died, and another took his place."

"Very well. Is the ruling monarch of this State despotic or constitutional?"

"I do not understand what you mean."

"This is what I mean. Has the ruling monarch of this State the power to do anything he pleases without any opposition, or is there another power that can oppose and correct him if he makes a mistake?"

"The Omanhene is the highest power in the State, but in his capital there are some elders, including the Queenmother, who can correct and oppose him, or depose him if he does not obey them."

"Very good. And in the State?"

"In the State his principal adviser and corrector is the Adontenhene. He is the Omanhene's right hand, and in some cases it even appears that he has control over the Omanhene."

"What do you mean by that?"

"I mean that there are some State ceremonies which the Omanhene cannot possibly perform without the Adontenhene."

"Give us some examples."

"At the Annual Yam Festivals, it is the Adontenhene who puts mashed yam three times in to the mouth of the Omanhene before he is given permission to eat some of the new yams."

"Is that all?"

"No. Any gift of liquor must be handled and blessed by the Adontenhene before it becomes sacred for the use of spirits of the departed Chiefs. At least, it was so in the ancient times."

"Is that all?"

"When the Stools are to be sanctified annually in the stream, the Omanhene cannot perform the ceremony unless the Adontenhene is present, and if he hesitates or shows reluctance to be present, precious gifts are lavished on him to persuade him to come."

"This appears to be a digression from the main point," interposed the judge, addressing Akotua. "Questions should be confined to the matter in hand."

"I must crave your Lordship's patience. These questions are by no means without bearing on the case, as will shortly appear." Akotua turned to the witness again. "When the land was presented to Akrofi, was the Adontenhene informed?"

"Certainly."

"Do you think the Stool Elders in the capital, including the Queen-mother, knew about it?"

"The Omanhene could not give the land without their knowledge."

"But if he wished to sell the land, could he do so without their knowledge?"

"Any sale of land without their knowledge or permission is not legal."

"But if they know of the sale and agree to it?"

"Then it is legal, and cannot be disputed."

"That is all I want to know. Thank you."

Akotua now produced a document and handed it to the Judge. It read as follows:

"WHEREAS Akrofi applied to us, four years ago, for a piece of land for farming.

"AND WHEREAS at first the land was given to him freely because he is a free citizen of this State.

"AND WHEREAS he has farmed extensively and it appears to us that he has become the possessor of the land now in his hands.

"NOW THEREFORE We the undersigned think it expedient to transfer the land to him by sale; and from this day onward, the land extending from a point on the right bank of the River Odihun southwards to the Odum Tree, measuring 9,756 feet, more or less, and from the said Odum Tree east wards to an Owawa Tree, measuring 8,867 feet, more or less, and from the said Awawa Tree westwards to the aforementioned point on the right bank of the River Odihun, measuring 9,876 feet, more or less, has become the property of the said Akrofi, his heirs and assigns. We have received from the said Akrofi the sum of £5,007 in full payment for the said land, and no other person whatever has any right to dispute his ownership of the Land. The land has been sold with the consent and concurrence of the Adontenhene of Kwahu, the Queen Mother, the Krontihene, the Akyeame-hene and the Gyaasehene. This sale and purchase is therefore complete in its entirety, and cannot be defied, altered or gainsaid by any of our successors.

"Dated at Abene in Akuamoa Panin Fie, this tenth day of September the year of our Lord 1918, in the second year of our reign. . . ."

The Judge, having read this document, asked Barrister Okulola whether his client were the accredited representative of the Omanhene of Kwhau, and was told such was the case. He then asked Barrister Akotua to produce the jar in question as the second exhibit. Akrofi told the Court that he had left the jar at home, and begged that some trustworthy men might be sent to fetch it.

Akintola Chipalsi, the Senior Superintendent of Police, with a police-sergeant and six constables, was ordered to bring the jar within three days, as no further time could be given to the case.

On the afternoon of the third day, the famous jar was produced in Court. Its appearance caused great surprise to all who had heard the speeches for the prosecution and the defence. It was dirty, its size was about that of the thigh of a medium sized person, and obviously it could never have contained the articles enumerated by Okulola, for its neck was only eight inches wide. It held some gold dust and nuggets, but none of the regalia previously mentioned.

The Judge read to the Court the document ratifying the sale and purchase of the land, and asked the [plaintiff] if he knew those persons whose signatures were appended. He replied that he did and that they were the chief powers of the State, and so he knew that he had lost the case.

Judgment was pronounced in favour of Akrofi and against the ruling Omanhene, and Akrofi thus became sole and undisputed owner of the farm.

His lawyer was well paid, and Akrofi and his wife returned home happy and contented.

Of Water and Spirits

Sandra E. Greene

Colonialism in Ghana was more than European economic avarice in the pursuit of land and labor, and the material luxuries that both produced. European colonialism often required that local populations reorient or challenge their own spirituality and core cultural ideas. For many in the Gold Coast and on its peripheries, sacred bodies of water or groves of trees held special meaning in their spiritual worldview. The arrival of Europeans, with their almost insatiable demand for natural resources, often resulted in situations where local understandings of these natural elements assumed new meanings in light of the socioeconomic and political changes brought by European contact. In the following excerpt from her monograph, Sandra E. Greene, a professor of history at Cornell University, explores these matters among the Anlo people of southeastern Ghana by focusing on how their understandings of key water bodies in and around that region shifted over time.

To enter the central district of Anlo is to journey into a land of water, where lagoon and sea, pond and creek are ever present, where even the location of farms and fields exist as reminders of where waters once stood. All that separates the littoral residents from the Atlantic Ocean and the inland Keta Lagoon is a narrow sandbar (not more than a mile wide), on which the Anlo villages are clustered "like beads on a string." Water is at the center of Anlo culture. As a liquid, it is seen as necessary for life itself, yet it is also believed to be capable of bringing great hardship. Death from drowning and the destruction caused by the waves of an ever-encroaching Atlantic Ocean have been an all-too-common reality of life since at least the nineteenth century. Periodically, the Keta Lagoon also overflows its banks, bringing destruction to fields and crops. This has profoundly shaped land-tenure patterns and residential development. Yet water is also part of everyday life. From the normative offer of water to visiting guests to the use of this substance in the many rituals surrounding birth, death, and religious worship, water is believed to have the power to cool the hearts of men and gods, mediate relations between humans and the spiritual world, and purify the physical both

An *ɔkyeame*, a speech intermediary and cultural repository, performing libation (*yi mpaeɛ*) at a groundbreaking ceremony in the Brong-Ahafo Region of Ghana. Photograph by Clifford Campbell, Techiman, July 2009.

literally and ritually. In its natural state, it has evoked in the imaginations of the Anlo awe and respect, but at the same time it can be so ubiquitous as to be taken for granted. . . .

Tagbamu and the Potable Water Ponds of Anloga

The existence of freshwater ponds in an area otherwise saturated with salt water has been a phenomenon of some interest to both Western-trained scientists and the Anlo who live in the area . . . Scientists, for example, state that the sandy soil of the spit on which the Anlo live is actually a former sandbar. After centuries of geologic activity, this sandbar enclosed the body of salt water that later became known as the Keta Lagoon. In the lengthening and widening process, the bar developed different elevations: some places rose higher above the saltwater table formed by the ocean and the lagoon, other places were lower. All, however, had a thick layer of sand, which allowed rainwater to percolate down to the saltwater table. Because fresh water has a lower specific gravity than salt water, it does not mix with the latter but instead "floats as a layer on top, rather as oil does on water." In those areas where the elevation was low, fresh water existed as a standing body, easily accessed without even digging below the sand's surface. Such is the scientific explanation, one concerned with relative specific gravities, soil types, and geological change.

Anlo oral tradition, of course, offers a very different explanation. . . . According to these traditions, the very existence of fresh water, easily obtained and seemingly permanently available, was critical to the decision by the Anlo's ancestors to settle on the coast. . . . Perhaps in recognition of the critical nature of these water bodies, and hoping to ensure their continued existence, the Anlo imbued these sites with spiritual significance. All were associated with a set of deities known as the *dzokpleanyiwo* that are said to have been the first inhabitants of the area. It was these gods who are said to have created the ponds that later became known as Welifome, Klalavime, and Atsiwume. . . .

More significant, the spiritual meanings associated with these three ponds—so critical as sources of drinking water for the residents of Anloga—seem to have been forgotten except by the most elderly residents of the town. . . . Only one, Atsivu, has been permanently preserved as a means of protecting it from being destroyed by residential development. The others have been largely ignored. . . . Similarly, the memories of even the most elderly residents of Anloga more often recall the ponds as part of the quotidian rhythms of the community. . . . That sacred quality that so influenced how the Anlo understood, interacted with, and remembered these early sources of drinking water no longer exists. . . .

The same can be said of the memories and meanings associated with the Keta Lagoon. Known locally as Tagbamu, this body of water is well remembered in Anlo oral traditions as the first major water body that the Anlo encountered on their arrival in the area in the early to mid-seventeenth century. . . .

Despite this central presence in the everyday activities of the Anlo, Tagbamu was more than a waterway for communication and a rich source of fish and salt. Its expansiveness, its periodic flooding and drying, its seeming unpredictability as a source of both abundance and destruction prompted the Anlo to associate it with several deities, one of whom is remembered today as Tovuntsikpo. It is said to have once been a very powerful god, for "no matter how heavy the rainfall . . . its shrine [in Anloga] near the lagoon . . . would never be submerged. Tovuntsikpo stopped the floodwaters from occupying the town. It also generated more fish in the lagoon." Associated with the Lafe clan, Tovuntsikpo protected the entire town, just as it offered its harvest of fish and salt (collected to the east and north of Keta) to any male who wished to tap its resources. Women—whether on their menses or not—were barred from entering the lagoon. Individuals who had recently eaten leftover food were advised to stay clear of Tagbamu if they wished to avoid weakening Tovuntsikpo's ability to provide abundant harvests of fish. No one was allowed to travel on the lagoon at night. These beliefs and practices—like those associated with the ponds of Anloga—held sway in Anlo, governing everyday practices through much of the colonial period. Yet over the remainder of this last century they too have come to occupy a meaningful place only in the memories of the very elderly. Why this is the case has much to do with the influence of missionary education and the technological efforts on the part of the British colonial government to "domesticate" and "modernize" the meanings and memories associated with Anlo's watery landscape.

Missionary Teachings and Western Technology

The majority of the missionaries who operated in Anlo during the late nineteenth and the early twentieth century were associated with the Norddeutsche Missionsgesellschaft, North German Missionary Society (NMG), also known as the Bremen Mission. . . .

The struggles of the Bremen missionaries to convert the Anlo to Christianity are well documented in their many reports published in the mission's publications. Of interest here is the way in which this conversion effort impacted Anlo views of their own physical environment, for one of the principal goals of the missionaries was to convince the Anlo that the spiritual forces that they believed occupied material substances were either manifestations of the Devil or simply did not exist. In 1909, for example, Bremen missionary Forster participated in what he and other Christians in Anlo considered to be a massive achievement: the baptism of the first converts from Anloga, the political and religious capital of Anlo, a town considered to be both a "bastion of heathendom" and a major impediment to the spread of Christianity. In describing the baptism, Forster noted that an especially important aspect of the ceremony was the public disavowal of any ritual objects that the converts once believed had efficacy. Each baptismal candidate was thus asked to hand over to the missionaries their "fetishes and magic things" before a crowd of more than 1,000 "heathens." The purpose: "to show all the people that [these objects] were harmless," that they had no power to predict the future, protect one from harm, or cause harm to others. . . .

A more focused attack had to await the development of an Anlo Christian community that had the power to enforce more broadly throughout Anlo (and not just among the community of converts) a different understanding of the natural environment. This occurred in 1907. In July of that year, the elders of the Adzovia clan installed Bremen Mission–educated Cornelius Kofi Kwawukume under the name of Fia Sri II as the *awọamefia*, or political and religious leader of Anlo. They were guided by the conviction that only with the ascension of a mission-educated king would the Anlo be able to direct what they felt was the necessary "modernization" of Anlo. . . .

On his ascension to office, Sri II immediately embarked on a campaign to challenge the power of the Anlo priests and their gods to dictate how the Anlo were to understand the material and spiritual world. He refused to participate for the full six months that had customarily been used to spiritually fortify any new *awọamefia* before they officially assumed office. And thereafter he also refused to remain in seclusion, as had also been the tradition for the Anlo *awọamefia* since at least the late seventeenth century. Instead, he traveled freely and openly throughout Anlo, riding a bicycle from one end of the littoral to the other. He supported the opening of Anloga to Christian churches and schools. He defied the ban on sewn clothing that had been imposed in the early nineteenth century by the Nyigbla religious order by allowing anyone who wished to wear European-style clothing in Anloga [to do so]. Most significant . . . he challenged traditional religious control over the water bodies that existed in Anlo. In 1906, for example, priests associated with two of the most well-known and influential deities in Anlo (Mama Bate and Togbui Nyigbla) declared a ban on the use of sails on the canoes that traveled on the Keta Lagoon. . . . In 1914, eight years after the ban and seven years after his installation . . . Sri ordered his subchiefs to allow canoes with sails to be once again used on the lagoon. . . . Sri launched a second challenge shortly thereafter when sand accumulated in the channel that connected the Keta Lagoon to the Volta River, blocking what was at that time a vital means of communication between Anlo and the rest of the Gold Coast. According to the priest of the Anlo god, Gbotonya, the barrier had been erected by this god and therefore was not to be disturbed. Sri defied this religious pronouncement by summoning workers and then personally supervising the removal of the barrier.

In pursuing these actions, Sri directly and deliberately challenged the authority of the priests who had been so influential in shaping the political and religious culture of Anlo. . . . The result was a gradual secularization of the Keta Lagoon and Anlo's potable water bodies.

AFRINHYIA PA O-O-O!

T. E. Kyei

In 1945, noted anthropologist Meyer Fortes led a three-member team that undertook a social survey of Asante "under the auspices of the West African Institute." Thomas E. Kyei (1908–99), a schoolteacher who compiled extensive records on Asante history and culture, served as "principal research assistant" on Fortes's survey and contributed copious amounts of material to the project. His autobiography, which focuses on his childhood days in rural Asante, provides insights into the quotidian activities of the period and place where he was reared. Kyei's work is valuable because it represents a firsthand account of the colonial experience in a former empire. In the excerpt below, Kyei describes the sociocultural activities connected with the relatively new celebrations of Christmas and the New Year.

To me, as a child, Christmas (*Buronya*), the festival of the birth of Christ, was an occasion of one solid week of merry-making which occurred once a year. It started in the afternoon of the day on which the Christmas tree was put up, nostalgically called "*Buronya-dua si da*," the Christmas round-off day, and ended a week later on a day that was to us children, "*Da a yɛyi Buronya ano*." The New Year's Day was not seen as a separate occasion marking what I later grew to know to be the start of a New Year, but the tail-end of Christmas festivities.

Buronya was a period of great expectation and a happy fulfilment. . . . For men . . . it was the time that they were expected to present the wife or wives with at least two sets of "*ɔsoro ne fam ne kaba*" (up-piece, down-piece and cover-shoulder piece) cloths, complete with headkerchiefs to match. A marriage could [flounder] if a husband neglected unreasonably to discharge that marital obligation. . . .

We, the children, likewise expected from our fathers at least one or two different piece-cloths (*ntama*) of three- to four-yard cut-lengths and a *pieto* (underwear). With luck we might have a pair of trousers or shorts (we called them knickers) together with a long-sleeved white cotton shirt. Some boys of "progressive" fathers could expect to receive a pair of trousers or white drill trousers and a coat complete with a white shirt for Christmas. A provident father therefore started preparing for Christmas weeks before the actual day of festivities. He got the required piece-lengths purchased and cut ready for presentation any time before the day. . . .

It was the wife's responsibility in those days to provide all food items except meat. The husband supplied game meat (*mpunam*) or fish (*adwene*) which he bought from a male meat seller's stand at the market (*konko-pon ho*). Many a time, he succeeded in trapping or killing some small game or big birds which went to the wife or, if a polygamist, was shared as equally as possible among his wives. The sale of meat, like most other items, was then the proper function of men. . . . A wife therefore started her preparations for the provision of quality food in sufficient quantity for Christmas weeks before the start of the festivities. Every industrious woman in Agogo at that time worked two or more farms. She worked on her own foodcrop farm (*mfikyi-fuo*), which was situated within a mile or so from the town, and at the same time, assisted her husband in working his cash-crop farm (*kwae-fuo*) some distance away from the town. . . .

My mother had an *mfikyi-fuo* at Nkwantam on the Agogo-Hwidiem road on a site about three hundred yards from the present Agogo Magistrate's court building. . . . It was a well-cultivated and neatly kept food-crop farm. . . .

Mother harvested her yams a few weeks before Christmas and had them preserved on a *putuo*, a wooden rack erected on the farm in the cool shade of a tree. . . . Tubers reserved for immediate consumption were not stacked on the rack but were kept separately in a heap at the foot of the *putuo*. Among the reserved lot were those to be selected specially for Christmas (*nea yɛde bedi buronya*), including those to be presented to friends and relatives on the morning of the great day. . . .

Our preparation for Christmas, as children, took the form of firewood stockpiling. Weeks before the great day we went in groups to the bush in search of dry outer coverings of *atewa* seeds. *Atewa-ahena*, as the husks were called, were hard and highly combustible and offered an ideal fuel for bonfires on Christmas Eve and New Year's Night.

The day before the Christmas Day itself was particularly busy for us. It was the normal practice that we accompanied our mothers to farm in the morning of that day to fetch the last batch of foodstuffs or firewood that would be needed for the celebration. We did not stay long in the farm and were usually back home before midday. All the afternoon was left free for us to go in search of a Christmas Tree (*Buronya Dua*). . . .

The still evening air was stirred by the church bell ringing, "*Kron-kron!*

Kron-kron! Kron-kron!" to summon all to the church room to hear the good tidings of the birth of the Saviour of the World. It was the same old church bell that I heard ringing, but on that particular evening the sound it made was exciting, cheerful, exhilarating—surprisingly extraordinary.

The Agogo Basel Mission little church building was filled to capacity by the time the third bell ceased ringing that "Holy Night."

The church service was programmed for adults whose hymn singing continued all the time with breaks for the reading of passages on the birth of the Little Lord Jesus from the Bible. Most of what was said or read did not interest us children in the least. We were looking forward eagerly to the end of the service and, on hearing the final "A-M-E-N!," rushed to an open space behind the church where our pile of *atewa-abena* (husks of *atewa* seeds) was set ready for our Christmas bonfire. . . .

At cock's crow, our leaders organized us for the annual early morning house to house carol singing to wish inmates in Salem houses *AFRINHYIA PA!* (Merry Christmas). . . .

Back home we rushed to the riverside thrice to fetch water. Then followed one of our most pleasant filial Christmas duties: that of carrying Mother's gifts to her friends and relatives. . . .

Presentation of gifts over, we bathed, dressed and got ourselves ready for the Christmas Day church service. As always, but particularly on such an important occasion, Mother saw to it that we had bathed ourselves thoroughly, shea-buttered every part of the body evenly, and that our talcum powder application was just right. Having been "passed" as properly dressed we set off to church, which was only a few steps away from our house. Everything we wore that day was new: our cloths were new, our *pieto* underwear was new, and our singlets were new. One thing, however, was puzzling to me on that day of days. It was the incongruous behavior of almost all adults in Agogo, but particularly the women of Salem. On a day that was, we had been told several times before it arrived, the remembrance day of the birth of Christ the Saviour, when all were bidden to "be glad," those same grown-ups were mourning! They mourned, grieved and wept irrepressibly, we heard, for the loss of some dear relatives who passed away a long or short time before that day! Because of the incomprehensible action of many of the adult members of the Agogo community, the atmosphere of Christmas Day itself was rather unhappy and funereal.

In town, the situation was no better, if not worse. It was a day of hard drinking and wanton drunkenness. The attendance at the church service that morning was, in consequence, seriously affected, with most of the few members present dozing most of the time.

The day after Christmas Day itself was the real merrymaking day in Agogo—a day of unbounded jollity. Animals bred for Christmas were slaughtered: fowls in their tens by the very ordinary folk, and sheep and goats in their numbers by the relatively well-to-do, who distributed some parts of the mutton to friends and relatives. In every home in the town that day, it was fresh meat consumption. She was regarded an odd fad of a woman who did not prepare Christmas Soup (*Buronya Nkwan*), but cooked the common, everyday soup of lean meat and smoked herrings (*ɛman*). The exception was, of course, in the case of sick persons on diet including venereal disease patients. It is worth observing that chicken soup (*akɔkɔ-nkwan*) was highly valued because it was an uncommon meal in those days. It was prepared and eaten on special occasions, particularly in times of gladness when one could truly say: *"Asɛm yi dɛ nti, mekum akɔkɔ madi"* ("For such a happy news, event or occasion, I will kill a fowl for a meal"). Another occasion for *akɔkɔ-nkwan* was to honour a distinguished guest (*ɔhɔho pa*). . . .

The slaughter of a sheep or a goat by an ordinary person for home consumption was quite unusual on an ordinary day except on an occasion such as Christmas. It was, in fact, a notion widely upheld that *"Wukum odwan di a, wo ho dwan wo"* ("He who killed a sheep/goat for his own consumption brings a nuisance unto himself"). In the case of sheep-slaughtering in particular, the involved procedure of obtaining the Chief's prior consent through an *okyeame* (linguist) militated against any desire, however strong it might be, for killing one for household consumption. Christmastime, therefore, offered an opportunity, once in a year, for anyone who had a domestic animal, including sheep, goats or pigs, to kill and enjoy it as part of the festivities, without any restraint or inhibition. Hence the added extraordinary cheeriness of the occasion. . . .

The New Year's Day (Afe Foforo Da)

It took me some time to comprehend that Christmas and the New Year's Day celebrations marked two separate occasions. My conception (or was it misconception?) was that the New Year's Day was celebrated to round off festivities called *"Buronya"* (Christmas). The traditional Asante practice of commemorating certain events on the eighth day of their occurrences might have led me to such a conclusion. . . . The view that Christmas day marked the start of *Buronya* and the New Year's Day, the end of *Buronya*, might have again been reinforced by the fact that only one form of greeting was heard expressing the wish of everybody anywhere during the season.

It was *"Afrinhyia Pa"* all through the eight days of *Buronya* festivities. One never heard of any other proper Twi equivalent of "Merry Christmas."

One other point was that the pattern of celebration of what I later learned to be the New Year's Day was almost identical with that of Christmas: an evening church service preceded a forenoon service on each of the two days. . . . The attendance at the service held on the New Year's Eve to welcome the incoming year (*Yɛkɔsare Afe*) was heavy and included many once-a-year churchgoers. It started soon after nightfall and continued, non-stop, till past midnight. The program consisted of community hymn singing, addresses by the Catechist and some church Elders, as well as prayers which were interspersed with *Mfante-nnwom* sung by some of the elderly members of the congregation. . . .

The time for the arrival of the New Year was fast approaching. Members of the congregation knelt and, in silent prayer, communed individually with God in the dead silence of the cold early January night. An alarm clock standing on the Catechist's table and set to ring precisely at twelve o'clock midnight kept tick-tocking the seconds and the minutes as the Catechist, in a clear staccato voice, kept announcing at short intervals: *"Ɔ - re - kɔ, Ɔ - re - kɔ - O - O! Afe dada no, rekɔ. Ɔ - re - kɔ - O - O, Ɔ - re - kɔ - O - O - O - O!"* ("It is passing away. The Old Year is passing off. It is going. It is g - o - i - n - g!"). Meantime four young men with flint-lock Dane guns, led by Kwasi K. (N), the freed slave and handyman of the Agogo Basel Mission community, had stationed themselves a few yards away from the church building. At exactly midnight, the alarm clock rang its shrill sound, "K - R - R - R - R - R!" signaling to the gun-men who, with guns cocked and muzzles pointed upward, shot volleys into the sky to usher in the New Year.

Reminiscences: The Hill of Knowledge

Kosi Kedem

Kosi Kedem was a member of the Ghanaian parliament from 1993 to 2005 in the Volta region of Ghana. His memoir, The Chance of a Lifetime, *recounts his childhood and the Ewe traditions and values. The excerpt below focuses on the Yam Festival: Kedem provides readers with a first-person account of the richness of Ewe spiritual culture connected with the growth and the harvesting of yams in his hometown. The cultivation of specific foods, especially the ubiquitous root crop of yams, is common to the histories of several cultural groups in Ghana. Among the Ewe in the Volta Region, the ritual consumption of yam at the Yam Festival before harvesting a new crop is the most important ceremony pertaining to food in their traditional calendar. The participation of the entire community at this festival underscores the importance of rites engrained in tradition and in local political culture.*

The Big Yam Festival

The [Holy Village] is perched firmly on a hill facing the Agumale and Gemi mountains. And it overlooks the biggest man-made lake in the world, the Volta Lake, and its basins. Because it is on a hill, access to the village is difficult.

To compensate for this geographical limitation God endowed the Holy Village with beautiful scenery and healthy environment as well as a hospitable people. The weather is most accommodating and pleasant. Its spring waters are cooling to the palate and soothing to the heart. Visitors who struggle to climb the hill to get there find it so friendly that they reluctantly leave the place. That is why despite its geographical difficulties people find an excuse to visit the place.

One of the excuses is to visit the waterfall and the limestone formation. The other reason is to participate in the annual yam festival. . . . Of all the crops, yam is the most difficult to cultivate. A lot of care, energy and time are devoted to its cultivation. It has to be carefully tended and handled. It exacts maximum attention from the farmer. Lazy people do not, and cannot, cultivate it successfully. Invariably, to be a successful yam farmer in the Holy Village earns a person the accolade of a successful and hardworking farmer. . . .

After the land is prepared, the yam mounds are made. But at the Holy Village where there are many stones and rocks in the soil, mound preparation is a very difficult task. First the ground is dug either by hoe or pickaxe, roughly, to the depth of two feet. All the stones and rocks are then extracted from the soil before it is put back into the hole, and then the yam mound raised on it. It is a backbreaking laborious job.

After the mounds are raised the farmer will then slice the seed yams according to desired sizes before they are planted. To plant the seed yam an opening measuring about six inches deep is made in the mound. The seed is put in it and then covered with soil. The mound is then properly reshaped and some dry straw is put on the peak to give moisture and coolness to the seed yam.

The seed yams are planted during the time of intense heat and dryness. Since there are no rains at that time, the yam seed depends on dew to help it survive and germinate. The farmer erects a pole of about eight to nine feet beside every mound in order to gather the branches of the yam tendrils. Sometimes two or more mounds could share a pole. The tendrils and the branches of the yam are very tender and delicate and they have the tendency to spread wildly so the farmer requires the patience of a midwife to gather them carefully around the pole. The tenderness of the yam tendril has given rise to many proverbs in Ewe such as "Beauty of conduct is like the tender climber of a yam, it needs constant minding." This means good conduct is cultivated and does not come effortlessly. It has to be nursed carefully, and therefore you should be prepared to make the necessary effort to be good. . . .

Yam is the most delicious of all the food crops, and therefore the most prized. It is not just an edible crop; it is also used for performing rituals for the ancestral black stool. It has a great spiritual value in the Holy Village. That is why every year special rituals are performed for the ancestors, the gods and God before anyone could harvest and eat yam. . . .

Before the new yam is harvested and eaten, special rites are performed, but it is not just any yam, which is used to perform these rites. There is a special yam called "Nyagasi" the king of yams. It is white, smells sweet and very delicious. The texture of cooked nyagasi is delicately soft and melts easily on the tongue. It is grown only by selected members of the royal family.

In the first week of September of every year, this special yam is the first to be harvested and brought to the chief's house. No woman in her menstrual period is allowed to touch the yam. To be on a safer side, only women in their menopause are selected to handle and cook the yam. The cooked yam is then mashed and a little salt added to it. Some of the mashed yam is mixed with red palm oil. The plain mashed yam is put in one big bowl and the one mixed with palm oil is put in a separate bowl. Three hard-boiled eggs are put on the mashed yam in each of the bowls. A piece of white calico, signifying peace and harmony, is tied around each bowl. At about five thirty in the morning, these two bowls are taken to the stool-house where the elders of the town are already assembled. The talking drum is beaten to alert the village to the commencement of the purification rites. This is followed by singing of a traditional song called the "odze." The rites are then started. Attendance at the purification rites is strictly by invitation, and is greatly restricted to the members of the royal family and the elders of the town. No one who attends the purification rites would have had sex the previous day or night. A ram, preferably a white one, is sacrificed and libation is poured with gin, or schnapps, or palm wine to the ancestors to solicit for peace, good health, and prosperity.

The pouring of libation is completed by pouring water on the ground, and the priest would say, "Those of you who don't take alcohol I have not yet invited you to take it. Here is water for you." Yam is considered a symbol of fertility. So during this festival, special prayers are offered for fertility and abundance of life. After libation is poured, the ram is raised to the sky three times accompanied by the incantation, "Oh God! Oh God! Oh God!" before it is slaughtered. The third invocation of God symbolizes life, and the sky in this context refers to the Almighty God. The blood of the slaughtered ram is poured at the entrance of the stool house. The ram is dressed, and the meat shared to the chief and his elders strictly according to a prescribed traditional formula.

Next, the officiating priest takes some of the white mashed yam and molds it into a ball. He does the same thing for the red mashed yam. Holding one in his left palm and the other in his right palm, he sprinkles them one at a time on the stool and then the entrance of the stool house. He then takes some of the white and the red mashed yam, adds one boiled egg and touches the lip of the chief three times (the third time signifying life) and gives them to the chief to nibble. Nibble, because chiefs are not supposed to eat in public. As he does that the priest recites words of blessing and prosperity for the people in the village. He asks especially for a peaceful year and adequate rains for the crops. He invokes, for everybody, the blessing and protection of the ancestors who are believed to be in the midst of the living all the time.

Next, the priest puts some herbs, including the one called "anyinya" into a bowl, which is placed on a forked pole erected at the entrance of the stool house. He adds water, which is fetched by a chaste teenage girl who has had neither sex nor her period before. This holy water is fetched from a sacred stream at a place called "Ombuetsi" where the stool is normally purified. . . .

The priest takes the holy water, mixed with herbs, from the bowl placed on the forked pole, prays over it, sips some and washes his face with it. He gives some of the water, first to the stool father, the chief's father and then the chief himself. They sip a little bit of it and wash their faces. The other elders, made up mainly of clan heads, follow suit in performing this water purification rite. The priest dips a short broom-like object into the water and sprinkles the holy water on the rest of the people present at the ceremony. The rites are concluded amidst the singing of more "Odze" songs. The talking drums are also beaten, accompanied by the blowing of animal horns, to signify the end of the rites and to announce to the rest of the village that new yams can be harvested and eaten. The remaining mashed yam is shared out. The priest would then lead a team, accompanied by Akpi or Adevu war drummers, to sprinkle the red and white mashed yam at some specially designated spots in the village.

The stool father ensures that every clan head is given some of the mashed yam to be taken to his clan members. After the rites, all those invited to the ceremony, apart from the elders, are allowed to sip some of the water and wash their faces with it. They are also allowed to dip the tips of their toes into the sheep blood poured at the entrance of the stoolhouse. It is believed that the holy water and the blood purify and cleanse people of evil, give prosperity, blessings and give or restore fertility to barren women. During this time too, people are allowed to go to the stool house to request for favors of the stool and the ancestors and to make pledges, which they will redeem if, in the course of the year, their requests are granted. . . .

The rites normally begin on a Thursday. On the following Friday, the whole town is spiritually fortified against witches, malevolent spirits and men, deadly diseases and hostile neighboring towns. Powerful medicine men and priests do this fortification. It is done when the whole village is dead asleep. At daybreak, newly erected fortified poles, adorned with "anyinya" creeping plants, are found at vantage spots in the town. The mission station, called "Kpodzi," is exempted from these fortification rites because the Church regards them as pagan rites. . . .

On this same Friday, at dawn, the war palanquin is sent to "Ombuetsi," the ancestral sacred grove for purification and for fortification. Our palanquin is not a ceremonial one. So no ordinary person, except the chief or a powerful medicine man can ride in it. The palanquin itself is more or less a god and so special rites are performed anytime it is used in public. In the olden days it was used only during wartime by the chief.

These days when there are no more wars the chief or any royal can use it during festivities like the Yam Festival. During festivals, everybody, including the guests of honor, would be seated before the palanquin would appear. The palanquin is carried on the head by strong young men who have also been properly fortified spiritually. It carries only the chief and the "soul of the palanquin" who is normally a small girl of about six or seven years whose body is smeared with kaolin lotion and dressed in beautiful heavy beads and jewelry. The soul sits in front of the palanquin facing the chief. The girl or the soul signifies purity and power. The chief normally wears a dyed smock adorned with many amulets. He could, at intervals and if he is brave, stand up and dance. He is coached to dance with grace and it is a rare spectacle to see him dance. . . .

The palanquin is always followed by a robust troupe of Akpi or Adevu war drummers. A powerful medicine man walks ahead of the palanquin to direct and protect the chief and the soul of the palanquin from any spiritual harm. . . .

The Saturday following the fortification day is the durbar day, the actual Yam Festival. On this occasion many dignitaries, especially government officials and members of the diplomatic corps, are invited to witness and partake in the celebrations.

The ARPS and the National Congress, 1901–30

David Kimble

David Kimble (1921–2009) was a British political scientist who spent his career teaching in different countries in Africa. His first major book, A Political History of Ghana: The Rise of Gold Coast Nationalism 1850–1928, *provides an account of the roots of early nationalism and pan-Africanism in the colony. Ghana was a focal point for the independence of other African countries and for pan-Africanism during the period of decolonization. However, this was not a new phenomenon that emerged from the efforts of Kwame Nkrumah, Ghana's first prime minister and president. Nationalism and indeed the idea of regional political integration were noticeably expounded before the Nkrumah era. These were expressed in the agitations of the Aborigines' Rights Protection Society (ARPS) and the National Congress of British West Africa (NCBWA). The excerpts below shed light on these proto-nationalist movements and chart their evolution, showing how the NCBWA developed a completely different agenda from the ARPS as the former was concerned more with what Kimble describes as "a fundamental change in the colonial relationship than with the preservation of traditional rights."*

During the twentieth century the Aborigines' Rights Protection Society retained the same guiding principles as had sustained it during the Lands Bill agitation, and continued to apply these to the changing political situation. For example, the leaders took for granted that the Society would continue to act as the main medium of communication between the Government and the people, and hardly seemed to notice that both the form of government and the peoples under its rule had changed beyond recognition during the few years 1897–1902.

The ARPS appeared to believe that the political leadership of this wider national unit would automatically remain in the hands of a small circle in Cape Coast, and that the Government was bound to respect the united opposition of the Fanti Chiefs, with their educated advisers and spokesmen. They also continued to oppose all legislation affecting lands and forests, often assuming wrongly that the economic interests of the Chiefs were identical with those of the country as a whole. Consequently, the Society failed to adapt its structure and tactics to the changed circumstances of the twentieth century; and its leaders hardly realized that power was slipping away from them, in favor of those who were more concerned with a fundamental change in the colonial relationship than with the preservation of traditional rights. . . .

The Idea of West African Unity

The concept of a West African nationality preceded the ideal of Gold Coast nationhood as an active political force. This can be partially explained by the obvious disparity between the three regional units so recently grouped together under the Gold Coast Government. More important was the fact that educated West Africans from the various British territories had more in common with one another than with the illiterate peasants of their own countries. Education was apt to breach tribal barriers; but it was also likely to establish a community of interest, stretching beyond the new and artificial colonial boundaries, between Africans in neighboring territories. Another important aspect was the growing "African" consciousness of the 1920's, which began to encourage the expression of national sentiment in terms of race and color.

"British West Africa" was itself an artificial concept, but *rapport* with neighboring French West Africans, though it might even then have been politically and psychologically feasible, was practically ruled out by the barriers of language, education, and different political systems. These were the very factors which facilitated contact between the politically conscious minorities in Nigeria, the Gold Coast, and Sierra Leone. Other predisposing factors were the relative ease of east-west coastal communications, compared to the difficulties of travelling inland, the established habit of crossing colonial boundaries in search of education or employment, and the intermarriage of several educated families in the various British territories.

J. E. Casely Hayford, for example, who supplied the inspiration for a united West African movement, was the first to see that a sense of unity could be most readily awakened by an appeal to race or color, and fostered by the growing consciousness of political disabilities under colonial rule, regardless of territorial divisions. Thus he wrote in 1913:

> One touch of nature has made all West Africa kin. The common danger to our ancestral lands has made us one—one in danger, one in safety. United we stand divided we fall. . . . United West Africa . . . shall take her true part among the nations of the earth.

This was the dream behind the formation of the National Congress of British West Africa. Although there was never any question of mass support, for in fact it was little broader-based politically than the ARPS, yet it was more of a "national movement" than the Society had ever been, in that its political horizons were wider and that it was working towards a fundamental change in the colonial relationship.

A conference of leading men from the four British West African colonies was probably first suggested during 1914. Casely Hayford talked the plan over with Dr. R. A. Savage of Nigeria, who was then editing *The Gold Coast Leader,* and they asked F. W. Dove, a barrister friend in Freetown, to discuss the matter with influential people there, including the editor of *The Sierra Leone Weekly News.* But they thought it unwise to press the idea of such a conference before the war ended. It might have been expected that any fresh initiative would be taken through the ARPS. In fact Casely Hayford fell out with the Society as soon as he suggested united West African action. Why was this? And why did he find it necessary to form a completely new organization? The answer lay partly in the structure of the ARPS itself, and partly in personal rivalries.

Casely Hayford's first brush with the ARPS hierarchy came as soon as the war started. With the help of Savage he initiated the Sekondi Gold Coast Imperial War Fund, which had an immediate success. The Governor set the seal on its respectability by agreeing to act as patron and making a personal donation. By December 1914 over £3,700 had been forwarded to London. But the leaders of the Society in Cape Coast were outraged because the idea had not been referred to them first—more especially as they had taken the lead in 1900 by contributing £100 to the South African War Relief Fund.

Determined not to be outdone this time, the ARPS launched their own fund, "to demonstrate in a practical form their gratitude and loyalty to His Majesty's Government"; they appealed especially to the Natural Rulers not to be persuaded into subscribing to any scheme other than the one organized by the Society, "through whom they have always expressed their national will and desire." Theirs was to be a fund for the aboriginal inhabitants only; Casely Hayford was attacked for collaborating too much with Europeans, and for claiming to have promoted the scheme from an imperial point of view (although that word itself had not yet become a term of political abuse). . . .

It was against this background of jealousy and recrimination that Casely Hayford was formulating his own plans for a conference. Meanwhile, the idea of West African unity was gaining ground. The inclusion of a representative from India at the Imperial War Conference prompted queries from Gold Coast newspapers, "Why not West Africa as well?" *The Gold Coast Leader* in 1917 recalled the separate deputation sent to London from the Coast and Nigeria some five years earlier which might have common cause. Now, it claimed, West Africa could be as easily represented as India or any of the Dominions. *West Africa* publicly doubted the possibility, owing to a number of races, and the difficulty of choosing any one man to represent the whole "country." But these doubts culminated in a challenge from the London editor "to prove us mistaken by letting the British public see and know that West Africa has public men" who would command the support of the great bulk of the people. Such articles were closely followed by Gold Coast leaders—and leader-writers. . . .

The Gold Coast Nation, referring to criticisms that the ARPS had been "conspicuously reticent" concerning the latest proposals for a wider political movement, agreed that there was a need throughout British West Africa for major reforms in "this hoary system of Crown Colony Government," especially the grant of the franchise. But the Society was not necessarily willing to participate in joint political action unless its own leadership was recognized. It claimed to have surmounted "insuperable" problems of domestic bickering and jealousy, and to be "a living aboriginal organization to be reckoned with." In any case it would have been difficult to persuade an association acting in the name of the Gold Coast Colony Chiefs, many jealous of their own local dignity, to accept the unknown implications of a still wider association. No decision was reached at the time, but it was clear that the Cape Coast leaders were not pleased with the steps Casely Hayford had already taken on his own initiative. . . .

In May 1919 a final attempt was made to get the backing of the ARPS and the western Chiefs, who were again in conference at Cape Coast; but they simply reiterated their refusal to associate themselves with the other colonies of West Africa to bring about the reforms desired. They also demanded that Casely Hayford should "satisfy" both E. J. P. Brown and the executive of the Society with substantial gifts of cash and drinks, in order to settle the strained relations between them. Casely Hayford was particularly taken to task for having written to Sierra Leone and Lagos before consulting the executive committee. *The Gold Coast Nation* later added fuel to the fire by reporting verbatim some of the plain speaking of the Chiefs: "You must know you are *not* the King of the Gold Coast, and that if even you were, you would have your big men to consult with first." The writer commented loftily that men with education could be very useful to their country in political movements; but this should not encourage them "to create a following and *condemn authority of their Natural Rulers* and thus sow seeds of the spirit at the present moment upsetting Europe, namely, Bolshevism." It was repeatedly emphasized that the Chiefs were the recognized political representatives through whom the British Government administered the affairs of the country. . . .

The 1920 Conference and Deputation

In March 1920 six representatives from Nigeria, three from Sierra Leone, and one from the Gambia with a Gold Coast contingent of over forty assembled in Accra for the first West African Conference. In view of the allegations that were soon to be made concerning the unrepresentative nature of this movement, it is useful to examine the initial support from the Gold Coast. There were seventeen lawyers, in addition to a sprinkling of Chiefs, clergy, journalists, doctors, merchants, and "independent gentlemen"—all from the Colony. Casely Hayford was at pains to analyze in public detail the extent of his support. He went on to claim, significantly, that this was a movement of the intelligentsia—the educated classes of British West Africa. It would never be possible "to dissociate the educated African from his uneducated brother (Cheers)"; but as advances were made in education, naturally he would become the leader of his people. This was a clear break with the past; previous organizations had always relied on support from the most influential Chiefs, or used them as intermediaries. Hutton Mills then developed a novel claim to leadership: since each delegate belonged to a "Distinctive African Family," with rights of property, they were the natural leaders of the people, and had in themselves the right to appeal to His Majesty's Government for "such constitutional reforms as in their judgement are necessary."

The Government initially welcomed the Conference as an opportunity "to find out what was really wanted"; and Guggisberg said that he would personally have attended every meeting, if he had not been away from Accra on tour. His deputy attended the opening and thought that the speeches were characterized by extreme moderation of tone. He had reservations about the representation from other colonies; but as far as the Gold Coast delegates were concerned, he had no doubt that they represented "a fairly large body of the educated Coast natives."

At the close the Conference resolved itself into a permanent National

Congress of British West Africa, to be composed of the several committees already established; its headquarters would be in Sekondi—the home of Casely Hayford at that time—and the next session would be held in Sierra Leone. The number of resolutions passed reached the remarkable total of eighty-three. First, and foremost, these put forward requests for constitutional reforms, both in central and local government. It was resolved that half the members of the Legislative Council should be elected, and half nominated. The Executive Council should remain as it was; but a new House of Assembly, with special financial powers, should be created. This should consist of all the members of the Legislative Council, together with six other elected representatives; there would thus be an elected majority for controlling finance. The methods of election were left somewhat vague; they were to be held through "such local groups as may be found most convenient and expedient." But where indigenous institutions did not provide a ready means of ascertaining the will of the people, property or educational qualifications would be necessary. For municipal affairs, corporations with full powers of local self-government were to be established in each principal town.

Women's Conjugal Strategies in a World of Cash and Cocoa

Jean Allman and Victoria Tashjian

In their assessment of how colonialism affected Ghanaians, historians Jean Allman and Victoria Tashjian depart from the analytical binary of the colonizer versus the colonized by engaging the oft-neglected women's perspectives in the most prominent polity brought under colonial rule, Asante. They examine the evolution of women's experiences against the backdrop of the attendant changes engineered by colonialism such as an imposed court system and a burgeoning cash economy driven by a boom in the world demand for cocoa—the production of which placed significant labor demands on women. The authors demonstrate how women in colonial Asante "challenged the meanings and makings of marriage and childbearing" within this context of cocoa and capitalism. The excerpt below from their scholarly book explores how these women negotiated control of their "productive and reproductive labor" in a local economy integrated into a global market.

Conjugal expectations, obligations, and responsibilities became sites of ongoing contestation as women and men sought to reshape marriage and parenting to the demands of the expanding cocoa economy. For Asante wives the burdens were particularly heavy, as the growth of the cocoa industry was predicated largely upon the exploitation of unpaid, often conjugal, labor. By the 1920s, however, many wives were making the move from being the most common form of exploitable labor during the initial introduction of cocoa to themselves exploiting the new opportunities for autonomy and security afforded by an expanding cash economy. . . . In order to safeguard their precarious positions, wives of this generation began to formulate new conjugal strategies in the interwar years and to redeploy older ones in struggles that were, more than anything, about control over their productive and reproductive labor. . . .

Old Strategies / New Contexts: Seduction and Divorce in a Cash Economy

For much of Asante's history . . . marriage between free commoners was a fluid process of transaction and reciprocity. The husband provided meat and other foodstuffs, as well as clothes, and the wife, in exchange, provided farm produce, prepared food, performed other domestic services, and allowed her husband exclusive sexual access to her. That a husband's care was absolutely central to the transactions of being married meant that the ending of marriage (*gyae aware*) was often tied to claims of improper care. Divorce, which had long been relatively easy to undertake for both men and women, thus continued to be one of the primary conjugal strategies utilized by Asante women in the tumultuous interwar years. Just as women in the nineteenth century utilized divorce to end marriages in which they did not receive proper care, women in the colonial period, as care increasingly assumed cash value, opted for divorce as a strategy to gain and/or defend economic security. . . .

As in earlier times, divorce in the colonial period was undertaken for a range of reasons, and even for no apparent reason at all, though in a vast majority of the cases initiated by Asante's first generation of colonized women, improper care seems to have been at the heart of the proceedings. Pragmatic reasons for seeking divorce for both women and men continued to include problems with childbearing. But most commonly women now blamed divorce upon a husband who did not care adequately for them and their children. . . .

It is important to note that not all women of this generation directly associated a decline in levels of care with the demands of the expanding cash economy. Many remembered that care declined simply because a marriage lasted a long time, or because a husband took another wife. In both of these instances, divorce was considered a viable option. "When you get married to somebody," Ama Sewaa Akoto remarked, "in the initial stage he will be treating you fine, but if later it turns sour, you just have to divorce him. . . . When you become exceedingly annoyed, you just end it."

The idea that women would and should actively look for good care was not of recent invention. It was central to the long-recognized art of seduction or *bɔ asɔn* (a man's active wooing of a married woman in an attempt to persuade her to divorce her husband and marry him). . . .

Obviously, a woman dissatisfied with her husband's care might be receptive to such inducements. Since *bɔ asɔn* was predicated upon improving the financial state of the woman involved, the man who persuaded her to leave her husband also assumed responsibility for paying off any debts she owed her husband at the time of their divorce. Given the often economic appeals of *bɔ asɔn,* this only made sense, for if the woman had to repay the debts herself, the cost of leaving her former husband might make divorcing and remarrying an unappealing course of action. As Aduwa Yaa Ama of Oyoko explained, "Some women were not bothered about the things the man would reclaim [at divorce]. . . . It could be another man who will pay for that and marry her."

Seduction is significant for the overt connection between marriage and economic interests, particularly expectations of care, that it continued to embody in the colonial period. It was not simply a matter of a woman's extramarital sexual affairs. Rather, seduction remained a process through which a woman could attain a state of material well-being superior to that afforded by her current marriage. . . .

In being seduced by promises of better care or in opting for divorce on the grounds of improper care, Asante women in the first decades of the twentieth century were utilizing conjugal strategies not unlike those of their mothers or grandmothers before them. But they were utilizing those strategies to protect far more and at a far greater price than their mothers could have imagined. Women increasingly connected the notion of improper care to their unrewarded labor on a husband's cocoa farm, and such uncompensated investments became a major reason for divorce from the 1920s onward. Likewise, the disposition of conjugally worked cocoa farms at the time of divorce became a significant and ongoing source of contention, and it remained so throughout the colonial period.

Whether or to what extent women should be compensated for diverting their labor to their husbands' farms was an area of immense social and customary ambiguity. Though women remembered having expectations that they should be given a share of conjugally developed farms, they also understood that husbands were under no absolute, enforceable obligation to share them out. Many recalled that whether a husband did so or not was entirely discretionary: "They were doing whatever they pleased then. They were not compelled. It was dependent on the goodwill of the man." As one man remembered, "In our time you gave the wife according to how you felt." Faced with this ambiguous reality, women who had agreed to work on their husbands' cocoa farms increasingly opted for divorce when it seemed likely they were not going to be adequately compensated for their labor. Divorce was a strategy that allowed women to withdraw their labor and invest it in their own enterprises, most commonly a farm of their own or small-scale trading. While this strategy did not result in any compensation for the time and effort woman had already put into a husband's cocoa farm, it did allow her to cut her losses. Thus a wife's power—like that of her mother and grandmother—lay in her ability to easily remove herself and her labor power from her husband's control. However, in so doing, she accepted a loss for the years she had labored without recompense. . . .

Women, Divorce, and Colonial Courts

Initiating divorce proceedings or redirecting labor power were two strategies employed by Asante's first generation of colonized women that were consonant with tactics employed by their mothers or grandmothers. Other strategies were new, however, shaped by the specific context of British colonial rule. Quite early on, for example, some women turned to the courts—first to the courts of colonial officials and later to the native courts that were established after 1924. The first women to test this strategy tended to have some connection with Asante's first missions, either the Basel or the Wesleyan. The missions had long argued against what they perceived to be the injustices of matrilineal inheritance and advocated that wives and children each be given one-third of a man's property upon his death. Thus women who were members of Asante's first Christian congregations, even if they were not married in the church, were also the first to challenge the inequitable distribution of conjugally worked properties in cases of divorce and inheritance. Perhaps one of the very first of these cases was heard before the district commissioner of Juaso in 1915. Emilia Boakruwa claimed £48 from her husband, Emmanuel Frimpong, as her share of the cocoa farms they had jointly developed and tended. Emilia stated that Frimpong was her husband but had divorced her. Together they had made ten farms—seven in cocoa and three in plantain. "When he divorced me," she reported, "he refused to give me any money for the farms. I have had five children, two are dead and three alive, one male, two females. As he has divorced me, I came and sued him for half of the farm so that I can look after myself and my children. . . . I kept the children." Frimpong responded that the claim was groundless: "When you marry a woman she ought to help you make a farm, but it does not mean she should take a share in it." For added measure, in case the court did consider that labor invested warranted a share of the property, Frimpong added: "When I married her I hired men with my own money to make the farm. . . . She never cleared and planted cocoa. When she was leaving she said the only thing she wanted was that the children go to school. As she said she did not want anything, I gave her nothing." Two witnesses then testified that Frimpong had a lover in town and that his wife had found out and therefore wanted a divorce. The Rev. C. E. Martinson of the Basel Mission was then called to testify, and he reported that the case had been brought before him and the church elders and they had urged the man to apologize. By that point, however, Frimpong had decided he wanted the divorce. Martinson reported that he had written to mission headquarters for advice, but they could offer none because "it was the first case in the district . . . [so] they cannot give me any definite instructions." In the end, Martinson advised Emilia and her family to bring the case before the district commissioner. After hearing the testimony, Commissioner G. H. Sumner Wilson ordered that the value of the farms be divided, with one-third going to Emilia, one-third to her children, and one-third to Frimpong. "As the woman is keeping the children," he concluded, "the woman will get one-third plus one-third and the man one-third."

With the Native Jurisdiction Ordinance of 1924, the government created the infrastructure for a native court system, and cases like Emilia's were meant to be heard in "native tribunals," rather than in the courts of colonial officials. That so few cases appear in the record books of those tribunals during the interwar years may very well be indicative of women's perception that the chiefs' courts would be hostile to their claims.

Not until the 1940s did many women begin to bring to Asante's native courts their divorce claims for portions of farms they had helped their husbands create, and the reasons behind the shift remain uncertain. Perhaps women were moved by the Asante Confederacy Council's discussions of inheritance in 1938—discussions in which many members argued in favor of wives being allowed to inherit one-third of a husband's property. The fact that in some inheritance cases women were beginning to win claims for portions of a deceased husband's estate probably provided an additional impetus. For whatever reasons, the numbers of cases brought by women to the court increased dramatically in the 1940s, though only on rare occasions in that decade did the chiefs recognize a divorced woman's claims. . . .

Not until the 1950s did women's claims in divorce cases stand a greater chance of success, though the wide disparities in the disposition of cases from even this decade point to the utter lack of a consensus over how divorced women's complaints should be treated. . . .

Though the native courts of the postrestoration era came to acknowledge in principle the legitimacy of divorced women's equity claims to a portion of any jointly produced cocoa farms, in fact, more often than not, they turned down divorced women's claims on procedural grounds. If the divorce was already finalized, women lost their suits. Of course, in the vast majority of these cases, the divorce arbitration had already occurred, for it was precisely because they were unable to force husbands to share properties with them in arbitration that women turned to the courts. Granted, some men did voluntarily share conjugally produced properties with their wives before divorce, recognizing this practice as only fair, and some women were able to gain a portion of conjugally produced farms by begging for it during divorce arbitrations or by pressing their claims before a sympathetic native court. But with no legal bases for their claims, divorced or divorcing women of this generation found that they would continue to have no legally enforceable mechanism to guarantee a return on the labor they had expended on their husbands' farms.

Report on the Riots of 1948

Commission of Enquiry into Disturbances in the Gold Coast

In February 1948, a group of unarmed ex-servicemen in Accra marched toward the Osu castle, the seat of government at that time, to petition the governor for their still-outstanding pension. The police fired on the group, killing three of the ex-servicemen; this precipitated riots throughout the city. These riots soon assumed national significance: people participated in them to express other grievances, such as the general dissatisfaction with the prices of imported goods. Consequently, during the ensuing fracas, rioters and looters alike targeted the shops of foreign merchants. The British authorities managed to quickly suppress the riots, appointed a commission led by Aiken Watson to investigate the unrest, and promptly arrested the leaders of the fledgling political party, the United Gold Coast Convention, on suspicion of instigating the disturbances. The riots therefore brought to the surface the serious underlying political tensions in the country. Not surprisingly, scholars now consider the 1948 riots the point of departure for the process through which Ghana gained political independence from Britain, as the subsequent investigation by the Watson Commission paved the way for constitutional reforms. The excerpts here outline the contents of the commission's report to the British government.

In the main, the underlying causes may be divided into three broad categories: political, economic and social. There is often no clear dividing line between them and they are frequently interrelated. . . . The remedy for the distrust and suspicion with which the African views the European, and which is to-day poisoning life in the Gold Coast, demands an attack on all three causes. None of them may be said to take precedence. . . . These may be summarized as follows:

A. Political.

(1) The large number of African soldiers returning from service with the Forces, where they had lived under different and better conditions,

made for a general communicable state of unrest. Such Africans by reason of their contacts with other peoples, including Europeans, had developed a political and national consciousness. The fact that they were disappointed with conditions on their return, either from specious promises made before demobilization or a general expectancy of a golden age for heroes, made them the natural focal point for any general movement against authority.

(2) A feeling of political frustration among the educated Africans who saw no prospect of ever experiencing political power under existing conditions and who regarded the 1946 Constitution as mere window-dressing designed to cover, but not to advance their natural aspirations.

(3) A failure of the Government to realize that, with the spread of liberal ideas, increasing literacy and a closer contact with political developments in other parts of the world, the star of rule through the Chiefs was on the wane. The achievement of self-government in India, Burma and Ceylon had not passed unnoticed on the Gold Coast.

(4) A universal feeling that Africanization was merely a promise and not a driving force in Government policy, coupled with the suspicion that education had been slowed up, and directed in such a way as to impede Africanization.

(5) A general suspicion of Government measures and intentions reinforced by a hostile press and heightened by the general failure of the Administration in the field of Public Relations.

(6) Increasing resentment at the growing concentration of certain trades in the hands of foreigners, particularly at the increase in the number of Syrian merchants.

B. Economic.

(1) The announcement of the Government that it would remain neutral in the dispute which had arisen between the traders and the people of the Gold Coast over high prices of imported goods and which led to the organized boycott of January–February, 1948.

(2) The continuance of war-time control of imports, and the shortage and high prices of consumer goods which were widely attributed to the machinations of European importers.

(3) The alleged unfair allocation and distribution of goods in short supply, by the importing firms.

(4) The Government's acceptance of the scientists' finding that the only cure for Swollen Shoot disease of cocoa was to cut out diseased trees,

and their adoption of that policy, combined with allegations of improper methods of carrying it out.

(5) The degree of control in the Cocoa Marketing Board, which limited the powers of the farmers' representatives to control the vast reserves which are accumulating under the Board's policy.

(6) The feeling that the Government had not formulated any plans for the future of industry and agriculture, and that, indeed, it was lukewarm about any development apart from production for export.

C. Social.

(1) The alleged slow development of educational facilities in spite of a growing demand, and the almost complete failure to provide any technical or vocational training.

(2) The shortage of housing, particularly in the towns, and the low standards of houses for Africans as compared with those provided for Europeans.

(3) The fear of wholesale alienation of tribal lands leaving a landless peasantry.

(4) Inadequacy of the legal powers of Government necessary to deal with speeches designed to arouse disorder and violence. . . .

In putting forward many of our proposals, particularly those dealing with political reform, we are conscious of certain risks brought to our notice by Africans as well as Europeans.

It would be idle to ignore the existence of bribery and corruption in many walks of life in the gold coast, admitted to us by every responsible African to whom we addressed the question. That it may spread as further responsibility devolves upon the African is a possibility which cannot be denied. No nation can rise to greatness upon any such foundations. It is a challenge, therefore, to the Gold Coast Africans to set their house in order and a challenge which we believe will be taken up under the weight of responsibility. In any event, in our view its existence cannot be accepted as a barrier on the road to self-government.

Again, in discussion with many Africans, we found a marked disinclination to face realities. A tendency existed to take refuge in ill-founded optimism that things would come right in the end, or that someone would find the answers. This was exemplified in their attitude towards Swollen Shoot, a belief that Government funds were inexhaustible, and a blithe disregard of the complexities of modern economic organization and the like. The hard truth that every penny of Government expenditure comes out of the taxpayer's pocket, has nowhere penetrated public understanding.

Save among the older population, there is an unconfessed desire for Europeanization, at least in many aspects. We say, unconfessed, because, while undoubtedly growing, it is not yet strong enough to cast off the shackles of tribalism. But the hands of the clock cannot be put back. The movement is gathering momentum, even if cloaked at times by anti-racial expressions. We doubt if it is sufficiently realized what problems these changes entail. Native authority in its widest sense is diminishing. The old religions are being undermined by modern conceptions. Earlier disciplines are weakening. Others must be devised to take their place. . . .

So far as the economic life of the country is concerned, we were struck by the high costs of production ruling in the Gold Coast. Many of the commodities, both industrial and agricultural, the export of which it is hoped to develop in the future, would be too costly to compete in world markets. It is essential, therefore, if the commercial aspirations of the people are to be realized, that productivity be increased. . . . Upon such increase depends the means to pay for all social services and for the creation of a higher standard of life. . . .

We are satisfied that in the conditions existing today in the Gold Coast, a substantial measure of constitutional reform is necessary to meet the legitimate aspirations of the indigenous population. The fact that . . . the Colony, Ashanti and the Northern Territories present, in some aspects, different problems, by reason of the varying stages of cultural, political and economic development at which each has arrived, does not in our view provide a valid excuse for delay. . . .

In so far as our proposals are acceptable, we recommend them as the basis of constitutional reform for a probationary period of ten years. At the end of that period the whole matter should be reviewed in the light of the experience gained. We do not believe that an atmosphere of stability would be created by any shorter period of trial.

The new Constitution, ushered in with such promise in 1946, was no doubt well intentioned. Its weakness, in our view, lay in its conception. It was obviously conceived in the light of pre-war conditions. . . . In [the post-war] background, the 1946 Constitution was outmoded at birth. . . .

The concession of an African elected majority in the Legislature, in the absence of any real political power, provided no outlet for a people eagerly emerging into political consciousness. On the other hand, it provided an effective stimulant for intelligent discontent. The real and effective political government remained in the hands of the Executive Council. Composed of *ex officio* and nominated members, it was the instrument of power. The Legislature was largely a Chamber of Debate.

The 1946 Constitution did nothing to decentralize the machinery of government. Government continued to concern itself with the details of preeminently local affairs. The District Commissioner still controlled matters of local concern. Africans, thus, even at lower levels, were still deprived of the school of political experience to be found in local management.

Only in Native Administration, residing largely in a hierarchy of vested interests, jealously guarded by Chiefs and Elders, was the African provided with an approach to political expression. Even where an enlightened Native Administration admitted some fresh entrants into the fold of the State Council, it was conceded as a great privilege and not conferred as an elementary right.

We have no doubt that this policy of rule through the Chiefs possessed many advantages. But . . . great questioning has everywhere arisen, particularly among the classes with little or no say in affairs. . . . We have found an intense suspicion that the Chiefs are being used by the Government as an instrument for the delay if not the suppression of the political aspiration of the people. The fact that destooling—once the absolute privilege of a dissatisfied people . . . has been made the subject of a well-defined code, under the supervision of Government, is itself the object of grave suspicion. The view is advanced that so long as the chief accepts and supports the government policy he will receive Government support, however much he has become the object of dislike to his people. That there is no evidence to support this view, is beside the point. . . . Nothing impressed us so much as the volume of evidence we received, not alone from the more forward sections of the community, of the intense objection to Chiefs being elected to and sitting in the Legislative Council. We were constantly reminded that the place of the Chief was among his people. Apart from this, we found great difficulty in getting any universal agreement on the precise place to be occupied by the Chief in any new political system. . . .

While for ourselves we are unable to envisage the growth of commercialization in the Gold Coast, with the retention of native institutions, save in a form which is a pale historical reflection of the past, we do not think we are called upon to make any immediate recommendation for the solution of a matter upon which Africans themselves are not in agreement. Our sole concern is to see that in any new constitutional development there is such modification as will prevent existing institutions standing in the way of general political aspirations. . . .

The moral justification for Britain remaining in the Gold Coast lies in this: out of a population of approximately four and a half million Africans . . . barely ten percent is literate. We have no reason to suppose that power in the hands of a small literate minority would not tend to exploit the illiterate majority in accordance with the universal pattern of what has happened elsewhere in the past throughout the world. His majesty's Government therefore, has a moral duty to remain until

(a) The literate population has by experience reached a stage when selfish exploitation is no longer the dominant motive of political power, or
(b) The bulk of the population has advanced to such a stage of literacy and political experience as will enable it to protect itself from gross exploitation;
(c) Some corresponding degree of cultural, political and economic achievement has been attained by all three areas, now part of the Gold Coast.

Pending the happening of these events, two matters in our view call for immediate attention:

(i) The Constitution and Government of the country must be so reshaped as to give every African of ability, an opportunity to help to govern the country, so as not only to gain political experience, but also to experience political power. We are firmly of opinion that anything less than this will only stimulate national unrest. Government through advisory committees, as a measure of reform, in our view would be quite unacceptable.
(ii) A forward policy of Africanization must take place in the public services, so that in all appointments or promotions, having laid down the standards of qualifications, the first question to be asked is "Is there an African capable of filling the appointment?"

Their constitutional recommendations include:

Local authorities in which provision is made for an African elected element; regional councils for the Colony, Ashanti and the Northern territories, with executive powers for, e.g. Health, Education, Housing, local communications and social services; members to be elected by the local and town councils; an extension of town councils.

A house of Assembly of 45 elected (⅓ from each region) members and 5 nominated, as well as *ex officio* members, chosen for four years (unless dissolved earlier on advice of the Board of Ministers). A Board of 9 ministers, 5 being African members of the Assembly and 4 *ex officio*; nominated by the Governor and approved by resolution of assembly; African ministers removable on a ¾ vote of censure.

History and National Development: The Case of John Mensah Sarbah and the Reconstruction of Gold Coast History

D. E. Kofi Baku

By the turn of the twentieth century, an elevated British self-image and an attitude that Africans and their culture were comparatively inferior led to British versions of local histories, which informed how the British formulated policy toward indigenous Gold Coast peoples. John Mensah Sarbah (1864–1910), a lawyer trained in Britain and an intellectual nationalist, "decolonized" and ably marshaled local history to fashion a nationalist character. In the excerpt below from a scholarly article, D. E. Kofi Baku, professor and former chair of the history department at the University of Ghana, shows how Sarbah effectively challenged the established British narrative of the Gold Coast and its peoples as well as the political and economic relations between the two by foregrounding indigenous institutions of governance and how these institutions shaped the nature of that relationship.

The role of history in national development has been acknowledged. In this regard, it is generally believed that History does not only equip the Historian adequately to understand his environment but it also informs him of the alternatives available for the purposeful harnessing of the resources of his environment for development. . . . Indeed as early as 1898, *The Gold Coast Aborigine*, the mouth piece of the Aborigines' Rights Protection Society, perceptively recognized this point. It declared in its very first issue,

> The people of the Gold Coast have a past and the rising generation must be instructed in the history of their country, for we do not know of a better weapon to be wielding in any political struggle for existence than a smart acquaintance with the history of the country, backed by a clear intelligence of the laws of the land.

Twenty years later in the 1920s, other African nationalists mirrored this same point. It was articulated by Solanke, the Nigerian nationalist as follows: "How is the spirit of a people to be formed and animated and cheered but out of the store house of its historical recollection."

From the foregoing, it is obvious that for History, Historical writing and Historical studies to achieve their desired objectives, they have to take specific forms. For Africa, the choice is clear. Many scholars have referred to the need to decolonize African History. What has generally not been acknowledged is the fact that this decolonization process began in some parts of Africa from the middle of the 19th Century. . . .

Eurocentric Historical Writing and Colonial Expansion

[In 1874,] British forces conquered the hinterland kingdom of Asante and declared a protectorate over the Coastal areas and the interior. . . . The era of formal colonialism in the Gold Coast thus began and with it came a renewed interest in its affairs. For in that same year some sixteen books of historical nature were published in Britain by British authors on Gold Coast and Asante affairs. These books were, in the main, written by soldiers, adventurers, missionaries, colonial administrators and journalists, men who were at best, ill-acquainted with the Gold Coast and its socio-cultural and political affairs. . . .

These books shared certain basic characteristics. First, they presented distorted versions of Gold Coast and Asante history, a history in which the progressive role of the traditional leaders and their societies were either totally ignored or denigrated. . . .

These books soon assumed the status of manuals for the British Colonialists and colonial administrators. Lugard's *Dual Mandate in British Tropical Africa* is probably the classic example of this. It was published at a time when colonial administration was undergoing self evaluation and Empire builders in the colonies and in London desired a "Universal" formula for colonial administration which would be applicable in all colonies. . . .

Sarbah and the Decolonisation of Gold Coast History

John Mensah Sarbah was born at Anomabo near Cape Colast in 1864. He was educated at the Wesleyan Primary and High Schools in Anomabo and Cape Coast. In [1878], at the age of 14, he was sent to England and was educated for four years at Queen's College, in Taunton, Somerset. In early 18[8]4, Sarbah returned to the Gold Coast only to set sail for England again in the middle of that same year. On the 25th of June, 1884, he was admitted to the Lincoln's Inn to study Law and was called to the Bar three years later, on 4th May, 1887. At the tender age of 23 he had become what is probably, Gold Coast's first Barrister.

Back in the Gold Coast, Sarbah set up a lucrative legal career, became a leading member of the "Mfantsi Amanbuhu Fekuw" or the Fante Political Society and the proprietor and editor of the *Gold Coast People.* He pursued a career which soon marked him out as a patriot and a nationalist agitator. More importantly, Sarbah like other Gold Coast nationalist intellectuals was quick to realize that the success of the practical politics of the British in the Gold Coast rested, in the main, on their control over what they considered the desirable versions of the histories of the Gold Coast and Asante. . . . He, therefore, published respectively in 1897 and 1906, *Fanti Customary Laws: A Brief Introduction to the Principles of Native Law and Customs of the Fanti and Akan Districts of the Gold Coast, With Report of Some Cases Therein Decided in Law Courts (hereafter Fanti Customary Laws)* and *Fanti National Constitution: A Short Treatise on the Constitution and Government of the Fanti, Ashanti and other Tribes of West Africa, Together with a Brief Account of the Discovery of the Gold by Portuguese Navigators, A Short Narration of the Early English Voyage and a Study of the Rise of British Gold Coast Jurisdiction, etc. etc.* (hereafter Fanti National Constitution). Indeed, both books . . . were well received. . . . As for the latter book it was a tour de force with a special section which reviewed Anglo–Gold Coast relations and argued out that illegality of the extension of formal British power and Jurisdiction in the Gold Coast. As a consequence the British colonialists in the Gold Coast became profoundly aware of the fact that there were alternative versions to the histories produced on the Gold Coast, which if known would not only embarrass them, but would also lead to a challenge of their authority. Not surprising, therefore, there soon developed carefully orchestrated moves to obstruct the production of such facts and histories. In December 1890, for example, the Governor of the Gold Coast issued instructions "for the collection and destruction by fire or sinkage in the sea of all old records, papers and other matters which can no longer be of any use." In an interesting passage, Sarbah reveals how he managed to buy some valuable historical records which were being burnt by African workers at the Cape Coast Castle in the preparation of their "noonday meal." According to Sarbah,

> In the year 1888, the Supreme Court being in Gothic House, Cape Coast Castle, I found some Kru boys one day cooking their midday meal, and burning as faggots several bundles of papers. On the ground

> were many more. Asked where they got them, they replied from a big box close by and the contents of which they were at liberty to use in any manner they pleased. It was the Gold Coast version of an old, old story over again: Knowledge through patient and frugal centuries, enlarging discovery, and recording it; ignorance, wanting its day's dinner, lighting a fire with the record, and flavouring its one roast with the burnt souls of many generations. On enquiry, the District Commissioner said the box was full of rubbish, and the Kru boys had spoken truly. Next day, for three pence, two of those bundles changes hands; examined, they were found to contain papers, the most important whereof are now published. The remaining contents of the box were shortly afterwards pitched into the sea, it was said, by order of an high official. The archives of the colony have been mostly destroyed.

This deliberate act of vandalism was soon followed by the withdrawal of the permission granted to Sarbah to use the facilities of the European archives in the castles along the Coast. . . . These acts did not at all leave Sarbah in any doubt about official Colonial mind on indigenous versions of Gold Coast history. For Sarbah, therefore, "history is sometimes troublesome; historical facts are often embarrassing in West Africa, and nothing so facilitates a spirited indefinite policy as a clean foolscap sheet of paper. . . ."

Thus beginning from about 1887, "Sarbah published a number of weighty books and articles in prestigious African oriented British journals. Taken together these books and articles covered some 400 and more years of Gold Coast history which focused attention on some important aspects of the Gold Coast and African past." Four very important and closely interrelated arguments were developed by Sarbah.

Firstly, Sarbah pointed out that Gold Coasters, and more specifically, the Fantes had from time immemorial inhabited the lands on which they lived before their contact with Europeans in the last quarter of the 15th century. Secondly, Gold Coasters have developed their own distinctive social, economic, political and legal-constitutional system and practices before their contact with Europeans. Some of these, according to Sarbah, had despite the ravages of colonialism survived in their basic essentials. Thirdly, for the whole period of European contact with the Gold Coast, Europeans had rented, but never owned the lands upon which their trade forts and castles stood. Fourthly, the relations between Gold Coasters and Europeans had always been carefully defined by treaties, such as the treaty of 1831 and the Bond of 1844. Thus any extension of European political and judicial authority beyond the confines of their rented forts and castles had to be covered by prior agreements between Gold Coast chiefs and Europeans and these were confined in the form of treaties. . . .

The success of Sarbah's books as Africanist "counter history" was demonstrated by the fact they soon acquired the status of authoritative texts . . . and were used by the colonial administration as reference texts for the determination of colonial administrative and judicial policies. They were also used in the courts of law, in commissions of inquiry into local and municipal government disputes and in legislative council debates. In this regard, Sarbah's books became instrumental in protecting local African interests particularly where questions of control over land and the imposition of direct taxation were concerned.

The Administrative Problem

J. E. Casely Hayford

Joseph Ephraim Casely Hayford (1866–1930) was an author, lawyer, and politician. Born in the Cape Coast region, he pursued his college education in Sierra Leone at Fourah Bay College, where Edward Wilmot Blyden (1832–1912), a well-noted pan-Africanist, heavily influenced him. Casely Hayford studied law in England, and apart from his practice in the Gold Coast, he was involved in newspaper publishing and political activism. Casely Hayford took the British to task over the issue of land ownership under the aegis of the Aborigines' Rights Protection Society, of which he also served as president in 1910. In his writings, he championed the cause of indigenous governing institutions and challenged the British to recognize the employment of these institutions as a viable way of governing the Gold Coast. In the excerpt here, from his book Gold Coast Native Institutions: With Thoughts upon a Healthy Imperial Policy for the Gold Coast and Ashanti, *Casely Hayford explores this "administrative problem."*

Africa, I believe, has been compared somewhere by Dr. Blyden in his writings to the Sphinx of old, which, sitting by the wayside, calmly propounded riddles. Trouble and great confusion to the nation, European or otherwise, which would attempt to read them without her aid. It could only mean disappointment bitterer than Jordan apples.

The analogy holds good with regard to the attempt on the part of Great Britain successfully to administer the Gold Coast and Ashanti without the cooperation of the sons of the soil. Indeed, the very difficulties which beset the path of the British Administrator can be correctly indicated sometimes only by the intelligent ones of the country, and the method, if not the means, of solution must also be with them. I venture here to indicate the problem.

It is desirable, at the outset, to clear our minds of certain impressions which recent writers upon the Gold Coast have sought to create. It has been assiduously inculcated that the only object of Great Britain of the Gold Coast is trade—legitimate trade, if you please. It is then urged that, since trade follows the Flag, and civilization trade, the Aborigines of the Gold

Coast cannot but be benefited by the presence of the British upon their soil. This is true to a certain extent but let me point out in what way it is not wholly true.

There is a keen pleasure in the sense of possession. *My* land, *my* house, as contradistinguished from *your* land, *your* house, will remain, till the end of time, worthy objects of ambition. As with the individual man, so with the individual nation. . . . Whether you call them spheres of influence, territories, possessions, protectorates, or colonies, there is hardly a European power which will not fight for their acquisition, even though there is derived from holding them not one farthing's worth of profit, taking the outlay it involves into consideration. I believe Mr. Andrew Carnegie has shown conclusively in an able article how comparatively unprofitable for purposes of trade are some of the colonies and protectorates of Great Britain, let alone the so-called possessions or spheres of influence. There is, in some cases, an insane thirst for territorial acquisition, cost what it may.

To state the proposition broadly, it is simply the primitive instinct of acquisitiveness in man which operates in the case of nations, no matter the extent of their boasted civilization. Primitive man in primitive society says: "I will have your land, or your hut, if you will give it to me. If not, I will take it. When I have taken it, and you cannot retake it, of course, I will keep it." The civilized nations of the world are to-day like unto primitive man, else international courts of arbitration would more frequently be sitting in one European capital or another, and the weak nations of the earth would have a little peace, if not a little justice.

If you are inclined to deny the foregoing proposition, then I ask you to accept this, that commonly, there are two ethical sanctions to the fact of possession. In the first place, you must come by your possession honestly, and secondly, you must bear manfully its responsibilities; which two sanctions are generally not observed, if recognized at all, by the great nations of the earth.

Since, however, the world is as we know it to be; since the weak must go to the wall, and the fittest survive, irrespective of what is right or wrong, fair or unfair; it is, I confess, but practical philosophy that the weak should side with the strong.

From this point of view, always remember, the Aborigines of the Gold Coast triumph in the wave of imperialism which at present sways the public sentiment of Great Britain. It may overwhelm them, and play havoc with all that is dear to them of law, custom and practice; it may reduce them to the condition of bondsmen and captives in their own fair domains; it may denationalize them and make them a people of no reputation, a by-word and a reproach among men; but, for all these things, they would rather have the ills that they know of than fly to others that they know not of. It is nothing but common sense. . . .

Now, since we have the British with us, and the object of an enlightened Government should be to promote the healthy national development of the governed by conserving and not destroying the institutions of the people; and since in the past the tendency has been toward disintegration rather than towards conservation—we have the right to say to them: "You have disorganized our institutions, you shall help to reorganize them; you have enriched your homes with the luxury that the Gold Coast has afforded, you shall help us to rebuild our homes; you have made here princely fortunes, you shall help us live peaceably in our own vineyards and under our own fig trees"—it is about time, I hold, that the Authorities at Downing Street confine themselves more to external administration, leaving the internal government of people to develop upon the natural lines of their own institutions. Will the Public opinion of Great Britain insist upon this being done, or will it allow the work of spoliation to proceed? This is the problem in its naked form. The people of the Gold Coast observe that for nearly a century you have been trying to mold for them their institutions, and that you have most signally failed. They see in the civilization you offer much that is fair, but cannot fail to perceive the weak spots and blemishes in the same. They say to you, "We are anxious to take part in the race of nations towards the attainment of higher ideals, if you will only give us a chance to work out our own salvation." But no, you will continue to regard them as innocents, and they, the pigmies, must march with you, the Colossus, whether it is expedient or not. This is not right or fair. It is not even common sense. Therefore, with all earnestness, I humbly urge that henceforth the Aborigines and their Protectors should adjust themselves respectively to their proper spheres of work. Let them do this, and the problem of a century will readily be solved.

But how about this adjustment? you will ask. Permit me to ask you to go to history and to science, and they will teach you what to do. Science will tell you that there can be no healthy growth except from within; and the history of the Gold Coast will disclose to you the facts and circumstances which must guide such internal growth. This has been the stumbling-block all along, this want of adjustment of the proper spheres of work of the parties concerned. It must be removed now. Let us see how.

Truly, the present is a critical moment in the constitutional history of the Gold Coast and her hinterland. He who runs may see that the time has come to determine what policy shall govern the administration of the coun-

Government building, Accra, Ghana. Unidentified photographer, ca. 1910. EEPA 1995-018-0070. Ghana Photographs [between 1885 and 1910], Eliot Elisofon Photographic Archives, National Museum of African Art, Smithsonian Institution.

try by the Colonial Office in the commercial interests of Great Britain and in the practical uplifting of the native tribes in the scale of civilization.

But unhappy recollections surround the name of the Colonial Office in the mind of the historian. That hoar-headed institution, generally dormant and lethargic, occasionally erratic and irrepressible, if not irresponsible, will have much to answer for in the day when the public intelligence of Great Britain will awaken to the golden opportunities which the Empire has lost on the Gold Coast and in Ashanti through its blunders.

Let me at once clear this matter, namely, the blunders of the Colonial Office, of all misconceptions. The custom has grown up, within recent years, that the moment the Colonial Office is mentioned the mind of the reader instinctively flies back to the right honorable gentleman who at present presides over that institution. He is at once fixed, rightly or wrongly, with all the blame, past and present, attributable to that office. This is not fair; and I will say this, that the Aborigines of the Gold Coast, in their criticism of the methods of the Colonial Office, disclaim the propriety of attacking any particular Cabinet Minister who, in past, present, or future Administrations, was, is, or will be, Secretary of State for the Colonies. . . .

If, therefore, you complain of Mr. Chamberlain, you only complain of the circumstance the Unionist Government, for once, has done the Colonies the unique honor of placing at the head of their affairs and the direction of their destinies a first-rate man, who has the courage of his convictions, and who presses such convictions to their logical conclusions. Hence the crisis. . . . For, pray, remember that, whatever the capacity of a Colonial Minister, and with the best of intentions in the world, he cannot be expected to be fully acquainted with local conditions, native peculiarities, past constitutional history of the Gold Coast.

Unlike Australia, Canada, and other of Great Britain rightly so denominated, here, on the Gold Coast, you have to deal with an aboriginal race with distinctive institutions, customs, and laws, which, now and again, European writers may attempt to portray, but which they can never fully interpret to the outside world.

It follows, therefore, that a Colonial Minister has to gather information, as guide for his conduct, second-hand. Now, what are the sources of information open to a Colonial Minister? There is principally the Colonial Governor, whose tenure of office is so uncertain, and who, during his administration, be it long, or be it short, is somehow generally surrounded with officials not always the best qualified to inform him accurately concerning the significance and hidden meaning of Native institutions. He, the Colonial Governor, sometimes supplements the erroneous ideas he thus acquires by desultory reading of authors who, in writing, seek not the making of history, but that of their own ephemeral fame. In his dispatches he freely makes use of such information; and the Colonial Minister, when pressed for a division in the House of Commons, presses into his service the ill-digested lesson he has learnt from the dispatches. Thus, between the Colonial Minister and the local Governor, ignorance at times reigns supreme as to the real merits of a given issue. This adds to the difficulty of the problem under consideration.

What, for example, could have been more pitiable than the excuses put forward by the Colonial Secretary in the "Golden Stool" debate in the House of Commons on the 19th of March, 1901? Speaking of the cause of the rising in Ashanti, the right honorable member for West Birmingham said: "The earlier expedition was so far successful that it was concluded without a single drop of blood having been shed. And when you ask what is the cause of the subsequent disturbance, I have no hesitation in saying that it was the bloodlessness of the previous expedition. The people of Ashanti, in common with every savage tribe, hold it to be a point of honor to fight for their chief, and to fight for their cause. They are ready to accept defeat, but they are not ready to accept the consequences of defeat without being actually defeated." Unhappy Ashanti, a nation steeped in grossest barbarism, addicted to human sacrifices, slave-raiding, and the breaking of treaties! You must be thankful for small mercies; for, until the Colonial Secretary spoke, we, your brethren on the Gold Coast, could not believe that you could be guilty of such a thing as a point of honor! But there it is in black and white. Who told Mr. Chamberlain this? Did he read it in books, or in Sir F. M. Hodgson's dispatches? I have never seen this in any authentic book on savage tribes, and so it is just possible it was from the dispatches.

Or, again, take this bit: "Sir Frederick Hodgson did not ask my permission to go for the golden stool, but, speaking now after the event, I entirely approve of his attempt to secure it. The golden stool is of very great moral and intellectual value (laughter). It is not loot in the sense the honorable member supposes. It has no great pecuniary value. But in the opinion of the tribe, and according to the custom of the tribe, the possession of the stool gives supremacy. And if, therefore, we should secure this stool, we would be doing more for the, peace of Ashanti than, probably, by any armed expedition, therefore, it was of the greatest importance to get hold of this symbol of sovereignty, if we could possibly do it."

Again, how came the Colonial Secretary by this *ex-post facto* explanation? This time I have read somewhere something very similar. Here it is: "The stool appears among the Ashantis and neighboring peoples to be the emblem of possession, for the expression 'to succeed to the stool' is applied not only to a king on his accession, but also to private persons when they inherit property. Hence a conquered country is not considered to be fully subjugated until the royal stool has passed into the hands of the conqueror. It was for this reason, no doubt, that King Ajiman of Jaman exhibited such eagerness when he spoke to me of his desire to invade Ashanti and recover the Gold Stool, and this is also the probable explanation of the fact that in neither of the British invasions of Ashanti has this stool been allowed to fall into the hands of the invaders."

The first point to note in reading these two passages is that, from Dr. Freeman's account of the King of Jaman's eagerness to recover the "gold stool," the said stool must once have been the stool of Jaman, otherwise there could be no need to "recover" it. That being so, the reflection is reasonable that, upon Jaman losing her "gold stool," she did not cease to be a nation, or to possess a stool, "gold" or otherwise, upon which subsequent kings sat, down to the time of Ajiman.

The second point to note is that the Colonial Secretary disclaims having directed Sir Frederick Hodgson to go for the golden stool. It is very unlikely, therefore, that Mr. Chamberlain knew till "after the event" of the great "moral and intellectual value" of the golden stool. But Sir Frederick Hodgson must have known of it, or he would not have, unsolicited, gone in quest of it. I am sure he did not get his information from any of his advisers, for his conduct in this matter has received the severest condemnation alike of officials and the general public of the Gold Coast. It is charitable to assume that the good Governor probably misread Dr. Freeman. Dr. Freeman, like the careful writer that he is, speaks of "appears," "no doubt," [and] "probable explanation." He kept an open mind in the matter. Perhaps later observation and experience might show that, after all, there was no virtue in the "golden stool." But when these tentative propositions pass through the official mill, they come out in a debate in the House of Commons as positive facts.

This sort of thing, or anything like it, is a source of danger, and adds to the difficulty of the problem before us. We want an intelligent and scientific study of Native Institutions, and a right understanding of the nature of the work Great Britain is called upon to do in the Gold Coast and Ashanti, and the limit of her capacity to carry out such work apart from the Aborigines of the country. When once this principle has been fully grasped and an attempt made to work it out, we shall, at last, be on the way to a successful administration of the Gold Coast and Ashanti.

The Employment of Men: Clerks, Police, Soldiers, and Teachers, 1930–1951

Stephan F. Miescher

Western schooling largely took roots in Ghana through the efforts of Christian missions. Consequently, schools in Ghana are often linked to Christian denominations. Christian-based schooling altered the traditional avenues of upward socioeconomic mobility for men in Ghana. This schooling shaped the lives and livelihoods of those who were able to partake as it stridently sought to recast them in the mold of British men. A net effect was that it transformed the meaning of manhood in Ghana as "educated men" sought to define a new socioeconomic niche for themselves in colonial Ghana. In the excerpt below from his monograph, Stephan Miescher, associate professor of history at the University of California at Santa Barbara, explores the nexus between Christianity, schooling, manhood, and employment in colonial Ghana.

In colonial Ghana of the 1930s and 1940s male students who had passed the Standard VII examination were called in Twi *krakye* (pl. *akrakyefoɔ*). The word is derived from the English word "clerk" and is often translated as "scholars." *Akrakyefoɔ* were mainly trained in mission schools to work as clerks, cocoa brokers, storekeepers, pupil teachers, and, if they pursued their education, as certified teachers and pastors. They had "a high prestige in the community due to their wealth, occupation, or literacy" and exercised "an effective influence in the political and social life of the community corresponding to their enhanced status." The subjective meaning of belonging to the *akrakyefoɔ* affected these men's selection of employment and self-presentation. *Akrakyefoɔ*'s habitus, their "systems of dispositions" rooted in individual and collective experiences of hometown *mmusua* (matrilineages) and education, not only structured their work but [also] shaped their notions of masculinity and its enactment. As pivotal middle figures in colonial encounters, *akrakyefoɔ* maintained a balance between home and host communities, between employers, government officials, church leaders, and salaried colleagues and friends. These men shared the following characteristics: literacy, a community of peers, ambivalence about politics, and consumption of certain goods. Different forms of employment, such as clerks, soldiers, policemen, and teachers, placed them into intermediary positions, which affected their social, economic, and political standing, as well as their individual experience.

As members of intermediary classes, *akrakyefoɔ* experienced a double social exclusion. Most of them were neither part of the older and established chiefly elites who as "traditional rulers" were in charge of local administration under indirect rule, nor did they belong to the highly educated and financially secure intelligentsia. This was the lawyer-merchant class, who controlled an increasing number of African-owned newspapers and gathered in exclusive social clubs in cities, while waiting to inherit the colonial state. Still, *akrakyefoɔ* had political, social, economic, and cultural aspirations. Many hoped for a share of power and sought to be part of a modern and increasingly urban world. . . .

Akrakyefoɔ claimed a special socioeconomic status. In the 1930s Standard VII certificate holders looked for wage labor appropriate to a literate *krakye.* In middle school parlance, they entered "the world." But during the post-Depression years they faced difficulties securing clerical employment with the government, with banks, or as a shopkeeper for a European company. Some *akrakyefoɔ* sought to join the police force, the railway or sanitation department, or the less secure job of a tribunal registrar. All were positions that required literacy, preferably a Standard VII certificate. Others looked for employment as teachers; only a few continued their education at a secondary school or a teacher training college. All these jobs, except primary school teaching and some clerical work, were reserved for men since women's education emphasized domestic skills. In becoming a *krakye* men looked for professional careers that were privileged compared to women's options in wage labor. Colonial education was "reinforcing" women's "subordinate position." In newspapers, literate men expressed an ambivalence about women "taking the place of men as clerks," and warned about "the competition for employment between the sexes." In her women's column, "Marjorie Mensah" (pseud., Mabel Dove) noted that "many a girl would like to take up a business course in book-keeping, shorthand and such subjects that would engage her to get a job and earn good money."

Joining the ranks of the *akrakyefoɔ* meant a new notion of masculinity. Because they became part of a migrant social group while remaining connected to their home communities and extended families, they were subjected to conflicting expectations. They had to redefine their selves within work environments and create a professional identity that was also mean-

"Superintendent Ellis & Mrs. Ellis & Revs. Glandfield, Morris & other & native pastors, Wesleyan Mission, Cape Coast," Ghana. Unidentified photographer, ca. 1910. EEPA 1995-018-0045. Ghana Photographs [between 1885 and 1910], Eliot Elisofon Photographic Archives, National Museum of African Art, Smithsonian Institution.

ingful to their wider network of social relations. Many of these middle figures left a paper trail, a "tin-trunk literacy" that has been overlooked by Africa's social historians. . . .

Akrakyefoɔ and Writing

In 1935 the *Gold Coast Times* published a letter deploring the "Plight of the African Mercantile Clerk." The writer, himself a clerk, referred to *akrakyefoɔ* working for European firms like the United Africa Company (UAC), the United Trading Company (UTC), or the Société Commerciale de L'Ouest Africain, whose stores were run by an African manager. Unlike clerks in the African civil service or working for a bank, mercantile clerks had a "precarious existence" without a standard grading system, regular increments to salaries, or security for old age. Rather, their wages fluctuated "like shares on the Stock Exchange." In the "slump" of the 1930s, mercantile firms were "understaffed and their overworked clerks underpaid," while European employees departed for their vacation "with clockwork precision." Still, many school leavers with aspirations as *akrakyefoɔ* envisioned themselves in clerical employment or as shopkeepers.

Graduating from the Abetifi Boys Boarding School in 1935, Boakye Yiadom wrote in his "Autobiography: My Own Life" that he now had entered the "life of the world." He traveled to the Central Province where his *wɔfanom* (uncles) Kwadwo Opong and Kwabena Mensa Opong worked as tailors. He hoped they would provide the capital of at least one hundred pounds to become a store manager for one of the European firms. Failing to receive support, Boakye Yiadom went to stay with his mother, Ntoriwa, who had married Kwasi Obeng, the *dekuro* (headman) of Kurofa. As a "well-known cocoa broker," the stepfather introduced him to W. F. Neizer, a cocoa buyer for UAC, "the commercial colossus of West Africa," in nearby Konongo. After examining his arithmetic skills, Neizer presented Boakye Yiadom to the *oburoni panyin,* the senior European. Having attended "a good school," he was hired as Neizer's second assistant cocoa-weighing clerk in 1936. The UAC manager considered Abetifi a "good town" because of its Presbyterian schools; Boakye Yiadom's Standard VII certificate counted as reliable qualification for clerical employment. Following standard procedure, Boakye Yiadom did not receive any pay during the first year of training. By 1937 he earned one pound a month, increased by ten shillings in each of the following three years. This salary enabled him to buy some furniture, as well as shoes, clothes, a hat, toiletries, and writing paper. Such goods, reflecting new needs, aided in the public display of his *krakye* status. . . .

Writing cards and letters, or keeping a diary, was common among *akrakyefoɔ*. Boakye Yiadom started his first diary together with classmates, including Bruce Breko, at the Abetifi Boarding School. E. K. Addo kept a written record of his work as a storekeeper. Unlike most *akrakyefoɔ,* Addo acquired literacy outside the classroom. In 1928 his older brother, J. K. Kwakye, had set him up as a store manager in Nsawam, a market center twenty miles north of Accra. Influenced by J. E. K. Aggrey's motto that "any person who wishes to learn can learn," Addo sought help from Achimota teachers to improve his written and oral English skills. They frequently came to his Nsawam home at weekends or during holidays. As part of writing exercises, Addo began keeping a journal. Among his papers are two diaries covering the years from 1932 to 1934; one appears to be a draft of the other. Addo followed a practice introduced by Pietist missionaries and popularized in Presbyterian schools. It resembled the "station diaries" kept by Presbyterian pastors and catechists. Addo wrote daily entries of at least a few lines, at times covering more than one page. Unlike the Pietist model, his entries were seldom introspective but rather served as a logbook. They provide a rare window into the everyday life of a storekeeper during the Depression and show how Addo embraced Presbyterian masculinity.

The diaries document Addo's activities as a trader. From Monday through Saturday he opened his shop as early as 6:40 a.m. and closed after 5 p.m., "when the sun sank to the horizon." The early 1930s were difficult years. Complaining about "very poor sales," Addo was greatly concerned about "the world depression." Since cocoa prices had plummeted, not reaching the level of 1930 until 1946, his Nsawam clients, all connected to the cocoa industry, suffered. Addo considered his sales "fair" as long as he made two pounds a day. They picked up toward the end of the year, when cocoa farmers started selling their crops; they peaked in the days before Christmas, reaching twenty pounds in December 1933. Addo shared profits with brother Kwakye who had provided the initial capital. Seeking to improve returns, Addo hired two itinerant traders from Kwawu; one woman, Adjeiwah, was particularly successful. Addo had a keen ability to acquire items not available from his competitors. When he made six pounds, he attributed this to offering "nice clothes that people desire most." Still, sales remained dependent on local economics *and* social activities. One Saturday he noted that "the only goods sold were collars and ties because dance is to take place tonight." Addo did not attend the dance but went straight to his residence. In the evening he usually "stayed indoor to study." Unlike other *akrakyefoɔ*, who frequented the recently opened "Mikado Picture House" at Nsawam, Addo disapproved of the moral content of movies. The only leisure activity he permitted himself was watching a boxing tournament, "occasionally" staged at the Mikado.

Addo's devotion to the Presbyterian Church is well represented in the diaries. He attended church service on Sundays, sometimes twice, and then recorded the Bible texts and commented on the preaching, which was usually in Ga for Nsawam's multiethnic congregation. Echoing the proverb "*Asɛm pa tiawa*" (A good message is brief), Addo preferred short sermons, which "did not waste time of the listeners" but "inspired hearts." He participated in preaching journeys and joined the Easter Monday picnic. When traveling, Addo attended Presbyterian services. On a journey to Kumase, he not only praised a "very short and inspiring" sermon by Rev. I. Bellon of the Basel Mission but visited Mmofraturo, the new Methodist kindergarten and women's training college, which prepared students for Christian motherhood and womanhood. Impressed by this school, Addo attended his first Methodist service the following Sunday. Reverend Acheampong "preached very well," invoking metaphors like "Bible is best [*sic*] than Gold and Silver." Still, Addo remained faithful to the Presbyterian Church. . . .

The outbreak of World War II had an impact on many *akrakyefoɔ*. With the Gold Coast serving as military hub for the Allied war effort, trader Addo saw his business volume rise. In 1944 he managed to return the capital of 150 pounds to brother Kwakye. The latter declared in a written statement that his "heirs, executors, administrators, or assigns have no claim or interest whatsoever in the above named business." Having established himself an independent businessman, Addo aspired to big-man status. Others like Ɔkyeame Kwabena Asante and Boakye Yiadom enlisted in the Gold Coast Regiment (GCR). Becoming soldiers affected their sense of self; the uniform strengthened their *krakye* identity since literacy qualified them for certain positions in the regiment. . . .

Conclusion

Akrakyefoɔ formed a distinct group that considered itself different, at times superior, from men and women with less or no schooling. The *akrakyefoɔ* enacted this difference in dress, in leisure activities, in the organization of space, in the consumption of goods, and in the practice of reading and writing. . . .

For *akrakyefoɔ*, literacy meant more than an employment qualification. Literacy skills enabled them to participate as members of the reading public, contributing to political and moral debates in the Gold Coast. . . . Some, like Addo, preferred involvement and leadership in their church over the increasingly politicized scholars' unions.

Achimota: From the Story My Mother Taught Me

Abena P. A. Busia

When the name "Achimota" is mentioned in Ghana, it is usually in reference to the noted Achimota School, the colonial government's attempt to compete with religious denominations in providing a first-class educational institution for its colonial subjects. Achimota enjoys a revered history as a formidable educational institution that at one time held the title of most prestigious in the country. Many prominent academics and public officials today affiliate themselves with the school as past students. In the following poem, Abena Busia, poet and professor of English at Rutgers University, takes the reader away from this obvious meaning of Achimota and explores the undertold historical meaning of the area that gave rise to its name. Though it is now within the sprawling metropolitan area of Accra, when the school was built in the early twentieth century, it was some distance away from the city. Centuries before that, the area was dense uninhabited forest that carried a spiritual significance for the Gã peoples, hence the appellation Achimota, which loosely means "We do not mention people."

There is a place between Accra and the Legon hills
where they built the famous school.
Everyone thinks of that
today
when the name Achimota
is heard.
Yet the new school takes the name
of the place
but does not reveal what the name means.
The name is A-chee-mo-ta.
It is a forest still, beside the school,
the roads, the railways, and the streetside markets.
But the forest came first,

and has always been there.
The trees still stand,
but they do not speak the history they have seen;
A-chee-mo-ta-no, not at all.
And only the name remains the remainder
of who we are, what we have been,
and what we have been through.
Sometimes it seems we are forgetting,
but so long as there are people alive who remember,
we will remember the meaning:
Here we came, fleeing
to a place of shelter,
escaping the chains and lash
we would not submit to,
and these trees hid us.
So, when travelling through
here, searching,
you do not call
by name
in this place.
A-chee-mo-ta;
you do not call,
by name,
out loud,
no, not here.

The "underground railroad" had its precursor,
long, long before, on this side of the world.
No one will tell you that today.
We too have been taught forgetting.
We are schooled in another language now
and names lose their meanings, except
as labels.

We are being taught forgetting.
But some remember still
Achimota, and its history
a forest, and its meaning—
the place, and its silence.

Women and Their Organizations during the Convention People's Party Period

Takyiwaa Manuh

Before 1949, women in Ghana were not actively involved in politics but this changed with the emergence of Kwame Nkrumah's Convention People's Party (CPP) in 1949. Indeed, the CPP and Nkrumah introduced a new paradigm in Gold Coast politics when they implemented strategies to involve the youth, the grassroots, and women in mainstream politics. In "Women and Their Organizations during the Convention People's Party Period," a chapter in a scholarly book, African studies professor and lawyer Takyiwaa Manuh examines the contributions of women to the CPP's struggles for office and ultimately the eventual attainment of political self-determination for Ghana. In the excerpts below, Manuh also explores the roles of women in the independent state and their relationship with Nkrumah's government. Finally, she focuses on the dominant women's organizations such as the National Federation of Ghana Women and the National Council of Ghana Women and their efforts to empower Ghanaian women.

Introduction

Women cannot be ignored in any assessment of the "Life and Work of Kwame Nkrumah," since it is clear from even a cursory study of the Convention People's Party (CPP) period that they played a significant part in events as well as constituting an important base for the CPP. Nkrumah himself suggests this by his axiom that "the degree of a country's revolutionary awareness may be measured by the political maturity of its women." . . .

Women in Ghanaian Society

The Convention People's Party, which came to power professing to speak for the masses, had women among its strongest supporters. C. L. R. James notes in his book *Nkrumah and the Ghana Revolution* that "in the struggle for independence, one market woman . . . was worth any dozen Achimota graduates . . ." Together with the workers, young men educated in primary schools and the unemployed, women became some of Nkrumah's ablest, most devoted, and most fearless supporters. Women followed Nkrumah across the country on his speaking tours, vigorously championing the struggle for independence. . . . These women fed Nkrumah and his followers and financed them, and it is alleged that without the support of some of these women, Nkrumah could not have survived in Accra. In addition, they were efficient organizers who could bring thousands of people together for a rally at the shortest possible notice. . . .

Women in the Anticolonial Struggle

With the return of Nkrumah to the Gold Coast and his breakaway from the United Gold Coast Convention (UGCC) to form the CPP, women's involvement in politics on a national scale became possible for the first time. While some of the women in the towns had identified with the UGCC, the lack of a mass base of the UGCC to successfully prosecute the struggle for independence had prevented meaningful action, and some of the first women to join the CPP had started out with the UGCC. With the birth of the CPP, a Women's Section was formed almost simultaneously, and these women worked tirelessly within it, for the achievement of "self-government now." Women such as Mabel Dove Danquah and Akua Asabea Ayisi worked side by side with Nkrumah on the *Evening News* writing articles, demanding independence and exposing themselves to the risks attendant on political activity in a colonial regime. Women took part in the "Positive Action Campaign," and Leticia Quaye, Akua Asabea Ayisi, and others went to prison. Memorable among them was an old lady in her sixties, Arduah Ankrah, who used to call herself "Mrs Nkrumah," and who was convicted for the contempt of exhibiting unruly behavior in court during the trial of some of the campaigners. . . .

Nkrumah recounts in his autobiography that

> much of the success of the CPP has been due to the efforts of women members. From the very beginning, women have been the chief field Organisers. They have travelled through innumerable towns and villages in the role of propaganda secretaries and have been responsible for the most part in bringing about the solidarity and cohesion of the party.

While Nkrumah was in prison, he had learned that at a rally in Kumasi, a woman party member who had adopted the name "Ama Nkrumah" got up on the platform and ended a fiery speech by getting hold of a razor blade and slashing her face. She smeared the blood over her body and challenged the men present to do likewise, in order to show that no sacrifice was too great in their united struggle for freedom and independence. . . .

In May 1951, the CPP appointed four women, namely, Mrs. Leticia Quaye, Mrs. Hanna Cudjoe, Madam Ama Nkrumah, and Madam Sophia Doku, as Propaganda Secretaries. They travelled around the country, enrolling men and women into the CPP and into its Women's Section and Youth League. Wherever there were CPP branches, women's wings proliferated, and these women's wings sponsored rallies where the Propaganda Secretaries spoke about CPP policies and collected contributions for the Party. . . . Inasmuch as independence sought to end colonial domination and create better conditions of life for the population in the form of more schools and hospitals, better drinking water and greater access to all of these amenities, women had more to gain from independence. . . .

Political and Civic Rights

In 1959, the Representation of the People (Women Members) Act was passed. This Act made special provision for the election of women as members of the National Assembly, and reflected the conscious desire of the newly-independent state to have women participate in national affairs at the highest levels. It made provision for the election of ten women as additional members of the National Assembly who were to hold office and be subjected to the same rights and disabilities as elected members of parliament under the Electoral Provisions Ordinance of 1953. New legislation in 1960 repealed the 1959 Act and provided for a different method of election for new women members. Elections were held in June 1960 for the special Women's seats, and the names of the new members were published in the *Ghana Gazette* in July, 1960.

Accordingly, ten women parliamentarians took their seats at the first session of the First Parliament of the Republic of Ghana. This move was not without its critics. The Honourable Mr. Victor Owusu, Opposition Member of Parliament, in his comments on the President's Sessional Address, referred to the women parliamentarians as "a sprinkling of 'lip-sticked' and 'pan-caked' faces of doubtful utility to the deliberations of the House." This was met with a swift rebuttal from Sophia Doku, woman member for the Eastern Region, and he had to apologize hurriedly.

Nkrumah catapulted women onto the political scene in a way that was new both in Ghana and Africa. For him, this was part of the attempt at projecting the African Personality and at raising the status of African Womanhood. Thus, in addition to the women parliamentarians, a woman deputy minister and women district commissioners were appointed. It was not without significance that the woman deputy minister hailed from the North. For long isolated from the rest of the country in political, social, and cultural terms, the Northern Territories had functioned as a labour reserve under colonialism and was at a lower level of development than most other parts of Ghana. . . .

Women were appointed to serve on the boards of corporations, schools, and town councils. Most of these women had been with the party from its inception, and their occupations as teachers, housewives, and the like, reflected the class composition of the CPP. The main criterion for appointment seems to have been loyalty to the party, a principle similarly applied to the men who rose into prominence with the CPP. . . .

Educational, Economic, and Social Measures

As well as enhancing women's political and civic roles, the CPP government pursued measures to advance women's educational levels and enhance their social and economic roles. . . . The access of girls to education, particularly at lower levels, was facilitated, and by 1965–66 girls constituted nearly 44 percent of total primary school enrolments, 35 percent in middle school, and 25 percent at secondary school. In addition, many elderly women participated actively in the mass education campaigns of the period.

The policy of providing segregated education for girls in mission schools was combined with the establishment of mixed secondary schools which provided places for the increased numbers of girls leaving middle schools. At the level of training colleges, however, no such policy seems to have been pursued, and many women's training colleges opened during this period to meet regional needs. One of these was the Tamale Women's Training College, and in a speech to inaugurate its opening, Nkrumah recounted the hitherto existing difficulties in the way of Northern girls who had completed Standard VII and wished to teach. Nkrumah noted his gratification at the presence of "a lady of Northern extraction on the staff of the college."

More women entered the Universities and higher institutions of learning, and others were sent abroad, together with men, to pursue courses in medicine, dentistry, and other technical courses to meet the requirements of the development plans. Women went on short courses to Israel, the Soviet Union and other Eastern-bloc countries for courses in co-operatives, trade unionism, and fisheries, among others. These courses meant diversification in the fields of employment open to women, and while the result of colonial education had been that the principal profession open to women was teaching, women could now be found working in many other areas. By the end of CPP rule (1966) there were a number of women doctors, dentists, lawyers, graduate teachers, administrative officers, parliamentarians, and a judge of the Supreme Court. . . .

In addition to the educational and economic measures, we may note briefly certain socio-cultural and moral matters affecting women which Nkrumah and the CPP attempted to resolve. The first concerned the state of nudity which existed among women in parts of then Northern Territories. While this state of affairs reflected environmental and cultural factors, it was also seen as a manifestation of a state of under-development. Nkrumah was concerned about it, and instituted measures to deal with it. . . .

The National Council of Ghana Women (NCGW)

In the period between 1953 and 1960, there were two predominant women's organizations. One of these was the National Federation of Gold Coast Women. . . . The other was the Ghana Women's League formed by Mrs. Hannah Cudjoe. In addition there were many women's benevolent associations, mutual aid and church groups.

The Ghana Women's League seems to have been very political, and concerned itself with local, nationalist, and continental issues. Its leader, Mrs. Hannah Cudjoe, who was also a CPP Propaganda Secretary, appears to have combined the insights gained in the nationalist struggle with her work among women. The League toured the Northern, Brong-Ahafo, and Central regions and gave talks and demonstrations on nutrition, childcare, and the distribution of cloths. . . . The League also saw its task as explaining issues of national concern to women, and it toured the Northern Region in March, 1960, to explain the impending national census.

In addition to these national issues, the League engaged itself with more general issues of immediate import. Such an engagement was over the French atomic tests in the Sahara, and it led a demonstration of over six hundred people including market women against the French atomic test. . . . The Cape Coast branch of the Federation organized a house-to-house educational campaign to explain the census in the fishing areas of Cape Coast. However, there were differences between the two organizations consisting mainly in the avowedly political nature of the League and the politically neutral posture of the Federation. This was to come to a head in the proposals for a merger between the two organizations and other smaller ones to form the National Council of Ghana Women.

In 1960, a conference was called of all women of Africa and of African descent. Before this conference took place, it was considered necessary to unite the various women's groups into one organization, operating as an integral wing of the CPP. To this end, invitations were sent to the Federation of Ghana Women led by Dr. Evelyn Amarteifio and to the Ghana Women's League of Mrs. Hannah Cudjoe. As well, invitations went to several women's benevolent associations. . . .

The Council was inaugurated by Dr. Nkrumah on 10th September, 1960, as the only recognized body under which all Ghanaian women were to be organized to contribute their quota to the political, educational, social, and economic reconstruction of Ghana. Branches were soon established throughout the country under the party's auspices. As an integral wing of the party, it had representation on the Party's Central Committee and participated in its programs with some of its members wielding considerable influence in national affairs. In what has become known as the Dawn Broadcast, it was decided that there should be no separate membership cards for the integral organizations of the party, the party membership card alone being sufficient. As well, it was decided that all appointments to the Council and to the other integral organizations would be made by the Party's Committee and that with the formation of the NCGW, the women's section of the Party had ceased to exist. . . .

Through the auspices of the Council, many young women were sent abroad for further studies and to pursue short courses. Others were found employment in state organizations and corporations as a reward for services to the party or more commonly, through family connections and other nepotistic practices. Market women constituted a big proportion of the membership of the Council, and mention has already been made of their control of space and goods within the markets. These women contributed vast sums of money to the party and were vocal at party gatherings and were fanatical in their support of the CPP. They could be seen spreading clothes on the ground for party functionaries to walk on at rallies and harassed opponents of the party and its policies. Typical of such tendencies was the "CPP Emashi Nonn," described as "a militant women's group with headquarters at Bukom (a quarter of Accra) which sprang up as a reaction to the adverse criticisms of the 1961 budget." Basil Davidson referred to the CPP as a "traders" party with a trader's attitude to politics, and these women played no mean role in it. . . .

Ghanaian Women and African Unity

In July, 1960, the Conference of Women of Africa and of African Descent was held in Accra. It was opened by the President, who used the occasion to make an appeal to African Women. He declared that the women of Africa had a mission to fulfill by creating better conditions of life for their sons and daughters. They were therefore to work hand in hand militantly with their men to end colonialism and imperialism. He asked the women to reflect on the burning issues of the time—why women of South Africa had to be in possession of passes in order to go about their ordinary business; why the apartheid overlords should mow down defenseless women and children; the French presence in Algeria, and South Africa's disregard of the United Nations resolutions on Namibia. . . .

In furtherance of the Ghana-Guinea-Mali Union, a Council of Women of the Union of African States was formed. Meetings were held in member countries for the promotion of the foundation of the movement, which would co-ordinate and harmonize the activities of organizations of African women throughout the continent. . . .

At the end of the Conference, the Council of Women of the Union of African States reaffirmed once more its strong desire to strengthen its efforts towards the realization of the total liberation of Africa as well as her unity and social and economic reconstruction. In a communiqué, the women pledged to work for the effective liberation and rapid emancipation of African women, to fight against illiteracy, which is one of Africa's greatest setbacks, to protect children and safe-guard their interests and to harness all their efforts towards the establishment of world peace.

Ghana: The Pioneer Guards the Gate

Frederick Cooper

Many commentators in and outside of Ghana have rightfully recognized Ghana's role in Africa's decolonization process as one of the pioneer independent states. In the following excerpt from one of his monographs, Frederick Cooper, professor of history at New York University, describes Ghana's political progression from the decade leading up to political independence and through the successive coups, which culminated in the fourth republic, led by Jerry Rawlings. This narrative is interwoven with the evolution of the country's economy from one dependent on cocoa exports with substantive state involvement to a market-oriented economy under the aegis of international lending agencies.

There is a particular poignancy to the history of Ghana because it was the pioneer. Kwame Nkrumah was more than a political leader; he was a prophet of independence, anti-imperialism, of pan-Africanism. His oft-quoted phrase "Seek ye first the political kingdom" was not just a call for Ghanaians to demand a voice in the affairs of state, but a plea for leaders and ordinary citizens to use power for a purpose—to transform a colonized society into a dynamic and prosperous land of opportunity.

But even when Nkrumah became Leader of Government Business in 1951 and prime minister of an independent country in 1957, he was operating under serious constraints. His government, like its colonial predecessor, depended on cocoa revenues for its projects to diversify the economy. A clash with cocoa farmers was virtually inevitable, as the government retained in its Cocoa Marketing Board accounts up to half of export earnings. . . . Nkrumah had by 1959 suppressed the cocoa farmers' own organizations; he had also banned all regional political parties, and hence eliminated the Asante-based National Liberation Movement. Meanwhile, the world price of cocoa was falling, farmers' income plummeting, and incentives to maintain and replant cocoa trees diminishing. After 1965 cocoa production fell by half as farmers turned to growing food crops, depriving the Ghanaian state of its main source of revenue for everything it was trying to do. Meanwhile, Nkrumah's biggest project [designed] to challenge the "neocolonial" monocrop export economy, the Volta River dam and aluminum processing industry, actually put much of the Ghanaian economy into the hands of multinational aluminum companies, which had the needed technology, and of the international financial institutions, which had the money.

By 1958 Nkrumah was ruling by decree. He changed his political underlings frequently. His stature abroad, as the pioneer of African independence and as a spokesman against imperialism, was high, but his most principled and ardent supporters at home were disillusioned. Wage workers, in the eyes of the CPP, went from allies to sources of subversion. The autonomy of the trade union movement was severely curtailed; leftist trade unionists were detained or forced out, strikes all but made illegal. Nkrumah told workers that their "former role of struggling against capitalists is obsolete" and that their task now was to "inculcate in our working people the love for labour and increased productivity." In 1961, nevertheless, a general strike erupted, led by railway workers. By the mid-1960s, the export agricultural economy was in collapse. In 1966, a military coup overthrew Nkrumah while he was abroad.

For many years afterwards, Ghana underwent a cycle of military coups, of governmental efforts to deal with basic problems which neither the British nor Nkrumah had solved, of frustrated military governments turning rule over to civilians and frustrated civilian leaders falling to military coups, and of each generation of rulers accusing the previous one of corruption and failure to help the common people. Ghana was ruled by military governments in 1966–69, 1972–79, and 1981–92. Flight Lieutenant Jerry Rawlings finally made a successful and apparently stable transition from military ruler to civilian and elected president. First taking power by force in 1979, he allowed elections and a civilian government to take office, then staged a new coup in 1981. In 1992 he again allowed elections and was himself the successful candidate for president, as he was in the next election in 1996. After his term was up, Rawlings stepped down, and he accepted defeat of his party's candidate for the succession, allowing a peaceful governmental transition to take place.

Government policy swung from Nkrumah's statist orientation in 1957–66 to a market-oriented economic approach under military and civilian rulers from 1966 to 1981, and then a populist direction under Rawlings between 1981 and 1983. Rawlings was critical of wealthy Ghanaians and their foreign partners, using socialist rhetoric and seeking policies aimed at helping the poor. In some ways, he followed a cyclical pattern started by Nkrumah: an invocation of the common citizen and an opening toward participation, followed by fear of the exercise of citizenship and repression. But unlike Nkrumah, Rawlings changed his policy as well as his mode of governance, and he received considerable outside support for doing so. He became the favorite of the International Monetary Fund for his willingness to cut back government expenditures, discard subsidies aimed at fostering urban consumption, privatize state-run corporations, and in general follow the rules of the structural adjustment policy. He had something to show for this: Ghana's debt burdens have been reduced, its growth rate has turned modestly upward after years of stagnation and regression, and it is attracting outside investment. Critics argue that the ultimate question—whether years of curtailing government services have made the common citizen any better off—remains unanswered. Rawlings implemented these policies in a period of tight control; a critic dubbed them an experiment on neoclassical economics "untroubled by popular democracy." That Rawlings could in 1996 make a case for his reelection on the basis of market-oriented economic reform, and that in 2001 a reasonably open campaign and honest election could take place in Ghana, provide a ray of hope that such serious issues can, at last, be debated.

Birth of Ghana

Lord Kitchener

Arguably the foremost calypsonian of the twentieth century, Lord Kitchener (1922–2000) was born Aldwyn Roberts in Trinidad. Even after migrating to Britain in 1948, Kitchener continued to be a major force on the calypso scene in the Caribbean. By its nature, the musical genre of calypso often involves social commentary and addresses topical issues. Calypsonians used the genre to express their varied concerns, including their affinity for African independence. In 1952, for instance, the Sekondi Morning Telegraph *newspaper reported that calypso musicians in London had composed a special song for Kwame Nkrumah. Calypso found a place of prominence in the musical landscape of Ghana and its melodies were often incorporated in Ghana's own indigenous popular music, highlife. Remarkably, despite the abundance of different local musical styles in Ghana and notwithstanding the existence of the popular music forms such as highlife and gome, it was Kitchener's calypso composition that captured the imagination and spirit of Ghana's independence. "Birth of Ghana" is considered an essential part of the "soundtrack" of Ghana's independence celebrations, and the reason for this is evident in the song's lyrics, presented here.*

This day will never be forgotten,
The sixth of March 1957.
When the Gold Coast successfully,
Get their Independence officially.

Ghana! Ghana is the name.
Ghana! We wish to proclaim.
We will be jolly, merry and gay,
The sixth of March, Independence Day.

Doctor Nkrumah went out his way,
To make the Gold Coast what it is today.
He endeavored continually,
To bring us freedom and liberty.

Performers at the Accra Carnival, 2013. Carnival is one of many imports from the Caribbean and the broader African diaspora in the Americas. Photograph by Clifford Campbell, Accra, June 2013.

Ghana! Ghana is the name.
Ghana! We wish to proclaim.
We will be jolly, merry and gay,
The sixth of March, Independence Day.

The Doctor began as agitator,
Then he became popular leader.
He continued to go further,
And now he is Ghana's Prime Minister.

Ghana! Ghana is the name.
Ghana! We wish to proclaim.
We will be jolly, merry and gay,
The sixth of March, Independence Day.

The national flag is a lovely scene,
With beautiful colors, red, gold and green.
And the black star in the center
Representing the freedom of Africa.

Ghana! Ghana is the name.
Ghana! We wish to proclaim.
We will be jolly, merry and gay,
The sixth of March, Independence Day.

Congratulation from Haile Selassie,
Was proudly received by everybody.
He particularly comment
On the Doctor's move to self-government.

Ghana! Ghana is the name.
Ghana! We wish to proclaim.
We will be jolly, merry and gay,
The sixth of March—Independence Day.

V

Independence, Coups, and the Republic, 1957–Present

In the eyes of many, Ghana in the late 1950s and 1960s was a nation synonymous with Kwame Nkrumah's staunch pan-African and socialist stance. However, Ghana's political culture actually challenges this perception by fostering a robust debate over whether or not Nkrumah even deserves his accolades, especially the status of the nation's "founding father." This debate has its roots in the development of the country's bifurcated political tradition, which began when Nkrumah decided to form his own party to agitate for independence, giving rise to a political culture now known as the Nkrumahist tradition. This alienated local indigenous leaders (popularly called "chiefs") and the educated elite, who banded together to form what scholars call the Danquah-Busia tradition, a noteworthy counterbalance to Nkrumah's populist and inclusive politics. Thereafter, strict adherence to either of these two political traditions characterized national politics, which is further complicated when combined with the oft-omitted factor of "ethnic" pride and identity. This combination of politics and ethnicity remains a primary and ongoing concern in the forging of the Ghanaian national identity.

The posturing of and fear that certain ideological or cultural groups would dominate the nation were undeniable consequences of lumping together diverse peoples—cultural strangers, migrants, enemies, kinfolk—into an emergent nation-state built around notions of oneness and consolidation. This process of nation building did not resolve the animosities between such groups; rather, it further complicated those matters already enmeshed in a political binary where "ethnic" belonging and the political divide combined to strongly influence Ghana's postcolonial history. Matters of "ethnicity" and politics were and are played out in the nation's favorite sporting pastime: soccer. In Ghana, the emotions connected to soccer are enough to either unify or divide the country. Nkrumah recognized this early and formed the national team, the Black Stars, to foster a sense of unison. Since then, despite various inherent differences in the people that make up Ghana, the country remains most united through support for its national team, the Black Stars, in international soccer matches.

A series of military coups punctuated the post-Nkrumah years, beginning in 1966, when the National Liberation Council, an amalgamation of military and police forces, overthrew the Nkrumah government and ruled the country until its return to civilian government in 1969. After three years of civilian rule, in 1972 the National Redemption Council—also comprising police and military personnel—assumed control of Ghana. This military government renamed itself the Supreme Military Council in 1975 and remained in control of the country until 1979, when a military junta, the Armed Forces Revolutionary Council (AFRC), ousted them. The AFRC returned governance of the country to civilians that same year. In 1981, the Provisional National Defense Council (PNDC) led another military coup and assumed control of Ghana until 1992. Since then the country has enjoyed a stable period of civilian democratic rule, the longest since political independence in 1957.

Despite the wide range of cast members featured in these episodes of military and civilian governments, some threads ran throughout: rising inflation, devaluation of currency, failed structural adjustment schemes, indebtedness, and "ethnic" conflicts. By the 1992 presidential election, Ghana's inequalities and antagonisms flourished beneath a veneer of democratic progress, and in 1994 "ethnic" rivalries over land and political authority exploded in what was perhaps the bloodiest conflict of its kind in the history of the nation. All this and more occurred in the context of Ghana's almost unquestioned acceptance of things foreign and an attendant view of North America as "God's country."

Independence Speech

Kwame Nkrumah

Ghana's first prime minister and later first president, Kwame Nkrumah (1909–72), was born Francis Nwia Kofi Ngonloma (mistakenly recorded as "Nkrumah") in Nkroful, Ghana. His speech delivered on Ghana's independence, March 6, 1957, served as the first official public utterance of the new Ghanaian nation—which alone ascribes great importance to it. The real significance of Nkrumah's speech, however, was its overt pronouncement of a pan-African agenda and Ghana's role in it. For Nkrumah, the country's independence was a harbinger of Africa's freedom from colonial rule. The excerpt from this speech below recognizes the various groups whose contributions culminated in the country's independence and captures the hope of the country's leadership.

At long last, the battle, has ended! And thus, Ghana, your beloved country is free forever! And here again, I want to take the opportunity to thank the chiefs and people of this country, the youth, the farmers, the women, who have so nobly fought and won this battle.

Also, I want to thank the valiant ex-service men, who have so co-operated with me, in this mighty task of freeing our country from foreign rule and imperialism!

And, as I pointed out at our Party conference at Saltpond, I made it quite clear that from now on, today, we must change our attitudes, our minds; we must realize that from now on we are no more a colonial but free and independent people! But also, as I pointed out, that also entails hard work. I am depending upon the millions of the country, the chiefs and people, to help me to reshape the destiny of this country. We are prepared to build it up and make it a nation that will be respected by every other nation in the world!

We know we are going to have difficult beginning, but again, I am relying upon your support. I am relying upon your hard work. Seeing you in these thousands, it doesn't matter how far my eye go, I can see, that you are here in your millions, and my last warning to you is that you are to stand firm behind us, so that we can prove to the world, that when the African is given chance, he can show to the world that he is somebody!

Black Star Gate. This was built as part of the architecture of nationalism to commemorate Ghana's birth as a nation. Photograph by Clifford Campbell, Accra, June 2013.

We have awakened, we shall no more go back to sleep anymore! Today from now on, there is a new African in the world. That new African is ready to fight his own battle, and show that after all, the black man is capable of managing his own affairs. We are going to demonstrate to the world, to the other nations, young as we are, that we are prepared to lay our foundation. As I said in the Assembly just a few minutes ago, I made a point, that we are going to see that we create our own Africa personality and identity! It is the only way in which we can show the world, that we are ready for our own battles.

But today, may I call upon you all, that on this great day, let us all remember, that nothing in the world can be done, unless it has the purport and support of God. We have won the battle and again rededicate ourselves not only in the struggle to emancipate other territories in Africa, our independence is meaningless unless it is linked up to the total liberation of the African continent!

Let us now, fellow Ghanaians, let us now, ask for God's blessings. And for only two seconds, in your thousands and millions, I want to ask you to pause only for one minute, and give thanks to Almighty God, for having led us through obstacles, difficulties, imprisonments, hardship and suffering, to have brought us to our end of trouble today. One minute silence.

Ghana is free forever. And here, I will ask the band to play the Ghana National Anthem.

The Nkrumah Government and Its Opposition

Kwame A. Ninsin

In the years leading up to independence, especially after the 1951 elections, the Convention People's Party (CPP) emerged as the dominant political party and faced the arduous task of determining the political direction and social character of the new state. Discussions on these matters centered around such issues as the distribution of material resources, the need to bridge the gap between the rich and poor regions, and how to treat the institution of chieftaincy—a local political system of governance, greatly weakened and, in some cases, eliminated, first by the British colonial administration and then by the Nkrumah administration. The ensuing debates exposed the divisions within the "ruling classes" and the competing paths that the new state should take. In the following excerpts from a chapter in a scholarly book, Kwame Ninsin, professor emeritus of political science at the University of Ghana, illustrates how the opposition parties constructed their arguments around the issues noted above.

The Issues

From 1951 when the CPP formed the government of this country, the controversy about what form the structure of state power should take assumed growing importance. From that time the Opposition persistently accused the CPP of antidemocratic tendencies. To check this suspected tendency the Opposition made a number of stringent political demands. Those demands may be summarized as follows: (i) protection of chieftaincy as a viable indigenous institution for local government; (ii) diffusion of state power from the centre to regional political organs; and (iii) control over cocoa revenue. These demands were interrelated at the level of concrete political struggle and factional debate. . . .

Democratization [versus] Chieftaincy

The first major confrontation between the CPP government and the Opposition occurred during the debate on the Local Government Ordinance of 1951. That moment exposed the contradiction between the government and the Opposition concerning the structure of the state power.

The government's position was determined by the need to democratize the machinery of government down to the grassroots. This, it was argued, had become necessary in view of the need for "a definite separation of the authorities responsible for ceremonial, ritual, constitutional and customary functions from those responsible for the administration of local government services." Local government institutions must therefore not only be modern; they must also be democratically constituted. In order to ensure that the new popular local government organs possessed the necessary financial means, they were also vested with power to manage stool lands—as estate agents, and not as owners.

It was evident that the bill was not intended to divest chiefs of their right as trustees of communal land. The Opposition nevertheless disputed the need to vest powers of control and management of stool lands in the proposed councils. . . .

The Opposition's view transcended the mere sentimentalism often expressed by Danquah, who defended it "because I love the institutions of this country. . . . I feel strongly that . . . it is chieftaincy over which or around which our institutions are built." Their position sprang from pure political considerations. . . .

Control over Cocoa Wealth

The relationship between cocoa revenue and land is an intimate one. Both contain property rights. Hence Danquah could lament that the Local Government Ordinance violated "that sacred right to enjoy one's own property" in the same way as the Gold Coast Cocoa Marketing Board (Amendment) Ordinance infringed the full enjoyment of private property.

This is the crux of the matter! If cocoa revenue and land could be legitimately considered as private property rights then whenever there was the slightest sign of violation of their private enjoyment the grounds for "rebellion" became incontrovertible. Then rebellion against constituted civil authority, that is, appealing to a higher justice, became justified. The agitation for a federal state system and bicameral legislature underscored this philosophical viewpoint. And so did the events which immediately preceded the

Billboard advertising centenary celebrations in honor of Ghana's first prime minister and president, Kwame Nkrumah. Photograph by Clifford Campbell, Accra, September 2009.

formation of the National Liberation Movement (NLM), the highest organized expression of that agitation.

Federal [versus] Unitary State Power

By 1954, the agitation for a federal state system had erupted into a full-scale rebellion—almost a civil war. The dynamics of that rebellion and its philosophical underpinnings bore a strong semblance to the rebellion of the American colonies against imperial Britain. For example, Danquah had, on the question of independence for Ghana, argued passionately for the colony to assert its "residual political sovereignty in the chiefs and people" to set up a constituent assembly. He had argued that this act of rebellion to "dissolve the political bonds which have connected them with another" was justified whenever citizens are convinced that the end of government has become destructive of their inalienable rights. The declaration that gave birth to the NLM was nourished by this philosophical claim. For the Opposition, it signaled the resumption of this residual political sovereignty which is presumably inalienable and latent. . . .

Two factors precipitated the federalist outburst. First: the failure of the Opposition in the 1954 general election, the first ever to be held on the basis of universal franchise. The Opposition had emerged from it as a weak, essentially tribal-regional group. Second: the Cocoa Duty and Development (Amendment) Ordinance, 1954. "The objects of the Ordinance were to provide for: (1) the establishment of three further development funds, (2) the allocation of amounts of money from general revenue, into which export duty on cocoa is paid to these new development funds, and (3) the alteration of the rate of export tax on cocoa. . . ."

The birth of the NLM fused the struggle for a federation and for a higher producer price for cocoa farmers. The two were labeled as a struggle for liberation from the misrule and dictatorship of the CPP; from a government that expropriated cocoa farmers, and that was above all corrupt. . . .

The CPP government's view was the exact opposite. For them land and cocoa wealth are social property and should be utilized for the benefit of the whole. The measures which the government instituted to control land and cocoa revenue were aimed at ensuring the unencumbered realization of this goal. . . .

The vision of society held by the CPP government was one that would be united and free from tribalism and all feudal remnants; strong and prosperous. The latter was necessary for forging national unity and making the nation strong. These collective social purposes were a value far greater than individual or private advantage.

Africa's Resources

Kwame Nkrumah

After independence, Ghana's development faced the specter of neocolonialism, as erstwhile colonial overlords and other "developed" countries sought to control Ghana's natural resources along the same exploitative lines developed during British colonial rule. Foreign countries controlled the market for Ghana's major export, cocoa, and all its mineral wealth. Kwame Nkrumah recognized that this problem was common throughout soon-to-be and newly independent African states and addressed it in his book Neo-Colonialism: The Last Stage of Imperialism. *In the following excerpt from this book, Nkrumah outlines how neocolonialism operates in Africa, while simultaneously making a case for greater African unity along economic lines.*

Africa is a paradox which illustrates and highlights neo-colonialism. Her earth is rich, yet the products that come from above and below her soil continue to enrich, not Africans predominantly, but groups and individuals who operate to Africa's impoverishment. . . . We know that iron reserves are put at twice the size of America's, and two-thirds those of the Soviet Union's, on the basis of an estimated two billion metric tons. Africa's calculated coal reserves are considered to be enough to last for three hundred years. New petroleum fields are being discovered and brought into production all over the continent. Yet production of primary ores and minerals, considerable as it appears, has touched only the fringes.

Africa has more than 40 per cent of the world's potential water power, a greater share than any other continent. Yet less than five per cent of this volume has been utilized. Even taking into account the vast desert stretches of the Sahara, there is still in Africa more arable and pastureland than exists in either the United States of America or the Soviet Union. There is even more than in Asia. Our forest areas are twice as great as those of the United States.

If Africa's multiple resources were used in her own development, they could place her among the modernized continents of the world. But her resources have been, and still are being used for the greater development of overseas interests. . . .

Although possessing fifty-three of the world's most important basic industrial minerals and metals, the African continent tails far behind all others in industrial development. . . .

On the whole, mining has proved a most profitable venture for foreign capital investment in Africa. Its benefits for Africans have by no means been on an equal scale. Mining production in a number of African countries has a value of less than $2 per head of population. As *Europe (France) Outremer* puts it, "It is quite certain that a mining production of $1 or $2 per inhabitant cannot appreciably affect a country's standard of living." Affirming correctly that "in the zones of exploitation, the mining industry introduces a higher standard of living," the journal is forced to the conclusion that mining exploitations are, however, relatively privileged isolated islands in a very poor total economy. . . .

The reason for this is seen in the absence of industry and manufacture, owing to the fact that mining production is destined principally for exportation, mainly in primary form. It goes to feed the industries and factories of Europe and America, to the impoverishment of the countries of origin. . . .

The assumption also ignores another important fact, namely that wages of manual workers, low as they are, are partly spent on goods manufactured abroad and imported, taking out of the primary producing countries a good part of the workers' wages. In many cases, the imported goods are the products of the companies associated with the mining groups. Frequently, they are sold in the companies' own stores on the mining compounds or by their appointed agents, the workers having to pay prices fixed by the companies.

The poverty of the people of Africa is demonstrated by the simple fact that their income *per capita* is among the lowest in the world. . . .

In some countries, for example Gabon and Zambia, up to half the domestic product is paid to resident expatriates and to overseas firms who own the plantations and mines. In Guinea de Sao, Angola, Libya, Swaziland, South-West Africa and Zimbabwe (Rhodesia), foreign firm profits and settler or expatriate incomes exceed one-third of the domestic product. Algeria, Congo and Kenya were in this group before independence.

On achieving independence, almost every new state of Africa has developed plans for industrialization and rounded economic growth in order to improve productive capacity and thereby raise the standard of living of its people. But while Africa remains divided progress is bound to be painfully slow. . . .

Africa is having to pay a huge price once more for the historical accident that this vast and compact continent brought fabulous profits to western capitalism, first out of the trade in its people and then out of imperialist exploitation. This enrichment of one side of the world out of the exploitation of the other has left the African economy without the means to industrialize. At the time when Europe passed into its industrial revolution, there was a considerably narrower gap in development between the continents. But with every step in the evolution of productive methods and the increased profits drawn from the more and more shrewd investment in manufacturing equipment and base metal production, the gap widened by leaps and bounds. . . .

There are, however, imperialist specialists and apologists who urge the less developed countries to concentrate on agriculture and leave industrialization for some later time when their populations shall be well fed. The world's economic development, however, shows that it is only with advanced industrialization that it has been possible to raise the nutritional level of the people by raising their levels of income. Agriculture is important for many reasons, and the governments of African states concerned with bringing higher standards to their people are devoting greater investment to agriculture. But even to make agriculture yield more the aid of industrial output is needed; and the under-developed world cannot for ever be placed at the mercy of the more industrialized. . . .

A continent like Africa, however much it increases its agricultural output, will not benefit unless it is sufficiently politically and economically united to force the developed world to pay it a fair price for its cash crops. . . .

So long as Africa remains divided it will therefore be the wealthy consumer countries who will dictate the price of African cash crops. Nevertheless, even if Africa could dictate the price of its cash crops this would not by itself provide the balanced economy which is necessary for development. The answer must be industrialization.

The African continent, however, cannot hope to industrialize effectively in the haphazard, *laissez-faire* manner of Europe. In the first place, there is the time factor. In the second, the socialized modes of production and tremendous human and capital investments involved call for cohesive and integrated planning. Africa will need to bring to its aid all its latent ingenuity and talent in order to meet the challenge that independence and the demands of its peoples for better living have raised. The challenge cannot be met on any piece-meal scale, but only by the total mobilization of the continent's resources within the framework of comprehensive socialist planning and deployment. . . .

When the countries of their origin are obliged to buy back their minerals and other raw products in the form of finished goods, they do so at grossly inflated prices. A General Electric advertisement carried in the March/April

1962 issue of *Modern Government* informs us that "from the heart of Africa to the hearths of the world's steel mills comes ore for stronger steel, better steel—steel for buildings, machinery, and more steel rails." With this steel from Africa, General Electric supplies transportation for bringing out another valuable mineral for its own use and that of other great imperialist exploiters. . . .

That exploitation of this nature can take place is due to the balkanization of the African continent. Balkanization is the major instrument of neo-colonialism and will be found wherever neo-colonialism is practiced.

Ordained by the Oracle

Samuel Asare Konadu

The Gold Coast was home to several indigenous and migrant cultural groups, and this multiculturalism grew even more by the time of the country's independence. Peoples with long-standing histories in what became Ghana were joined by successive waves of migrants, merchants, and missionaries from Europe, Asia, the Caribbean, and the West African region—each with their own cultural histories and traditions. Adhering to established local protocols is quite pervasive in the indigenous Ghanaian cultures, and many persons therein, in varying ways, continue to engage in practices that served their ancestors well. In Ordained by the Oracle, *Ghanaian journalist and novelist Samuel Asare Konadu (1923–94), who also went by the name Asare Konadu and the pseudonym Kwabena Asare Bediako, foregrounds the interwoven nature of tradition and so-called modern life. For the Fante, like most other groups that comprise Ghana, the funerary rites that follow death are venerated, and there are specific cultural rituals associated with the death of a loved one. In the following excerpt from his novel, Konadu immerses the reader in some of the rituals that must be undertaken by the husband of a deceased Fante wife.*

So passed Boateng's first night with his dead wife. But that was only the first out of the forty in which he was to mourn his wife and carry out customary practices and sacrifices. It was, however, his second encounter with a ghost. The first was when he was a young lad of about eighteen. . . .

But what was happening in connection with his wife's death was out of proportion with his earlier experience which was the result of his imagination playing on his mind. He could not say the same with the watch over the dead body of Dora and the other rituals that were to follow. They were to be carried out in the dark and in circumstances in which a ghost was likely to be seen. And now he was not even to speak. . . .

"Will you sit down and wash your feet and hands," the old woman said, producing from under her cloth a small earthenware pot with some of the herbal waters.

Boateng sat down on the first landing of the wooden staircase and dipped his hand seven times into the pot washing each foot and each hand. He scooped some of the water and washed his face too. The water was cold and he could feel the skin contract under its touch.

"You must not look back from now on until you have been cleansed in the sea. Follow me," the woman beckoned. . . .

From now on it was a march of the fit and filled with the weak and hungry and it reflected in the steps that they took. Boateng's difficulty was aggravated by the fact that he was not wearing any sandals and he was walking barefooted in a lane in which stones spiked out about two inches high. Each step brought pain to his feet and shook his stomach. He bent at times but he was not to turn round so he did not know how close those behind him were, and it was too dark even to see them, but he could hear their footsteps and he knew he was not alone. . . .

What awaits him? What was the cleansing ceremony like? He kept thinking this as every step brought him nearer to the sea. . . .

"Will you stop?" the man behind him said. Boateng halted and he ran into him before steadying himself.

"This is the ceremony to cleanse yourself of any association spiritually and bodily you have had with your wife. What you did last night was to say good-bye to her. That over, you must part company and you must wash yourself in the sea which takes everything," he said.

The old woman who was leading had stopped too and turned to face Boateng now. When she spoke her voice came very close to his ears and he could feel her breath against his neck.

"The longer you stay in the sea the cleaner you become and you must not rush out until you are sure every part of you has been washed clean. Where is your hand?" she asked.

Boateng stretched his hand towards her. She took it in one of hers and he could feel her thrusting some grains into it with the other. They were so small in size that he had to close his fingers together tightly to be able to hold them in his palm.

"Those are the ghost grains of departure. Before you dip yourself in the water bite into each and throw them against the seven wings of the winds, repeating after them a wish or a heart's desire," she said.

"Have you understood that?" the man asked. He nodded but wondered if they saw his face and got the signal.

"Now we are going to wait here and you should walk down to the sea alone. Walk up into the water deeply, standing up to your waist before you start the ceremony."

Akyeame (speech intermediaries) carrying *akyeamepoma* (*akyeame* staffs) laden with the coded wisdom of the indigenous cultures. Photograph by Clifford Campbell, Techiman, July 2009.

Boateng took the first few steps. He stopped as he heard other footsteps behind him. But he dared not turn because he had been warned earlier on. . . .

Boateng stopped and looked over the dark waters for any sign of life. A dark cloud seemed to take over the scene now and before him everything started to lose its shape.

"What is this?" he thought. Just then he remembered that it was *Krofa sum*, the darkness that surrounded the earth just before dawn. It came suddenly cutting everything before it and leaving Boateng in complete isolation.

For a brief moment he felt he should turn and run back but he feared not what the spirit of Dora would do to him then but what chain-effect it was likely to have on his life. It grew darker and darker. . . .

"*Kwaa*," a bird cried over his head. Boateng opened his eyes and found that he had walked right to the edge of the water. . . .

Boateng entered the water carefully testing each foothold before moving on. When he stopped the sea water came up to his knee. He bit into two of the grains. "Aarr," he groaned. Their bitter aroma spread all through his mouth and it was difficult to hold the saliva in his mouth. He opened his mouth and let it run out. He threw the rest of the grain on the four winds without biting into them, repeating after them: "Dora, my love, take away with you all the poverty and disease which you left us and bring us prosperity and riches. Do not let any mishap come our way and in the years ahead let our dream of building our own house at Elmina come true. You knew how I suffered with you. If it is true there is a place where people go when they die, let us truly see that you still live and look after us."

Boateng felt all the fear departing from him. His heart was now filled with sorrow. The tears were coming again and he put his head through the water to avoid them. When he came out, his mouth and nostrils were filled with salty water. He stood up to allow the water to drip before walking to the boat to pick up his *kuntunkuni*. Then he heard a big roar. He knew it was a wave but how big it was he could not see because once he had turned facing the town he should not turn back to look at the sea. It came nearer, he could feel it. Just then he jumped to get it through his feet as he had done when a boy. He felt the waters towering over him and then he was on the ground, a deep pain going through his head where the wave had lashed.

"Aah," he shouted with all the strength in him before he fell. . . . He could not raise himself from the ground and he kept his face down to avoid water entering his nose and mouth. He knew then he had become a victim of a tradition not created by his hands or the hands of the people before him, but the hands of long ago. . . .

Boateng had not been able to keep the utter silence which the ceremony of cleansing demanded and if his shout of pain had been heard by the people who stood guarding the heritage and the culture, then he would not be free but required to go through it again. . . .

"Aah, can't someone save me," he shouted again. He could feel the water as it passed over his body raising the padlock up and down. It hit him on the buttocks and it would have been a relief to pull it off. He raised his hand but he could not reach it. The pain in his head was increasing and . . . "aaa," he shouted, falling back. It was the last he saw.

Flight

Kwame Dawes

"Flight" is the culminating part of an ambitious book-length poem, Prophets, *which appeared in 1995. The poem has some autobiographical elements, as professor of English and poet Kwame Dawes was born in Ghana during the government of Kwame Nkrumah, but it is important to note that the speaker is a woman, a Pentecostal preacher, the product of the cross-cultural dynamics of an African origin and a Caribbean experience. In her effort to reconcile the conflicted history of colonialism, and her sense of reconnection to a past of anomie and memory, she addresses the antagonists of her sense of worth and identity and finds comfort in the sincere engagement with this complex combination of faith and political engagement. At the haunting center of the poem is the remarkable historical fact of the Middle Passage and its repercussions, and the poem arrives at a conclusion that is energizing, comforting, and unsettling: "Culture is flux, flux is culture; we are changing inside." It is in this lyric moment that Dawes found the language containing his own history as a Ghanaian-born New World migrant.*

i

And when I die, I will fly. What promises you have for me?
Call it a bargain basement faith, but I have to find
something what can fit my broad hip and match my
complexion. What you have for me? When I die
my pains will be no more; I will touch clouds
damp with next week's storms, over
the cedars and pines, above the smooth green
thighs of the Blue Mountains and, when I dip like a bucket,
the water from the rocks will be cool blue.
My watertight goatskin satchel will carry
smooth stones, cooling pebbles for under my tongue
when the harmattan dries the Atlantic
air waves. I will fly over Cuba

and say a prayer for Fidel (stroking my chin), for
despite the bad press, defecting daughters, etcetera, I dig
the man for his cynic's wit and mannish ways. Look the
boat-load of criminals he liberate on Miami's
red, white and oil-blue shore, and see how blood flow—*sangre de dios*—
in the palmetto beachhead when each defectee
prance the golden roads with scar-face badness,
dusting the green with coke like wedding rice.
Though hesitant, I will pit-stop over Babylon,
in some third world barrio like South Carolina's low country
or them turtle-green islands where they preserve
the tongue of Africa, lodged in seed and stomach,
static magic swirling on Sycorax's fantastic Bermudes,
where black man Caliban still howls his panting heart.
Then it's east, for the cold bite hugging too tight
the Atlantic rocks. East it is, for this soulful flight,
looking, looking for soil to plant in—looking, sniffing.
East along the channels of air, warm Gabon air,
smelling the *akra*'s mellow smoothness, the sweet
kelewele, calling, calling, drawing me along the warm
currents. I'm flying west for the fleshpots
of Cairo, the sphinx, the pyramids—not home,
just legacies of gifts we have left, simple skeletons.
There on Cairo's streets, panoramas of faces
whip by like old statues of ancient times,
while the Black American intellectuals sip sweet coffee
in the cafes, retrieving their lost heritage in the colonizer's
tongue. Ah, the relics of our lost histories, the things
we have lost—seeking out a Black Atlantis so far, so far
from the conclave of huts and the circle of the griot's music
in the south, where green explodes in mountains
rising out of the brittle grit and dust of the Sahara.
Whitewashed memories are shored up in colourful texts
and clichés of a glorious race. Divided is Africa;
the Egyptians wince at the kente and dashiki.
Fly, I must, from this museum of broken dreams;
fly, I must, south to the antiphonal howls of the
Mahotella Queens, the magic of the Mokola daughters,
the flaring nostrils of the township shabeens,
speaking easy their histories in the firelight;

their eyes staring far like the Masai's gaze.
This is my dignity, this my familiar earth, this my arrival,
still damp with the dew of tomorrow's rain.
I alight without fanfare from the blue; the earth
reaches up its red fingers and sucks me, legs first,
deep into the blooming bottom-land. This yank
tautens my neck like a kite rope, my head a dignity flag.
This is my dignity, constructed by so many journeys.
Why must I stay satisfied with rumours
of old women's proverbs and the *brujo*'s sharp
recognition of healing in each weed, bush and turning
leaf? Return I must to that old shrine, now broken,
for those left behind forgot to feed the soil.
Shrine of my deepest fears, whose fingers reach
across the centuries and touch my eyes, my offspring
wrestling with the Holy Ghost found in the mountain chapel;
shrine of my deepest fears, split in my devotion
from the earth that beckons me with her smell of seed
to the new libation of bloodshed for remission of sin;
shrine of my deepest fears, have you not heard that I wept
and felt the fingers on my cheek wiping, wiping;
that I have dreamed of another land, comely, home?
shrine of my deepest fears, path to my distant time,
not that path which would find me back in Jericho,
or as nigger Simon on Golgotha staring at the black sky;
shrine of my deepest fears, what wind is blowing now
to meet my uneasy mind? I feel the travail in my bones.
What do you have to offer, dare I fall open before you?
Then, land I have heard about,
will you rise before my face from the spread
of desert and thick bush, Kilimanjaro
probing the cloud cover? Is this my
Eden, my heaven? Have you something better?
Have you a truth to plant me like a tree?

ii

Culture is flux. Flux is culture. Absolute spirit.
Is spirit absolutely true? Heart is not history. Heart of stone.
Heart is the fire caught-up within my bones.

Heart is prophecy frothing to the stomp and rattle
of the gospeller's Sunday. Heart is the word spoken
so deep in the stomach, so jealously protective of my soul.
Heart is my eye peering into our collective pasts
and, finding that ancient shrine in some broken hut,
drawing me. I arrive a stranger. I arrive dead. Sleep
never comes easy, for the trees of the mountain sanctuary
rustle their hymns, calling me back, calling me back.
Flux is culture. Culture is flux. We are changing inside.

iii

The dashiki I wear is a flag.
Calls me dignified. The kente, a gift
from the Ghanaian attaché, my banner.
The sandals and the dust, my contact
with the earth. There is no burden of guilt
in my history; I will not share the blame for the callous
whip; the gospel of enslavement,
justified sardining of humanity
in our own juices, value packaged
and shipped with the blessing and guiding eye
of the all-seeing papal man; nor for the stolen gold;
the satchel of smallpox and rude disease;
the blood spilt; the betrayal and slaughter of Toussaint;
Sam Sharpe bleeding in the cane fields;
the dangling of Bogle; the black and white churches;
the rejected cornerstones falling, falling in the
black water of your hell; the silencing of my songs.
I will not be no beast of burden for you no more.
I reject twilight schizophrenia; illusions
of white Jesus with his red heart
enshrined in thorns, and his hippie
hair smoothly permed as he stands propped by
his Anglo disciples with thin, stiff upper lips;
I reject, too, the Academy of Regret;
your constant belief in the beauty and joy
of Colon's accidental landing; the perpetual admonition
to avoid the backward glance for your sake;
as if it were I facing the judgment

of salt and fire, as if I had left nothing
of beauty in the old village by the sea.
No, I will not deny the prophet with
wicked locks and a Trench Town bob
in his rhygin walk who says look back,
for that yoke is easy and the burden light,
and our legacy is more than the homelessness
of the sea—I have planted seed and it has sprouted
in this new soil, I have wailed to the hills
and my voice has returned dew soft
with clear melody and the harmony
of new trees, new brooks, new light;
the antiphonal prayers of old bones
calling me to take shelter in the green.
So there's nothing strange here;
nothing odd in my ancient garb,
and the path of my metaphors.
You have, I know, heard it all before,
and more sweetly spoken, I am sure;
but I repeat the litany to clear the table
so we may start afresh. Now, clean as I am,
plealess; now that we know the lay of the land,
offer me what you have for me—go on. I am listening.
You see, I've always known this stuff—this stuffing of history—to be
the baggage of your sterile sermons;
secretly concealed behind those curtains
while you down the best part of the wine
after we've just dipped and sipped small;
behind your Oxford tongue, acrobatic
around that clean sermon of bloodless salvation;
locked up in some closet, all this stuff
is sitting there, and if it wasn't for that smell,
that thick muggy smell seeping through,
I would never know you had all this stuff.

iv

I have come like this to see you point me
out in my cloth from Togoland and my
raggamuffin gait. Finger me now, I don't

give a damn who sees. I won't cause no
trouble. Tell the ushers to stay cool. I will smile
'cause I come to find a path—and this won't be
a path you make, it will be a path you may offer,
then I will decide and either walk the asphalt
or ride the cobalt sky on that chartered journey back.
See me sometime as your old black ancestor
before Peter at the door, proffering her
letter of recommendation to be relayed up
the ladder to God's desk or to his well-paid
letter writers: the risen popes, paul, newton, augustine
of the burning groin. Like her, I come
like a comma to replace the closure
of your periods, screwing up the text
until the end is somewhere in the middle.
Now, tell me, what you have for me,
for this Sowetan gum-boot dancer,
this Akan mother transported like a scroll,
discovered here where the bush still parts
for her footfall, slowly marching
from the sea inland to the sound of the drum?
What you have to offer me to break this miasma
of uncertain homes? What promises can speak above
the smell clamouring behind the curtains?
You see, the path you raise your left finger to
is a false path, o false prophet. This I have
seen. My morning songs lift me beyond
the chaos of your many and twisted roads.
Flying comes so natural to me these days
as I ride this sun-full, misty morning to Heartease.

v

I am reluctant to leave it like this;
the tricks, the sin, the betrayals, as if this was all.
My journey has drawn me astray and, remiss,
I am turning to the old songs. Marley's call
from the darkness is pure light and hope
despite the countless dead by unbelief.
This song has wallowed in its grief

as if there was no music in the bright aftermornings,
no prayer caught in the mist's delicate sieve.
Now, rising up like a fisherman's weighted seine
to God, the tambourines celebrate the joy of faith rewarded,
the sickly child awakening after prayer,
sight returned to a warped cornea,
hope in a miracle of a child born intact.
How green is the island when it rains!
This song has lamented like a spoilt child,
yet how can I turn from these miracles
without tears of thanksgiving in my eye?
I write these poems with trepidation,
as if this tantrum might bring down the wrath
of the Almighty. But the prophets no longer groan
through the stinking city. Their feet skip on the mountains.
The cleansed are dancing on the hill's broken path.
Now, there is laughter and belief in mornings.

Everything Counts

Ama Ata Aidoo

Ama Ata Aidoo is one of Ghana's most prolific novelists. "Everything Counts" is one of several short stories that appear in her No Sweetness Here and Other Stories, *set in early postindependence Ghana. "Everything Counts" confronts the influence of the Western world on notions of beauty in Ghana. Set in a time when wearing a wig and skin bleaching was prevalent in Ghana, the story articulates these themes through a Western-educated Ghanaian woman grappling with the pervasiveness of Western culture in Ghana. The excerpt below tackles the notion of Africans appreciating themselves and celebrating their aesthetics against the prevailing European standards of beauty. In many ways the story recognizes that a revolution of the mind was necessary to reorient African views about themselves vis-à-vis Western cultural influence and values.*

She used to look at their serious faces and laugh silently to herself. They meant what they were saying. The only thing was that loving them all as sister, lover and mother, she also knew them. She knew them as intimately as the hems of her dresses. That it was so much easier for them to talk about the beauty of being oneself. Not to struggle to look like white girls. Not straightening one's hair. And above all, not to wear the wig.

The wig. Ah, the wig. They say it is made of artificial fibre. Others swear that if it is not gipsy hair, then it is Chinese. Extremists are sure they are made from the hairs of dead white folk—this one gave her nightmares. . . . And she would shiver for all the world to see. At other times, when her world was sweet like when she and Fiifi were together, the pictures that came into her mind were not so terrible. She would just think of the words of that crazy *highlife* song and laugh. The one about the people at home scrambling to pay exorbitant prices for second-hand clothes from America . . . and then as a student of economics, she would also try to remember some other truths she knew about Africa. Second-rate experts giving first-class dangerous advice. Or expressing uselessly fifth-rate opinions. Second-hand machinery from someone else's junkyard.

Snow-ploughs for tropical farms.

Outmoded tractors.

Discarded aero planes.

And now, wigs—made from other people's unwanted hair.

At this point, tough though she was, tears would come into her eyes. Perhaps her people had really missed the boat of original thinking after all? And if Fiifi asked her what was wrong, she explained, telling the same story every time. He always shook his head and laughed at her, which meant that in the end, she would laugh with him.

At the beginning, she used to argue with them, earnestly. "But what has wearing wigs got to do with the revolution?" "A lot sister" they would say. "How?" she would ask, struggling not to understand.

"Because it means that we have no confidence in ourselves." Of course, she understood what they meant.

"But this is funny. Listen, my brothers, if we honestly tackled the problems facing us, we wouldn't have the time to worry about such trifles as wigs."

She made them angry. Not with the mild displeasure of brothers, but with the hatred of wounded lovers. They looked terrible, their eyes changing, turning red and warning her that if she wasn't careful, they would destroy her. Ah, they frightened her a lot, quite often too. Especially when she thought of what filled them with that kind of hatred. . . .

As for imitating white women, mm, what else can one do, seeing how some of our brothers behave? The things one has seen with one's own eyes. The stories one has heard. About African politicians and diplomats abroad. But then, one has enough troubles already without treading on big toes.

After a time, she gave up arguing with them, her brothers. She just stated clearly that the wig was an easy way out as far as she was concerned. She could not afford to waste that much time on her hair. The wig was, after all, only a hat. A turban. Would they please leave her alone? What was more, if they really wanted to see a revolution, why didn't they work constructively in other ways for it?

She shut them up. For they knew their own weaknesses too, that they themselves were neither prepared nor ready to face the realities and give up those aspects of their personal dream which stood between them and the meaningful actions they ought to take. Above all, she was really beautiful and intelligent. They loved and respected her. . . .

Really, she had found it difficult to believe her eyes. How could she? From the air-stewardesses to the grade-three typists in the offices, every girl simply wore a wig. Not cut discreetly short and disguised to look like her own hair as she had tried to do with hers. But blatantly, aggressively, crudely. Most of them actually had masses of flowing curls falling on their shoulders. Or huge affairs piled on top of their heads.

Even that was not the whole story. Suddenly, it seemed as if all the girls and women she knew and remembered as having smooth black skins had turned light-skinned. Not uniformly. Lord, people looked as though a terrible plague was sweeping through the land. A plague that made funny patchworks of faces and necks.

She couldn't understand it so she told herself she was dreaming. Maybe there was a simple explanation. Perhaps a new god had been born while she was away, for whom there was a new festival. And when the celebrations were over, they would remove the masks from their faces and those horrid-looking things off their heads.

A week went by and the masks were still on. More than once, she thought of asking one of the girls she had been to school with, what it was all about. But she restrained herself. She did not want to look more of a stranger than she already felt—seeing she was also the one *black* girl in the whole city. . . .

Then the long vacation was over and the students of the national university returned to the campus. O . . . she was full of enthusiasm, as she prepared her lectures for the first few weeks. She was going to tell them what was what. That as students of economics, their role in nation-building was going to be crucial. Much more than big-mouthed, big-living politicians, they could do vital work to save the continent from the grip of its enemies. If only for a little while: and blah, blah, blah.

Meanwhile, she was wearing her own hair. Just lightly touched to make it easier to comb. In fact, she had been doing that since the day they got married. The result of some hard bargaining. The final agreement was that any day of the year, she would be around with her own hair. But she could still keep that thing by for emergencies. Anyhow, the first morning in her life as a lecturer arrived. She met the students at eleven. They numbered between fifteen and twenty. About a third of them were girls. . . .

And yet she was there as a lecturer. Talking about one thing or another. Perhaps it was on automation as the newest weapon from the industrially developed countries against the wretched ones of the earth. Or something of the sort. . . .

It was then she noticed the wigs. All the girls were wearing them. The biggest ones she had seen so far. She felt very hot and she who hardly ever sweated, realized that not only were her hands wet, but also streams of water were pouring from the nape of her neck down her spine. Her brassiere felt too tight. Later, she was thankful that black women have not yet learnt to faint away in moments of extreme agitation.

But what frightened her was that she could not stop the voice of one of the boys as it came from across the sea, from the foreign land, where she had once been with them.

"But Sissie, look here, we see what you mean. Except that it is not the real point we are getting at. Traditionally, women from your area might have worn their hair long. However, you've still got to admit that there is an element in this wig-wearing that is totally foreign. Unhealthy."

Eventually, that first horrid lecture was over. The girls came to greet her. They might have wondered what was wrong with this new lecturer. And so probably did the boys. She was not going to allow that to worry her. There always is something wrong with lecturers. Besides, she was going to have lots of opportunities to correct what bad impressions she had created. . . .

The next few weeks came and went without changing anything. Indeed, things got worse and worse. . . .

Fiifi had not arrived in the country yet. That might have had something to do with the sudden interest she developed in the beauty contest. It wasn't really a part of her. But there it was. Now she was eagerly buying the morning paper to look out for the photos of the winners from the regions. Of course, the winner on the national level was going to enter for the Miss Earth title.

She knew all along that she would go to the stadium. And she did not find it difficult to get a good seat.

She should have known that it would turn out like that. She had not thought any of the girls beautiful. But her opinions were not really asked for, were they? She just recalled, later, that all the contestants had worn wigs except one. The winner. The most light-skinned of them all. No, she didn't wear a wig. Her hair, a mulatto's, quite simply, quite naturally, fell in a luxuriant mane on her shoulders. . . .

She hurried home and into the bathroom where she vomited—and cried and cried and vomited for what seemed to her to be days. And all this time, she was thinking of how right the boys had been. She would have liked to run to where they were to tell them so. To ask them to forgive her for having dared to contradict them. They had been so very right. Her brothers, lovers and husbands. But nearly all of them were still abroad. In Europe, America or some place else. They used to tell her that they found the thought of returning home frightening. They would be frustrated. . . .

Others were still studying for one or two more degrees. A Master's here. A Doctorate there. . . . That was the other thing about the revolution.

Story: Patience and Pleading

Gracia Clark

Market women are often the most unrecognized factor in any analysis of the Ghanaian economy even though they are responsible for a sizable portion of the "informal" economy. They played a crucial role in the independence movement by financing Nkrumah, providing him with invaluable logistics and organizing supporters. They are the agents responsible for exchanging most of the country's farm produce directly with consumers. Consequently, they handle a significant amount of money collectively. Most of these "unschooled" women possess a thorough working knowledge of the local economy and how they fit into it. The following excerpt from a scholarly monograph demonstrates this through the voice of a market woman, Abenaa Adiiya, in conversation with Gracia Clark, professor emeritus of anthropology at Indiana University, as the former talks about the evolution of the economy and the cost of doing business.

At first, the world was good, and as for me, I know what I know, in my own mind. What I mean is, the Bible says that this is not true, and if things are good now, times will come that are bad. First of all, I know that my mind tells me that the Bible said that when the world is coming to an end, conditions will be hard. That's how I know that very time has come.

When you first came, and you and I used to play around, about four years ago—

MA [Mary Appiah, research assistant/interpreter]*: About ten years*

About ten years ago—

GC [Gracia Clark]*: It was about fourteen years ago.*

Well, at that time fourteen years ago, when you and I were going to Bolga, how much did the car even charge us? Five hundred cedis [local currency]. We boarded the State Transport bus, and it was five hundred. Today the fare to Bolga is six thousand cedis. I mean, the world is going up [*kɔ so*]. Everything is going up finally, too, the people are too many. If we are too many, then problem will set in with everything. At first, in trading, the people who were trading were not many, only a few people. The more we get, the more everyone struggles to get into trading. Nowadays, for ex-

Takyiman (Techiman) market in the Brong-Ahafo Region of Ghana. The market is one of the largest in Ghana and West Africa, attracting thousands of producers, traders, and consumers each week. Photograph by Kwasi Konadu, 2007.

ample, look at this handbag I am holding now. If I were selling it and not many people come around, I could not raise the price very high. *Wahu?* If you come by, and Akua comes by, and someone else also comes by, I know that someone will surely buy it, and this lets the price go up.

OK, it is partly due to petrol, too. I mean, what makes things get expensive is petrol. At first, when I was starting to travel, the car charged me 2,500 cedis. Then they raised the price of petrol, and when they raised the price, they raised the fare to 3,000. Just the other day it went up again, and now they charge 3,500. That's why I know very well that if they change the budget and raise the petrol price again, they will raise the fare again to 4,000. These days, very high prices of things are really due to petrol. I mean, if they raise the price of petrol, it affects everything. I mean, people have to take a car. If you sell things, you need to take a car, you see? That's why foodstuffs and everything, cloth or clothing, everything is so expensive. Everything really depends on petrol, really. That's why I say the rising price of petrol has caused all of the problems in Ghana today. A person cannot pick up this chair and, with your own strength, walk with it for half a mile. You cannot carry this table. Whatever happens, you have to take a car. *Wahu?*

A few days ago I went to buy yams at Ejura. When we first went to buy, for every hundred yams the car charged two thousand cedis. Today, if you go to buy a hundred, they charge five thousand. Just like that, they raised it three thousand cedis. That's why, if at first I sold the yams for two hundred each, now I cannot sell them for two hundred. I have to sell them for about three hundred each. So as for the hard times, really it is because they are raising the price of petrol so very fast. Petrol makes everything hard. Today food is also hard. All of it ends up this petrol business.

In the old days, as a poor person, if you had even five hundred cedis to take to market, you could eat. Today, take me and these children of mine. Now, even if I haven't bought much I have spent eight hundred cedis, only for staples, before you have gone to look for meat. And sister, the work you do, if you work for one day, how much will you earn? How much will you get? That's why, as for me, the thing I know is that it all, mostly, is because of petrol. Petrol has made the prices of things get very, very high, and as soon as they raise it, it affects everything. OK.

I mean, they say they have raised the price of cocoa, and then the prices of things have got very expensive. As for cocoa, I don't have any myself; you don't have any. None at all, none of my relatives have ever planted cocoa at all. But if they raise the price of cocoa, and the prices of all other goods go up, it affects all of us. So, the things that have changed in this world, they are due to cocoa and petrol, the two of them. That's what is on my mind. . . .

GC: When you were young, was it this hard?

No, not at all. At the time I was a child, when I grew up enough to be buying cloth, I paid three hundred. . . . I gave birth, we named my child, they gave me six hundred. With the six hundred, my mother bought three cloths for three hundred each. Even the really expensive cloth she bought was four hundred cedis. *Wahu?* But today, if you wear European cloth, if you are buying it and you don't have fifty or fifty-five thousand cedis, you won't be buying any. . . . So between the old days and these days there is no comparison.

When I had just married . . . my husband gave me five shillings. Only five shillings, and I did a lot of shopping. . . . But sister the way I am living now, when I go to market, I can take three or four thousand, and it is not enough for my shopping. So I mean, in time, everything is going up. As time passes, everything goes up.

Rebellion, Revolution, and Tradition: Reinterpreting Coups in Ghana

Maxwell Owusu

The hope with which many Africans embraced independence faded as the continent was plunged into decades of political instability characterized by military interventions. Ghana was no exception to this phenomenon. Kwame Nkrumah was overthrown through a military coup d'état on February 28, 1966. From that time to 1992, when the nation adopted multiparty democracy, government was dominated by one military regime or another, as outlined in the introduction to this part. Instead of rehashing the economic and political factors often cited as the major reasons for this phenomenon, Maxwell Owusu, professor of anthropology at the University of Michigan, places these moments in a broader cultural context. In the following excerpt from a scholarly article, he connects the "tradition" of coup d'états in Ghana with the indigenous culture of opposition to established political orders through such organized groups as the Asafo.

The Relevance of the Past: Culture and People's Power

The postcolonial political experience of Ghana, the first black African country to achieve independence, is very illustrative of the rapid succession of coups, and the alternation of civilian and military regimes typical of many contemporary African states.

The endemic political instability in contemporary Africa has naturally been the subject of a flood of scholarly studies and publications, which has generated a variety of interpretations and explanations of the causes and outcomes of African coups.

The dominant analytical perspectives . . . have two major problems. First, they derive from images and views of change largely associated with Western historical experience. These tend to obscure or distort the great historical and cultural differences between African and European local sociopolitical realities. . . . Second . . . existing accounts underplay or ignore the central role of traditional beliefs and practices, indigenous political ideology, attitudes and outlooks. . . .

A. L. Adu has correctly observed that though European values, attitudes, and institutions have had profound effect on the politics of African societies, "they have not been strong enough to create lasting institutional and attitudinal basis for political development." Accordingly, no contemporary coups in Ghana . . . can be properly and fully comprehended as a political phenomenon, unless due account is taken of their total cultural setting and how they fit into the history of popular anticolonial and antichief protests and rebellions going back to the early period of colonial rule, including the Asafo risings of the interwar period in Ghana and the growth of mass parties and decolonization in the postwar era. . . .

The impact of colonialism and Western influence in general on African society has generated, nurtured, or reinforced two related local traditions. First, there is a persistent tradition of a strong desire among African leaders and peoples to cultivate, preserve, and adapt a viable African racial and cultural identity. . . .

Second, and more importantly, there exists a strong popular tradition of resistance, revolt, and rebellion against any form of injustice, and above all, against imperialism and foreign domination, as relevant case studies have conclusively demonstrated. In Ghana, the early and later forms of African nationalism grew and spread from this tradition of popular political consciousness, at once combining communal and emergent class elements, particularly among major ethnic groups of southern Ghana: the Akan, the Guan, the Ga, and Ewe.

The Asafo: Tradition in Transition

"The military is not in to take over. We simply want to be a part of the decision-making process in this country," proclaimed Flight-Lieutenant Rawlings in his first broadcast speech to the nation on 31 December 1981 soon after his coup. About five and a half years before this, Colonel Acheampong launched his famous Charter of Redemption, which he saw as an instrument to make Ghanaians "recapture, once again, our moral virtues, the good qualities, of our traditions and our sense of values," and proceeded to submit a proposal for a union government. It was to be a government without political parties, and one in which the army, the police, and civilians shared power. The parallels between the politicized role of the army, as proposed by both Acheampong and Rawlings, and the traditional role of the Asafo are too striking to be ignored.

The Asafo, the traditional warrior organization (*sa* "war," *fo* "people") of the Akan and other coastal peoples of southern Ghana, goes back at least to the early seventeenth century. . . . As a traditional institution, it is basic to the whole Akan culture.

Though the Asafo is primarily a warrior organization, the name is used for all male adults united for any purpose. In its wider sense, it is, according to De Graft Johnson, "a socio-politico-military organization embracing both men and women, including stool-holders or persons holding positions ordinarily recognized as forming part of the political constitution of the *Oman* [the traditional state and its divisions]," as well as "all other persons capable of defending in any way the common honor and integrity of such *Oman*. . . ."

It is particularly the last sense of the Asafo and its political role that is of primary concern here. . . .

As De Graft Johnson points out, the chief is, first and last, the servant of the traditional *Oman*, and the Asafo "form the bulk, the essential and most articulate part of the *Oman*." Traditionally the Asafo served as independent outlet for popular dissatisfaction and protest. It has always thus formed an "essential part of the traditional system of checks and balances upon the authority of the chief. . . ."

The Asafo also protected the polity against internal and external enemies. . . .

The Asafo in Colonial Politics: The Age of Rebellions

The interwar period—the crucial decades of Indirect Rule in the Gold Coast (Ghana)—was characterized by a spate of Asafo risings and frequent destoolments of corrupt and authoritarian chiefs throughout Southern Ghana, the area most affected by capitalist penetration and westernization. . . .

The most famous of the commoner rebellions took place in the Kwahu and Akim-Abuakwa areas of the eastern province of the Gold Coast. A broad discussion of the nature and principal objectives of the Asafo populist movements indicates the close parallels between them and contemporary military coups in Ghana. Despite their suppression by colonial authorities, the Asafo persisted as a potential political force that could be readily mobilized, or its spirit and ethos evoked (either in the service of African mass nationalism or to justify and legitimize contemporary corrective-reformist coups).

As Hobsbawm points out in his discussion of peasants and politics, when a sympathetic reformist or revolutionary government, inspiring leadership, or a single nationally organized and effective political party unify the masses—in this case, the Asafo, and youth organizations—"their support may make the difference between success and failure for national revolutions."

The early phases of Acheampong's NRC and Rawlings's PNDC regimes provide good examples of this. Soon after the coups, both regimes, proclaiming themselves to be "revolutionary" and populist, won the wholehearted support of students and youth organizations across the country and successfully mobilized them for involvement in their programs. Students contributed significantly to the effective implementation of Acheampong's policy of self-reliance, notably to the Dawhena irrigation project. Under the PNDC regime, a task force of students and members of other youth groups provided vital communal labour, assuming the role formerly performed by the traditional Asafo. . . .

Rituals of Rebellion and the Dilemmas of Class Action

Whatever the range of personal and sectional motivation involved, contemporary coups and popular revolts in Ghana may be interpreted as kinds of communal or civic sanctions which could be and are used to enforce moral obligations or responsibility of leadership in societies with communal bonds embedded in complex networks of multiplex relationships (kinship, affinity, ritual, locality) that are still strong. This important cultural dimension has been missed in nearly all the existing explanations and interpretations of coups in Africa. It is significant that *The Directive Principles of State Policy* of the PNDC in Ghana is committed, among other provisions, to "the adaptation and development of traditional cultural values as an integral part of the growth and development of society. . . ."

Thus modern coups and other popular rebellions and threats to political stability, at least in Ghana, may be correctly linked to what Max Gluckman has called "the frailty of authority." Gluckman argues that positions of leadership in Africa carry high, often contradictory, ideals, like justice, mercy, bounty, and integrity that in Ghana find expression in the chief's oath of office sworn during election and installation ceremonies and embodied in basic customary law doctrines of trusteeship.

It is my contention that, particularly in African states like Ghana, where communal values and ties are highly respected, the rituals of rebellion, like coups, symbolically state and try to resolve the perennial conflict and contradictions between the ideals of leadership and the realities of the exercise of power—the common "frailty of authority." The seemingly endless cycles of coups and countercoups that provide clear instances of the intractable problem of succession to high office could be shown to be historically and culturally connected, according to the peculiar institutional characteristics of African polities. These include a persistent tradition of populism, and African conceptions of the role of the state, of power and its legitimate exercise.

Miracles and the Message
(1983 Drought in Ghana)
Kwesi Brew

Between 1981 and 1984, West Africa experienced a severe decline in annual rainfall, which resulted in food shortages in Ghana. The military coups in 1979 and 1981 led by Flight Lieutenant John Rawlings meant that the country was trying to cope with yet another martial regime, further compounding the problems. In addition, there was a mass deportation of almost 1 million Ghanaians from Nigeria back to Ghana. These returnees added further tension to the political climate and affected the country's food resources. Combined with numerous bushfires in 1983, the picture was indeed one of desolation; hope or help from a supernatural source seemed a viable, if not the only, alternative. Kwesi Brew captures this hope in the following poem.

In the heat of this afternoon
Someone is working over across the dry river bed,
Starting a farm on his faith in miracles
Of abundant rains, sleeting and blowing cold
In a long period of drought;
In a land flooded with ubiquitous mirages
Where fires, without mothers, like crocodiles, dinosaured,
Gifted with fires instead of tongues crawl ungovernable
Throughout the land along implacable trails blinded by smoke;
Of heavy crops of maize, yellow, white, parti-coloured, and even blue;
In a harvest splashed with the prosperity of the gold of dryness,
Land sprinkled with yams mashed with red red oil and eggs offered
As thanksgiving to the Supreme Being whose day is Saturday.
"Listen papa, listen," Baaba calls out at me,
"Someone is working over across the dry river bed
There will be rain soon; rain, rain, my Papa!"

I hear the tubercular coughs of the cutlass
Rasping continually, quickening with hope, over tough seedy dry grass
Which had lost hope of being cut to grow
And sees at last the man come along
Who will cut to release and inspire life.
And I wonder what all these could mean for him who wielded the
cutlass.
Have faith, have faith, my people, the cutlass seems to assure.
Miracles are the sons and daughters of faith;
Miracles hover just beneath the gossamer of air around us
Awaiting the invocation of faith
To staunch the tears of those who find the burden wearisome
And are breaking under its weight,
Not because they have no will to wait for the unthinkable to happen
But weariness has shut the door
To visitation of visions and the breath is fading
With the vain beating of broken wings.
But here was the faith of one man;
The faith of all those who never lost hope.
And all the while the cutlass sang,
Have faith, have faith, have faith, my people.
My people, my great great people do not faint.
Have faith.

Win the Match and Vote for Me

Kevin S. Fridy and Victor Brobbey

Soccer in Ghana is more than just a game. In a country that is an amalgamation of numerous cultural polities, imbuing a sense of national Ghanaian pride and a feeling of belonging can prove an arduous task. However, this is not the case when the national soccer team takes to the field. On such occasions, the country merges into a solid unit of support without regard for ethnicity, politics, or socioeconomic standing. On the domestic front, however, soccer is not perceived in that same manner. Political scientist Kevin Fridy and Ghanaian lawyer Victor Brobbey examine the complex interplay between "ethnicity," politics and soccer in Ghana. They show how important the sport is while underscoring the fact that Ghana is indeed a nation of many "nations" in which people still cling to "ethnic" concerns, often privileging those concerns over national matters. The following excerpt from a scholarly article investigates how politicians have harnessed this "ethnic" tenacity and fanatical support for soccer to create a divide of national proportions in Ghana.

[Accra Hearts of Oak] and [Kumasi Asante Kotoko] are the two best professional soccer clubs in Ghana. . . . Between them, Hearts and Kotoko have collected forty of the Ghanaian premier league's forty-nine titles, and neither club has ever been relegated or even seriously faced the possibility of relegation. This supremacy has given the clubs a national following, such that, when matches involving Kotoko or Hearts were moved from Kumasi and Accra during scheduled renovations of the national football stadiums in anticipation of hosting the 2008 African Cup of Nations, smaller venues dispersed throughout Ghana's regions overflowed when hosting the clubs' league matches. . . .

Phobia: "Never say die 'til the bones are rotten"

Hearts records its official date of establishment as 11 November 1911, when they introduced their kits to the public and played their first official match.

. . . In 1957, Hearts joined the first nationally organized league competition of the newly independent state of Ghana and won the inaugural tournament, going on to win nineteen domestic league titles and two continental cups.

Hearts has always had strong connections to the Ga state and Ga traditional authority in Accra, but never to the same degree as Kotoko with the Asante nation. In the early days of the Guggisberg Shield competition, Nii Tackie Tawiah II took the field for Hearts. The man who would become Ga Mantse (head of the Ga traditional state) later took the post of club chairman until his enstoolment in 1944. Another Phobian who would rise to political prominence after his playing days were over was Joseph Ankrah. In the late 1930s and early 1940s Ankrah was Hearts' stand-out right wing. In 1966 he would become the first, and at present only, Ga speaker to take up the position of head of the Ghanaian state, when his National Liberation Council (NLC) overthrew Nkrumah's Convention People's Party (CPP) government. . . .

Fabulous: "Wo kum apem a, apem be ba"

Having won twenty-one domestic league titles and two continental championships, "Fabulous" Kumasi Asante Kotoko was established initially under the moniker Ashanti United in 1924 and then rechristened the Kumasi Titanics a few years later. The name of the club was changed yet again to Kumasi Asante Kotoko in 1935, a particularly important year in Asante history. It was the year that the Asante Confederacy, dissolved in 1901 by the British, was restored, and the Asantehene (the king of the Asante) returned to the ceremonial stool. That the club was in this year dubbed Asante Kotoko and given the porcupine as its mascot, a name and symbol synonymous with the Asante military wing, was no coincidence. The name Kotoko evoked not just Asante pride, but a populist form of militant Asante nationalism which, like the porcupine's quills, is thought to be an inexhaustible source of strength. Nana Agyeman Prempeh II, Asantehene at the time and a fixture at Kotoko's early matches, was appointed the club's "Life Patron," with final authority concerning club decisions resting exclusively in his lap.

From newspaper accounts of their early matches, it is apparent that when Kotoko played, it was seen as representing all of the Asante nation rather than merely the municipality of Kumasi. . . .

A History of Mixing Soccer and Politics

In the period immediately after independence, the government of Ghana recognized the importance of sports in general, and soccer in particular, as a vehicle for nation-building. Soccer played an important part in the independence celebrations of 1957, as Nkrumah encouraged English footballer Stanley Matthews to join Hearts for a few matches to publicize the creation of an annual national soccer league competition. . . . Clubs were chosen, and in some cases created, from all over the country to take part and to give the league its national character. . . .

In the period immediately before and after independence, the National Liberation Movement (NLM), led by J. B. Danquah and his supporters in the Asanteman Council, became the most vocal component in Ghana's anti-Nkrumah oppositional forces. As the movement derived much of its support from Kumasi and its environs, the NLM and the Danquah-Busia political tradition that would follow it became closely associated with Kotoko in the 1960s, as it has been ever since.

This politicized sports history ultimately had an effect on what it meant to be a fan of a particular club, or the adherent of a particular political tradition. Thus, for a Kotoko supporter, the extremist fan/conspiracy theorist would suggest that the CPP government, and later those led by Rawlings, were against them. . . . These governments, by their acts of oppression and discrimination against Kotoko, were not just attacking a soccer club, but attempting to suppress the social identities, specifically the Asante ethnic identity in this case, wrapped up in the club's persona.

For a Hearts fan, the conspiracy theory would be that the NPP [New Patriotic Party] government and its earlier incarnations in the Danquah-Busia tradition and Ghana's Akan business and political establishment are firmly in the camp of Kumasi Asante Kotoko and, therefore, do not want to see Hearts succeed. Disputes over players that are resolved in court, investigations of irregularities in player transfers, hearings of the disciplinary committee of the Ghana Football Association, investigations of incidents at stadiums by various committees, and indeed all other actions or decisions that require governmental input, are resolved in Kotoko's favour when the Danquah-Busiaists are in power. . . .

The Hearts/Kotoko Political Rivalry

The politicization of the rivalry between Hearts and Kotoko is a reflection of two overlapping phenomena: the bifurcation of Ghana into two dominant political traditions, and the failure of the soccer clubs to put in place independent institutional structures to sustain themselves financially. Despite their large support bases, covering operation costs for both Kotoko and Hearts is dependent on the generosity of wealthy and influential patrons. Traditionally popular perception holds that the two clubs have attracted a different, and arguably rival, set of sponsors. Personalities who have held influential positions in Kotoko have largely been members of Kumasi's traditional and business elite. When they have dabbled in politics, they have for the most part been strong supporters of the Danquah-Busia tradition. The personalities behind Hearts have mostly been Accra-based businessmen and political leaders. They have tended to support the Nkrumahist political tradition. Today, with the demise of the Nkrumahists as a political force and the supplanting of the Nkrumahist tradition by Jerry Rawlings's regime, the leading personalities of the Hearts have tended to come from the NDC half of the political divide.

The (P)NDC and Accra Hearts of Oak

In 1992, a new constitution was promulgated, and Rawlings assumed the presidency as a democratically elected leader under the banner of the NDC. As with the CPP, the primary locus of opposition to the (P)NDC was the Ashanti Region, and Kotoko again assumed its role as the club of the opposition. Rawlings made it clear that Hearts was the club of the establishment by showing up to matches between Hearts and Kotoko wearing Hearts' well-known "rainbow" colors.

The NPP and Kumasi Asante Kotoko

The connections between Kumasi Asante Kotoko and Ghana's . . . NPP [party] . . . are equally clear. The NPP is the modern-day party of the Danquah-Busia tradition. . . . Patrons of the club, such as George Adu-Poku and Kennedy Agyepong, are also big donors to the NPP. Kotoko, despite Hearts being the club of the establishment for the twenty-year period of the (P)NDC regime, is perceived as wealthier and better run than Hearts. . . .

Clash of the Titans

The Hearts/Kotoko rivalry shares similarities with other sports rivalries around the globe. It is always intense and occasionally violent, it is based on a perceived sense of alienation and persecution by both clubs at various stages in their histories, and it has been exacerbated by national politics. . . .

Such is the association between the two clubs and the two parties that, in the run-up to the 2000 elections when John Kufuor, then presidential candidate of the NPP, offered Hearts a donation to assist the club in its preparations towards the African Club Champions campaign, it was initially refused. During the same election cycle in 2000, a banner was reportedly unfurled during a soccer game at the Accra Sports Stadium stating that the Hearts were solidly behind the NDC's presidential candidate Professor John E. A. Mills. A few months later, in the aftermath of the 9 May Stadium disaster which resulted in the death of 127 fans, those who felt justice was both slow and poorly served were keen to point out that the newly installed government was NPP and most of the fans who perished were supporters of Hearts. More recently, in 2003, an antigovernment demonstration organized by the NDC to protest against the policies of the NPP went through the streets of Accra and ultimately ended up at the training grounds of Accra Hearts of Oak, at which point both Hearts and NDC songs were sung.

The 1994 Civil War in Northern Ghana

Artur Bogner

The Northern Region is the largest among the ten regions in Ghana. In terms of peopling, it has over thirty linguistically and politically distinct cultural groups. The imposition of "chiefs" on indigenous northern groups without a history of such a system and the favoring of one group over the other by British colonial administrators created divisions and tensions among these groups. Artur Bogner, professor of sociology at the University of Bayreuth (Germany), examines the ways these tensions have manifested themselves over the years. In this excerpt from his chapter in a scholarly book, the author explores how minority groups such as the Konkomba have sought to assert their political independence in the region and how their attempts at doing so have resulted in conflicts, the largest being the 1994 conflict between them and their "overlords," the Dagomba and Nanumba.

Since 1981 the region around the Oti River, on the border of Ghana and Togo, has been the scene of five ethnic conflicts—the bloodiest clashes in Ghana since its founding. These conflicts (one of them on Togolese territory) can be seen as a series. Although up to 1994 they each occurred in a different place with different opponents, they all involved members of one ethnic group in particular, the Konkomba. . . .

The Konkomba have been classified as a "chiefless" group, in contrast to their opponents. Even today they have no ruling nobility above the village level. Compared to their neighbors they are reputed to have an unbroken tradition of an agricultural way of life, a lower standard of education and higher birth-rates. . . . In 1978 the Konkomba represented the largest ethnic group in the Nanumba District with an estimated 46 percent of the population. In East Gonja they represented the second largest group, with an estimated 29 percent. Prior to the war these districts, which had earlier been scarcely populated and are known for their fertile soils, had become the most important centers of yam cultivation in Ghana. In 1992 and 1993 the two districts alone produced almost a fifth of the entire national yam crop.

A Muslim resident of northern Ghana on bicycle. Bicycles are very popular on the flat roads of northern Ghana, where male Muslims will ride to mud-and-stick mosques for prayer. Photograph by Kwasi Konadu, 2007.

It is assumed that the Konkomba contribute in an overproportional manner to this production. . . .

There had already been tensions between the Konkomba and the so-called "majority tribes" (Dagomba, Nanumba, Gonja, and Mamprusi) before 1994, particularly because of the earlier conflicts. When taken separately the last three groups each has a smaller population than the Konkomba. What gives them their special status is their alliance with the largest group, the Dagomba, and the fact that, since the time of the British protectorate, a formalized and theoretically comprehensive system of recognized chiefs existed, with the noble families of these four groups at the head of the hierarchy. . . .

In these circumstances the Konkomba leaders' demand for an independent Paramount status for the Chief of Saboba exploded like a grenade. It was raised in a petition to the president of the National House of Chiefs in June 1993—circumventing the Dagomba king, the Ya Na, who would be directly affected by it, and who, according to the rules of protocol, would have been the first one to be addressed. In the petition it was *inter alia* asserted that the Konkomba inhabited the whole Oti basin as early as the seventeenth century—thereby calling into question their status as immigrants in Nanumba and East Gonja, where their actual presence today is mainly due to relatively recent waves of migration. In some passages the privileged position of the "majority tribes" was described as an artifact of colonial rule. . . . The Ya Na's reply in October, in the form of a letter to the National House of Chiefs, was a clear refusal. In it he claimed that the Konkomba living in Ghana were immigrants from "French Togoland" (that is, present-day Togo). . . . After the war the Ya Na explained his argument more precisely in a document submitted to the government-appointed negotiation team; he claimed that the Konkomba had been driven out of what is now Ghana by the Dagomba, who conquered them "some 600 years ago," but the Konkomba "have over the years been sneaking into Dagbon in trickles"—that is, into the land under his sovereignty.

According to the first reports in the media, which cited the leader of the district administration, the violence started on 31 January 1994 when a Konkomba and a Nanumba got into a brawl over the sale of a guinea-fowl at the Nakpayili market near Bimbilla. . . . In the physical fight that followed, the Nanumba bit off one of the Konkomba's fingers and taunted him with it. Another behaved in such a way as to challenge his opponents to a physical fight. The son of the injured Konkomba, who lived at another settlement nearby, killed this man in an individual action on the next day. According to the Konkomba "Position Paper," the village headman of the culprit ordered him to wait for the police to arrive. Before this could happen, however, this settlement as well as other Konkomba locations were attacked by Nanumba. . . .

Two explanations for the conflicts dominate public debate in Ghana. The first goes back to the widely accepted stereotype of the Konkomba as an "uncivilized and warlike" people. . . .

The second explanation blames the conflict on the quasi-feudalistic, and at times discriminatory, relations between the chiefs of the majority tribes and the rural Konkomba. . . .

Both prejudices clearly contain an element of truth and, at the same time, both should be taken with a pinch of salt. The propensity to respond to an individual attack with collective retaliation played a role in all of the recent conflicts; however, this propensity is not one-sided, as the escalation of violence in the Nanumba District both in 1980–81 and in the period before the outbreak of war in 1994 shows. In this respect there is little difference between the groups in conflict in northern Ghana—both amongst themselves and when compared with parties involved in other civil wars around the world.

"That All Konkomba Should Henceforth Unite"

Benjamin Talton

Over the years, Ghana has recorded several ethnic conflicts, despite its externally projected image of peace and stability. The Northern Region in Ghana is one of the areas where these conflicts have resulted in immense destruction, loss of lives, and a shift in established political relationships. The 1994 conflict between the Konkomba and the Dagomba is representative of these issues. In Politics of Social Change in Ghana: The Konkomba Struggle for Political Equality, *Benjamin Talton, associate professor of history at Temple University, examines the relationship between the centralized and so-called noncentralized states of the region using the Konkomba as a case study. The following excerpt from his monograph explores the effects of the 1994 conflicts on the relationship between the Konkomba and their neighbors and the process of instituting central leadership among a hitherto decentralized people.*

Conflict disrupts economic progress and development. During the ten years that followed the 1994 conflict, Kpandai remained cut off from support from Bimbilla after alienating Nanumba leaders. The strength of chieftaincy in Northern Ghana, the lack of viable economic development, and political isolation contributed to the entrenched political inequality in the Northern Region. Compared with the south, chieftaincy remained popular in the north and, prior to the 1980s, there was no opportunity for a strong business or professional class to emerge that might have posed a counterweight to chieftaincy for shaping ethnic politics. Party politics in the postcolonial period also helped to sustain political inequality in the region. The dominant political parties devoted their energy on candidates and potential candidates from the historically centralized societies even when they were minorities in their constituency, which made room for Konkomba candidates of minor parties to win elections in majority Konkomba constituencies. In 1996, in Bimbilla, a Konkomba won the parliamentary seat because he ran for a minor party, while the majority parties divided the Nanumba vote.

Leading to the second democratic election of the Fourth Republic Jerry Rawlings's National Democratic Congress suffered severe bruises from corruption and sex scandals that threatened to undermine Rawlings's image as the champion of democracy and Ghana's economic recovery. Most of all, perhaps, the administration's failure to effectively address the conflicts in Northern Ghana between Konkomba and their historically centralized neighbors threatened to terminally derail their prospects to gain a second term. Konkomba and Dagomba leaders blamed the Rawlings administration for its inadequate response. In addition, Konkomba leaders had long mistrusted Mohammed Ibn Chambas, MP for Bimbilla and first deputy speaker of parliament. They accused him of providing arms to Nanumba combatants. Before the fighting broke out there was palpable tension between the two groups, which pointed to the potential for a repeat of the violence of 1981. . . .

In the years that followed the 1994 conflict, Konkomba leaders continued to pursue recognition for a Konkomba paramount chief, but it was more than the Ya Na's resistance that stood in their way. Even if the Ya Na accepted the Konkomba request, there was little agreement among Konkomba with regard to which *ubor* should be the Konkomba paramount chief. There was no single *ubor* or individual leader whose authority was recognized throughout Kekpakpaan. KOYA [Konkomba Youth Association] enjoyed broad respect in the political realm, but with regard to traditional authority—issues of land, social relations, and death—no organization or individual wielded such influence.

The absence of a strong central leader who exercised broad and consistent authority was, in many respects, an advantage for Konkomba. With no leadership hierarchy, historical precedent and protocol were irrelevant in Konkomba politics. Western-educated professionals and business leaders were able to push forward a political agenda for Konkomba without advice or oversight from an entrenched, hereditary political class. Consequently, social and political transformation occurred more rapidly among Konkomba than among their centralized neighbors. The obstacles to Konkomba change were the state—with its support of chiefs and chieftaincy—and groups with an established system of chieftaincy, who jealously guarded the privileges that came with such a system. The opposition that Konkomba encountered for their social and political reforms precipitated their dominance in fields outside of the more common paths to political power. Party politics and commercial farming in Ghana were not regulated by ethnicity in the way that traditional politics was.

Today, Konkomba generally recognize that their economic gains were a result of their embrace of Western education and hard work. Few Konkomba cite increased political power, commercial success, and population growth in historically Nanumba and Gonja areas as sources for the 1981 and 1994 conflicts. Rather, most cite chieftaincy affairs, which suggests that Konkomba regard the issues at the heart of the conflicts as tangential to their immediate concerns. In addition, there continued to be few Konkomba who list chieftaincy as a significant issue within their communities. It was not the case, however, that thousands of Konkomba rallied around an issue that the majority regarded as inconsequential. In fact, although many Konkomba explain that chieftaincy was the cause of the 1994 conflict, for those who participated in the fighting the conflict was about their right to freely define their political character and status.

However, the consequences of the conflict extended far beyond the issue of chieftaincy. Most Konkomba residents of Yendi, Tamale, and Damanko were forced by their Dagomba and Gonja neighbors to flee. Many Konkomba continue to be reluctant to spend long periods in Yendi and Tamale. The main road to Saboba from the south passes through Tamale and then through Yendi, but after the conflicts, a longer route from Accra that passes through the Volta Region and connects to Yendi via Bimbilla became a popular alternative to traveling through Tamale, for Konkomba travelers.

The conflicts also affected northern politics. While most northerners present a picture of improved ethnic relations and, in some areas, ethnic harmony, for many politicians violence or the threat of violence has become a card to be played for political leverage. This tactic carries the potential to inspire actual violence because having experienced the conflicts, violence then becomes a viable option for resolving disputes when there is an existing perception that the threat of violence is real. In recent years, there have been several political disputes that carried the potential for larger, violent conflicts. . . .

These developments are further evidence of the continued primacy of chieftaincy and ethnicity in local politics in Northern Ghana. Ethnicity remains a tool with which political stakeholders compete for political and economic gains. These recent disputes also point to the failure of Ghana's government, since the end of British colonial rule, to properly ensure social and political equality. With the responsibility left to individuals and groups to secure their own access to the privileges of Ghanaian citizenship, it carries the potential for conflict because power gained by some is inevitably seen as power lost by others.

I Am Not Brainwashed

Asirifi Danquah

As we have already noted, Ghana's political history recognizes two local political traditions: one represented by Nkrumah's Convention People's Party, and the other by those who oppose it. To most observers of history residing outside Ghana, Kwame Nkrumah is almost infallible, and little or no attention is paid to certain of his policies that proved to be draconian. Neither is much attention devoted to the writings of his detractors. In the months leading up to the celebrations to mark the fiftieth anniversary of Ghana, the extent of the political divide in Ghana was played out in the major newspapers as journalists jousted over the legacy of the country's first independent leader. Set within this context, veteran Ghanaian journalist Asirifi Danquah defends himself against some of his detractors in the following newspaper article by arguing that his critique of Nkrumah is well founded. Danquah supports his position by recalling personal experiences and foregrounding some of the reasons that Nkrumah and his regime were not without flaws.

I have been compelled by the unwarranted abuses rained on me by Messrs. Michael Nunoo and Kwabena Bomfe in the *Daily Graphic* issues of November 21 and December 6, 2006, respectively, in response to my article headlined "Origin of Violence in Ghana Politics."

In fact, people without any political bias for the CPP would readily admit that I was careful not to utter any word of insult against Kwame Nkrumah and any member of the CPP. I just presented the facts as I could remember.

Unfortunately, both critics of my article ignored the substance of the issue and rather launched vicious attacks on my person. I should have treated their attacks with the contempt they deserve; nonetheless, there are a few distortions and falsehoods which must not be left to remain as part of Ghana's political history.

There are two main statements which portrayed Nkrumah's intention to establish a one-party state in the country. In his own autobiography, Kwame Nkrumah confessed that he accepted the offer to become secretary of the

United Gold Coast Convention (UGCC) because he wanted to form a different type of political movement.

In pursuit of this evil intent, he took advantage of his position as a general secretary to use the structures of the UGCC to form the Convention Peoples Party (CPP) barely one year of holding that post, a mark of dishonesty indeed.

Thus, Nkrumah's inordinate lust for power exposed his premeditated agenda to set up a one-party regime in the country. This became clear when, at the inauguration of his party (CPP), he threatened to chase the chiefs out of the country. He declared, "The chiefs will run away and leave their sandals behind." Had the chiefs threatened his life to warrant the passage of the obnoxious law, the Preventive Detention Act (PDA)?

The chiefs had not thrown bombs at him and members of his newly formed CPP, and yet he could not hide his ingrained agenda to rule the country as an untouchable monarch. Thus, the only way to achieve this objective was to destroy any perceived opposition to his course.

True to his word, he did not only chase some chiefs out of the country, but Nkrumah reached the height of his threat when he stripped the Okyenhene, Nana Sir Ofori Attah II, of his title "Osagyefo" and banished him from his area of jurisdiction. He arrogated to himself the title "Osagyefo" and assumed the role of the kingmakers and thereby enstooled and destooled chiefs by the stroke of his pen.

Chiefs who were found to be anti-CPP were removed just by a gazette notice, the official machinery for withdrawing [the] government's recognition of chiefs.

Censorship

The next group of people who became victims of Nkrumah's arbitrary rule were the intellectuals and professionals, as the tides of political liberty ebbed away with the arrest and incarceration of all classes of the citizenry; principal among such victims were journalists, authors, and students who were critical of his policies.

For example, the expulsion of Bankole Themothy of the *Daily Graphic* from the country for posing the question "Kwame, what next?," after the passage of the PDA gave a signal of what was ahead of journalists in and outside the country.

This was followed by the forced closure of the *Ashanti Pioneer*, the only known opposition newspaper, and the detention of journalists such as Kojo Dumoga, Kwame Kesse Adu, A. D. Appiah, all of the *Pioneer*; Lovelace Johnson of the *Daily Graphic*; [and] Henry Thompson and others, which marked the beginning of the end of democracy in the country.

Apologists for Nkrumah have no evidence to justify the incarceration of the journalists except that the despot did not tolerate criticisms. Consequently, all the news media, including the Ghana Broadcasting Corporation, were compelled to toe the party's line. Both columnists and radio commentators extolled the tyrant and everything that he did. Books written on government and politics from the Western world were banned from the newsstands, and their places taken over by books of Karl Marx, Lenin, and some other communist authors.

Under such circumstances, nobody could subject any of Nkrumah and his CPP's policies to any critical analysis without being landed in Nkrumah's concentration camp. He then employed authors who shared the same communist ideas he upheld to write books which portrayed him not only as a saint, but also as a visionary, burdened with the task of liberating his people from oppression, the opposite of what he practiced.

He embarked upon a systematic brainwashing of the youth and the adults by establishing institutions such as the Young Pioneer Movement and the Kwame Nkrumah Ideological Institute at Winneba, the purpose of which was to deify him.

The Young Pioneers became the instrument of arbitrary arrests and detention for the least discussion of politics in which Kwame Nkrumah was mentioned. This became the only justification for one's detention, as J. B. Danquah's detention was based on a hearsay that he was planning a coup against Kwame Nkrumah.

Brainwashed?

Most unfair to my integrity is Bomfe's insult that I might be "suffering from selective amnesia and or have been brainwashed to accept falsehood as the truth and might also have not spent quality time to search diligently for what can be accepted as the truth that can stand the test of time."

Bomfe has misfired woefully for ranking me among those allegedly brainwashed to accept anything false about Nkrumah as true. This accusation is false and the following events will prove to my critics and the world at large that I cannot be brainwashed.

At twenty-seven, I, Asirifi Danquah, was the Chairman of the Sunyani Areas Local Council and member of the erstwhile Brong Ahafo Central District Council, an equivalent of the now district assembly.

I was seventy-six on September 28, 2006, and can say that I am a living witness to the period during which Kwame Nkrumah toyed with the lives of Ghanaians. Besides, my major employers, the Graphic Corporation, has abundant evidence on record to support my claim to the knowledge of Ghana's political history, particularly during the reign of Kwame Nkrumah and beyond.

Moreover, I have not only spent quality time to search for the truth about the hostilities that existed between Kwame Nkrumah and J. B. Danquah, but I have been a living testimony of all major events which took place before and after Nkrumah's overthrow.

Records at the archives of the *Daily Graphic* show that I was the first journalist to accompany the army to capture Kwame Nkrumah's subversion camps at Obenemase in Ashanti and also the leader of the team comprising both local and foreign journalists to cover events at the subversion camps.

I was also present when representatives of all the foreign missions in Ghana visited the Obenemase subversion camp to see for themselves nationals from other Africa countries who were being trained to carry out subversive activities against their governments.

I interviewed the inmates who confessed that they were trained to go back to their respective countries to subvert their own governments, which appeared not to agree with Kwame Nkrumah's ambition to become the President of Africa.

I also witnessed large quantities of explosives, bombs, dynamites, and all sorts of sophisticated weapons which dissidents recruited from all over Africa were trained to handle.

Torture

I was an eyewitness to the release of hundreds of detainees from Nkrumah's concentration camps, maimed, blind, and crippled as a result of brutalities they suffered at the hands of prison officers on the orders of Kwame Nkrumah.

It was not surprising, however, that the director of prisons committed suicide on hearing of the overthrow of Kwame Nkrumah's dictatorial regime, for fear of retribution for torturing Nkrumah's political opponents. He could not face the consequences of his inhuman treatment to such great men as Dr. J. B. Danquah, Obetsebi Lamptey, and others, who opposed Kwame Nkrumah's dictatorship.

No fair-minded Ghanaian can deny that I had the privilege to cover for the *Daily Graphic* some of the commissions of enquiry set up to probe Nkrumah's corrupt practices, particularly the NADECO, a special company established to receive 10 per cent commission on all contracts awarded by the CPP government, the evidences of CPP stalwarts and Nkrumah's financial advisers like W. H. Halm, Aye Kumi, Krobo Edusei, and Kofi Boako, who told the world about things like the twelve gold bars sent through Krobo Edusei to Nkrumah's wife in Cairo, Egypt, the bribes taken on the value of import licenses issued, as well as the huge sums of money released from the Consolidated Fund to Nkrumah's girlfriends and concubines such as Miss Genoviva, and a massive acquisition of wealth by Kwame Nkrumah the Socialist.

There is no doubt in my mind that with such abundant evidence, Bomfe and his cohorts will describe Asirifi Danquah as having been brainwashed to accept falsehood as the truth.

Hydro-Power and the Promise of Modernity and Development in Ghana

Stephan F. Miescher and Dzodzi Tsikata

Ghana relies heavily on hydropower as the main source of electricity. Before the construction of the Kpong and Bui hydroelectric plants, the Akosombo Dam remained the largest supplier of hydroelectric power in the country. Until the National Patriotic Party assumed office in 2001, subsequent governments after Kwame Nkrumah suspended the construction of the Bui Dam. Like the Akosombo Dam, the construction of the Bui Dam project was supposed to fast-track the nation's development by providing a lasting solution to the persistent energy crisis. In the following excerpt from a scholarly article, historian Stephan F. Miescher and social scientist Dzodzi Tsikata compare the rhetoric of "development" and "modernization" evoked in the construction of the Akosombo and Bui dams and the effects of both projects on the people in the immediate environs.

In 2007, as Ghanaians were suffering another electricity crisis with frequent power outages, President J. A. Kuffuor celebrated in a festive mood the sod cutting for the country's third large hydroelectric dam at Bui across the Black Volta in the Brong Ahafo Region. The new 400-megawatt (MW) power project promises to guarantee Ghana's electricity supply and to develop neglected parts of the north. . . .

Although there is more than a forty-year gap between the commissioning of Akosombo in 1966 and the beginning of work on the Bui Dam, the two projects have striking similarities in the discourse of modernization and development they have generated among government officials and in local communities. . . .

On the ground in many African countries since early independence, politicians, policy makers, and popular writers have expressed in vivid terms not only the expectations of modernity but also relied on the notion of modernization when outlining their goals and hopes for the emerging nation. . . . We are interested in how "the idea of modernization was *used* in

The Akosombo Hydroelectric Project, which sits on the Volta River in southeastern Ghana. Flickr: yingke, 2011. Courtesy of the photographer.

particular context," and how the usage of this idea has changed over the last fifty years. We argue that Akosombo and Bui have served as a gauge of relevance of modernization discourse in Ghana and as a reflection of the crucial players and ideologies. . . . Modernization and its related aspirations have not lost their luster in Ghana, but have maintained distinct meanings at different times.

The Volta River Project

The Volta River Project represents different understandings of development and modernization in the history of Ghana. In 1915, when travelling downstream by canoe, the geologist Albert Kitson had the idea of damming the Volta at Akosombo in order to produce hydroelectric power for processing the country's bauxite into aluminum. Ten years later, Kitson (1925) published a survey on the Gold Coast's mineral and water-power resources, which included the possibility for a second dam at Bui as a way to electrify a railway to the north. . . . The rising demand for aluminum during World War II created an interest in the project. . . . In 1952, a British white paper echoed this sentiment by rallying for the project with the call for the "need for a new Sterling Area Aluminum Smelter," emphasizing the project's benefits for empire and commonwealth.

In the 1950s, nationalist leaders shifted the rhetoric around the Volta River Project. Nkrumah, an early and enthusiastic supporter, described it in a Legislative Assembly debate as "a gigantic project for the industrial development of our country—a scheme which can change the face of our land and bring wealth and a higher standard of living to our people. . . ."

Promises of Akosombo

In a speech to the National Assembly in 1961, when seeking approval of the Master Agreement between Ghana and VALCO [Volta Aluminum Company], Nkrumah articulated the objective of creating an industrial sector that would balance Ghana's agricultural production (cocoa). "Newer nations," he declared, "which are determined by every possible means to catch up in industrial strength," must select a "large-scale industrial advance. Electricity is the basis for Industrialization. That, basically, is the justification for the Volta River Project. . . ."

Resettlement

Promoting Akosombo, Nkrumah's government sought to highlight the positive aspects of resettling 739 villages into 52 townships. A VRA booklet noted that although "homes and lands would be destroyed, this very destruction could be turned to account if better living conditions and more efficient farming methods could be provided instead. . . ." Resettlement should serve Ghana's anticipated transition from tradition to modernity. . . .

The experience of resettlement was traumatic. Most people did not believe that their homes and farms would be flooded. . . . The Akosombo resettlement program failed to deliver the promises expressed by the planners. Changes in agriculture, such as the introduction of mechanized and cooperative farming, did not yield the anticipated results of moving people from a subsistence to a cash crop economy. . . .

Still, the livelihoods of lakeside settlements became superior to those of older communities in the Lower Volta. . . . Akosombo, and its promise of modernization, turned out to be a mixed blessing for the communities of the Lower Volta.

Building Bui Dam

In November 2005, the NPP government signed a memorandum of understanding with the China Water Resources and Hydropower Construction

Group (Sinohydro) and Chinese financiers to build the Bui Dam. . . . Advocating Bui, the government evoked the promises once associated with Akosombo. The discourse on modernization that has accompanied the Bui Dam was in evidence at the sod-cutting ceremony in August 2007. Energy Minister Joseph Adda announced that the $622 million project would generate 400 MW of electricity to address shortages across Ghana, improve the security of electricity supplies to Northern Ghana, and enable the country to supply electricity to Burkina Faso and Côte d'Ivoire. . . .

In its effort to promote Bui, the government erected large billboards along the road from Accra leading to the dam site. The most prominent billboard depicted Bui City as a modern settlement with high-rise buildings, tree-lined streets, and public fountains situated against a background of massive Bui Hydro-Electric Dam, featuring open floodgates and three penstocks feeding the turbines. . . . As is well known, some of the modernization promises of Akosombo, including industrialization and irrigation, did not come to pass. In this case the chances of realizing Bui City in the image of the billboard are even more uncertain, as it is not clear who will pay for this urban center. . . .

There is also a qualitative difference in the modernization paradigm that accompanied the two dams. While Akosombo was being constructed in a period of state-led development of the 1950s and 1960s, Bui is being constructed in a situation of private sector–led strategies. Thus in the case of Akosombo, rural people were to be ushered into the modern world through irrigation agriculture under the guidance of the Volta resettlement project. In the case of Bui, local people and their chiefs are being entreated to position themselves in order to exploit the opportunities of the project. . . .

Postscript: Modernization in Question

Despite this history of shortcomings in the treatment of dam-affected communities in Ghana, it remains striking that the backers of the Bui Dam continue to fall back on the lofty rhetoric of modernization whenever they promote the dam, or when they try to convince those who will lose the most to support this infrastructural project. . . . Thus, ideas and aspirations of modernization in relation to large dams are very much alive in today's Ghana—even if they are evoked in different historical context from the one half a century ago, when Nkrumah had advocated Akosombo as a route to achieve the promise of modernity.

The Ghanaian Media and National Unity

George Sydney Abugri

In March 2007, Ghana celebrated its fiftieth year as an independent nation. The national festivities were dubbed Ghana@50. Given the histories we have showcased thus far, these celebrations included as well as excluded certain individuals or groups based on political affiliation, gender, and locality. The narrative of the nation, the promotion of national unity and a shared identity, were literally controlled by those who excluded others from orchestrating or fully participating in the "national" celebrations. Some of the excluded challenged these assertions over the present and the future of Ghanaian nationhood. In August 2007, award-winning Ghanaian journalist George Sydney Abugri at the Daily Graphic, *Ghana's largest newspaper, featured in his weekly column, "Letter to Jomo," the following article, titled "The Ghanaian Media and National Unity." In it he takes aim at the aforementioned issues, providing a subtle yet poignant analysis of the state of national unity and the role of media on the occasion of the country's fiftieth anniversary.*

In the year of the Golden Jubilee of our independence from British Colonial rule, political economists are no doubt assessing the level of socioeconomic progress made in fifty years. A major concern of peace-building advocates and activists will however relate to the question of how much has been achieved in terms of national unity and integration fifty years after independence.

Integration refers to a combination of various components and parts needed to make a harmonious whole. In this article, national integration will refer to the harmonious coexistence of the country's different ethnic, political, social, religious, and other groups, in a spirit of oneness and unity.

In his book *Ghana: Peace and Stability*, K. B. Quantson recalls that the struggle for independence had been marred by an acrimonious, ruthless, and violent war between Dr. Kwame Nkrumah's CPP and the opposition parties led by Dr. Kofi Abrefa Busia. "The scale of the violence was unthinkable. The human and material damage was incalculable. In some cases, it was sheer madness. Houses and official functions were bombed or dynamited. Axes and machetes were used to hack down political opponents. At some level it was a demented affair." Such political violence may not be occurring on a scale reminiscent of the situation in many African countries today, but the threat of negative political activity and discourse to national unity and integration fifty years after independence is evident in the acrimony that has characterized partisan politics in the country.

A frequent observation by many has been that fifty years after political independence, Ghana is acutely polarized along partisan political loyalties and sympathies. The political polarization of the nation, as explained in the quotation from Quantson's book above, has its roots in the last days of the struggle for independence and the immediate postindependence years.

Fifty years later, ethnic and chieftaincy conflicts may not have led to [the] disintegration of our nation, but in the decades since independence, they have killed thousands of our people. Many ethnic hostilities still simmer in an atmosphere of deceptive calm. There are scores of potential trouble spots throughout the country security categorized by the national security establishment as "flash point."

The political threat to national integrations is often evident during national elections. The 2004 elections were relatively more peaceful, but in the run-up to and during the 2000 elections, one could quite literally reach out and touch the fear and tension in the air.

Fifty years after independence, political affiliation and loyalties in the country are based on tribal affiliations, and it is often predictable that during partisan political elections people of one ethnic group in any political constituency will vote for this or that political party.

Some ethnic groups engaged in disputes with the potential to escalate into serious conflict have tended to belong to particular opposing political parties. Alleged meddling by political forces has been cited as a cause of some of the chieftaincy and ethnic conflicts. Ethnicity, partisan politics, and chieftaincy thus appear to be linked in their common threat to national integration.

Our discussion of the question of level of national integration achieved in fifty years zeroes down unavoidably to the country's media. As disseminators of information, the media has always been a potential tool for the promotion of national integration or division and acrimony. Let us consider radio: Radio phone-in programs have their usefulness as mediums for public education and for the promotion of freedom of expression and democratic debate. They serve as a safety valve for the healthy expression of opinions on national issues, which people feel strongly about.

Paradoxically, radio phone-in programs have also become communication tools for the propagation and promulgation of negative political propaganda and ethnic sentiments with the potential to divide the nation.

Of particular note in this regard is the phenomenon of so-called "Serial Callers" to radio phone-in programs. These are actually political activists who call into the phone-in segments of as many radio programs as possible, in a bid to disseminate political propaganda as widely as possible.

They have been a significant threat to national integration, inasmuch as they have used radio to make derogatory, insulting, and sometimes threatening remarks about individuals and groups whose views and actions they do not approve of.

The destructive power of radio in this regard should not be underestimated: Few will forget the infamous case of Milles Collines Radio, which in the midst of ethnic tension in Rwanda persistently and loudly called on Hutus in Rwanda to rise up and kill the *inyenzi*, a Hutu word meaning cockroaches, which was used in reference to Tutsis.

Milles Collines Radio actually went on to set a deadline of May 5, 1994, when it said the country must be cleansed of all Tutsis. Although the ethnic conflict had by then begun to gather momentum, the radio broadcast sent Hutu militias combing the hillsides of Rwanda and killing every Tutsi in sight.

Newspapers, rather than promote national unity, have sometimes tended to endanger national unity. The following is a slightly abridged extract of a letter a reader wrote to the radio of one of the national dailies on the matter: "One is alarmed by the sort of tribal politics being preached in the print and electronic media in Ghana these days. It was with disgust and contempt that I read a story in one of the leading newspapers."

In the report, the impression was given that the Fantes and Gas [Gã] at the Tema Oil Refinery are very unhappy because the Ashantis [Asante] have been put at the top hierarchy of the refinery. This is a very dangerous ground on which newspapers like this are treading. It seems we in Ghana are not learning from the mistakes of others. Tune in to any one of the radio stations in [the] morning, and you will often hear people commenting that this tribe is like this or like that. Most of these hasty generalizations (about "tribes") have no substance or relevance. They are usually the imagination of dangerous journalists and callers into radio phone-in programs. In the run-up to one [of] the presidential elections, there was agitation for what some people called "regional balance" in the choice of political party candidates and their running mates. Some people were of the view that if a party chose someone from the south of the country as presidential candidate, it would be appropriate for the candidate to choose someone from the north as a running mate.

One privately owned newspaper published an article in which the author wrote that people from the north of the country had always been known to be "subservient and willing to follow rather than lead."

The writer added that the people of the north had always accepted their social status willingly. He or she was therefore surprised that they were now asking to share in national leadership. This is a true story and while it may be one of the extreme cases, it nonetheless exemplifies the extent to which the media has sometimes threatened national integration. The media has sometimes not been sensitive to the need to disseminate ideas and information in such a manner as to make all social, political, religious, and cultural groups feel they are an integral party of the nation with a common destiny.

That some sections of the media lack a basic knowledge of the people from northern Ghana are often identified in the media by the tribes. This is never the case when the press refers to people from the southern part of the country. Thus while you often read about "Adongo Frafra," "Awuni Kusasi," and "Peter Dagarti," you are unlikely to come across any reference to "Kwaku Fante," "Kofi Ashanti," or "Nortey Ga."

To the disappointment of people in the north of the country, newspapers and radio sometimes mix up geographical locations of places in northern Ghana. Erroneous references may for example be made to "Bolgatanga in the Upper West Region" or to "Jirapa in the Upper East Region."

To the chagrin of many traditional rulers in the north of the country, the media continues to mix up their royal titles as if they did not matter as traditional rulers. They mix up the chieftaincy titles of Naba, Naab, Naa, and Kuoro. The chief of Tumu is referred to as "Tumu Naba" instead of "Tumu Kuoro" and the chief of Sandema as "Sandema Naa" instead of "Sandem Naab." In reflecting on the level of national integration achieved fifty years after independence, it is only honest to argue that the desired level of national integration and cohesion has yet to be achieved. The media therefore needs to employ its power more consciously, for promoting tolerance, love, peace, and respect for one another's dignity, as cardinal virtues for the achievement of the unity and nation hoped for at independence.

VI

The Exigencies of a Postcolony

If one considers the intersection of the prime meridian and the equator as the center of the world, then the Ghanaian capital of Accra is the closest major city to this global focal point. Indeed, and apart from geography, Ghana has garnered the world's attention from several quarters—peoples, ideas, and products all flowing in and out of this "postcolony" at rates that make any predictions about its future tenuous.

Notable among these flows is the increased incoming traffic of African descendants, Eurasians (e.g., Indians, Lebanese, Chinese), continental Africans, and the outgoing traffic of Ghanaians, all forming paths that crisscross Ghana, which remains a composite "homeland" for different peoples and for different reasons. The African diaspora, who originate largely in the Americas, identify Ghana as a possible place of ancestry and belonging, a place to reconcile memory and transatlantic slavery, or a "home" away from the "madness" of the "modern" Western world. Ghanaian migrants flock primarily and ironically to the very parts of the world that incoming African descendants or diasporic Africans are seeking to leave—Europe, North America, and Canada. The offspring of these migrant Ghanaians socialized in Western sociopolitical contexts challenge existing Ghanaian sociocultural norms but also find themselves experiencing the racism, exclusions, and violence long known among African descendants who live in the Western Hemisphere.

Ghanaian officials, especially those in tourism and economic development, project Ghana as the "gateway" to Africa and, for many diasporic Africans seduced by this image, a place for their "return" to the continent. This incoming flow of diasporans complicates the dual citizenship debate and its implications both for immigrants and for those who seek to return to Ghana as a "homeland," not to mention the realities of Ghanaian peoples' material condition and their aspirations arising from it. As Ghana seeks to serve as the gateway to Africa, especially for diasporic Africans, the country can no longer put off the necessary dialogue between its citizens and those of African descent, especially individuals descended from enslaved Africans in the Americas, some of whom are viewed locally as paragons of material success.

Ghana also faces the allure and challenge of "modernizing" without losing its axes of identity and becoming a homogenous "underdeveloped" nation that simply imitates or reproduces Western sociopolitical ideologies, especially in light of the nation's increasing multicultural population of citizens, visitors, strangers, and so on. Now, we not suggesting that Ghanaians are unaware of these tensions; rather, readers who may one day travel to Ghana or interact with Ghanaian nationals should have some awareness of them and how they factor into behaviors that seem at odds with the local cultural specifics that actually draw visitors and others to Ghana in the first place. For example, most Ghanaians have now transformed their local marriage ceremonies into "engagement ceremonies" that precede a Christian or Islamic wedding; the former was open to all community members, whereas the latter are usually restricted to those of either faith, thus excluding "others" and undermining Ghanaian cultural notions of community bonds and belonging. Most Ghanaian Christians, in fact, will not recognize couples, including kin, who undergo *only* an indigenous marriage ceremony as "married." But there are others in Ghanaian society who, like the country's burgeoning film industry, demand a certain level of adherence to and appreciation of cultural specifics, norms, and etiquettes that do not fit well into accepted notions of "modernization" and "development."

While recognizing that some foreign influences are embedded in aspects of Ghanaian culture, Ghana continues to grapple with outside influences that may seem harmless but erode core cultural understandings, notions of social relations, and locally defined appropriate behaviors. Closely related to this is the European import of Christianity that is rapidly undergoing a mutation informed by the exigencies of life in a so-called developing nation. The result is a charismatic, "Africanized" Christianity rooted in prosperity gospels and exorcisms; this new iteration of Christianity threatens to usurp long-established European forms—as exhibited in Catholicism, Presbyterianism, Methodism, etc.—as well as ancient cultural ideas and practices now seen as "demonic" through Christian lenses. Pentecostal Christianity, in fact, is quickly becoming the frame through which many Ghanaians make sense of their social, political, and economic lives.

Ghana has continued to remain squarely at the center of global economic interests through the recent discovery of substantial amounts of crude oil offshore. This has precipitated competition once more among foreign countries for influence and opportunities in Ghana, eerily reminiscent of earlier scrambles for Africa and along the economic fault lines of valuable commodities. Today, however, the scenario is markedly more complex, as China has emerged as a major participant in the competition for Ghana's resources and favor. Ghana therefore faces the real threat of being the site of an intense diplomatic and economic contest between Western (European) nations, who are themselves in competition with each other, and a China that has risen to challenge the global economic dominance of these nations. Viewed from this perspective, Ghana is at risk of becoming the proverbial grass in the African adage "When elephants dance, the grass gets trampled."

Conversely, Ghana might be able to use its worldly position and the world's attention to her benefit. Historic diasporic communities have contributed to the nation, and contemporary ones can meaningfully do the same. Such contributions have already helped to spawn important musical and cultural creations in Ghana, such as highlife and hiplife. The inflow of foreign ideas and institutions might necessarily be reexamined with the abatement of Ghanaian intellectual capital outflow and in light of what the nation ought to be. Additionally, international competition for the country's economic resources might be effectively managed for the benefit of its broad populace at various strata rather than for kleptocratic officials and their in-country and international associates. Though the nation's official word to all who care to visit is *Akwaaba*! (Welcome!), that invitation lies somewhere between how the worlds that forged Ghana came to be and what these people and this part of the world will become.

The Return of the Native

Kwesi Brew

There is dissonance between members of the African diaspora and Ghanaians on the matter of transatlantic slaving and its legacies. More often than not, the empathy of Ghanaians is not adequately perceived by diasporic Africans, who often seek an overt welcome and explicit acknowledgment that their concerns about the circumstances surrounding the export of their ancestors—effectively and affectively a severance from an African homeland—is adequately recognized. Substantial numbers of diasporans "return" to Ghana to reconnect with their African roots, though the ports of Ghana may not have been those through which their ancestors departed. That journey is spiritually profound and of great significance to them. In the following poem, Kwesi Brew empathetically welcomes "home" fellow poet and noted diasporan Dr. Maya Angelou (1928–2014).

(To My Dearest Sister, Dr. Maya Angelou)
There are dungeons in the Cape Coast Castle
Now without their cast-iron gates
Where, all the evil spirits of slavers, pirates,
And buccaneers,
Suspended head-down in brown incarceration
Under the frowning vigilance
Of Nana Tabir, the first of equals among the tutelar gods.
Seventy-seven, of this ancient town of Efutu;
There in dank misery condemned to be
Unsunned
For the period of their lives
And the lives of generations after them and those after them
Till the end of time; judged and condemned
Their souls are coffined in the bodies of the bats,
Whose eyes burn like smoldering coals but see nothing
And they languish as bats in that hole.
Where they can hear the hissing and booing of the rollers

Of the Atlantic Sea
But sail on it no more; No passage for the wicked, says the Sea.
There in that dungeon they stagnate.
In the worm-infested turpitude of their crimes;
And the worms multiply by leaps and years;
And tadpoles scorn the pollution of the puddle.
Only the mosquito, guerrilla of days,
Immerses its larvae hanging them aslant in the water
With their probosces drawing pure air for life
To gain life to destroy life of intruders:
Thus our land was saved.
Not for them any more the cool comfort of the crescent
Smile of the moon as it glides across the silvery expanse
Of the heavens.
Beaming its chubby matronly approval on pale nights
Upon the maidens playing *ampe*, lithe flicks of black legs
In the lucency of happy and open hours, full of song,
And cheered by cracking reports of clapping hands:

II

Not for them the leisurely sight of old men,
Scions of the blind days drowning the shame
Bequeathed to them by our forebears
As our share of the burden
In endless games of *oware*:
The pebbles, they drop by tally pensively into the holes
As men descending into the murk of graves,
Are moistened by remorse.

III

How can we explain should they want to know
What crimes, what new crimes, they committed to bring on themselves
This punishment heavier and more damning
Than the wages of sin:
What if the cruel yoke had broken bone and soul
And none had lived to tell the tale.
But there are no hard thoughts here as blood flows into blood.

Where two minds meet in soft sessions of harmony
Peace is born, love, and joy.
For if the happenings of the past
Could be unraveled by the mind of man
we would all be God;
One seed of maize would not be planted to rot
For us to take a cob grinning with
Four hundred and twenty seeds at harvest;
And Joseph would not have been the ruler of Egypt
In the time of famine
To feed father and the brothers who sold him into bondage
And glory.

IV

Today those who made the grim passage
Now with sandaled feet, heads sparkling
With gold-studded fillets; *aggrey* beads on their wrists;
Clothed in the splendour of their indomitable spirit;
Our kinsmen, have crossed the threshold,
Drank the water of welcome and are seated
On their stools of precious wood
Telling their story
In the compounds of their ancestral homes.

V

The children of Adam have come to see their kinsmen:
Like the great heavens of African evenings
The shade of the doorways are peopled
With bright and shining curiosity:
The children are whispering their regrets
For five hundred years is a long time to be gone.

VI

The gold rings, the outdooring gift of belonging,
They held in the palm of the hands,
Their fingers are too gnarled and knotted
By beast labour for painless decoration.

VII
Now are we free
Being sons and daughters of God;
Free people with one destiny.

VIII
Wrapped in the fearless colors
Of our kente, the pride of our loom
Here we stand,
United in heart in mind and in blood
And none so bold,
None daring—and none dares,
To make slaves of us again!

Toward a Pan-African Identity: Diaspora African Repatriates in Ghana

Obiagele Lake

Large numbers of English-speaking diasporans view Ghana as the gateway to Africa. The country's role in the political independence of African nations combined with the personality of one of the foremost pan-Africanists, Kwame Nkrumah, has further served to cement this image—an image propagated by the Ghana Ministry of Tourism and others. Accordingly, the Gold Coast / Ghana, which once served as a slaving port for captive Africans exported by the centrifugal forces of European slaving and capitalism, is now a key point of return for the descendants of the enslaved. Anthropologist Obiagele Lake characterizes this movement back to the continent and especially Ghana as "a centripetal response to the diasporization of African slaves to all corners of the globe." The following excerpt from a scholarly article centers on a conversation with a "returnee" for whom pan-Africanism was a driving force behind her decision to relocate to Ghana.

In the late 1960s Kwame Toure (formerly Stokely Carmichael) proposed that diaspora Africans—that is, people of African descent born outside of Africa—and indigenous Africans are "one people." My research among diaspora repatriates in Ghana, West Africa, revealed that diaspora Africans construct their identities along a broad spectrum of pan-African identities. While most repatriates identified with their diaspora African nationalities, they also saw themselves as belonging to a wider African community. . . .

Compared to eighteenth- and nineteenth-century repatriations of diaspora Africans, contemporary migrations are smaller, but still significant in their capacity to inform struggles for racial, cultural, and national integrity. In political and academic circles nationalist struggles and identity politics on the continent of Africa have often been argued within the context of pan-Africanism. This discourse most often emphasizes the continental aspects of pan-Africanism, which has as its major goal the political-economic

Dr. Julius Garvey addresses the Nkrumah centenary celebrations in Accra in 2009, flanked by members of the African diaspora who have made Ghana their home. Photograph by Clifford Campbell, 2009.

amalgamation of African nations for the purposes of cultural and political self-determination. . . .

Diaspora African Identities

My concentration on informants' ideas about pan-Africanism and how they integrated, culturally and socially, into Ghanaian life grew out of an interest in the "fit" between diaspora lives in Africa and pan-African theory promulgated by Kwame Toure, which defines all people of African descent as "one people." Toure believes that diaspora Africans will never attain equal rights unless they have a land base from which to negotiate their demands. According to Toure, this land base must be Africa, the land of diaspora Africans' ancestors, and a land in which other people are fighting for similar freedoms within their neocolonial boundaries. My conversations with informants sought to assess whether diaspora Africans in Africa held similar opinions.

I divided informants into three categories based on the proximity of their views to the notion of "one African people." The positions they assume range from thinking of themselves as belonging to Africa as much as indigenous Africans do to focusing on global affiliations. I refer to the first group as "Africanists" and the second as "citizens-of-the-world." The majority of informants, whom I call "Diasporafricans," feel a strong attachment to their places of birth, but are also in the process of forming connections and new identities in Africa. I use these categories for heuristic purposes, since there are areas of overlap and gradations within and among them.

Several informants either concentrated on their national identities or expressed more diffuse identities. . . .

Other informants' comments lie at the center of the pan-African discourse insofar as they raise questions about the meaning of pan-Africanism: Who is African? What role can diaspora Africans play in Africa? Although all offered their views on the potential effects of political connections between Africa and the diaspora, one informant had given these issues more attention. Nguyen, who came to Ghana in 1967, placed a great deal of emphasis on race, and secondarily on culture, in formulating her views on pan-Africanism and the role diaspora Africans have to play in that process:

NGUYEN: Pan-Africanism to me means a united Africa. Well, it's supposed to be the whole of Africa including North Africa, but I don't think those Arabs think of themselves as Black or Africans. They're only Africans when it's their interest politically. They really don't identify with Black Africa. So I think the idea that Nkrumah had was beautiful, but I don't think the Arabs adopted it as such. So I think that we have to somehow limit that pan-Africanism to sub-Saharan Africa. We should be able to communicate with the Northerners, but I don't think it's going to be integrated, united like the United States of America was envisioned. I don't think it's possible because the two cultures are too different, you know. And it's such a different race of people.

LAKE: Do you think that diaspora Africans have a role to play in the development of pan-Africanism in Africa?

NGUYEN: Yes, certainly. And we have the heroes who started long before even Nkrumah had the idea of pan-Africanism. That West Indian . . . Marcus Garvey, he had the idea. You know, I admire him. And there are others. Frantz Fanon, he's a Black. So indeed, we should bring in all our people. If they're in the Caribbean or wherever they're from. As long as they are Black they have a role to play in uniting Africa—I mean sub-Saharan Africa.

Other Ghanaians with whom I spoke who also felt that there needs to be a stronger relationship between diaspora and indigenous Africans and that coming to live in Africa is one way of reestablishing that link. These responses to repatriation are at variance with the scholarly rhetoric, which tends to situate the experience and goals of diaspora and indigenous Africans as separate if not antithetical. Although there are cultural and political differences between indigenous and diaspora Africans, there are also similarities.

Though indigenous and diaspora Africans share a history of oppression by people of European descent, local affinities sometimes take precedence over broad-based notions of identity. Many Ghanaians have, along with feelings of affinity with diaspora Africans, views of diaspora Africans not in terms of descent, but in terms of separate national origin. Droller calls this nationality difference "culture color":

> There has been quite a movement from America and the Caribbean. Just as *your people* [informant's way of referring to the diaspora; emphasis mine] on that side have gotten a distorted idea of life in an African community, Africans have gotten a distorted idea of Black Americans. So when you come into this town, he [a Ghanaian] sees you as some kind of White man. He doesn't see you as a skin color, but rather as a culture color. And it takes him a little while.

Although many Ghanaians address diaspora Africans as brothers and sisters, and tell them that they are glad that we have "finally come home," others regard them solely as American or West Indian and believe that they carry the same values and privileges as people of European descent in these regions. Ghanaian reference to diaspora Africans as *oburuni* is an important indication of these indigenous perspectives. While this term was initially used to refer to people of European descent, it has since been extended to mean "foreigner." While many Ghanaians who use this term mean no offense (the word is also used as a term of endearment to refer to African children who are light skinned or who have curly hair), others do. Diaspora Africans often take it as an offensive remark, since they view themselves as sharers of an African heritage.

Nguyen, who is married to a Ghanaian, expressed her disappointment at the disparities between her self-identity and the perceptions of her hosts:

NGUYEN: I find that people still see me as an Afro-American. For instance, there was a woman I met here in the early seventies. She was from Costa Rica. And I asked her, "Do you know that people still refer to me as being White?" I said, "Look at my skin." And she said, "Oh, don't worry about that, I've been here for thirty-five years and I'm still considered 'White.'" And she was browner than me. She was an old lady married to a Ghanaian. I said, "But maybe it's because I don't speak the language."

> She said, "I speak fluent Ga, it doesn't matter. They know you have a western culture so when they say 'White,' they mean that your culture is different. They're referring more to culture than color." Because, you know, I didn't like being called White. Here you think you're coming home and you're called White.

In analysis of diaspora African incorporation to Ghanaian society, the ideologies and cultural habits of the host society constitute the other half of diaspora/indigenous encounters. Most diaspora Africans agreed that Ghanaians accepted them socially, but not culturally. As is painfully clear from historical and recent events in Africa, ethnocentrism has played a major role in conflicts in all African nations. Viewed in this context, the acceptance, or lack of it, of diaspora Africans is not completely different from the way other cultural groups or other nationals are accepted. Oburuni, as mentioned above, is not only a term used to mark the different cultures of diaspora Africans, but also different skin-colors among Ghanaians. Non-Ghanaian Africans are also referred to as oburuni. The fine lines drawn by Ghanaians are also used for differentiating the offspring of diaspora/indigenous couples from Ghanaians.

Slavery and the Making of Black Atlantic History

Bayo Holsey

Ghanaians generally do not speak about the "slave trade," and this is often to the bemusement of diasporic Africans who descended from slaves. In Ghana, "slave ancestry" is not celebrated because of the negative stigma attached to being "kinless" in a society where clan/family belonging is central. Consequently, in some cases it is considered impolite and taboo to broach the topic. Conversely, in the African diaspora, "slave ancestry" is explicitly known and, for some, celebrated as a testament of one's ancestors having survived perhaps the most brutal system of human exploitation centered on "race." The "slave trade" and things associated with its memory is contested terrain in Ghana. The historical significance of the "slave castles" that mark Ghana's coastline, for example, has become embroiled in this dual vision of how they and slavery should be interpreted. Even so, the "slave trade" serves as the moral and psychological bedrock on which heritage tourism in Ghana is constructed and marketed to the African diaspora, particularly those in the United States. The "slave trade" is also used as a reason for diasporic Africans to visit Ghana in order to find their "roots." In the following monograph excerpt, Bayo Holsey, associate professor of African and African American studies and cultural anthropology at Duke University, delves into the debate surrounding the "slave castles" at Elmina and Cape Coast.

Making a Black Atlantic Discourse

The development of diaspora tourism has been the outcome of an extended conversation between Ghana and segments of the African diaspora, particularly African Americans. It is the product, in other words, of a black Atlantic conversation. . . .

In 1911, J. E. Casely Hayford, a key figure in Fante cultural nationalism, published a book entitled *Ethiopia Unbound: Studies in Race Emancipation,* which he dedicated "To the sons of Ethiopia the world wide over." Inspired

Inner courtyard of Elmina Castle, which is now a (contested) tourist attraction for a range of visitors interested in its transatlantic slaving or colonial history. Photograph by Kwasi Konadu, 2005.

by [Edward W.] Blyden, he writes, "Afro-Americans must bring themselves into touch with some of the general traditions and institutions of their ancestors, and, though sojourning in a strange land, endeavor to conserve the characteristics of the race," arguing that Africa provided cultural grounding for African Americans and using more generally the notion of Ethiopianism to call for the unification of black people throughout the world.

Several decades later, Kwame Nkrumah would shift the emphasis in black Atlantic discourse from culture to development. When he visited the United States after becoming president of the newly independent Ghana, he invited African Americans, but specifically black professionals such as teachers, doctors, and dentists, to move to Ghana and to help develop the nation. Rather than stressing African Americans' connection to Ghana as a result of their African ancestry and forcible removal from the continent through the slave trade, Nkrumah focused on their potential future connections through a commitment to the goal of African development. The access that the African American professional class had had to American educational opportunities, in the same way that he himself had had such access in the United States, could, he argued, be put to use in the service of

Ghanaian development. In this vein, in 1958, he also hosted in Ghana the All African People's Conference. Many African Americans responded to this call, although Ghana never saw an organized back-to-Africa movement of African Americans like those to Liberia and Sierra Leone. Nevertheless, as a result of more individualized travel, since the late 1950s Ghana has received the most African American expatriates of any African nation. Many prominent African Americans visited Ghana during this period as well, including Richard Wright, Malcolm X, Maya Angelou, and Martin Luther King Jr. In addition, W. E. B. Du Bois moved to Ghana late in life and was buried there.

The greater affordability of air travel as well as the expansion of the black middle class in the United States allowed more and more African Americans to travel to Ghana to explore this history once the market responded to their burgeoning interest with the development of what has come to be known as diaspora tourism.

Castle Histories

The popularity of slavery narratives among African Americans was a major factor in the Ghanaian tourism industry's decision to focus on the slave trade, and there were few sites more fitting for this endeavor than Ghana's Cape Coast and Elmina castles. The sheer size and structural integrity of Cape Coast and Elmina castles provided the main arguments for their centrality to such narratives. They are massive structures, occupying nearly 100,000 square feet each, that sit on the shoreline of each town. They are made up of former storerooms, soldiers' quarters, apartments for the governors, churches, courtyards, watchtowers, and ramparts that are still lined with cannons trained at the sea. The *Maison des esclaves* on Gorée Island in Senegal as well as *La route de l'esclave* in Benin are other sites of such commemorative work. However, because these are French-speaking nations, undoubtedly many American tourists choose Ghana over Senegal and Benin to experience this history. The grand scale of Ghana's castles coupled with the nation's status as an English-speaking, politically stable West African nation has led to its emergence as a primary imagined homeland among African Americans, despite the fact that it accounted for only 13 percent of the British slave trade. . . .

Although they dominate the landscape of Cape Coast and Elmina, prior to the 1980s the castles had not received a great deal of attention as important historical monuments. Before their conservation, they served primarily mundane functions including housing the post office and law court. An article in the *Ghana Teacher's Journal* in April 1958 suggests that students visit the castles as "places of historical interest," although no further information is given as to their specific significance. . . .

Conserving and Commemorating the Slave Trade

The significance of the castles and of the slave trade in general began to change in 1989 when the then regional minister Ato Austin traveled to the United States under the sponsorship of the Ministry for the Central Region to explore the options for the development of Cape Coast and Elmina castles as tourist sites. During this visit, he and his delegation met with various organizations and were eventually awarded $5.6 million from USAID for the implementation of the Natural Resource Conservation and Historic Preservation Project for the conservation of the castles. . . . This grant led to the castles' becoming major tourist sites, with serious attention being paid to the history of the slave trade. As such, they became extremely popular destinations for diaspora tourists, and African Americans in particular.

When the castles' conservation began, in addition to stabilizing the castles and providing modern plumbing facilities, the preservation team applied a mixture of lime, sand, and cement to the castle walls to remove the black mold stains that result from exposure to the coastal salt air, a process known as whitewashing. Members of the African American community in Ghana immediately responded to this act, concerned that it was an attempt to beautify the castles and thereby erase all evidence of the slave trade. Some charged that the whitewashing of castle walls and other improvement efforts were an attempt to whitewash history and, essentially, to erase the history of the slave trade. In particular, plans to clean up the dungeons met with fierce opposition. . . .

The debate surrounding this and other issues reached such monumental proportions that in 1994, a conference on the preservation of the castles as well as of a military fort in Elmina was held. Dr. Robert E. Lee, another quite prominent member of the African American community in Ghana, delivered a paper entitled "On the Meaning of the Slave Forts and Castles of Ghana." In it, he argued that Africans in the diaspora, as the descendants of slaves, some of whom passed through the castles, are the most important stakeholders in the matter of the castles' conservation and interpretation. . . .

In southern Ghana, where the slave trade invokes forms of discrimination against certain family members and particular regions, and where discussions of race have historically involved the condemnation of "Africans" as an undifferentiated category for their participation in the slave trade, the notion of commemorating the slave trade struck many as a dangerous proposition. For this reason, several Ghanaian officials sought to reduce the amount of focus on the slave trade in the interpretation of the castles. In one report, they stressed the importance of representing the castles' "total history" and not just the history of the slave trade, noting that the castles "started as trading posts, changed into slave castles and then into administration centers."

An alternative interpretation of the castles as sacred space was addressed during the conference. In the report of the committee on philosophical and historical considerations, committee members listed the following as one of its philosophical considerations: "The Committee views the monuments as places that are 'sacred' places of pilgrimage and high cultural and spiritual importance for Ghanaians, West Africans, and the African diaspora. The centers are not secular and mundane places and should thus be regarded as 'special places' when it comes to the matter of usage." The committee also recognized the African American diaspora (a telling reduction of the African diaspora to African America), along with the local Ghanaian population, companies, and traditional authorities, as important stakeholders in the conservation of the castles. The influence of African Americans in the interpretation of the castles as sacred space proved to be profound.

The committee concluded that the castles should be developed as tourist sites; they should be "an organic museum and not a cemetery." But while they decided that tourism should be encouraged, they agreed that a certain degree of sensitivity must be employed at the castles and that inappropriate activities and usages should be stopped, including the holding of "musical extravaganzas" and the existence of a restaurant above the male dungeon in Cape Coast Castle. They also agreed that the dungeons should be left intact. The committee compromised on the significance of the slave trade at the castles. Some members argued that the castles should be marketed for the slave dungeons. Of particular interest, some committee members noted that highlighting the history of the slave trade could remove the aura of fear that surrounds it in Ghana. The report includes a reference to this fear that states, "There was [*sic*] general concerns that among local Ghanaians and the African diaspora for a long time, the old people have tried to discourage the children from enquiring into the historic past of the slave trade. There was concern that the bitter truth about the past be ascertained, documented, and disseminated. . . ." Making the castles into sites of pilgrimage in a narrative of slavery, sites to construct the horrors of the slave trade and to evoke the suffering of black people, was conceived of by many African Americans as a prelude to the redemption figured in stories like *Roots*.

The Return through the Door of No Return

Seestah IMAHKÜS

The Cape Coast Castle is one of the most visited places in Ghana. Diasporic Africans have made this site quite popular, and visiting it is akin to a pilgrimage by those who see it as the point at which their connection to the African continent was broken. Going there in many respects allows such persons to reconnect with an ancestral homeland while giving them a sense of appreciation for being the progenies of those human captives who survived the atrocities of transatlantic slaving. In the following excerpt from a book based on personal experiences, author and hotelier Seestah IMAHKÜS offers some visceral insights into the experience of a diasporan coming to Africa—Ghana, to be precise—for the first time. It details a visit to the infamous slave-trading site at Cape Coast, the point of departure for a significant number of human captives to the Americas.

We continued to work our way slowly through the streets towards the Cape Coast Castle Dungeons, savoring the pleasure of being home and interacting with folks along the way. Even though we didn't understand the language, we were still enjoying ourselves, while making new friends.

Ahead of us loomed this enormous, foreboding structure. The sight caused me to tremble; I almost didn't want to go inside. The outer walls were chipped with a faded and moldy white exterior. The sea had eaten away some of the mortar. It was gray and dismal as we climbed the steep steps, following the sign leading to the reception area. When we entered the reception area of the Cape Coast Castle Dungeons a smallish man with a bright smiling face met us. His name was Mr. Owusu and he had been working there as a receptionist and sometimes Guide, for many years.

"Akwaaba," he said, "we are happy that you have come home. We don't get many African-American visitors, only white people, they come all the time," he continued.

We all laughed and told him that we were equally, if not more happy than he was, for we had worked, planned and saved for many years to make this journey. Most of us will be in debt to the Credit Card companies, VISA

Seestah IMAHKÜS, author, entrepreneur, and diasporic African who now lives in Ghana. Photograph by Clifford Campbell, Accra, September 2009.

and Master Charge. "Plus some of us borrowed money from friends who we will have to re-pay when we get back to our homes in the United States," I told him. But for years many of us had spoken of Afrika [the spelling derives from the KiSwahili language], our "Mother" land and finally all our discussions and dreams had become a reality.

Debt-be-damned, nothing is greater than this, I said to no one in particular.

After introductions were made all around, Mr. Owusu, our Guide, began the tour around the Castle. Entering the inner part of the castle overlooking a large courtyard, our guide gave us the background history of the Cape Coast Castle Dungeons. This was one of the more than sixty castle dungeons, forts, and lodges that had been constructed by European Traders with the permission of local rulers (the Chieftaincy) and stretched for 300 miles along the West Coast of Afrika to store kidnapped Afrikans, until a shipload of enslaved Afrikans could be assembled. Twenty-seven of those houses of misery were located in Ghana.

Various European oppressors had occupied the Cape Coast Castle Dungeons during the Trans-Atlantic European Slave Trade. It began with the Portuguese in the 1500's, followed by the Dutch, then the Swedes, the Danes and finally the English who occupied it in 1665. It remained under their control, serving as the seat of the British Administration in the Gold Coast

(Cape Coast) until they relocated their racist regime to Christianborg Castle in Accra in 1877.

Our next stop was the Palaver (which means talking/discussing) Hall, the meeting place of slave merchants, which also served as the hall used in auctioning off our ancestors. The room was huge, the only light coming from the windows which lined both sides of the walls; one side facing the ocean, the other side overlooking the town; a bare room, echoing the voice of our Guide, a haunting echo, which reverberated off the walls, as the Guide explained how they bargained and sold us. When slave auctions were not going on, Palaver Hall was used as a meeting place for the Governor, Chiefs and other visitors.

We then moved on to the Governor's apartment and the church, which I felt like burning down!

But nothing could prepare me for what we would experience next. We descended the stairs into a large cobble-stoned courtyard and walked through large double wooden doors, which lead into a long, dark, damp tunnel. The stench of musty bodies, fear and death hung in the air. There was no noise except the thunderous crashing of the waves against the outer walls and the roaring sound of the water. Deeper we walked, into large, dark rooms which had served as a warehouse for enslaved Afrikan people awaiting shipment to the [Americas] and Caribbean.

This was the Men's Dungeon. As we stood in that large cavernous room the air was still, the only ventilation that was available came from small openings near the 20-foot high ceilings. Our ancestors had been kept underground, chained to the walls and each other, making escape impossible. The mood of the group was hushed, as several people started crying. We were standing in hellholes of the most horrific conditions imaginable. There were no words to express the suffering that must have gone on in these dungeons.

I became caught up, thrown back in time. I was suddenly one of the many who were shackled, beaten and starved. But I was one of the fortunate souls to have survived the forced exodus from their homelands to be sold, branded and thrown into those hellholes, meant to hold 600 people but which held more than 1,000 enslaved Afrikans at one time. The men separated from the women, as they awaited shipment to the Americas. According to our Guide, the chalk marks on the walls of the Men's Dungeon indicated the level of the floor prior to the excavation of the floor, which had built up over years of slavery with feces, bones, filth, etc.

As the Guide continued to describe the horrors of these pits of hell I began to shake violently; I needed to get out of there. I was being smothered.

I turned and ran up the steep incline of the tunnel, to the castle courtyard, the winds from the sea whipping my face, bringing me back to the present. I couldn't believe what I had just experienced. How could anyone be so cruel and inhuman?

Gradually, the others began emerging from the dungeon, subdued looks on their faces; many tear-stained . . . no one was talking.[1] Following the Guide we proceeded across the massive courtyard and down another passage way to the Women's Dungeon, a smaller version of the Men's Dungeon but not so deep underground, it had held over 300 women at any given time. As we entered that dark, musty, damp room, the sound of the crashing waves was like muffled, rolling thunder. A dimly lit, uncovered light bulb hung from the ceiling on a thin, frayed wire. After standing silently for a time in this tomb, the Guide began to lead the group out. I was the last person left in the room when the Guide turned and said he was continuing the tour.

"Please," I said, "I'm not ready to leave, just turn off the light for me and I will join the group shortly."

As the group walked silently away, the tears would not stop flowing. I dropped to my knees, trembling and crying even harder. With the light off, the only light in that dungeon came through one small window near the very high ceiling, reflecting down as though it were a muted spotlight. Darkness hung in every corner. As I rocked back and forth on the dirt floor, I could hear weeping and wailing . . . anguished screams coming from the distance. Suddenly the room was packed with women . . . some naked, some with babies, some sick and lying in the dirt, while others stood against the walls around the dungeon's walls, terror filled their faces.

"My God, what had we done to wind up here, crammed together like animals?"

Pain and suffering racked their bodies, a look of hopelessness and despair on their faces . . . but with a strong will to survive.

"Oh God, what have we done to deserve this kind of treatment?"

Cold terror gripped my body. Tears blinded me and the screams wouldn't stop. As I sat there violently weeping I began to feel a sense of warmth, many hands were touching my body, caressing me, soothing me as a calmness began to come over me. I began to feel almost safe as voices whispered in my ears assuring me that everything was all right.

"Don't cry," they said, "You've come home. You've returned to your homeland, to re-open the Door of No Return."

Gradually the voices and the women faded into the darkness; it was then that I realized that some of the screams I'd heard were my own. The eerie light beaming down from the window was growing dimmer as day began fading into night. As I got up from the dungeon floor I knew that I would never be the same again!

After years of wandering and searching, I had finally found home. And one day, I wouldn't be leaving again.

My ancestors were truly a strong, courageous and determined people to have survived that holocaust but they had warmly received me.

Note

1. The ellipses in this selection are original.

Citizenship and Identity among Ghanaian Migrants in Toronto

Takyiwaa Manuh

In recent decades, the inflow of diasporic/immigrant groups to Ghana is often surpassed, in sheer volume, by the outflow of Ghanaian nationals to Europe, the United States, and Canada. A few relocate to other parts of Africa. The Ghanaian diaspora is quite prominent and often serves as a conduit for diasporic African travel to, or eventual residence in, Ghana. Ghanaians abroad see themselves as an integral and active part of Ghana and have lobbied in recent years for recognition of dual citizenship and voting rights. Interestingly, living in host societies quite different from Ghana allows these diasporic Ghanaians to challenge normal relations as defined by their culture, especially social ranking and gender relations within one's cultural group. In the scholarly article excerpt here, Takyiwaa Manuh looks at these issues associated with the Ghanaian diaspora in Toronto.

Ghanaians in Toronto

Since the late 1980s Toronto has become a major hub for Ghanaians who left Ghana to escape economic and social crisis. An estimated twenty thousand Ghanaians live in the greater Toronto metropolitan area, although official census figures are lower. Because a military regime in Ghana (1982–92) suspended the constitution and abrogated many civil liberties, many Ghanaians claimed (and were granted) refugee status on arrival in Canada. In addition to the influx of immigrants during the 1980s, other Ghanaians have lived in Canada since the mid-1970s, many of whom have become citizens of Canada and call themselves Ghanaian Canadians.

Ghanaian migrants in Toronto include members of nearly all social classes and ethnic groups in Ghana, although northern Ghanaians tend to be in the minority. Some are highly educated and are fluent in English, while others can barely communicate in the language. Migrants include individuals who were formerly petty traders, artisans, schoolteachers, and junior civil servants. Women migrated both autonomously and as wives. Ghanaian migrants maintain close ties with one another through their living arrangements, work situations, family or hometown relationships, churches, and other associational ties. Important rites of passage such as births and deaths give rise to expressions of solidarity and gift giving according to particular Ghanaian cultural norms. Such events affirm shared notions of cultural practice, solidarity, and identity (though such notions are contested in other realms). In addition, Canada's adherence to a policy of multiculturalism since the 1970s and its support for community organizations through local grants has encouraged the formation of Ghanaian migrant organizations to support the Canadian cultural mosaic.

Some migrants expected their stay to be temporary, but many have been forced to remain in Canada. Conditions there and in Ghana have made it impossible to accumulate sufficient capital to enable them to return to Ghana and live comfortably. As a result, many migrants have adopted a transnational existence as a way of lessening the vulnerabilities they face in both societies. To buttress this choice and to be able to take advantage of opportunities that exist both in Ghana and abroad, Ghanaian migrants have sought Canadian citizenship. They have also lobbied for the recognition of dual citizenship in Ghana, justifying their request by citing their contributions to Ghana's development.

Migrants and the Canadian State

Having been exposed to immigration procedures in European countries before arriving in Canada, many migrants are adept at using both international and national law to their benefit. In addition to family and friendship networks in Canada, decisions to migrate there are based on the perception that Canada's refugee policies and practices are more liberal than those of other countries. Until 1992, however, many asylum claimants faced considerable delay in the determination of their claims, and there was a high rejection rate. (There is an extensive case record involving Ghanaian applicants who claimed "Convention refugee" status as defined by the Canadian immigration act.) At the time of my research in 1996, there were several people whose claims had still not been finally determined although they had been in Toronto for six years.

The Canadian state stands in marked contrast to the Ghanaian state, with which many migrants had had no dealings prior to leaving Ghana. As Ghanaians in Canada expressed it, Ghana was a "lawless" state, meaning a state with little documentation or extensive recordkeeping. These migrants take law in Canada and lawlessness in Ghana to mean the absence in the latter of firm, nondiscretionary rules of behavior and judgment, while in the former law and its agencies appear hegemonic. But migrants also experience the Canadian state as a benevolent source of rights and benefits (including protective labor regulations and unemployment benefits) that were not available to them in Ghana.

The work environment that migrants confront is also highly regulated; they must adjust to set hours of work and recreation and structure their social activities and relaxation time accordingly. The discipline of the labor process and place imposes strict limitations on migrants' time and space if they are to achieve their financial and other goals while abroad.

Highly regulated work processes, the expanded sphere of law and control, and the possibility of deportation make migrants extremely vulnerable. They actively seek Canadian citizenship to reduce this vulnerability and to expand their options. Citizenship is seen to confer all the rights and privileges of any Canadian, including the right to work in any government institution and the guarantee of social security and benefits in old age.

The possession of a Canadian passport also allows the highly desired mobility between Ghana and Canada as well as other spaces without time limitations and harassment at foreign airports. Janet Gilboy, for example, discusses the practices of inspection, interception, and return of "undesirable" travelers at U.S. ports of entry, which are mainly aimed at third world migrants. Gilboy notes the cooperation of airlines in such practices and highlights the moral assessments inspectors make when deciding whom to admit. Judgments (such as "decent," "bad," "don't deserve detention," and "criminals") are routinely made and influence case dispositions.

Many of the migrants who intended to return permanently to Ghana viewed Canadian citizenship in instrumental terms. It guaranteed the option of safety, health care, and protection in Canada in case of crisis or instability in Ghana. Given current conditions in the latter country, these calculations are seen as a rational means of guarding against the uncertainties of and lack of welfare from the Ghanaian state.

Ghanaians and Canadians: The Quest for Dual Citizenship

Beginning in the mid-1990s, Ghanaians in the United Kingdom and Canada began a struggle for the recognition of dual citizenship in Ghana. Citing their increasing contributions to the Ghanaian economy, they sent memoranda and delegations to Ghana to lobby opinion makers. Records from the Bank of Ghana indicate that private transfers have increased appreciably and are now equal to the value of official transfers, and that remittances from migrants form a large proportion of the former. In 1983, for example, private transfers were only $16.6 million, while official transfers totaled $72.4 million. Since 1991, private transfers have equaled or surpassed official transfers; in 1995, private transfers totaled $263.2 million compared with $260.0 million of official transfers. Other data from the Agricultural Development Bank, which is the correspondent for Western Union in Ghana, showed appreciable increases in remittances that are paid to recipients in Ghanaian cedis. These transfers increased from $3 million in 1994 to $12 million in 1995, $24 million in 1996, and almost $8 million in only the first quarter of 1997.

These remittances do not reflect other contributions in kind that migrants make to their natal families, relatives, friends, schools, and communities. Migrants send home durable consumer goods such as television sets, refrigerators, cars, cloth, and clothing, and they have built houses or acquired plots of land to do so. Through ethnic and school associations, migrants have donated money and equipment for hospitals and schools and have responded to specific requests for assistance following disasters or in other times of need. Specifically, they have outfitted hospitals, provided books and computers to local schools, and donated electricity plants and water pumps to communities. As a result of such contributions, relatives, schools, and communities have been able to maintain a level of well-being beyond what their own resources would permit. In a situation of low private foreign investment, these resource flows constitute important alternative sources of investment. Thus migration can be viewed as a privatized investment scheme to enable Ghanaians themselves to supply the necessary capital for national regeneration.

In late 1996 the Ghanaian Parliament adopted a constitutional amendment that recognized dual citizenship. The amendment, however, restricts the right of dual citizens to hold elective office and to participate in public life. These exclusions, which are perceived to be politically motivated, have bred discontent. Although migrants formulated their demands for dual citizenship in economic terms, they regard it as a quid pro quo that should entitle them to the full range of participation in Ghanaian society and economy, including the political institutions of the state. Having been abroad for years, migrants see themselves as the bearers of new ideas regarding rights and entitlements for all Ghanaian citizens. In their view, governments are obligated to provide certain services for their citizens to ensure their livelihoods and to foster development. Given dual citizens' increased expectations, the Ghanaian government may try to preempt challenges to its rule by keeping them out of politics.

In short, many Ghanaian Canadians regard their foreign citizenship as wholly instrumental and see their Ghanaian citizenship as an attribute of birth that can never be taken away. Moreover, they expect Ghana to be the beneficiary of the skills they have acquired during the time of their migration. Although it may be difficult for the state or anyone else to know which Ghanaians who live in Ghana are dual citizens, migrants would like restrictions on their political participation to be removed so that they are treated as Ghanaians in the land of their birth. Migrants have yet to challenge these exclusions; they may be waiting for a more favorable political environment in which to raise these issues.

Rights Consciousness and Gender Relations

Among Ghanaian men and women in Toronto there is deep contestation over gender relations and an evolving consciousness of rights among women. A persistent complaint among men is that the Canadian state is "spoiling" the women by making them conscious of their rights and that this consciousness is leading to high divorce rates. Men also contend that state benefits available to unmarried or divorced women with children (including the provision of housing and child support) undermine the authority and power of husbands to maintain particular kinds of relations with their wives. Indeed, some men believe there has been a complete reversal of roles in Canada, claiming that "women have become men, and men have become women." Whereas some men contend that physical spousal abuse is a cultural right in Ghana, in Canada it can lead to ejection from the home, restraining orders, and jail time. Moreover, women are willing to call the police to report such abuse. Noting that "this place is not Ghana," women express their willingness to take advantage of the laws that exist for their protection.

In addition to physical abuse, another key area of contestation is control over a wife's earnings. Financial autonomy of spouses is common in Ghana, with men and women each responsible for specific expenses for themselves and their children, but migrants recognize that the norm in Canada is for couples to pool their resources. Attempting (at least initially) to conform to this norm, many women then become disenchanted with the pooling of resources, alleging that husbands tend to treat the money as their own and make withdrawals (to benefit themselves or their extended families in Ghana) without their wives' knowledge and consent. As a result, many women refuse to maintain joint accounts and, instead, provide money for particular expenditures.

Women also note that among native-born Canadians housework is often shared. Ghanaian men, however, while willing to pool resources, are not willing to share in housework, child care, or other domestic chores. As one woman put it, when the men are ready to marry "the Canadian way" the women will also be ready. Until then, they intend to continue the Ghanaian practice whereby a woman's earnings belong to her exclusively and she has the right to determine how the money will be spent.

The changing terrain of gender relations has implications for women's autonomy and options in both Canada and Ghana. Although women sustain certain actions against men in Canada due to provisions in Canadian law, many women do not expect to receive the same protections in Ghana. For such women, citizenship claims and desires for political participation in Ghana have less salience and can affect their decisions to return to Ghana or to remain in Canada. Despite certain advantages to living in Canada, many women express a fear of growing old in Canada and point to older Caribbean women they have encountered, whom they see as having to fend for themselves without any visible social support network. Thus women face a dilemma in choosing between their desire for Canadian freedom from patriarchal practices and the respect and care that is accorded to the old within family and community structures in Ghana.

Chieftaincy, Diaspora, and Development

George M. Bob-Milliar

The institution of chieftaincy has proved quite resilient, surviving colonialism and subsequent challenges as Ghana emerged as an independent nation. This system of governance continues to evolve in innovative ways in order to bring "development" to areas under its control. One of the latest techniques used to source funding from persons outside Ghana is to award them the honorific of Nkɔsuohene/hemaa (development chief/queen mother). In Ghana, local "traditional" leaders have targeted persons of means, particularly from the African diaspora, who have obvious vested interests in contributing to various local causes. This in itself is ironic, for, as we have noted before, the descendants of "slaves" are not held in high regard. For example, in most of the extant "traditional" polities, descendants of slaves cannot hold any office or be appointed as customary state functionaries. Ghanaian political scientist George Bob-Milliar examines the installation of African Americans as "chiefs" in Ghana, contrasting how they and Ghanaians perceive their position, and the implications for the tourism industry, in the following excerpt from his scholarly article on this subject.

Chieftaincy and Development

Chieftaincy is an indigenous system of governance with executive, judicial, and legislative powers. The history of chieftaincy in Ghana is one of evolutionary tenacity and contradictions, but not refusal of change. It survived the exploitative British imperialism of the nineteenth century and has endured both civilian and military post-Independence regimes. Its endurance must be viewed within the larger political economy of Ghana. Eighty percent of land in Ghana is held by the various traditional authorities in trust for the subjects of the stool/skin in accordance with customary law, and central government has 10 percent for public development. Chieftaincy has come to serve two major functions: statutory (settlement of chieftaincy disputes and the codification of customary laws) and nonstatutory (socio-economic development). Chiefs are the custodians of the resources within their various communities. In resource-endowed areas, as is the case with most of the stools in southern Ghana, chiefs exploit the resources for the general good of their communities. Development may be seen in several ways. It may be the clearing of bushy paths or the provision of basic amenities such as drinking water, health centers, schools, and electricity. In trying to provide these basic socioeconomic necessities chiefs either mobilize the material and human resources of their various local and expatriate communities, or approach nongovernmental agencies for assistance. More recently, chiefs have identified diasporan Africans as a potential source of assistance for their development agendas. . . .

The dominant concept of development—based on the idea of human progress, with the broad aim of increasing the standard of living of people as a whole, a notion whose ownership has been claimed and hijacked by the West—has been practiced by Ghanaian kings, chiefs, and queens for generations. Perhaps what is "new" is that chiefs are employing very innovative and seemingly modern means to achieve this goal. It was in the spirit of providing for the material and nonmaterial needs of subjects within Asanteman's jurisdiction that the late Asantehene Opoku Ware II in 1985 created the *Nkɔsuo* stool division in Kumase. . . . Many chiefs have embarked on a new paradigm for chieftaincy, which is reshaping the institution in a manner that challenges its present ethos. A good number of chiefs are taking up the challenges of the twenty-first century, tackling very modern issues as diverse as children's rights, the environment, women's rights, and HIV/AIDS. These leaders perceive initiating development processes as their primary role today.

Historical Context: The Institution of Nkɔsuohene/hemaa

Traditional stools are not rigid or fixed portfolios; new ones are constantly being created and old ones modified as the situation demands. Barfuo Abayie Boaten conceptualized the framework within which the *Nkɔsuo* chiefship functions: *Nkɔsuo* is an Asante Twi word and it literally means "progress or sustained development." *Ohene* or *Ohemaa* in Twi translate as "chief" and "queen mother," respectively, and the same linguistic rule applies throughout the Akan cultures. *Nkɔsuohene* therefore literally means "development chief" and *Nkɔsuohemaa* is "development queen mother." . . . Boaten further states that it was not the responsibility of the *Nkɔsuohene/hemaa* to execute development projects single-handedly. The key concept here is full community participation and approval of whatever development is intended. For Tom McCaskie the title has been used in Asante "to describe responsible advancement through combined or communal effort." He adds that the stool was instituted by the late Asantehene Opoku Ware II to commemorate his reign, as is required of every Asantehene. The first Asante citizen to be honored with an *Nkɔsuo* stool was the wealthy businessman E. K. Osei, with the stool name Nana Osei Nkwantabisa. McCaskie's discussion of the *Nkɔsuohene/hemaa* concept in relation to Africans from the diaspora is illuminating:

> In private many Asante chiefs angrily mock Africans from the diaspora who think they have somehow returned home and been reintegrated because they wear cloth, speak greetings in Twi and *buy Nkosuo stools*. Painful though it is to say, and no one seems willing to say it, many Asante office holders regard returnees from the diaspora as the *unwelcome descendants of slaves,* as well as being people who proclaim themselves to be African but all too often behave like stereotypical "ugly Americans."

When McCaskie, one of the most prolific and influential scholars of Asante, makes such an assertion, it must be considered carefully. Do African Americans "buy *Nkɔsuo* stools"? The evidence for this assertion by Asante chiefs with regard to diasporan Africans is rather shallow. However, in a recent study, "African American Psychologists, the Atlantic Slave Trade and Ghana: A History of the Present," McCaskie's interest in the subject becomes clearer. He examines the work of African American academics who have occupied *Nkɔsuohene* stools in some communities and argues that Ghanaian chiefs initiate developments projects, extending an invitation to the African Americans to play a supportive role. The processes leading to the installation of an *Nkɔsuohene/hemaa* are in most cases initiated locally or abroad by Ghanaians. . . . Further, it is important to state that some Asante citizens who reside in the West court the friendship of wealthy African Americans and most probably extend a romanticized idea of African royalty in Asante. African Americans may be "sold" a dilapidated school structure in some rural community, the dire need for a health facility, or generally high poverty levels in the "motherland." Such appeals touch the conscience of diasporan Africans. Those with disposable incomes will usually respond by visiting Ghana. At this point, the unfree origin of diasporan Africans is not an issue. Most are welcomed with pomp and pageantry; the issue of their unfree origins is only discussed privately.

It is important to note in this context that the Asante are extremely secretive about an individual's ancestry. Emmanuel Akyeampong and Pashington Obeng write that "Asante proverbs like *obi nkyere obi ase* (no one should point to other people's [non-Asante/unfree] origins) emphasize the concept of wealth in people and Asante assimilativeness." McCaskie also makes this point clear when he notes, in relation to the affairs of Nkawie, that according to the historical record Asantehene Opoku Ware I "fined Bantama as it had spoken to reveal the origins of Nkawie which was forbidden by custom." According to McCaskie, it was strictly forbidden in Asante law and custom to mention the origins of another person publicly. This prohibition was among the laws of Komfo Anokye, and it has remained to the present. . . .

The Tabon and Fihankra Experience in the Ghanaian Development Context

The relevance of the discussion of the Tabon and *Fihankra* in this article must be seen in the context of diasporan Africans' attempt at reintegration. The two cases have similarities and dissimilarities within the chieftaincy institution. One important distinction for the Tabon, for example, is that they have been more or less completely integrated into Ga society over several generations. African American *Nkɔsuohene/hemaa* are not assimilated in this way. Similarly, the *Ye Fa Ogyemu (Fihankra)* township residency is strictly limited to African Americans, which, as some African Americans and Ghanaians have pointed out, contradicts the avowed aim of reintegrating African Americans into Ghanaian society.

The *Nkɔsuo* stool was created with community development as its main objective. The *Nkɔsuohene/hemaa* is theoretically a development initiator whose aim is to mobilize the community to undertake projects. The stool has been abused in several ways. For some subchiefs the presence of any Westerner in their community is the opportune time to offer the *Nkɔsuo* stool to such a person, and these discrepancies merit further examination. The Western media have shown a lot of interest in the installation of these African "kings" and "queens," and one wonders what the basis of this fascination is. News abounds in Western dailies of the installation of foreigners as *Nkɔsuohene/hemaa*. A news item in the UK tabloid *The Sun* proclaims "Brit Pair to Rule in Ghana." John Lawler was installed as *Nkɔsuohene* of Shia (with the stool name Torbui Mottey I) and Elaine Lawler as *Nkɔsuohenemaa* (Mama Amenyo Nyowu Sika). Another headline, in the UK *Telegraph*, drew attention to "Africans Still Waiting for 'Chief' Geldof's Help." In 2004, Bob Geldof, the Irish rock star turned Africa campaigner, visited the town of Ajumako-Bisease in the Central Region of Ghana and was promptly installed as an *Nkɔsuohene* with the stool name Nana Kofi Kumasah I. In Sir

Bob's case the installation was captured on film for his *Geldof in Africa* TV series, broadcast on BBC Television in 2005.

The honor of an *Nkɔsuohene/hemaa* is often misunderstood by white Westerners. For instance, in 2004 when Geldof was so honored, he accepted the responsibilities that came with the post. But after using the "crowning" ceremony as a photo opportunity for his documentary series, made in the run-up to the 2005 Live 8 concerts, Geldof somehow forgot all about the Ghanaian town—as its people pointed out in their counterdocumentary, *A Letter to Geldof.* Nana Okofo Kwakora Gyan III, who installed Geldof in 2004, after waiting for the *Nkɔsuohene* to no avail, followed him to London. Nana was surprised to see that he and other elders who had posed for a photograph with Geldof were featured in the book that accompanied the *Geldof in Africa* TV series, sold at £16 a copy. "I didn't know we would be sold in London," he says.

Westerners view *Nkɔsuo* stools from their cultural perspective and this sometimes conflicts with how chiefs see them—principally as development initiators. Whereas a traditional stool would mean very little to a white Westerner, for diasporan Africans the honor of an *Nkɔsuohene/hemaa* is more spiritual. Upon being enstooled as a Ghanaian subchief or queen mother for development, these Africans from the diaspora are reintegrated back into the ancient clan system of chieftaincy. The honors are also significant for many reasons, as they acknowledge the excellent leadership that these recipients provide to their chosen communities.

The *Asanteman* Council and the Ghanaian Parliament have been very concerned about what has become a habit at community festivals where foreigners are installed as *Nkɔsuohene/hemaa*. The traditionalists are concerned about the denigration of Asante norms and traditions, which, they argue, undermines the authority of the chieftaincy institution. In principle, however, the Asanteman Council is not against the concept; the concern is the uses to which the stools are put by nonindigenous *Nkɔsuohenes*. For example, it is alleged that some occupants of the stools have acted in their capacities as development chiefs in poverty-stricken Ghana to solicit for funds and other development aid in the names of deprived communities, but never delivered.

The developments undertaken by the *Nkɔsuohene/hemaa* are probably limited to southern Ghana. About one thousand African Americans live and work in Ghana, mainly in Accra, and the country annually attracts about ten thousand black Americans as tourists. Information on African diasporans adopting communities in northern Ghana was not available at the time of writing. However, some northern chiefdoms have from time to time honored foreign personalities who through their work have contributed to "poverty alleviation"—this could be in the provision of resources ranging from drinking water to microfinance. . . . The process of reintegration into the various African societies has a direct correlation with state power and level of economic advancement. Even though the "Back to Africa movement" was once championed by Marcus Garvey, a Jamaican, it is the middle-class African Americans who have responded. It is the black Americans, backed by American dollars, who are capable of embarking on a trip to Africa in search of their roots.

China–Africa Relations: A Case Study of Ghana

Dela Tsikata, Ama Pokuaa Fenny, and Ernest Aryeetey

In 2008, the Institute of Statistical, Social and Economic Research at the University of Ghana (Legon) prepared a study to examine the economic relations between Ghana and China. Regardless of new developments since the preparation of this study—and additional developments by the time readers encounter this book—the study nonetheless provides a basis for evaluating the nature of Ghana–China relations up until 2008. Though Chinese laborers were imported to the Gold Coast / Ghana at the end of the nineteenth century and in the first quarter of the twentieth, bilateral or diplomatic relations between Ghana and China began around the second half of the twentieth century—1960, to be exact. In the twenty-first century, now that Ghana has emerged from its recent history of military coups and leadership and China from communist rule under Mao Zedong (1893–1976), the two countries have restarted those relations. But recent incidents such as the deportation of 218 Chinese miners for illegal gold mining in Ghana continue to test the nature these relations, and the political, economic, and environmental implications of Chinese aid and the increasing inflow of Chinese workers paid through that "aid" for road and harbor constructions, gas pipelines, and other China-aided projects.

With the emergence of China as an engine of growth, it is expected that investment in different sectors like the consumer, agricultural, banking, logistics, and industrial sectors will grow. This will especially be the case in the extractive sector. Such investment may be a boon to a developing country like Ghana or alternatively may serve to stunt the development of local industries. The outcome depends on whether or not the particular country is able to respond proactively and take advantage of the new opportunities which emerge. An important first step in this process would be for the country (Ghana) to examine the nature of its relations with China, especially with regards to investment, trade, and aid.

In the area of investment, data shows that Chinese investment in Ghana has been growing steadily over the past decade. In the last two years, however, there has been a dramatic increase in Chinese investment. From 2004 to 2005, the value of Chinese investment increased from $3.09 million to $17.87 million. In 2006, there was a slight decrease to $15.2 million. Despite this ramping up of Chinese investment, China's share of total investment in Ghana is somewhat minimal and reached a maximum of 8.85 percent in 2005. Thus China is not a major investor in Ghana yet, but it is gaining increased prominence. Chinese companies over the past seven years have invested primarily in the manufacturing and general trade sectors of the Ghanaian economy. One notable feature of Chinese investment is that most of the funding has come from Chinese nationals, which raises the possibility that most of the profits gained from these operations will be repatriated to China. With respect to investment, one can tentatively say that Ghana is "losing" because of the Chinese investment's negative effect on the Ghanaian manufacturing sector and the fact that investment in the general trade sector is detrimental to the deepening of the local economy.

In the area of trade, a number of observations can be made. First of all, China's share of total exports from Ghana is very low. In fact, since 2000, China has consistently received less than 2 percent of Ghana's exports, and the total value of Ghana's exports to China have fluctuated from year to year. This is in stark contrast to the overall performance of Ghana's exports, which has shown a fairly consistent positive trend in recent years. For instance, between 2000 and 2006, the total value of Ghana's exports increased from $1,648 million to $4,145 million. Over the same period, exports to China only marginally increased from $25.8 million to $28.6 million.

On the import side, Ghana's imports from China have increased consistently over the past few years, from $96 million in 2000 to $503 million in 2006, mirroring the overall increase in Ghana's total imports. This increase has been largely fuelled by a growth in manufactured imports, and this observation has significant negative implications for the development of Ghana's industrial sector. On the other hand, however, the availability of cheap manufactured goods from China might increase the overall welfare of Ghanaians, especially low-income consumers. There is the need for critical cost-benefit analysis to determine the overall effect.

China has had a long-standing aid relationship with Ghana since the 1960s. However, it is only in recent years that the aid relationship has been taken to a new, higher level. Chinese aid is still, however, only a small percentage of the total development assistance received by Ghana. Figures for total amounts of Chinese aid to Ghana are not readily available but an examination of recently signed contracts gives some idea of the purpose of the aid and the amounts involved. The aid has comprised loans, grants, and technical assistance. Over the years, Chinese aid has been used to build physical infrastructure like roads (for instance, the Ofankor-Nsawam section of the Accra-Kumasi road) and buildings (for instance, the National Theatre). Chinese aid is also going into the construction of the Bui Hydro-Electric Power Dam, which is almost completed. However, in recent years, the focus has partly shifted to ICT development, and China is currently providing part of the funding for two key ICT projects (the National Communications Backbone Network Project and the Dedicated Communications Project for Security Agencies project). The important question is: Is Ghana gaining or losing as a result of Chinese aid? We can say, again tentatively, that overall Ghana is gaining. By not relying exclusively on Western donors, Ghana is thus able to negotiate at least to some extent for more favorable conditions for aid. The Chinese are serving a wide variety of infrastructure needs which it would be quite difficult and/or expensive for Ghana to meet on its own or have met elsewhere.

Ghana Market Women Pay the Daily Micro Man

Emily Bowers

As we pointed out in part V, market women in Ghana occupy a place of prominence in the country's economy. Nevertheless, there are few channels supported by the banking industry to finance these small-scale entrepreneurs, primarily because they are considered part of the informal economy. As such, it can be quite difficult for market women to access formal financing to start up or expand their businesses. Recently, however, microfinance institutions have filled this void, allowing these women access to formal loans, albeit small ones with high interest rates. Women's eNews correspondent and freelance journalist Emily Bowers, in the following news article, chronicles the stories of some women participants in microfinancing at the Makola market in Accra, one of the busiest in the country. In terms of the monetary amounts below, the reader should bear in mind both the redenomination of the Ghanaian currency (cedi) as a high-value currency unit some months after this article was published in 2007 and the fluctuating exchange rates between the Ghanaian (old) cedi and the U.S. dollar.

Margaret Agyeman watches as Nii Aryee Quaye opens her banking passbook and counts the five bills tucked inside. Perched on plastic chairs inside Agyeman's tiny market shop, Quaye takes her regular daily contribution to her savings account: 100,000 Ghanaian cedis, worth about $10.80. Quaye records the amount, hands her a receipt, and heads back out into the brilliant sunshine. It's a quick transaction, buffered by a few pleasantries. Quaye will do this up to seventy times each day, moving from stall to stall, greeting calls of "accountant" from vendors.

Accra's frenzied Makola market is in the heart of the city; thousands of traders mingle with shoppers, taxis, and tro-tros, or local minibuses. For several blocks, narrow paths of broken pavement and dirt wind through scores of tiny container shops selling everything from colorful African printed fabric to air conditioners and live chickens. Through this maze of shops, Quaye collects savings money from clients of his employer, Women's World Bank Ghana. He assigns some of the money to savings accounts, some to payments of microcredit loans they've taken through the bank.

The market women at Makola are among the estimated 60 percent of the Ghanaian population involved in the informal sector, and the Women's World Bank is one of scores of microfinance institutions operating in this West African country. A majority of the recipients here, as in many other developing countries, are women who have established an impeccable repayment record of up to 98 percent, according to microfinancing pioneer Grameen Bank in Bangladesh. Borrowers routinely pay high annual interest rates—of between 15 percent and 40 percent—reflecting the special costs of this type of highly negotiated credit, which reaches borrowers who don't qualify for standard bank loans and whose accounts must be serviced by itinerant loan officers such as Quaye.

Some critics decry the high rates of interest, but Aba Quainoo, who runs a microfinance consultancy business in Accra, justifies them with a familiar argument. The rates, she says, are far lower than the only alternative. "Women who can't access microfinance will go to a moneylender who will charge as much as 10 percent a month," Quainoo said. But while microfinance has proven itself to be cheaper than local moneylenders, the larger question is how the growing billions of dollars that are expected to flow into this credit system over the next few years will affect borrowers. Will the money fund economic development or just leave borrowers marginally better off?

Microfinance Network

After making his rounds, Quaye returns to the busy office of Women's World Bank, a microfinance network based in New York with affiliates around the world. Staff in a back room are sifting through piles of paper as they prepare to pack up and move to a new, bigger location. The bank was started in Ghana in 1983 and now has eight branches, including the Makola market branch, as well as a head office in Accra. There are some seven thousand members at the Makola branch, says manager Eleanor Ofosu-Addo, though not all of them are active. The minimum microcredit loan they give is 500,000 cedis ($54), the maximum is 100 million cedis ($10,800).

Before a woman can obtain a loan, she must first open a savings account and start putting some money away, Ofosu-Addo says. The idea is that women should get used to setting aside money on a regular basis, so that when it's time to take a loan, they can already have the habit of steady payments. Ofosu-Addo says the women are not expected to use those savings in repayment of their future loans, and if a woman is having trouble repaying, the bank will restructure the loan instead of taking from her savings.

Little Shop in Big Market

Agyeman, fifty-seven, has had her container shop in one corner of Makola for about fifteen years. Six days a week, she works from 8 a.m. to 4:30 p.m. and employs two workers as well. While her five children are all grown, Agyeman and other family members are looking after three young grandchildren and her savings from her business helps support them. She's been a member of Women's World Bank for about seven years and has twice taken loans from the bank: one of 10 million Ghanaian cedis ($1,080) and another of 20 million ($2,160). Subject to the whims of her business, repaying the loans on a steady payment rate isn't always easy, Agyeman said. "Sometimes you get it difficult, sometimes you get it easy, because of the market," she says. "But you manage to pay."

Agyeman says her business wouldn't have folded without the loans, since she does have some savings set aside, but it has allowed her to buy large amounts of products in bulk on trips to Nigeria. That means better bargains and better savings for her. "It helped me a lot," she says. "I use the money to buy goods and do so many things." Agyeman made biweekly payments on her first loan at a monthly interest rate of 3.2 percent, or about 38 percent annually. When she took out her second loan, the rate had fallen to 3 percent a month, or 36 percent annually.

Borrowing for Rent and Wares

Mary Darkoah, fifty-two, has just taken out her first loan of 25 million cedis ($2,700) to help stock her market business of stationery and school books, which she has run for fifteen years. She has recently moved to a new store location within the market and has used her money to pay rent on her second-floor shop. The loan has helped her fully stock her shelves with books. She's just begun repaying a daily rate of 250,000 cedis ($27). Darkoah says making the payment right now isn't too bad with her daily sales of between 1 million and 5 million cedis. "It's not all that difficult," she says. But it will take her nine months to pay off the loan, and Darkoah worries that things will get more difficult in a few months, when her sales of schoolbooks will taper off as students go on holidays.

And she's not putting aside any regular savings right now, since a lot of her profit is going toward paying her rent. She's paying installments of total rent of 65 million cedis for a ten-year lease, plus an extra 300,000 a month. Darkoah says her microcredit loan has helped her use the savings she has already put aside on paying some school fees for her children, and Agyeman has used her loans to expand her business selling household electrical items in bulk. Both women say it has given them more stability and financial flexibility. "At least I have some money inside (my account)," Agyeman says.

"The Slums of Nima" and "Fading Laughter"

Kwesi Brew

Nima is one of the prominent slums in Accra in terms of both its sheer size and its challenging living conditions. Slum life and its attendant ills normally serve to erode social conventions regarding privacy, ownership rights, and respect for the elderly. However, the culture of the peoples in Ghana is so profound that it challenges the very notions of how slums and poverty affect those who endure them. In the following two poems, Kwesi Brew paints a vivid picture of the squalor, rapacity, hardship, and violence that exist in the slum. He also demonstrates how even in these "typical" slum conditions, Ghanaians steadfastly adhere to certain cultural practices like showing respect for elders or clinging to the beauty and significance of kente cloth even though it might be old and faded.

The Slums of Nima

When I passed the windows yesterday
I passed into a night buttered
With stars like the yellow petals
Of the acacia on the black soil
On which it stands.
I plunged into a treachery of winding lanes
Into an eclipse of the sun.
I heard murmurs and groans of childbirth
And could not tell
From which unhinged door they came:
The doors were too close together.

Three neighbors met,
And after a hurried, "I give you rest"
The two young men stood aside for the old man
To pass and then picked their way
In the opposite direction towards the alley

A narrow passageway between houses in the residential town of Nima, Greater Accra Region of Ghana. Nima is home to a major market and well-known slums. Photograph by Clifford Campbell, Accra, July 2013.

On the left.
They were thieves who robbed with violence
But still they stood aside for the old man
And he thanked them.

In a bereaved world questions and comments
Fall on unhearing ears.
Only silence, understanding and
Belonging can put
A blind man's stick in the hands
Of a searcher in that night.

The crumbling walls have leaned
On their chests for decades!
The toll of breathing has shredded
Their lungs, and their eyes are sore
With the smoke of the wicker lamps.
And now we all stand at the edge
Of an abyss
Afraid to plunge headlong, or
Return to the dark of the night with them!

Fading Laughter

It is not all laughter, all the time.
Who can laugh when the roof leaks
And the walls give way to floods?
Laughter is the seasoning of salt, and
Salt is not food but a seasoning for food.
They have their sorrows, these men of the land.
Poverty stalks them by the hour
And the kente is a flash in their lives:
Handed down the rungs of years
From uncle to nephew through mother's stream.
Time's disintegrating fingers, have by stealth,
Loosened the threads
Where the
Weaver of
Bonwire
Had joined
The strips.
The dyes in the colors, red, blue, gold, and green
Sapped by the devilry of age,
Have paled to where they can fade no more.
But, to them, there is no matter for grief:
Life has other gifts.

Ghanaian Highlife

E. J. Collins

The musical genre of highlife is Ghana's most notable contribution to African popular music. While it is wholly Ghanaian, it also represents a musical bridge of sorts between Ghana and the African diaspora. Highlife music developed toward the end of the nineteenth century along the Fante coast as musicians incorporated the melodies of Caribbean soldiers stationed there. The musical fusion further deepened as local musicians chose to articulate this new sound with Western instrumentation such as brass sections and guitars. Later in the twentieth century, conga drums from Cuba, jazz from the United States, and calypso from the eastern Caribbean would further influence the evolution of the highlife sound. The composite nature of highlife allowed it to transcend the ethnic divide in the Gold Coast; it represented one of the earlier markers of unity among the colonized peoples that would achieve political independence as Ghana. As a cultural marker that transcended ethnicity, highlife was more than just a means of popular entertainment, especially in the period leading up to political independence and in the turbulent years that followed, as its popularity made it a viable mean of expressing various interests. Ghana's foremost highlife scholar and music professor, John Collins, offers insights on how highlife served as a platform for the expression of multiple social and political concerns in the following excerpt from a scholarly article.

Highlife presents a multiplicity of styles employing various musical ensembles and playing to very different audiences. . . .

The lyrics of many highlife songs are concerned with the rapid social changes that are occurring in Africa. One of these is migration. A . . . record by the African Brothers guitar band called *Obiba* (*Broke*) is about the social forces that compel young people to leave their village homes. "Nyimpa ne mber ara nyi" ("Man's time is short") by Kakaiku's guitar band concerns the problem of living in a strange town. Social stratification is another contemporary theme covered by highlife. In 1967, just after the anti-Nkrumah coup, the African Brothers released "Ebi te yie" ("Some live well"), a song in the form of a fable obliquely referring to corruption in high places and the division of society into rich and poor. "Yen nyina ye bow pepeepe" ("We all booze the same"), concerning a man who thinks that *akpeteshie* (a cheap local gin) is a good as any prestigious imported drink, lightheartedly makes fun of the pompous and wealthy. The Jaguar Jokers concert band recorded "Ahiame obi nwhe me" ("I am poor, somebody should help me"). The Gã highlife group Wulomei's "Walatu walasa" means in Twi that "you are digging and then shoveling it away," implying that only an idiot would do both. "Walatu Walasa" has become a popular phrase at a time when large numbers of workers have been employed by the government to build drains in Accra. To greet a laborer with this term is to insult him, for it demeans manual labor.

Highlife songs are often overtly political. During Nkrumah's imprisonment by the British in 1950, the Axim Trio wrote a play and song called "Kwame Nkrumah Will Never Die." E. K. Nyame welcomed Nkrumah out of prison with "Onim deefo kukudurufu Kwame Nkrumah" ("Honorable man and hero Kwame Nkrumah"). Other groups that openly supported Nkrumah and the CPP were Bob Cole's Ghana Trio, the Farmer's Brigade band, and the Worker's Brigade band. "Ebi te yie" not only deals with the problem of social injustice, but is also a good example of songs critical of political regimes. In fact, the African Brothers wrote another song about the same time, but it was banned by the government. Its refrain, translated from the Twi, is "Although the driver is different, the lorry is the same": adverse commentary on the government is usually disguised, but not always well enough. In 1964 Dr. K. Gyasi's band recorded "Agyima Mansa," in which the ghost of a mother laments that her children are not thriving. Nkrumah thought criticism of his regime was implied, and despite the composer's insistence that the lyrics were inspired by a dream, the song was never allowed to be broadcast on the radio. A very recent example of a politically motivated song is "Kanana," recorded by King Pratt and His African Revolution in 1974. The song sets some of Nkrumah's speeches to highlife music.

Many highlife lyrics influence social behavior and standards; for instance, the Stargazer's dance band number "Beenu Nkombo" ("Tete-a-tete") condemns gossip. Other songs positively affirm new Western norms. Iain Lang (1956) refers to a highlife refrain that goes, "Jagwah, been-to (i.e., to the West), houseful, earful, fridgeful," affirming everything that a successful man about town should have and be. Yet another example is E. K. Nyame's "Se wo ko na anny e yie a san bra" ("If you go and it does not work out, come back"). This love song explicitly mentions the wife's desire for her husband to return home and kiss her, a romantic topic never mentioned openly in traditional Akan society. Also on this topic of sexual norms, the Nigerian composer Omogbewa's highlife called "Man on Top" states that women are inferior to men; it is typical of many songs bemoaning modern trends among townswomen.

Highlife bears an important relationship to two social phenomena occurring in Africa today, social mobility and urban socialization. Highlife is relevant to horizontal (i.e., geographical) mobility because its lyrics, often concerned with the attractions of town life, contribute to urban pull. On the question of vertical, or social, mobility, highlife from its origins as entertainment for the indigenous elite in the coastal towns has come to be considered as a high-status ideal, as opposed to the concept of "bush," which embraces the unsophisticated and uneducated. In reality the situation is far more complex, for the highlife bands themselves hold differing social positions, from the high-status dance bands to the low-status guitar bands.

A second aspect of highlife's relationship to social mobility is generational. The emergence of new styles of traditional Ghanaian music often reflects the conflicts between generations, as in satirical musical commentary that criticizes village elders. The highlife-influenced Kpan-logo music, created in the early sixties, was banned by the Ga elders, who considered the dance indecent. The dispute was finally resolved, in favor of the young people, only by Nkrumah's intervention. Today, many young Ghanaians consider highlife itself to be part of the colonial mentality and oppose it with their own Afro music and culture.

Highlife plays an important role in the second phenomenon of urban socialization. With the rapid expansion of the towns, composed mainly of poor rural migrants, concerts have become popular again in the large urban areas, but it is a very different concert from the old vaudeville type found earlier in the coastal towns. Today, although the plays and songs are in Twi, they incorporate other local languages as well, creating much cross-cultural humor. Highlife thus affects socialization, both in the sense that it transmits Western urban ideas, aspirations, and values to its largely newly urban audience, and that it is a medium understood and appreciated by the ethnically diverse population.

The Western influences on highlife have been discussed. Yet it still retains many of the features of traditional folk music. Both musical forms include dance, and in fact highlife became popular precisely because its acculturated melodies and rhythms fit into existing local dance patterns. It is notable that the dance used in the Odonso style of highlife is identical to the traditional Akan Adowa. Besides traditional gong and dance rhythms, a number of indigenous instruments, such as local hand drums and idiophones, have been retained by the less Westernized guitar bands and Konkomba groups. The popularity of the guitar and its rapid assimilation in the Akan areas can be understood in the light of evidence offered by A. A. Mensah (1966), who has analyzed musical similarities between this instrument and the seprewa, or traditional Akan lute. Indeed, the popularity of highlife in general is due to the close approximation of the Akan seven-note scale to the European diatonic scale.

In addition to musicological features, highlife also continues some of the social features of traditional musical performance. There is traditionally a great deal of audience participation in the form of dancing, and even today it is unusual for an audience to simply sit and listen to [highlife songs]. The lyrics of highlife, almost always in a local language, often contain elements found in traditional music, such as local proverbs and religious beliefs. Like traditional music, highlife, in its songs of ridicule and praise, plays an active role in social control and the definition of social norms.

Finally, highlife treated as an organized syncretic subsystem operates within the broader social system, in both its traditional and modern spheres. It is a dynamic agent at work on new forms of traditional recreational (i.e., modern-traditional) music. One such variety, Dagomba Simpa, was banned . . . for six months, as the songs of the various Simpa groups aligned with the two opposing royal houses in a chieftaincy dispute were considered too inflammatory by the government. Highlife also affects the modern sector in its relevance to the rapid social changes taking place on the continent. In these ways, highlife represents a creative African response to the modern world.

Profile of Five Ghana Emcees

Msia Kibona Clark

The Ghanaian hip-hop scene is very diverse and includes emcees that vary in style and skill. As a genre that stands alone, separate from Ghanaian highlife and, more recently, hiplife, Ghanaian hip-hop features a wide spectrum of artists and sounds. The artists that call Ghana home reside both inside and outside the country and are helping to shape the international hip-hop scene. Indeed, Ghanaian hip-hop artists have helped catapult Ghanaian hip-hop onto the international stage, as outlined in the following essay by Msia Kibona Clark, African studies professor and coeditor of Hip Hop and Social Change in Africa.

While the diversity of Ghanaian hip-hop makes defining a typical Ghanaian hip-hop artist impossible, there are five emcees that offer a great representation of what Ghana has to offer. There are the fast Twi flows of Tema-based rapper Sarkodie, the Pidgin prankster and self-proclaimed African gypsy Wanlov the Kubolor, London-based multitalented emcee M3nsa, the classic hip-hop sounds emanating from the amazing flow of M.anifest, and the jazz-infused sounds of Brooklyn-based Blitz the Ambassador. All of these emcees are extremely diverse; they are all well respected for their lyrical content and for producing some of the best Ghanaian hip-hop music of the past five years. In addition, they all represent Ghanaian hip-hop on the international stage with followings that extend far beyond Ghana's borders.

I no be gentleman at all'o / I be African man original—Wanlov the Kubolor & M.anifest, "Gentleman"

Sarkodie's 2009 release "Borga" was directed at Ghanaians living abroad. In the song Sarkodie comments on the extent Ghanaians go through to put up the facade that they are living lavishly abroad. In the song he calls on Ghanaians to return, commenting on the many advantages of coming home to Ghana. Sarkodie's roots are in Tema, just outside of Accra. While the artist has signed a major record deal with Akon's Konvict Records, he remains rooted in his Tema neighborhood. During our interview and photo shoot the artist made it clear that the meeting had to take place in Tema and that his neighborhood, and the people in it, needed to be a part of the images taken. Sarkodie, often called the Tongue Twister of Ghana because of his quick lyrical style, raps primarily in Twi, and stands out as an artist that enjoys great local commercial success, as well as immense respect among hip-hop aficionados.

Modwene s eda fom, gyae nipa rebre / Obi te Canada, nee obei koraa, osre / Burgers yi bebree na entaa nka nokore / Anka mobehunu se amanone mpo ye fomkyere / Wote Ghana pam adee nya wo sika / Nea wobɛdi, woanya koraa wowo beebi da

Do you think this life is easy? Stop but we've really hustled! / Someone is in Canada he needs to go begging for his daily meal / A lot of these borga are not truthful you would have known life in the West is not that easy / You live and work in Ghana / At the very least, you have somewhere to sleep—Sarkodie, "Borga"

The Ghanaian hip-hop duo Fokn Bois has blazed a serious trail on the Ghanaian and international music scene. Comprised of Wanlov the Kubolor and M3nsa, the duo released what they called the first Pidgin-language musical film, *Coz ov Moni*, in 2010. The film is a comedic tale of two men (Wanlov and M3nsa) who get by hustling the people around them. The film presents a cautionary story of the problems that arise from living life in the pursuit of money. The film also features a tribute to past leaders from Africa and the African diaspora, including Kwame Nkrumah, Steve Biko, Malcolm X, Patrice Lumumba, Marcus Garvey, Cheik Anta Diop, Fred Hampton, and Thomas Sankara. Wanlov and M3nsa are currently working on the much anticipated sequel *Coz ov Moni 2*. Individually both artists have been responsible for several international hits, such as "Green Card," "Adjuma" ("Hustle"), and "Human Being." These songs question the benefit of struggling to get immigration papers ("Green Card"), address working-class struggles ("Adjuma"), and examine the interconnectedness of all of us ("Human Being").

I spoke with M3nsa recently about managing a career that has him traveling between England, Ghana, and the U.S. Coming from a musical family, M3nsa said he is firmly grounded in his identity and tries to bring that out in his music. M3nsa's debut solo album, *No. 1 Mango Street* (the location of the home M3nsa grew up in Ghana), features popular songs like "Fanti Love

Untitled graffiti art commemorating Ghana's hip-hop and R&B scene. Art by Martin Numadzi, 2009. Courtesy of the artist.

Song," "Asem Pa," and "Adjuma." With songs like "Adjuma" M3nsa is one of the few hip-hop artists to produce commercially successful "club" tracks that also contain important social commentary.

Wanlov the Kubolor, who has been open about his immigration problems in the U.S., voluntarily returned to Ghana a few years ago. The artist blends his experiences and background (he has a Romanian mother and a Ghanaian father) to stand out among other Ghanaian emcees. He keeps his hair locked, wears his trademark wrapper (skirt), and almost never wears shoes. Wanlov's line in the song "Gentleman" exemplifies his demeanor in the face of ideas on proper dress and behavior: "In our simplicity we are elegant / so to us your coat and tie are irrelevant / give up my culture for your religion? I can't."

Noted Ghanaian hiplife artist Wanlov the Kubolor. Hiplife is a Ghanaian musical style that combines hip-hop and highlife music. Photograph by Msia Kibona Clark, 2010. Courtesy of the photographer.

Wanlov the Kubolor's debut solo album, *Green Card*, featured lyrics about his past immigration experiences, including the deeply personal "Loredo," which talks about Wanlov's experience being detained by immigration officials in Texas. Both of Wanlov's solo albums, *Green Card* and *Brown Card*, offer views into the artist's state of mind and infuse sounds from his diverse backgrounds to create a signature sound.

We fought to get off the slave yard / Now we fight to get us a green card / Why do we work for this stuff so hard? / How you living and your working grave yard?
—Wanlov the Kubolor, "Green Card"

If M.anifest wanted to blend into the U.S. hip-hop scene, he could. His style and cadence is reminiscent of some of the best U.S. emcees. But he is a proud Ghana man. M.anifest's 2011 album, *Immigrant Chronicles: Coming to America*, announces that the artist identifies strongly with his Ghanaian roots. I sat with M.anifest just before his return to Ghana in 2011. He spoke of the importance for him of representing Ghana. But he also recognized that as a Ghanaian he was a part of a wider African community that included the African diaspora. He understood that his use of both Pidgin and African American vernacular in his songs made his music much more pan-African. Unlike many who use African American slang as a way to imitate American hip-hop, M.anifest often uses it to express his dual experiences, in the U.S. and in Ghana.

> Young dummy / thought it was the land of milk & honey / hunger pains in my tummy / why is everything about money . . . in Ghana I was a human being'o / here I'm an alien, a martian Mandingo—M.anifest, "Motion Picture"

Many would argue that M.anifest is probably one of the top Ghanaian emcees of all time. His lyrical timing, flow, and delivery are difficult to equal. His visual style is also unique. Like his lyrics, his style tends to use an African American swagger to represent Ghanaian styles. He is often seen wearing African print shirts and Ghanaian jewelry, with a classic hip-hop stance, or posing in a manner that suggests lived experiences outside of Ghana.

Lastly, Blitz the Ambassador has two full-length albums and three EPs to his name. He left Ghana after secondary school to attend college in the U.S. Before leaving Ghana, however, he had already begun his career in the country's budding hip-hop scene. After arriving "at JFK with one duffle bag and a dream," Blitz would emerge on the underground scene in Brooklyn, New York. Unable to get a record deal, Blitz started his own record label and began releasing his own music. Since the beginning the artist has infused jazz sounds and African rhythms into his music. Rapping in English, he established himself as a representative not just of Ghana, but of Africa. With lines like "I got the whole continent on my back," Blitz positioned himself as one of the leading African hip-hop emcees in the U.S. His topics have included his experiences in Ghana and the U.S., as well as broader introspections on everything from the image of Africa in the media to the mass incarceration of Black men. With his second full-length album, *Native Sun*, Blitz the Ambassador returned to Ghana, and the album includes several tracks of the artist rapping in Twi. Blitz also went home to Ghana to perform during that time, including a tour with the group Les Nubians. Blitz also took advantage of his time in New York City, the birthplace of hip-hop. He worked with several hip-hop legends, and his album *Native Sun* includes a track that features Chuck D of Public Enemy.

Incarceration is the new plantation / a new kind of slavery, a new foundation / and it wouldn't even cost you much / the project is the slave ship, the corner is the auction block—Blitz the Ambassador, "Ghetto Plantation"

Blitz the Ambassador is a multitalented emcee, musician, and graphic designer. He is also an extremely conscious emcee. He has used his music to bring attention to numerous social and political issues. Having conducted several interviews with Blitz the Ambassador over the course of his career, I have seen the artist emerge with feet firmly planted in the U.S., international, and Ghanaian hip-hop scenes.

All of the artists featured here have collectively spoken out on the experiences of Ghanaian migrants in the West, failed economic policies, love, struggle, and the forgotten visions of past African leaders like Kwame Nkrumah. They have all made a name for themselves on the Ghanaian music scene, as well as on the international music scene. The aim of this piece was to provide a closer look at five Ghanaian hip-hop artists that are as diverse as they are dynamic.

Kumasi Realism: Alex Amofa

Atta Kwami

A burgeoning body of West African artistic production draws on photography, advertising, graphic design, European art history, and Ghanaian history and culture but does not subscribe to the dichotomy between "traditional" and "modern" visual culture. The works of these Ghanaian visual artists constitutes a local "modernity" located in Kumase (Kumasi)—a vibrant trading city at the center of local, national, and international networks, and heartland of the historic Asante empire. Though the Ghanaian painters who practiced at Kwame Nkrumah University of Science and Technology (KNUST) in Kumase influenced the street art of individuals like Alex Amofa, one of Kumase's leading sign painters and the focus of this selection, Amofa's art uses indigenous and other techniques to produce a style that has life of its own. The following excerpt from Atta Kwami's book Kumasi Realism: An African Modernism *showcases the art and life of Alex Amofa.*

Alex Amofa experiments in fine art, which he regards as sharing the same materials and tools with advertising and commercial art. He worked with pastels over black-and-white Xeroxes from photographs in his efforts to arrive at Kumasi Realism. He paints social customs in acrylic and oil, sometimes in combination, on canvas. The underdrawings/paintings are done in chalk or paint, which is then meticulously developed to achieve his delicate touch. Landscapes in watercolour on paper are a favourite medium of Amofa, reminding us of his debt to Delaquis and the painter Philip Amonoo, whom he sought out in Winneba in the 1970s. Amofa has created murals based on the Stations of the Cross for St. Cyprian's Anglican Cathedral in Kumasi. Revered as the father of sign painters in Kumasi, he continues to inspire the young with his careful technique in picturemaking. The master of Supreme Art Works is one of the most popular sign painters in Kumasi, from a rating of 10 per cent by peers in 1999.

Alexander Amofa is five years younger than Samino [another leading sign painter]; he was born on 21 May 1940 at Apramaso (near Anwomaso), though his home town is Kwaso, also in the Asante region. There were four boys and two girls in the family and Alexander was the youngest. He came from a family of artists; four of his maternal uncles were goldsmiths. One of them, Kofi Berko, was a close friend of the late Asantehene, Sir Agyemang Prempeh II. Berko worked solely for the nobility. The king left the choice of design to his goldsmiths. Berko had the upper hand in a team of five designers at the palace. Goldsmithing or silversmithing was an early career option for Amofa, but he opted for painting and never relented. One brother became a farmer. It is worth noting that in Asante society some royals may train in a trade or work as taxi drivers before their enstoolment. And for Amofa painting was an introduction into the palace and high society, for he said: "I have always wanted to know more about art [and] successful people." Amofa established portrait paintings of Asante kings as objects for the palace.

Alex Amofa was educated at the Presbyterian Middle School, Kwaso, until 1957, when he received his middle school certificate. After school from 1957–62 Amofa did "commercial art." In an interview he said that he joined the workshop of Bob Eshun at Asem, Kumasi, in 1957, at which time Samino was also working there. When Eshun left for Côte d'Ivoire in 1959 and did not return, Amofa took over the studio. Amofa is fond of landscapes. While practising as an artist Amofa continued his education through correspondence courses abroad in general commercial art, most notably with Bennet College in Sheffield in 1969/70. He also took a course from a college in the United States in 1971. Correspondence art courses from Europe and the U.S. have been available and favoured for a long time and are not confined to sign painters. Several college-trained painters have taken them, such as Ato Delaquis, who took a course in France, and Dr. Alhaji Yakubu Seidu Peligah of the KNUST, who took a course in commercial art with the Rapid Results College in London in the 1970s.

Amofa took part in the first National Art Contest sponsored by Mobil Oil Ghana in 1968 in Accra. The exhibition that resulted from this was an opportunity to show his work alongside college-trained artists, such as Edmund Jimmy Kwame Tetteh, Ablade Glover, and Ato Delaquis. Amofa identifies with the work of Ato Delaquis, and some of the compositions he has painted (*Tomato Seller*, 1980s) are also similar to the market scenes of Kofi Antubam. When asked to name his favourite artists, he pointed out Ato Delaquis as "a very good draughtsman," and Owusu Dartey, who was renowned for his "strokes" in watercolour painting, adding, "We like E.V. Asihene's technique." Over and above all these he named Philip Amonoo as the one who influenced him with his "natural" works. In the early 1970s, Amofa travelled southwards to the coast, to Winneba, on a sketching trip during which the two artists met. Amonoo is a watercolourist of renown and for many years taught at the Winneba Specialist Training College (now the University College of Education, Winneba). Amofa stated: "I did some still lives in 1959. *Takai Dance*, a Dagomba dance, was first painted in 1959. Several versions were to follow. I took inspiration from Philip Amonoo, who was very good in all the mediums." Amofa told me that Antubam was his colleague: "I know Antubam. He came to my studio on about two occasions." Amofa's favourite media are watercolour, pastels, and oils. In his townscapes there are signs of experimentation with mixed media. This experimental work using acrylic and oil on canvas as well as pastels and watercolour on photocopied images enables him to achieve a delicate touch and flexibility for which former pupils revere him.

As a portrait artist Amofa has specialised in painting famous statesmen and royals. In 1968 his portrait of President Léopold Sédar Senghor of Senegal was sent to the Senegalese president courtesy of the Ghana News Agency, for which he received an acknowledgment from the presidential office. The same year the presence of a letter from N. S. Patrinos, a Greek patron, who wrote requesting to visit him in Kumasi on 27 January indicates something of Amofa's status in his late twenties. The following year he donated their portraits to President Houphouet-Boigny of Côte d'Ivoire, Otumfuo Sir Nana Agyeman Prempeh II, Asantehene, and a visiting Mossi king from Upper Volta (Burkina Faso). He also sent a portrait of the head of state of Niger through the *Ghanaian Times*. These public acts helped to establish Amofa's fame, to the extent that the artist is listed in the *Allgemeines Künstler Lexikon: Die bildenden Künstler aller Zeiten und Völker* (Leipzig, 1986). Three larger-than-life-size portraits made at De Afrique Arts studio in the late 1960s show Ghanaian military rulers in a style of hyperrealism: Lieutenant General Emmanuel Kwasi Kotoka and Generals Joseph Arthur Ankrah and Ignatius Kutu Acheampong. A half-nude painting from the same period depicts a black woman dressing her hair in what appears to be a flower garden.

A feature in the *People's Daily Graphic*, of 13 February 1987, describing Amofa as a forty-seven-year-old commercial and fine artist, recalled that "Mr. Alex Amofa yesterday presented a portrait of the late Osagyefo Dr Kwame Nkrumah, the first President of Ghana, to government at the Castle Osu." The work (showing the subject, in three "outlooks") was received by Mrs. Aanaa Enin, member of the Provisional National Defence Council government, and was illustrated in the paper. In certain respects Amofa's work appears to be modelled on that of a former state artist, Kofi Antubam, who like Amofa was constantly in demand, from bodies such as the Arts

Adowa demonstration. Adowa is a popular indigenous dance/genre performed at funerals and important social events, using a mixture of symbolic hand gestures and graceful body movements combined with instrumentation and call-and-response singing. Artwork by Alex Amofa, 2003. From Atta Kwami, *Kumasi Realism: An African Modernism* (London: Hurst & Co. Publishers Ltd., 2013), 212. Reprinted, with permission, from Atta Kwami, *Kumasi Realism*, copyright, Atta Kwami, 2013.

Council of Ghana or the Ministry of Culture, to represent Ghana at local or international events. Amofa was selected to represent Ghana at the 1971 International Trade Fair and the Second World Black and African Festival of Arts.

Amofa saw his art as a means to performing his philanthropic activities. He regularly mounted exhibitions for such charities as the Ghana Red Cross (as did Antubam before him in the 1950s), the National Trust Fund, and the Society of General Medical Practitioners (Ashanti Branch). In 1987 he was commissioned by the Society of General Medical Practitioners to produce work of art towards "the improvement of health delivery services in the country."

During his short lifetime Antubam imparted, through artworks, lectures, and writings, ideas on the African personality and African culture in

Ghana and abroad. Amofa, who emulates him, is also adept at promoting knowledge of Ghanaian customs through his images, which demonstrate a familiarity with the topic and factual information possibly extracted from a photograph, as in the picture *Hornblowers*, ca. 1998. The treatment of the faces closely follows Delaquis's technique. In *Adowa Demonstration*, 2002 [see accompanying figure], a closer rendition of the dancer's face does not deviate from a photographic resemblance. Amofa has explored the hornblower theme several times in different ways. The version shown in *Kumasi Junction* illustrates the sheer delight of working the white oil paint to form clouds, an abstract feature of the work. Amofa's painting boldly parades the musicians, contrasting white, yellow, red, and green adinkra cloths in a well-measured pattern.

In 1998, Amofa was commissioned by the Anglican Church to present the Stations of the Cross, which he executed with the help of his assistant Owusu Yaw. He achieves an unsettling atmosphere through a limited palette of blues and browns. The muscular soldiers wielding hammers that drive in the nails convey unusual violence for a picture destined for permanent church display. With reference to his images of these Stations, Amofa explained: "Art is more eloquent than speech, so when you paint people know your story at once. . . . Art beautifies." Regarding materials and tools and messages (visual communication), this is a significant observation by Amofa because he understood the medium of advertising.

According to Amofa, he established the Supreme Art Works at Asem, Kumasi, in 1959. He referred to an art school he had since 1961, probably relating to the one taken over from Eshun. He was building a bigger art school at Atonsu Agogo than the current one at the Supreme Art Works in Asem-Kumasi. The average duration of training is two to four years at a fee of 300,000 cedis; "I hope to bring it here." Amofa's verisimilitude is seen in certain billboard adverts and the canvas painting *Bimpeh Hill*, 1998, while his careful observation and skilful execution appear in small painted compositions of three or more figures, as shown in *The Musicians, or Hornblowers*, ca. 1998, and *A Game of Mind*, 2000. Amofa's preoccupation for rendering things as they appear leads him to abstraction, in a picture entitled *Reds and Browns after Harvest*, 2006.

Among his tools for painting, such as a set of poster colours, brushes and watercolour paper, can be found a small Instamatic camera on the coffee table in Amofa's living room. On the wall is a naturalistic painting of Otumfuo Osei Tutu II in *batakarikese* (battle dress). Another portrait of the current Asantehene painted in 2000 presents him in three different types of dress: in ceremonial battle dress, in Western suit with bow tie and appearing to be beyond gender, and in the dominant form of the king, wearing kente cloth. A respected portraitist in West Africa, Amofa has honoured contemporary Asante and Mossi kings with his work. In the past he had painted a landscape that reminded me of the work of Sam Ntiro, the Tanzanian master and diplomat. In two large paintings (*Super Peau* and *Ideal Plus*) for an Ivorian client, Amofa imbues his work with a smart painstaking approach that has become his hallmark. Amofa's naturalistic paintings have earned him the appellation "Father of Sign Painters in Kumasi."

Amofa, like Samino, has been fond of landscapes. Whereas Samino shied away from portraits, Amofa relishes them, working slowly from photographs in a delicate hand. His mixed-media pastel over black-and-white Xeroxes prove his desire to go the extra mile and take his work wherever he is pushed by his ideas. Both Samino and Amofa exhibit alongside college-based painters. In contrast to Samino, who has preferred to employ assistants on an ad hoc basis, Amofa's school has provided him with a stream of apprentices. By dint of study and hard work he has earned the respect of the younger generation of artists, who view him as a leader in sign painting. By the same token, he has adapted the model of art education from the university/college. He likes his profession and networks with fellow painters from the KNUST. . . . Amofa, widely regarded as the grand master of sign painting in Kumasi, uses his art to promote social customs and philanthropy in Ghana.

Paradigm Shift

Paul Gifford

While the number of churchgoers is steadily declining in the very parts of Europe that exported Christianity to the Gold Coast / Ghana, Christianity, in its various mutations, has grown to significant proportions, especially in Africa, Asia, and Latin America. Ghana is no exception. Faced with poverty and attendant life challenges, some Ghanaians have produced a brand of Christianity with which they identify—ironically using indigenous symbols, rituals, and musical forms they consider "devilish"—and which they hope will address their hardships. Consequently, they unabashedly resort to this "prosperity gospel" as only one of several recourses, including indigenous spiritualists, Islamic healers, and those somewhere in between. Paul Gifford, professor emeritus of religions at the University of London (SOAS), traces the development of Ghana's new Christianity in this excerpt from his monograph, exploring the pervasiveness of Christianity in Ghana and how it is being appropriated and put to local use.

The Mainline or "Orthodox"

In 1980 there were at least four recognizable strands of Ghanaian Christianity. First there were the Catholics, the biggest single church; secondly the mainline Protestant churches, the Methodist, two Presbyterian (stemming from the Bremen and Basel missions), and the much smaller Anglican; thirdly the established Pentecostals (Apostolic Church, Church of Pentecost, Christ Apostolic Church, and Assemblies of God); and fourthly the African Independent (or Initiated) Churches (AICs). The mainline churches have been of considerable significance in building the modern nation, particularly through their schools, to an extent probably unequalled in Africa. The schools—Mfantsipini, Adisadel, St. Augustine's, Prempeh, with the government-founded but very Christian Achimota (for historical reasons nearly all in Cape Coast rather than Accra)—have created Ghana's elite since the nineteenth century. This is well caught by the title of a centenary book by the distinguished academic . . . Adu Boahen, *Mfantsipim and the Making of*

Modern Ghana. Ghana's most distinguished son, the [former] UN Secretary General Kofi Annan, is a product of the Methodist Mfantsipim and, according to some public-school-conscious Ghanaians, "head prefect of the world."

The general cultural impact of Christianity is incalculable. It provided the images, metaphors, and concepts for the independence struggle, most clearly in Nkrumah's slogans like "Seek ye first the political kingdom." Another example is the Creed of his "Verandah Boys" (his followers, so called from the poverty of their living quarters): "I believe in the Convention People's Party, the opportune Savior of Ghana, and in Kwame Nkrumah its founder and leader, who is endowed with the Ghana Spirit, born a true Ghanaian for Ghana, suffering under victimizations, was vilified, threatened with deportation. He disentangled himself from the clutches of the UGCC and the same day he rose victorious with the Verandah Boys, ascended the political heights, and sitteth at the supreme head of the CPP from whence he shall demand full self-government for Ghana. I believe in freedom for all peoples, especially the New Ghana; the abolition of slavery; the liquidation of imperialism, the victorious end of our struggle, its glory and its pride, and the flourish [*sic*] of Ghana, for ever and ever." Today it is impossible to begin or end meetings of any kind without Christian prayer (in which Muslims seem ready to participate). Christian, rather than specially African, metaphors occur in public discussion. Officers of the Ghana Journalists' Association are sworn in by a bishop. Famously, Ghanaian shops are often given Christian names (Father, Son and Holy Spirit Ventures; For Christ We Live Brake and Clutch Linings; Lord of Glory Kebabs; By God's Grace Fresh Fish; Yahweh Fast Food; Holy Ghost Cosmetics; Sweet Jesus Hair Fashions). Slogans on vehicles are often Christian, even cryptic biblical references like "Dt 8.1" or "Is 41.10." The independent *Chronicle* always ran a scriptural quote along the bottom of its front page, denouncing what it considered the latest aberration of Rawlings or the NDC with quotes like "This son of ours is stubborn and rebellious. He will not obey us. He is a profligate and a drunkard" (Dt. 21.20) or "Woe to the wicked! Disaster is upon them. They will be paid back for what their hands have done" (Is. 3.II). The pervasiveness of this ethos was revealed at the Miss Ghana contest in 2001, where the contenders had not only to parade in their finery but also to answer questions on "health, education and religion," and debate among themselves whether "Mission schools be handed back to the Missions."

Ghana's mainline churches have also produced some of Africa's best-known Christians internationally: Kwesi Dickson, theologian and president of the All Africa Conference of Churches; Kwame Bediako, a theologian well known for his argument that African Christianity is no longer an import, but has been thoroughly internalized; and Mercy Amba Odu-yoye, for years at the World Council of Churches and now back in Ghana and the driving force behind the promotion of African women's theology. Besides the mainline churches' network of schools and clinics, they have also been involved in development work. Since independence they have been influential opinion-formers in political matters. They were probably most vocal against what were seen as the human rights abuses ("revolutionary justice") of the early Rawlings years. Their criticism was often sustained and courageous, and Rawlings did not disguise his antipathy towards mainline church leaders.

The mainline Protestants collaborate in a Christian Council, which is probably the best-run in Africa and as significant a national player as any such church body apart from the South African Council of Churches in the twilight of apartheid, and the Christian Council of Kenya. Even though donor funds are diminishing, this is not because of donor dissatisfaction with the Council. Through it in particular these Protestant bodies relate to and collaborate with the Catholics very closely. The Catholic-Protestant collaboration was evident in statements right from the early Rawlings years, and it gradually extended to Muslims, first the Ahmadiyya (particularly strong in Ghana) and then the traditional Muslims in FORB (Forum of Religious Bodies, very much a Christian-driven group).

If the development work of the mainline Protestants is considerable, it is dwarfed by the Catholic involvement, which is incalculable. Besides the initiatives of each diocese, Catholic Relief Services (CRS), with access to USAID money as well as American Catholic donations, is an important player on the national scene. The Catholics dominate many areas of development, from work with street children in Accra to health care in the Upper West. It must be said that development is the involvement that defines the Catholic Church in Ghana, not the human rights advocacy which characterizes them in some other parts of the world. Despite the pronouncements of the hierarchy early in the Rawlings era (when the *Catholic Standard* was banned for three years for its human rights stance), by the late 1990s they were less vocal. Some claim that under Rawlings the attempts to contribute in this way were simply counterproductive (Rawlings let it be known that he did not want to appear on the same platform as Bishop Peter Sarpong of Kumasi, who in those early years was chairman of the Catholic Justice and Peace Commission). Others say that it was becoming less necessary. Certainly, the Catholic Justice and Peace involvement is as weak as their commitment to development is strong.

The Newcomers

These mainline churches ("orthodox" is their label in Ghana) remain significant bodies. Nevertheless, in the two decades we are especially considering (1979–2002) they have in many ways been eclipsed by something quite new, the charismatic sector (here we will keep to the term "charismatic" although some in Ghana use the term "neo-Pentecostal"). . . . Everyone is aware of charismatic prayer centers, their all-night services ("All Nights"), their crusades, conventions, and Bible schools, their new buildings (or the schools, cinemas, and halls they rent), their bumper stickers and banners, and particularly the posters that everywhere advertise an enormous range of forthcoming activities. Everyone is aware of their media efforts. Above all, everyone knows of the new religious superstars Bishop Nicholas Duncan-Williams, Pastor Mensa Otabil, Bishop Charles Agyin Asare, Bishop Dag Heward-Mills—and the prophets like Salifu Amoako. If these are the most prominent or the household names, it is just as obvious that they are merely the tip of the iceberg or (to change the metaphor) the "premier division" in a multidivisional "national league." . . .

Nicholas Duncan-Williams (it is reasonably common, especially along the coast, for Ghanaians to have European names, even hyphenated ones) had led a somewhat wild youth, even stowing away twice on ships to Europe, before being converted in 1976 while in hospital after something of a breakdown. In that year he went to Benson Idahosa's Bible school in Nigeria, and on his return in 1979 founded Christian Action Faith Ministries International (CAFM), and his church Action Chapel International (ACI). . . . The church has twenty-eight branches in Ghana and abroad.

Pastor Mensa Otabil began his International Central Gospel Church (ICGC) in February 1984 in a rented hall in central Accra, and in December 1996 moved to his new church, still in the inner city. He draws about seven thousand on a Sunday to two services. His TV and radio preaching make him well known far beyond his own congregation; the church estimates that about twenty-five thousand watch his Sunday evening *Living Word* telecast. The church claims twenty-three branches in the neighborhood of Accra and about one hundred throughout Ghana.

Bishop Dag Heward-Mills, son of a Ghanaian father and Swiss mother, trained as a doctor, and his church grew out of his fellowship for medical professionals around Korle Bu Teaching Hospital. He left medical practice for full-time ministry in January 1991. His Lighthouse Cathedral is situated near the hospital, in inner Accra, but in the late 1990s the characteristic yellow signboards advertising Lighthouse Chapel branches began to appear all round the city. . . . He attracts about three thousand to his four services at his cathedral every Sunday. He claims about 120 churches in twenty-five countries.

Bishop Charles Agyin Asare was converted at the age of eighteen, attended Idahosa's Bible school in Nigeria, and returned to found in March 1987 his World Miracle Bible Church in Tamale, which had sixteen churches and an extensive ministry in the north before the ethnic disturbances there forced him in 1994 to shift his base of operations to Accra. . . . He attracts about four thousand to the four Sunday services at his headquarters, and the church (now the Word Miracle Church International, WMCI) claimed seventy-two branches in October 2000, including eleven in Accra.

Prophet Elisha Salifu Amoako was born to a poor Muslim family in Kumasi and had virtually no schooling, but as a young man he was converted and introduced to the Resurrection Power Evangelistic Ministry of the controversial Evangelist Francis Akwesi Amoako in Santasi, working in the latter's house until the evangelist was killed in a car accident in 1990. Salifu claims his mantle, hence both "Elisha" (to the evangelist's Elijah) and "Amoako." . . . On a Sunday he attracts about sixteen hundred to his one lengthy service, where the sermon is in English but much else in Twi. . . .

The other church in our premier division is Living Faith Church Worldwide, popularly known as Winners' Chapel. This is unlike the other churches just mentioned in that it was not founded by a Ghanaian, but is a branch of a Nigerian multinational based in Lagos. This was founded in September 1983 by Bishop David Oyedepo, and by 2000 had become active in thirty-eight African countries. Unlike the other churches mentioned here, Winners' in Accra is not identified with its pastor, who can be reassigned as in a mainline denomination. . . . In late 2001 it attracted about thirteen thousand to its two Sunday services.

These churches are not all the same. . . . Duncan-Williams's ACI is most obviously a faith/prosperity/health-and-wealth church . . . and Duncan-Williams has lately taken on a "spiritual warfare" emphasis. In Winners' Chapel, a general faith or health-and-wealth orientation has undergone a mutation into a concern almost exclusively for financial success. Heward-Mills's Lighthouse Chapel is characterized by a stress on church planting and lay leadership. Agyin Asare's WMCI concentrates on evangelistic and healing crusades, and although the diseases cured at these crusades would certainly be understood in terms of demonic causality, this is not greatly emphasized. By contrast, in Salifu's Alive Ministry the stress is on the demonic causality for all ills, and the remedy is the gifts of Salifu himself. Otabil is almost exclusively a teacher, with no emphasis on healing, and the demonic is hardly ever mentioned. All these strands, with their different though often compatible emphases, are part of the new charismatic revival, and illustrate at the outset the considerable range involved and the difficulty in talking about "charismatic Christianity" without qualification.

Nor are these churches the same in their clientele. They attract different categories of people. I have developed my own wildly subjective grading system based on such things as the number of Mercedes, BMWs, Pajeros, Landcruisers, and Patrols in the car park; the hairstyles and hair-coverings of the women; the number of men in formal traditional cloth; the use of English; and the obtrusiveness of mobile phones (Winners' has signs posted urging that they be switched off; Otabil's ICGC has computerized instructions flashing across a giant screen). A very rough guide to class (understood very loosely) is that if the affluent Catholic parish of Christ the King (President Kufuor's church) rates 10, Otabil's ICGC rates 9, Duncan-Williams's ACI 7.5, Winners' 7, Agyin Asare's WMCI 5.5, Heward-Mills's LCI 5, and Salifu's Jesus Alive 1.

Ghana's charismatic Christianity has not remained static. One can visualize developments in terms of waves. If for convenience we date the beginning of Accra's charismatic Christianity to around 1979, with Duncan-Williams leading the first wave, we can distinguish three further waves. The second is the teaching wave best illustrated by Otabil, the third is the miracle healing introduced by Agyin Asare, and the fourth and last the prophetic exemplified by Salifu. A complicating factor is the tendency for each succeeding wave to affect all existing churches, making "pure" or "non-hybrid" types hard to find. For example, Duncan-Williams's ACI is still best seen as a faith-gospel church, but even it had to advertise its 2000 annual convention as a "prophetic" convention—by 2000 *everything* had to be prophetic. Churches have not been influenced to the same degree, but the tendency is undeniable.

The Funeral as a Site for Choreographing Modern Identities in Contemporary Ghana

Esi Sutherland-Addy

Death in the indigenous Ghanaian worldview does not signify an end of life. Rather, it marks the transition from the physical to the ancestral or spiritual world. To help an individual make this transition successfully, certain rites of passage are performed. These rites vary depending on the status of the person making the transition to the realm of the ancestors. Consequently, funerals are occasions that highlight various aspects of Ghanaian culture, many of which, understandably, are performed only during such occasions. Interestingly, funerals are also opportunities to observe evolving trends and foreign influences on local cultural practices. In the following scholarly article excerpt, author and African studies professor Esi Sutherland-Addy takes readers through some of the various stages and significance of the funeral ceremony of an Akuapem royal in the Eastern Region of Ghana and identifies some of these "encroaching" changes.

Funerals in Ghana are elaborate commemorative ceremonies that not only mark the existential transition of the dead, but also crucially provide the opportunity for the reaffirmation and negotiation of complex social relations, political structures, and ontological identities. The death of a traditional ruler destabilizes these carefully calibrated systems and must necessarily offer the occasion for the expression of pathos that goes over and beyond the private mourning of the loss of an individual. It must also be the occasion for the restitution of balance through communally significant ritual. As the embodiment of the dominant communal ethos among a large majority of the peoples of Ghana, the traditional ruler is given a funeral that is the apogee of these commemorative ceremonies.

Furthermore, as a result of the chief's role as custodian of the arts and repository of its classical dimensions, his court is meant to display these arts and to engender innovation. At no time is this expected to be more apparent than during funeral celebration, when a full panoply of courtly performance and visual culture is in evidence. This article explores the powerful conjuncture between the institution of chieftaincy as custodian of the traditions and culture of the peoples of Ghana, and the intense funeral ceremonies through which many of these traditions are performed.

The following discussion is based on a multidisciplinary study conducted by the Institute of African Studies (IAS), University of Ghana, on the funeral celebration of Nana Wereko Ampem II, chief of Amanokrom in the Akwapim area of the Eastern Region, and former chancellor of the University of Ghana. During his lifetime, he straddled the global, national, and community spheres. . . .

The Funeral as Event

The funeral of Oyeeman Wereko Ampem II upheld the basic architecture of a royal funeral. It consisted of preparatory activities such as official announcements to appropriate relatives and associates, preburial activities such as the presentation of bath items, the lying in state, rites of separation, burial rites, and postburial family gathering.

Death in the ethnological present is seen as a journey to *asamando* (land of the dead). The ruler needs to be equipped with several items for the comfort of his journey. To maintain his identity and status, he must be dressed in full regalia reflecting his wealth and dignity. His colleague chiefs are expected to pay homage and swear to him in a predeparture ceremony bidding him farewell. His maternal and paternal relations, as well as his subjects and associates, do the same. The atmosphere is militaristic in character as he is the commander-in-chief of the traditional army. The *asafo* (warrior) groups come out in full battle regalia, firing musketry to salute and bid him farewell.

Indeed, for the success of this momentous event in which many interest groups wished to be seen to have participated, several formal and informal negotiations took place to allocate space, time, and roles. Physical preparations were very much in evidence. The palace was painted, roads cleaned, canopies mounted, and chairs arranged. A key aspect of the physical preparations of the funeral was the construction of a set in the ground-floor room of the two-story palace. This was in the form of a farmstead made of thatch and branches. Plantain and cocoa trees with lamps hanging from them were placed on the set. Palm wine pots and other items used by the chief were in place. In this model farmstead some attendants were seated beside an effigy of Oyeeman.

Generally, the impression created was that one was entering into a forest

The funeral procession for Nana Kwabena Mensa, *ɔbosomfoɔhene* (head indigenous healer) for Taa Mensa and the Techiman Traditional State, 2008. Photograph by Kwasi Konadu, 2008.

glade—a place of transition between the known and unknown worlds. In contrast, the top floor of the building was decorated with vases of exquisitely arranged flowers, a critical cultural innovation, in preparation to receive the ornate bier on which Oyeeman would eventually be placed. This was accompanied by an exhibition of the attire and insignia of the social, academic, and professional groups to which he belonged. The contrast between the decor on the two floors of the palace was only one example of the juxtaposition of aspects of the chief's life that was to recur throughout the funeral and that made the event so interesting as a site for observing and seeking to define modernities in contemporary Ghana.

Performing Modernities

The funeral provided the opportunity for observing different situations in which persons in various capacities engaged with multiple influences and initiated or participated in acts that maintained the spirit of heritage traditions and sought to create an amalgam of cultural expression. Modernity was played out in the most unlikely of circumstances. For example, quietly in the background, but in full control of the adornment of the chamber and the body, was the wife of Oyeeman, Mrs. Leticia Omaboe. In an interview after the funeral, she described with disarming charm her steely determination to ensure that her husband's tastes were respected. Again, the royal family of Amanokrom showed appreciation and deference to the immediate family of Oyeeman, who, during his life, had gone beyond the bounds of duty to support him to cater to the people of the traditional area in many ways. Thus they permitted Mrs. Omaboe to take a central role in a set of activities from which she would have been strictly proscribed according to traditional norms.

The performance of the funeral reached a crescendo on Friday when the burial ceremonies began. The state officially participated in these burial ceremonies, which more than any other element demonstrated the careful efforts of the funeral committee to create a modern Ghanaian funeral ceremony. The day began with the performance of drum poetry by the *atumpan* drums sounding *damirifa due* (condolences) and assembling of the elders. As the morning wore on, *fontomfrom* (royal) drumming and dancing was done in honor of Oyeeman and exquisitely executed symbolic movements connoted individual grief in unique ways. The *gyaase* and chiefs assembled and various delegations of government institutions, public and private organizations, and diplomats arrived, filed past the body and got seated for the burial service. The *gyaase, akyeame*, and family received the president, government officials, and dignitaries who filed past the body. On this occasion, a book of condolences set on a table decorated in kente cloth at the foot of the stairs leading to the room in which Oyeeman was lying embedded a European norm into the ceremony.

The Friday church service was attended by President J. A. Kufuor and Vice President Alhaji Aliu Mahama. It was officiated by high-ranking clergy from the Christian community, including the moderator of the Presbyterian Church of Ghana, the Anglican archbishop of the province of West Africa, the metropolitan Catholic archbishop of Accra, the presiding bishop of the Methodist Church of Ghana, and several other clergy from other parts of the country. The military band, the Akwapim Mass Presbyterian Church Choir, and other singing groups were in attendance. During this service, the Oyeeman's eulogy was read, as were tributes, including one for and on behalf of the people and government of Ghana. The program was designed as a formal cosmopolitan one which, when performed, communicated that Nana Wereko Ampem was a prominent national and international figure in public service, education, and international business.

In the middle of the night on Saturday, the final parting ceremonies were done, involving only the major chiefs and courtiers. The body was then moved to the burial grounds shrouded in secrecy. This was followed on

Sunday, 5 February, by a Christian thanksgiving service attended by a large congregation, which was held on the Amanokrom football field. Clearly, since Oyeeman had led a multifaceted life, both spiritually and physically, the funeral rites combined, with some dexterity, Akan traditional rites and Christianity. There is no doubt that Oyeeman's power and influence at the national level and his international reputation served as a mitigating factor for any misgivings the Presbyterian Church may have had against the ceremonies as a whole. These accommodations reached between the mainstream denominations of Christian churches and traditional institutions have developed over the years in Ghana and come to light at ceremonies such as those enacted at Oyeeman Wereko Ampem's funeral.

At this stage, an analytical eye might be cast back. The funeral of Nana Wereko Ampem was an extended performance symbolizing a complex system of values, a representation of historical alliances, and an interpretation of the impact of one man and his life. Various categories of people and their interests came into play at this royal burial, turning the funeral into a site where centers of power were being negotiated and balanced constantly.

Legitimacy, pedigree, and even sacredness are conferred by sticking to ancient ceremonial etiquette, modes of dress, and ritual procedure. In this respect, every effort was made by key players and the general public to observe these during the proceedings. This included the opening of the funeral in the middle of the night by paramount chiefs of the Akim and Akwapim states who are direct relatives of Wereko Ampem II.

The traditional priestess who cleansed the town just before the event began invited the evil spirits to take the sacrifice offered and to spare the people of the town and their visitors the tragedy of their greed. These words of exhortation were meant to be performative and to take effect for the duration of the festival. Again, all manner of regalia and apparel were brought out on the occasion, including skins, bark, and vines. These added to the mystique that was being carefully built around a personality who was deemed to be deserving of the highest honor.

On the other hand, there was an apparent snob value in the throw back to the precolonial. The most striking example found in one of the processions was the *bede*—a loosely woven palm frond receptacle in which kola nuts used to be carried. There were hundreds of nuts in the receptacle so the presenter could use the measure *bede ma* (one full *bede*) not symbolically, but literally. This was all the more striking because most donations of kola nuts would consist of fifty to one hundred nuts. Indeed, the language of presentation was full of reference to archaisms, such as in the measures of drinks or sums of money.

That modernities in Ghana cannot be discussed without mentioning the influence of European culture on Oyeeman's life was apparent in the various facets of the event ranging from church services in the English language to the adoption of modern management practice in the planning of the funeral and event managers in its execution. Apparel was again an important marker of European influence. Representatives of banks, lodges, and the diplomatic corps wore their European suits to make their identity distinct as part of the establishment of their elite organizations. As chiefs were indeed leaders of armies in the past, guns ranging from muskets to up-to-date rifles were in evidence.

Ghanaian society has made major adaptations and imported or borrowed culture. To name two obvious adaptations: schnapps and the cotton wax print, both originally imported from Holland, have been adopted, over the years, for use in a variety of ways, which the original manufacturers could not have imagined. During the funeral, schnapps was the drink of choice for complementing the numerous official announcements of the news of the funeral made by official delegations dispatched by the bereaved family. Likewise, all the delegations officially received at the palace paved the way for their interaction with the traditional authorities with schnapps. The drink was used repeatedly in the pouring of libation and in that sense became a medium of expression in important communication processes of the event. Turning to wax prints, the funeral was literally clad in a display of dozens of designed, color-coded cloths that were changed to suit the stage of the funeral and the status of the wearer. The varieties of white material with black motifs worn on the Sunday following the burial for the thanksgiving service provided a vivid visual marker of the transition from a total absorption with the rituals of death to a return to normalcy.

The United States, Ghana, and Oil: Global and Local Perspectives

Tom C. McCaskie

Gold from the Gold Coast / Ghana was part of the trans-Saharan trade, signaling the region's significance in a globalized economy that involved parts of Africa, Europe, and the Mediterranean. Since then, major European states have competed with each other for influence and control in the region, at one point extracting human captives that proved more profitable than gold. By the twentieth century, Ghana continued to be of global economic importance as the biggest producer of cocoa until eclipsed by Côte d'Ivoire—together, both countries account for about 70 percent of the world's cocoa. Ghana's continued global economic significance now lies in the 2007 discovery of "black gold"—oil. In the following excerpt from a scholarly article, Tom C. McCaskie, professor of African history at the University of London (SOAS), considers local Ghanaian and wider global reactions over the potentially valuable oil deposits in the context of Ghana–United States relations; local debates conditioned by ideas of providence, prosperity, and Pentecostal Christianity; and China's growing interest in Ghana.

Ghana, the Oil Industry, and the "New Gulf"

In 2004 the Halbouty Lecture was delivered to the AAPG's annual meeting in Dallas by Brian Maxted of the Texas-based independent oil company Kosmos Energy. . . . In the 1990s, declared Maxted, 40 percent of new oilfields with a potential yield of more than 500 million barrels were found in "deep water," and 30 percent of these were located off the Atlantic coast of western Africa. This was the "New Gulf," an area of supply for U.S. industries and consumers where extraction problems paled by comparison with those confronting the oil business in the Middle East since 9/11 and the invasion of Iraq.

Like all smaller independent oil exploration companies, Kosmos Energy tries to spread its risk. Founded in Dallas in 2003, its first contract to explore and drill was signed with Ghana in 2004. Under the terms of this seven-year lease it created a local affiliate called Kosmos Energy (Ghana) to operate its 86.5 percent working interest in the offshore West Cape Three Points Block. Its Ghanaian partners were Ghana National Petroleum Company (GNPC), a parastatal with a 10 percent participation share, and the EO Group of Ghana, with a 3.5 percent interest.

Ghana's Oil

Ghana has long felt lack of oil hindered its development, a view that has become more salient in very recent years as oil has climbed towards US$100 a barrel. However, lack of indigenous oil resources has also had an impact on the national psyche. In 1983 Ghana was at its lowest economic point. The country was bankrupt, and raging bush fires burned crops, creating shortages and hunger. In the midst of all this Nigeria decided to expel all Ghanaian economic immigrants. . . . There I talked with the late John Hagan, who had been put in charge of the relief supplies by the Rawlings government. In private he vented his anger at the Nigerians, saying that they behaved in a high-handed manner only because they possessed oil wealth . . . The world, he stated, ran on oil and Ghana had none. God, he concluded, had abandoned his country.

Many others in the parlous 1980s believed that God had withdrawn his blessings from Ghana. It was then that Ghanaians first turned to Christian Pentecostalist, charismatic, and other sectarian churches. This is a well-studied phenomenon. Of relevance here are two interlinked features of the "new Christianity." These might be described as the interface between beliefs about prosperity and providence. The new churches held out the promise of prosperity to believers, in extreme cases preaching a Prosperity Gospel in which riches were represented as the birthright or heritage of congregants. The idea of prosperity was mixed together with that of providence (which had a long history in Ghana's nineteenth-century missionary churches and their local successors). The "new Christianity" argued that prosperity would descend on God's people through the work of divine providence. That is, faith would encourage the Lord's providence to bestow the blessings of prosperity on Ghana. . . .

Ghana's blighted promise, its reduced international status, its tangled history of social, political, and economic underachievement, and its faith in a prosperity granted through the workings of divine providence shaped immediate response to the announcement of the first oil find in June 2007. In the Castle at Osu, Accra, President Kufuor gave an impromptu speech to the media with a glass of champagne in one hand and a glass of crude oil from the Mahogany-1 well in the other. He expressed "joy" that he would "go down in history" as the president during whose tenure oil was found. Oil, he said, was "a shot in the arm," and Ghana was now "going to fly." He said Ghana was going "to really zoom, accelerate," and "if everything works, which I pray will happen," then in only five years his country would "truly" emerge as an "African Tiger." "Ghana will succeed," he stated, "because this is our destiny." By October 2007, with a national election just over a year away, destiny had become more narrowly defined. Speaking at Asamankese, President Kufuor told his audience that God had given oil to the NPP "to be presented to Ghanaians."

Ghanaians echoed and enlarged on these opinions. The tabloid *Accra Daily Mail* produced the stark headline "Thank God. Oil at last. Thank God." Churches held services of thanksgiving for the discovery of oil. On the Internet, now an important element in Ghanaian life, people thanked God for blessing Ghana with oil. In many cases, commentators wove partisan politics into the workings of divine providence. God, so it was said, hid the oil from "Devil" Rawlings and his NDC and only chose to reveal it when the godly Kufuor and his NPP came to power. Finally, on 3 July 2007, GNPC Managing Director M. Boateng declared that studies showed Ghana had a "huge oil potential" of 1.23 billion tons of oil, currently worth US$560 billion, and that the Mahogany-1 strike was only the "tip of the iceberg." However, this public euphoria could not and did not last.

A national debate began almost immediately about what it might mean for Ghana to possess oil. One strand of this, again using providential language, took up the theme of oil as "curse" rather than "blessing." African oil states and Middle Eastern producers were brought into play to argue the point. Some Ghanaians said oil was a "curse," and even termed it "Satan's black gold," for it promised improvement and well-being but instead brought mismanagement, greed, and corruption. It was all at once a seductive temptation and a finite resource, and those who came to depend on it were mortgaging themselves to "a false God." Others, notably including President Kufuor and his NPP government, argued that oil was a divine "blessing" and that the key to its use lay in successful and transparent management. Kufuor declared: "Oil is money, and we need money to do the schools, the roads, the hospitals. If you find oil, you manage it well, can you complain about that?" NPP Information Minister K. Bartels stated that government was fully aware of oil mismanagement in other countries, and he was assembling inspection teams to visit and learn from such states so that, and again note the language, "we don't fall into the same pit."

Ghana's Energy Policy and Security

In May 2007 London's influential *Economist* Intelligence Unit produced a report on Ghana's energy policy. It noted that in 2006 the failure of the rains created a serious and still-continuing drought. This had severe implications. By March 2007 the water levels in Lake Volta were nearing an all-time low. Hydroelectric output from the Akosombo Dam was reduced to a point where supply was in shortfall and could no longer meet demand. The energy-intensive Volta Aluminium Company (VALCO) was forced to shut down its operations. The Electricity Company of Ghana was forced into extensive load shedding. Both power and water were in short supply. In addition, the infrastructure of both industries was ageing and beset by maintenance problems. The report said that the NPP government was looking at nuclear energy and reverse-osmosis water desalination plants, but concluded these were not realistic solutions. It urged investment in more orthodox solutions like additional dams and larger thermal plants to use gas provided by the West African Gas Pipeline when this finally came online.

In 2006–7 Kufuor's government faced first drought and then flood. Public misery was widespread and anger was palpable. Apart from spending money, and claiming it had things under control, the government's tactic was to ask for patience and to point to a brighter future. One item in that future was the West African Gas Pipeline (WAGP), an ambitious but environmentally controversial project. In 2004, the World Bank gave guarantees for the building of WAGP, a 681-kilometer onshore-offshore gas pipeline to run from Nigeria via Benin and Togo to Ghana. The gas itself was to be sourced from the Escravos area of the Western Niger Delta. This was a very expensive project. Capital costs were US$590 million, with running costs over twenty years of another US$110 million. The consortium contracted to build WAGP was led by Chevron and Royal Dutch Shell, which owned 59 percent of the equity between them. The four African states involved were minority shareholders, with Nigeria's National Petroleum Corporation holding the largest African stake, 25 percent. WAGP was originally scheduled to reach Tema in Ghana by December 2006. However, construction delays at Cotonou in Benin meant that completion was rescheduled for December 2007. . . .

Another controversial future energy source was the Bui Dam, to be constructed on the Black Volta River near Banda in the Ahafo region of west-central Ghana. This project was first mooted in the 1960s when the UK firm of Brown and Root was contracted to draw up site plans. For cost reasons, the Bui Dam remained unbuilt over the next forty years, and in 2001 the new

NPP government shelved the project. Then, in 2005, higher international energy tariffs persuaded government that building the Bui Dam was now cost-efficient in terms of energy self-sufficiency. An international outcry ensued, for it was argued that the dam would have disastrous consequences for the plant and animal ecology of the Bui National Park. The World Bank refused to underwrite the project. In 2006, however, President Kufuor went on a state visit to China. President Hu Jintao agreed to support the building of the Bui Dam by the Chinese companies Sino-Hydro and Exim Bank at an estimated cost of US$600 million. The Bui Dam was designed to generate 400 megawatts of hydroelectricity. The project has now gone ahead, although fears have been expressed that its output will be expensive and that, just as at Akosombo, it will mean the relocation of numbers of local people.

These two projects illustrate the dilemma facing an African country like Ghana in the global power struggles of the early twenty-first century. Essentially, WAGP is funded and operated by a U.S.-based oil multinational and its partners. The Bui Dam is a point of entry for China and its investment institutions into Ghana. On the one hand, Kufuor has to deal with the ongoing consequences of agreements that first bound Ghana to the World Bank and Western companies in the mid-1980s. On the other hand, he has said that Ghana is "serious in its desire to deepen its relations with China." This is a tightrope, and one forced on the NPP and any future government in Accra by a lack of national investment capital. This is the context in which Ghana's oil was discovered. If hopes and expectations of that resource are realized, then Ghanaians may well see an upturn in their economic well-being. If they do, however, it will be within the larger arena of international business competition and, now, US–China relations. Perhaps the rapid deflation of the national euphoria that greeted the first oil find in June 2007 was brought about, in part at least, by the sober recognition of the price that might be paid for becoming an object of international desire within the "New Gulf."

Conclusion: Ghana in the Here and Now

The discovery of significant oil potential offshore of Ghana has served to reinforce U.S. strategic interest in the country as a pivot of the "New Gulf." Ghana is now a civilian democracy, with two elections and a successful handover of power in its recent past. It is run by an elite that supports President Kufuor's "Golden Age of Business" and that increasingly educates its children at American universities. The United States has become a destination of choice for Ghanaians, and the diaspora there is ever larger. Ghana seems a long way from the *marxisant* politics of the early 1980s, and it now ticks many of the boxes on transparency and rights so beloved of U.S. legislators. It is or seems to be a "natural" ally of U.S. government and business, with the future of Ghana's oil reserves cementing that relationship. Washington has no interest in seeing China's presence in Africa extended to Ghana. As yet, Chinese influence and investment are still straws in the Ghanaian wind, but it is safe to conclude that the United States is monitoring the evolving situation closely.

Obama's Visit as a Signifier of Ghanaians' "Colonial Mentality"

Kwabena Akurang-Parry

The influence of industrialized countries on the cultural practices of Ghana is quite profound. Not surprisingly, these influences often come at the detriment of maintaining core cultural ideas and behaviors, as even the custodians of culture often go too far in imitating foreign cultural practices. The use of schnapps in the performance of libation and dressing in imported Dutch wax prints or Western suits at culturally significant occasions are just a few examples. Ghana's arbitrary attachment to cultural imports of its colonial past further complicates this. The general picture that emerges, then, is that the Ghanaian tends to extol all things foreign. In the following op-ed excerpt, Kwabena Akurang-Parry, professor of African and world history at Shippensburg University, addresses this tendency by giving examples of practices that seem to serve as harbingers of "cultural genocide."

"The only thing that Ghanaians probably do better than everybody else on our planet is to adopt a foreign culture and try to outdo the originators of that culture. The extent of our addiction to cultures other than our own is simply mindboggling." Quoted from Nana Akwasi Twumasi, "Ghanaians and Wedding: Are We Losing Our Mind?," Ghanaweb Feature Article of Sunday, 23 August 2009. Using President Barack Obama's visit as my unit of analysis, framed around and illuminated by relatable everyday stories and experiences, I offer some stories and incidences as reflections on Ghanaians' huge appetite for all things foreign and distaste for our own way of life, indeed, what we may conceptualize as pathways of cultural genocide. Let me offer a brief caveat: the stories and experiences offered here, exemplified by Obama's visit, do not present any precise chronology of our travels along pathways of cultural genocide. Rather, I have stitched together everyday experiences and stories to provide a cohesive account of what Kwame Nkrumah, among other things, theorized as neocolonialism and which Adu Boahen characterized as "colonial mentality"; indeed, both mirror the ways that Ghanaians dramatized Obama's visit. In sum, we are so taken in by foreign things to the detriment of our own culture and development as a nation. As a result, Ghana is now a petri dish in which the nurturing of one of the debilitating viruses of our time occurs: a tide of sustained self-fulfilling marginalization of Ghanaians and, by extension, Africans as a whole.

Excepting the attainment of independence in 1957, there is no doubt that no single celebratory event had focused so much global attention on Ghana as Obama's recent visit to Ghana. Undoubtedly, most Ghanaians appreciated Obama's visit; it made us proud, at least, knowing that Ghana is at the forefront of progress and stability in Africa. For those of us tucked away overseas, our gingerly hope is that the ways that the worldwide media showcased Ghana would enable our foreign hosts, at least, to fathom the spatial location of Ghana during casual conversations. In sum, the visit embodies moments of great possibilities and watersheds of excellence for the African world which Ghana championed during the heyday of the fruitful, empowering Nkrumah epoch.

At another level, and indeed the focal point of this essay, Obama's visit illustrates the tyranny of neocolonialism and how it has gripped the mind-set of Ghanaians in farcical ways. During the visit, state-sponsored special cloth imprinted with Obama's image went on sale. I would hazard that Ghana is the only place in the world where this could occur. Overnight, the American flag dominated masts everywhere and completely eclipsed the flag of Ghana. Schoolchildren, as in the colonial era, were forced to stand in the intimidating sun to honor the presence of Obama as if he was a provincial governor on tour of duty in a backwater colonized nineteenth-century world. Also, prepubescent females adorned with colorful traditional costumes flaunted their budding feminine assets as they danced to the de/cadence of politicized drums to welcome Obama. Unashamedly, members of Parliament and government officials, like children chasing butterflies in a playground, struggled among themselves to capture photos of Obama with their cell phones. Again, this is something that could only happen in Ghana! Our chiefs/kings were not about to be outperformed in the political theatrics that heralded Obama's visit. For instance, some chiefs rebuilt their durbar grounds, renovated palaces, regroomed their political space, pressured the government to renovate dilapidated state buildings, retuned their state drums, compelled *asafo mma* [so-called companies] to practice their craft, etc. Sad to say that in the end, some of the chiefs did not even get the chance to see Obama. Above all, Ghanaians hoped that Obama would bring a magic wand to solve all their problems, indeed, what one commentator aptly called our dependency syndrome. In nursery school, one of the

One of the many billboards in the Ghanaian capital of Accra signaling *akwaaba* (welcome) to President Obama on his visit to Ghana in summer 2009. Photograph by Clifford Campbell, Accra, 2009.

rhymes that was planted in our young, fertile minds was the best comes from the West. In the long term, such nursery rhymes have come to stay and are manifesting in several prophetic ways through our own agencies and in/actions.

Simply put, it was expected that Ghanaians would showcase their proverbial hospitality during Obama's visit, and we did, but went overboard, hence the whole visit, to use a metaphorical stretch, was like the Second Coming of Christ in Ghana. Not surprisingly, an ordinary president of a backwater American college who visited Ghana years ago as a tourist was able to gain audience with the president of Ghana! A Ghanaian professor plying his trade in America took his students on a study-abroad trip to Ghana. At the Kotoka International Airport, Ghanaian immigration officers bypassed the grey-haired Ghanaian professor, who had introduced the group as his study-abroad students from America to the immigration officers, and asked the white teenage students, to their surprise, about who was their real team leader.

For the sake of analogical clarity, let us summon additional hyperbolic stories as our embroidery for emphasis. Ghanaians now celebrate Mother's Day, Father's Day, Children's Day, Grand-Parents' Old-Age Days, etc. There may be Chinese Dog's Day in the pipeline. Very soon there will be Japanese Chopsticks Day and Italian Pizzas Day. The American flag and the Union Jack will soon become our national uniform! Valentine's Day is now our national festival; paradoxically, we have abandoned our indigenous practices like storytelling, *bragoru*, and *dipo*, which, among others, taught the youth about love, respect, reciprocity, and duty. Yes, we have latched onto Valentine's Day, which promotes capitalistic, orgiastic behavior. Certainly there is nothing wrong with celebrating these "global" days. The problem is that in the process of embracing foreign cultures and values, we continue to marginalize and abandon our local languages, communal values, festivals, ancestor reverence, rites of passage, and so on that sustain our collective well-being and ontological harmony.

Indeed, at the center stage of our looming cultural genocide is our fascination for and unquestioned acceptance of all things foreign, especially "white superiority." In 1997, I was traveling from Sekondi-Takoradi to Accra when we were told that a portion of the Beposo Bridge on the route had partially collapsed so all vehicles on both sides of the bridge had to stop for the necessary repairs to be made. After we had waited for several hours, a team of engineers arrived to repair the bridge. I made my way to the bridge to see what was being done and heard my nickname, "Agoro," echo off the bridge in the dimly lit environment. To my utmost delight, three of the engineers were my schoolmates at the Presbyterian Boys' Secondary School (PRESEC), Legon. But the happy encounter was quickly snuffed out of my system when I realized that the Ghanaian engineers were being supervised by two white men. Ironically, even in building local bridges (pun intended), we have to use the superior expertise of foreigners!

There are Ghanaians who have never been to the Ukraine, but have adopted some affected Ukrainian accents! American slangs are highly prized in Ghana. Just pick up the phone in the US of A, God's own country in the estimation of Ghanaians, to speak with Ghanaians in Ghana and you would come across concocted American accents! Someone asked me whether I was calling from the US of A because my accent was still Ghanaianized, but before I could respond, his adopted American accent departed from him like the sun parting company with darkness! Our television and radio hosts mimic foreign accents as if they have had plastic surgery to replace their Ghanaian tongues. I recently watched a Ghanaian film that has a bumbling "Americanized" character who kept calling everyone in the film "Nigger" this or that. Ghanaians like to imitate anything foreign, and we often overdo it: the fact of the matter is that even African American comedians and "gangster" rappers who deployed the N-word in recent times have now abandoned it. Rather surprisingly, the film was made in 2009.

In 2006, an Akuapem scholar eulogized his deceased father in Akuapem Twi, spicing his words with proverbs and symbols of local color in the hope that the assembled mourners would admire his "native" eloquence. But in the end, he disappointed the teeming mourners who had come to feed on a menu of American accent(s) conjured by their native son who teaches in America. The fact that he was literate in Akuapem Twi did not matter! What would have mattered was his use of "gonna," "wanna," "hey men," "ya knaw," even the N-word, etc.! You bet the disappointed family queried their son about why he had used Akuapem Twi in elegizing his deceased father, and he told them that Westerners spoke their own languages at funerals. The son's brief, but apt response, was paradoxically conceived as a signifier of too much education, and in the parlance of Ghanaians, he was "too known."

Not surprisingly during the celebration of the fiftieth anniversary of Ghana's independence President J. A. Kufuor entombed himself in some Italian-made and carpenter-built suit, with a flaunting nineteenth-century Victorian imperial waistcoat to match. It was as if President Kufuor wanted to remind the former imperialists, euphemistically called "colonial powers," that Ghanaians still looked up to them for leadership! The irony of it all is that foreign dignitaries adorned the Ghanaian kente! Well, on that day, Nkrumah turned in his grave and confronted the African elites that are now hegemonizing and privileging Western cultures! Anyone who has seen photos of our founding fathers and mothers, whose period spanned the golden age of decolonization from the late 1940s to about 1966, when the overthrow of Nkrumah by the CIA-induced homegrown forces dimmed the splendid history of emergent Ghana, would admire their luxuriant batakari, agbaja, kente, ntama, etc. Today, our parliamentarians, TV personalities, government officials, and even armed robbers show their stolen wealth and putative class by adòrning ovenlike woolen suits in spite of the mighty unrepentant sun that bakes Mother Earth in Ghana.

In order to develop, we have to source inspiration and empowerment from our indigenous cultures to serve as counterhegemonic philosophies. Indeed, we have to figuratively peel off the retrogressive wrinkles of neocolonialism and see Western cultures as mere compasses, devoid of divined self-fulfilling maps that always show the way to progress. Certainly, all societies are dynamic and go through phases of change predicated on renewal or decay and defined by the agency of continuity and discontinuity. Some Ghanaian sociologists and ethnographers, including Kofi A. Busia, G. K. Nukunya, J. M. Assimeng, Peter Akwasi Sarpong, and Kofi Asare Opoku, have shown that societies gain from diffusion of innovations and ideas that are osmotic worldwide at any given time, but that care is needed to sift through the various webs of change. For example, China and Japan have done remarkably well by plucking some good ideas from dominant, hegemonic cultures, but have also had the nationalistic capacity to reject fruits that are distasteful on the local tongue. For their part, African states and societies eagerly assimilate foreign influences which our neo/colonized mind-sets epitomize as Western values, synonymous with "civilization" and progress.

Oftentimes and rather paradoxically, the most educated people among us are the ones that construct and champion the pathways of cultural genocide. As noted, Boahen problematized this when he concluded: "But the last and the most serious negative impact of colonialism has been psychological . . . colonial mentality among educated Africans in particular and also among the populace in general." In sum, African states and societies continue to experience the effects of the Black holocaust–Atlantic Slave trade; European colonialism; what Kwame Nkrumah ably framed as neocolonialism; and now facets of hegemonic globalization beamed to Africans via Hollywood and the Internet, to mention a few. These avenues of domination, however defined, have enticed Africans to engage in self-depreciation. Indeed, the evidence suggests that Africans have internalized the inferior status imputed to them by Arabs and Euro-Americans. We would be stating the obvious by concluding that the upswing of "colonial mentality" of Ghanaians today appears to be more gripping than it was at the dawn of independence in the late 1940s.

Certainly due to the tyranny of space, we can't recount every story or incidence of cultural hegemony and its output of African self-depreciation—or, in fact, even self-hatred, which may be a variation on the above. Here and now, it is well to restate that there is nothing wrong with borrowing from other cultures. No society is static. In fact, change is a part of the human condition. Today, the processes of diffusion of innovations, ideas, cultures, etc. have been made easier via globalization, technology, and rapid travel. What is wrong is our collective failure to look deeper into our ontological pot so that we can retain what would make our society more workable. We are hastily dismissing our way of life, while happily borrowing other people's cultures even in some crusading and championing ways. The irony is that non-Africans look down upon African cultures: for example, local media accounts illustrate that the Chinese and Lebanese in Ghana think that they are better than Ghanaians. Perhaps those foreigners have come to learn that Ghanaians/Africans cherish foreign cultures and look down upon an African way of life. We need to frame a coherent empowering agenda for our cultural renewal.

Mobile Phones and Our Cultural Values

Kwesi Yankah

*Human cultures invariably and to certain degrees adopt from each other, though the conditions under which such adoptions occur often shape the tensions between existing and imported cultural ideas. In Ghana, European (specifically British) views and values have infiltrated foundational cultural wisdom and the practices that flowed from it. Imported liquor rather than locally produced alcohol (*akpeteshie*) is ubiquitous in the widespread performance of libation rituals. Likewise, the mobile phone, while greatly improving communication in a country without a wired infrastructure, encroaches on certain customary norms relating to the protocol of communication among a composite people who intractably cling to culturally conditioned communicative practices such as slightly bowing in front of a parent, elder, or "traditional" official. The excerpt that follows is from a keynote address by Kwesi Yankah, renowned linguistics professor and president of Central University College in Ghana, where he explores some of these issues in context of a marked increase in the use of mobile phones in the country.*

The notion that civilization must come from abroad pervaded Africa at the dawn of independence, as was made clear in the expositions of clergymen of the Gold Coast, like Attoh Ahuma, who, though proud of African culture, saw in Westernization the way out of darkest Africa. "The impenetrable jungle around us," he said, "is not darker than the primeval forest of the human mind uncultured." Thus Africa had to emerge from the savage backwoods and come into the open where nations were made. One area that underwent modernization was communication: an attempt was made to supplant or pluralize the legacy of indigenous language and face-to-face communication, highly cherished in Africa. Modern norms would seek to move Africa from an oral to a chirographic society, and to a world of print and mass media.

The issue becomes compounded by highly advanced systems of information technology that relocate the physical world into cyberspace and transmute the vast boundaries of the world into an electronic village. The move has been towards the globalization of culture, through the penetration of sovereign boundaries with an avalanche of uncensored Euro-Western values, all in the name of global sense of free speech, and rights of access to information. . . .

Custodians of Culture

Among the domains where the mobile phone culture has penetrated, I would like to highlight a few significant ones, to signal the extent to which the very core of indigenous tradition appears to have been permeated. I am referring to the following categories of people:

1) Those for whom privacy of communication, and general inaccessibility, is crucial for the effective exercise of their traditional responsibilities.
2) Custodians of our traditions, those responsible for preserving cultural values.
3) Those who conduct important rituals requiring intensity of silence.

The mobile phone by its very nature intrudes upon privacy and would ideally be avoided by functionaries whose duties are most effectively performed with minimum accessibility. I refer, for example, to traditional rulers, access to whom is normally restricted by a series of traditional protocol and rigid formal procedure. As a rule, the chief is not directly accessible to the public. Communication with him is routed through an intermediary, who receives and manipulates the message before relaying the information to its final destination. Partly owing to the crucial need to preserve the dignity of chieftaincy as an institution and avoid its vulgarization through direct exposure to mundane affairs, the Constitution has debarred chiefs from actively participating in politics, lest he compromise his neutrality and generally limited exposure to the hazards of worldly affairs.

Secondly, from time immemorial chiefs have been the custodians of tradition and are often the last bastion to be overcome by disruptive influences on tradition. Today, the mobile phone culture has virtually pervaded the chieftaincy institution. In places almost all chiefs and subchiefs have mobile phones, and use them regularly, sometimes receiving and transmitting messages while at serious meetings. And this is sometimes gleefully done without apologies, and would often demonstrate the wide network of contacts an individual has in the world of business. Sometimes, as soon as a phone rung, a chief would quickly exit and receive it; other times he would remain seated and take the phone call.

One chief in Ga told me the phone culture has caught on with his fetish priests, who all have mobile phones tugged in their pockets, even while conducting important rituals at the palace. But due to the disruptive propensities of the phones, he often announces that all phones must be turned off before any meeting commences. Even though the instruction would normally create inconvenience, they would all comply in the interest of the meeting.

It may therefore be said that the culture of mobile phones is gradually percolating through our way of life as Ghanaians, permeating areas of our traditional life and culture that have long been insulated against encroachment. In the domain of chieftaincy, one can easily say that the normal unavailability of chiefs for casual interaction has been defied by the culture of mobile phones. If you are lucky to have your chief's phone number, you may be lucky to catch him on the phone at a meeting of the traditional council, or house of chiefs, far away from your own location. The normal protocol of royal communication is temporarily suspended, and you may have a brief chat with your traditional ruler in the middle of a meeting, without the normal protocols. Whereas the transformation of chieftaincy into an accessible institution through modern technology makes for closer interaction between the chief and his people, it stands in danger of undermining the dignity and sanctity of the institution, since familiarity naturally breeds contempt.

Naturally the mobile phone culture has transformed lives and cultural values. The intensity of silence normally expected at funeral services, weddings, marriage ceremonies, and indeed traditional rituals can no longer be guaranteed. All it takes to undermine ritual intensity is a single phone intrusion. This is particularly significant since silence in certain settings, normally created ideal space for communication with the supernatural world. . . .

Text Messages

Significantly, contribution to the decision-making process has of late not been limited to phone communication from various distances. Text messages now have a semipermanent status on radio and television programmes, where times have been allocated for the reading of text messages on air. It is important to put on record here that a trend has started whereby text messages on radio are gradually being Ghanaianized. Not only are text messages occasionally interspersed with colloquial Ghanaian expressions and interjections. Several radio stations have told of text messages they have received and read in Ghanaian languages. This is indeed a major development that denotes our readiness to adopt current global technologies in the service of our culture.

In this case, the global communication technology has been used to add value to local languages. It is as if to say, even though current communication revolution is undermining cultural values, it can be very carefully cultivated in the services of cultural institution. Currently available are of course various Ghanaian language fonts on the computer, which afford the user the facility of writing messages in the original Ghanaian orthography, without using the Eurocentric approximations. Indeed, this has helped textbooks to be written in Ghanaian languages. Indeed, the Linguistic Department is in the process of finishing an Akan encyclopedic dictionary, in which all diacritics, including tone marks, have been indicated, all using modern software.

In a way the mobile phone technology, without the requirements of literacy, is easier to adopt and adapt. It has transformed communication habits and enabled access to individuals and places previously declared incommunicado; but it has also transformed cultural values; privacy is on the verge of being lost, and noise pollution in certain ritual and traditional settings requiring absolute silence and tranquility have been compromised. The youth, courtesy of mobile, have often inadvertently sometimes offended the dignity of elders with mobile phone interruptions during serious deliberations. They have rudely walked out during meetings and have privatized talk in forums that require open general deliberations. They have whispered and cupped their hands over phones, hoping their voices are out of earshot; but private conversation has now entered the public domain.

The world indeed is changing, for the phenomenon has permeated the most conservative institutions in our culture. But all these take place at the onset of a new century, a new millennium, where the indigenous cultural institutions themselves are changing and evolving. The chieftaincy institution is on the verge of losing its arcane disposition; chiefs are abolishing outmoded customs. Our chiefs indeed are now part of global partners working towards local and national development. The new dialogue the phone has wrought is therefore in keeping with changes taking place the world over, where all cultures are yearning to be part of the global village. It is up to us to adapt modern technologies in ways that move us forward in development, without undermining the foundations of our cultural values. The mobile phone culture is welcome, but must be carefully nurtured to fully agree with local cultural values.

Ghallywood or the Ghanaian Movie Industry

Ernest Dela Aglanu and Samuel Nii Narku Dowuona

Even in the inexorable march toward modernity, Ghana still clings tenaciously to certain cultural norms. Despite the Westernization of the society in many regards, Ghanaians maintain a healthy respect and appreciation for the articulation of matters of local relevance in a vernacular that the masses can easily understand. For example, radio stations often broadcast important matters in several local languages, with some stations broadcasting exclusively in a local language. This feature is exhibited unreservedly in some productions of the country's budding film industry, referred to locally as "Ghallywood." As the Ghanaian film industry strives to produce "modern" entertainment with a wide appeal, it has to contend with this multicultural and multilingual nature of the Ghanaian society. The following excerpts from works by journalists Ernest Dela Aglanu and Samuel Nii Narku Dowuona, respectively, shed light on this phenomenon by outlining how comments by a noted Ghanaian actor, ostensibly aimed at improving the quality of local films, offended the sensibilities of those invested in the maintenance and expression of stories in local languages on film.

"90% of Kumawood Movies Are Destroying Movie Industry" *(Ernest Dela Aglanu)*

Ghanaian actor Ekow Smith Asante says the majority of movies being churned out by movie producers in the local language are negating the progress of the Ghanaian movies industry. The local language sector of the Ghanaian movie industry, known as Kumawood, is responsible for the majority of movies being produced in Ghana currently, and many have credited it with reviving the industry, which had lost ground to the Nigerian movie industry. But speaking on the dwindling fortunes of the Ghanaian movie industry on *Rhythms A2Z* on Joy FM . . . the actor noted that Kumawood must also take the blame for the decline in standards in the industry.

Answering a question on whether Kumawood is helping or killing the Ghanaian movie industry, Ekow Smith Asante said, "About 90 percent of the Kumawood movies are destroying the movie industry. I will be emphatic on that." He explained that "sometimes when you talk to some of the producers, all they are interested in is the money not the passion for the business. Their passion is not for the creative arts, their passion is to make money."

"Their target market is not me and you sitting in Accra here," the actor said, and added that their target market is those in Ghana's interior and those people "don't know [anything] about lighting effects, about bad sound, about bad acting. They don't want to know, it's the story that is relevant to [them]."

"Now we need to find out, are we doing movies for money or are we doing movies for the creative industry?" he quizzed. Ekow Smith Asante lamented that if nothing is done to salvage the situation, the industry will continue to dwindle in fortunes and reputation.

"Ekow Smith-Asante in Big Trouble with Chiefs, People of Asankragua" (Samuel Nii Narku Dowuona)

Ace Ghanaian actor Ekow Smith-Asante may have meant well when he said 90 percent of the "Kumawood" movies (movies made in Kumasi) are destroying the Ghanaian movie industry.

But he definitely bit more than he could chew when he said the target market for those "inferior" movies are people in Asankragua, Sefwi Wiaso, "Yaw Wiaso," and other places "who do not know jack about lighting, sound, good acting and other things and they are not ready to know."

The ace actor also stated that Kumawood movies, according to the producers, are not made for educated people living in Accra, Cantonments, and other urban areas but for those in the hinterlands like the places mentioned earlier.

Those comments have rattled the cage of the chiefs and people of Asankragua, and they are asking for an unqualified apology from Smith-Asante or he would have himself to blame. Smith-Asante's comments, made on Joy FM's *Rhythms A2Z* show, was originally targeted at the producers of the "Kumawood" movies, whom he said were only passionate about making money and not developing the creative arts. He said the Kumawood moviemakers ignore everything that makes a good movie and only pay attention to the story lines based on themes like witchcraft and others, which people in Asankragua, Sefwi Wiaso, Yaw Wiaso, and the rest love.

His comments attracted an equal measure of response from some movie stars like Agya Koo, Kwaku Manu, and Akrobotu, who are major Kumawood movie characters. Kwaku Manu thought Smith-Asante is fading out so he wanted to say something to remain relevant, hence the "empty talk" about Kumawood movies. Agya Koo and Akrobotu disagreed with him, saying the Kumawood movies are more entertaining and educative than those movies Smith-Asante calls quality movies. Agya Koo described the English-based movies as "Indian movies" because the greater majority of Ghanaians do not fully understand the language and the story line, but they could easily relate to the Kumawood movies.

Kumawood moviemaker Paul Gee admitted that many Kumawood movies lack the needed quality. He also admitted that the target market is indeed people in Asankragua and other such areas.

Paul Gee, however, hit back at the so-called English-based quality movies, saying that they are worse because they contain lots of sex scenes, which promote infidelity, immorality, and other social vices.

He also noted that Smith-Asante had no business going on radio to criticize Kumawood movies because he has acted in some of them and he had been in meetings where the industry was discussed but he made no contribution.

ASANKRAGUA IS ANGRY

Smith-Asante's biggest trouble was not with the players in the movie industry, but with the chiefs and people of Asankragua, whom he described as people who did not know jack about what makes a quality movie and are not ready to know. The Gyaasehene of Asankragua, Nana Adu Boahene I, told Adom News the chiefs and people of the town feel very insulted by Smith-Asante's comments because "he is trying to say that we live in some hen coop in the remotest part of the country and we have no clue about what is going on around the world." He said it would be good for Smith-Asante to go through the proper channel and apologize to the chiefs and people of Asankragua, otherwise "he should wait and see what is coming at him." "Some people are determined to just call hinterland dwellers names and denigrate the chiefs but we will not sit by and watch them do that to us," he warned.

Smith-Asante has since apologized on radio but Nana Adu Boahene has hinted that the chiefs of Asankragua would not accept an apology on radio so if Smith-Asante knows what is good for him and he should get the right people and take them to Asankragua to apologize to the chiefs or be ready for the consequences. Some residents and citizens of Asankragua think being the big movie star that he is, Smith-Asante should have known better than to insult the sensibilities of a group of people in the country. They argued that, as a movie star from Ghana, he was expected to have mastered the cultural dynamics of the country and rather educated people on the implications of making such derogatory statements about any group of people in the country. Adom News is reliably informed that Smith-Asante is preparing to offer a proper apology to the chiefs and people of Asankragua for his comments.

Ghana's Philosophy of Survival

Kwesi Brew

In the following poem, Kwesi Brew pays tribute to the resilience of the Ghanaian peoples, extolling their ability to endure the machinations of transatlantic commerce, slaving, and European imperialism and celebrating the way they have deployed culture as a survival mechanism against cumulative trauma.

We are the punch bag of fate
On whom the hands of destiny wearies
And the shower of blows gradually lose
Their viciousness on our patience
Until they become caresses of admiration
And time that heals all wounds
Comes with a balm and without tears,
Soothes the bruises on our spirits.
This is the mettle of invisibility.
This is how we outlast and outlive
The powerful and the unwise.
Whether it is best to wait
Or engage the scarlet fury of battle
To stay the hand is for the wise to say,
And not the rashness of the moment.
But we have always been here
On this land of ours.
Our country is our home.
And will always be here at home
To watch, listen and take our suffering
Till true happiness comes naturally
And without bitterness.
Love of family kith and kin and brother-keeping
Has cast us in this mold:
That while we take the blow and seem unhurt,
Speechless, we also watch and wait.

Suggestions for Further Reading

Part I. One Nation, Many Histories

Amenumey, D. E. K. *Ghana: A Concise History from Pre-Colonial Times to the 20th Century.* Accra: Woeli, 2008.

DeCorse, Christopher R. *An Archaeology of Elmina: Africans and Europeans on the Gold Coast.* Washington: Smithsonian Institution Press, 2001.

Dickson, Kwamina B. *A Historical Geography of Ghana.* Cambridge: Cambridge University Press, 1969.

Farrar, Tarikhu. *Building Technology and Settlement Planning in a West African Civilization: Precolonial Akan Cities and Towns.* Lewiston, NY: Edwin Mellen, 1996.

Konadu, Kwasi. *The Akan Diaspora in the Americas.* New York: Oxford University Press, 2010.

Nketia, J. H. Kwabena. *Folk Songs of Ghana.* Accra: University of Ghana, 1963.

Owusu-Ansah, David, and Daniel Miles McFarland. *Historical Dictionary of Ghana.* Lanham, MD: Scarecrow, 2005.

Schaumloeffel, Marco Aurelio. *Tabom: The Afro-Brazilian Community in Ghana.* Barbados: Lulu.com, 2008.

Wilks, Ivor. *One Nation, Many Histories: Ghana Past and Present.* Accra: Anansesem, 1996.

Wolfson, Freda. *Pageant of Ghana.* New York: Oxford University Press, 1965.

Part II. Between the Sea and the Savanna, 1500–1700

Claridge, Walton W. *A History of the Gold Coast and Ashanti: From the Earliest Times to the Commencement of the Twentieth Century.* London: Frank Cass, 1964.

Doortmont, Michel René, and Jinna Smit, eds. *Sources for the Mutual History of Ghana and the Netherlands: An Annotated Guide to the Dutch Archives Relating to Ghana and West Africa in the Nationaal Archief, 1593–1960s.* Leiden: Brill, 2007.

Garrard, Timothy. *Akan Goldweights and the Gold Trade.* London: Longman, 1980.

Justesen, Ole, ed. *Danish Sources for the History of Ghana, 1657–1754.* 2 vols. Copenhagen: Kgl. Danske Videnskabernes Selskab, 2005.

Kea, Ray A. *Settlements, Trade, and Polities in the Seventeenth Century Gold Coast.* Baltimore: Johns Hopkins University Press, 1982.

Law, Robin, ed. *The English in West Africa, 1611–1699: The Local Correspondence of the Royal African Company of England, 1681–1699.* 3 vols. New York: Oxford University Press for the British Academy, 1996–2006.

MacGaffey, Wyatt. *Chiefs, Priests, and Praise-Singers: History, Politics, and Land Ownership in Northern Ghana*. Charlottesville: University of Virginia Press, 2013.

van Dantzig, Albert. *The Dutch and the Guinea Coast, 1674–1742: A Collection of Documents from the General State Archive at the Hague*. Accra: GAAS, 1978.

Vogt, John. *Portuguese Rule on the Gold Coast, 1469–1682*. Athens: University of Georgia Press, 1979.

Wilks, Ivor. *Forests of Gold: Essays on the Akan and the Kingdom of Asante*. Athens: Ohio University Press, 1993.

Part III. Commerce and the Scrambles for Africa, 1700–1900

Allman, Jean, and Victoria B. Tashjian. *I Will Not Eat Stone: A Women's History of Colonial Asante*. Oxford: James Currey, 2000.

Austin, Gareth. *Labour, Land and Capital in Ghana: From Slavery to Free Labour in Asante, 1807–1956*. Rochester, NY: University of Rochester Press, 2009.

Boahen, A. Adu, E. Akyeampong, N. Lawler, T. C. McCaskie, and I. Wilks, eds. *"The History of Ashanti Kings and the Whole Country Itself" and Other Writings, by Otumfuo, Nana Agyeman Prempeh I*. New York: Oxford University Press for the British Academy, 2006.

Debrunner, Hans W. *A History of Christianity in Ghana*. Accra: Waterville, 1967.

Der, Benedict G. *The Slave Trade in Northern Ghana*. Accra: Woeli, 1998.

Konadu, Kwasi. *Transatlantic Africa, 1440s–1888*. New York: Oxford University Press, 2014.

McCaskie, T. C. *State and Society in Precolonial Asante*. Cambridge: Cambridge University Press, 1995.

Sill, Ulrike. *Encounters in Quest of Christian Womanhood: The Basel Mission in Pre- and Early Colonial Ghana*. Leiden: Brill, 2010.

Smallwood, Stephanie. *Saltwater Slavery*. Cambridge, MA: Harvard University Press, 2007.

Sparks, Randy J. *Where the Negroes Are Masters: An African Port in the Era of the Slave Trade*. Cambridge, MA: Harvard University Press, 2014.

Part IV. Colonial Rule and Political Independence, 1900–1957

Agbodeka, Francis. *Ghana in the Twentieth Century*. Accra: Ghana Universities Press, 1972.

Arhin, Kwame, ed. *The Life and Work of Kwame Nkrumah*. Accra: Sedco, 1991.

Austin, Dennis. *Politics in Ghana 1948–1960*. New York: Oxford University Press, 1964.

Greene, Sandra E. *West African Narratives of Slavery: Texts from Late Nineteenth- and Early Twentieth-Century Ghana*. Bloomington: Indiana University Press, 2011.

Hawkins, Sean. *Writing and Colonialism in Northern Ghana: The Encounter between the LoDagaa and "the World on Paper," 1892–1991*. Toronto: University of Toronto Press, 2002.

Howard, Allen Marvin. *The National Congress of British West Africa: An Economic and Political Study of Gold Coast Society*. Madison: University of Wisconsin Press, 1963.

Kimble, David. *A Political History of Ghana: The Rise of Gold Coast Nationalism, 1850–1928*. Oxford: Clarendon, 1963.

Newell, Stephanie. *Literary Culture in Colonial Ghana: How to Play the Game of Life*. Bloomington: Indiana University Press, 2002.

Rathbone, Richard. *Nkrumah and the Chiefs: The Politics of Chieftaincy in Ghana, 1951–60*. Athens: Ohio University Press, 2000.

Part V. Independence, Coups, and the Republic, 1957–Present

Adjei, Mike. *Death and Pain in Rawlings' Ghana: The Inside Story*. London: Black Line, 1994.

Allman, Jean Marie. *Quills of the Porcupine: Asante Nationalism in an Emergent Ghana*. Madison: University of Wisconsin Press, 1993.

Asante, Clement E. *The Press in Ghana*. Lanham, MD: University Press of America, 1996.

Herbst, Jeffrey Ira. *The Politics of Reform in Ghana, 1982–1991*. Berkeley: University of California Press, 1993.

Lentz, Carola. *Ethnicity and the Making of History in Northern Ghana*. Edinburgh: Edinburgh University Press, 2006.

Lentz, Carola, and Paul Nugent, eds. *Ethnicity in Ghana: The Limits of Invention*. New York: Palgrave Macmillan, 2000.

Thompson, Scott. *Ghana's Foreign Policy 1957–1966: Diplomacy, Ideology and the New State*. Princeton, NJ: Princeton University Press, 1969.

Wright, Richard. *Black Power: A Record of Reactions in a Land of Pathos*. New York: Harper, 1954.

Part VI. The Exigencies of a Postcolony

Angelou, Maya. *All God's Children Need Traveling Shoes*. New York: Random House, 1986.

Busia, Abena P. A. *Testimonies of Exile*. Trenton, NJ: Africa World Press, 1990.

Clark, Gracia. *African Market Women: Seven Life Stories from Ghana*. Bloomington: Indiana University Press, 2010.

Gaines, Kevin Kelly. *American Africans in Ghana: Black Expatriates and the Civil Rights Era*. Chapel Hill: University of North Carolina Press, 2006.

IMAHKÜS, Seestah. *Returning Home Ain't Easy but It Sure Is a Blessing*. Bloomington: Trafford, 2009.

Plageman, Nathan. *Highlife Saturday Night! Popular Music and Social Change in Urban Ghana*. Bloomington: Indiana University Press, 2012.

Rawlings, Jerry J. *Selected Speeches of Flt. Lt. J. J. Rawlings: A Revolutionary Journey*. Accra: Information Services Department, 1983.

Talton, Benjamin. *Politics of Social Change in Ghana: The Konkomba Struggle for Political Equality*. New York: Palgrave Macmillan, 2010.

Yankah, Kwesi. *Woes of a Kwatriot: Reflections on the Ghanaian Situation*. Accra: Woeli, 1990.

Acknowledgment of Copyrights and Sources

Part I. One Nation, Many Histories

"Ancestral Faces," by Kwesi Brew, from *The Shadows of Laughter* (London: Longman, 1968), 52. Used by permission of Baaba Brew.

"The Holocene Archaeology of Ghana," by Ann Brower Stahl, previously published as "Innovation, Diffusion, and Culture Contact: The Holocene Archaeology of Ghana" in *Journal of World Prehistory* 8, no. 1 (March 1994): 83–84, 86–91, digitalized by Springer © 1994 Plenum Publishing Corporation. With kind permission from Springer Science+Business Media B.V.

"Quest for the River, Creation of the Path," by Kwasi Konadu, from *Akan Diaspora in the Americas* (New York: Oxford University Press, 2010), 27–29, 33–36, 40–43, 53–54.

"A Creation Story and a 'Beautiful Prayer' to Tano," by Robert S. Rattray, from *Ashanti* (New York: Clarendon Press, 1923), 146, 177–79.

"Folk Songs of Ghana," by J. H. Kwabena Nketia, from *Folk Songs of Ghana* (Accra: Ghana Universities Press, 1963), 55, 107.

"Bono-Takyiman Oral Traditions," by Dennis Warren and Owusu Brempong, from *Techiman Traditional State, Part 1, Stool and Town Histories* (Techiman: Institute of African Studies, University of Ghana, 1971), 57–61, 71–72, 75–76. Used by permission of the University of Ghana (Institute of African Studies).

"Oral Traditions of Adanse and Denkyira," by Kwame Y. Daaku, from *Oral Traditions of Adanse* (Legon: Institute of African Studies, University of Ghana, 1969), i–vi. And from *UNESCO Research Project on Oral Traditions of Denkyira*, no. 2 (Legon: Institute of African Studies, University of Ghana, 1970), 3–10. Used by permission of the University of Ghana (Institute of African Studies).

"An Account of Early Asante," by King Asantehene Agyeman Prempeh I, from "Part II: The Seychelles Writings, Chapter Five: Historical Pieces," in *History of the Ashanti Kings and the Whole Country*, edited by A. Adu Boahen et al., transcribed by Nancy Lawler, T. C. McCaskie, and Ivor Wilks (New York: Oxford University Press for The British Academy, 2008), 85–87. Used by permission of The British Academy.

"Fante Oral Traditions: Kwamankɛse and Komenda," by John K. Fynn, from *Oral Traditions of the Fante States: Komenda*, no. 3 (Legon: IAS, University of Ghana, 1976), i–iv. Used by permission of the University of Ghana (Institute of African Studies).

"Archaeological Reflections on Ghanaian Traditions of Origin," by Kwaku Effah-

Gyamfi, previously published as "Some Archaeological Reflections on Akan Traditions of Origin," *West African Journal of Archeology*, no. 9 (1979): 189–94. Used by permission of the West African Journal of Archeology.

"Prelude to the Atlantic Slave Trade," by Gérard L. Chouin and Christopher R. DeCorse, from *Journal of African History* 51, no. 2 (July 2010): 123, 125, 129, 133, 138, 142. Copyright © 2010 Cambridge University Press. Reprinted with the permission of Cambridge University Press.

Part II. Between the Sea and the Savanna, 1500–1700

"Encounter with Europe," by Kwesi Brew, previously published as "Don Diego at Edina (Elmina)" and "Don Diego at Edina (Elmina)—'The Great Rebuff,'" in *Return of No Return and Other Poems* (Accra: Afram Publications Ghana Ltd., 1995), 2, 4–5, 7–9.

"The Voyage of Eustache de la Fosse," by Eustache de la Fosse, from *Voyage a la Côte occidentale d'Afrique, en Portugal et en Espagne* (1479–1480), edited by R. Foulche-Delbosc (Paris: Alfonse Picard et Fils, 1897), 12–15.

"A View of the Gold Coast from the *Esmeraldo de Situ Orbis*," by Duarte Pacheco Pereira, from *Esmeraldo de Situ Orbis* (Lisbon: Imprensa Nacional, 1892), 68–70.

"Letter from Mina Governor to the Queen [Catarina]," by Afonso Gonçalves Botafogo, from *East of Mina: Afro-European Relations on the Gold Coast in the 1550s and 1560s: An Essay with Supporting Documents*, by Avelino Teixeira da Mota and Paul Edward Hedley Hair (Madison, WI: African Studies Program, 1988), 62, 64–66. Courtesy of University of Wisconsin–Madison, African Studies Program.

"A Report on Mina," from *East of Mina: Afro-European Relations on the Gold Coast in the 1550s and 1560s: An Essay with Supporting Documents*, by Avelino Teixeira da Mota and Paul Edward Hedley Hair (Madison, WI: African Studies Program, 1988), 75, 77–78, 81, 86–87. Courtesy of University of Wisconsin–Madison, African Studies Program.

"The Gold Kingdom of Guinea," by Pieter de Marees, from *Description and Historical Account of the Gold Kingdom of Guinea (1602)*, translated and edited by Albert van Dantzig and Adam Jones (New York: Oxford University Press, 1987), 41, 46, 47, 51–53. Used by permission of The British Academy.

"Letter 17," by Jean Barbot, from *Barbot on Guinea: The Writings of Jean Barbot on West Africa 1678–1712*, edited by P. E. H. Hair, Adam Jones, and Robin Law (London: Hakluyt Society, 1992), 331, 492–95. Used by permission of Hakluyt Society.

"Treaties between Gold Coast Polities and the King of Denmark and the Danish Africa Company," edited by Ole Justesen, previously published as "20th December 1659: Treaty between the Kingdom of Fetu, the King of Denmark and the Danish African Company," in *Danish Sources for the History of Ghana 1657–1754* (Denmark: gl. Danske Videnskabernes Selskab, 2005), vol. 1, 1, 9–11, 12. Used by permission of The Royal Danish Academy of Sciences and Letters.

"The Dutch and the Gold Coast," edited by Albert van Dantzig, previously published as "Plantations on the Gold Coast, March 14, 1707" and "Dutch Slaving on the Gold Coast and in Its American Colonies, September 17, 1710," in *The Dutch and the Guinea Coast, 1674–1742: A Collection of Documents from the General State Archive at The Hague*

(Accra: Ghana Academy of Arts and Sciences, 1978), 130. Used by permission of the Ghana Academy of Arts and Sciences.

"Denkyira in the Making of Asante," by T. C. McCaskie, previously published as "Denkyira in the Making of Asante c. 1660–1720," in *Journal of African History* 48, no. 1 (March 2007): 1–4, 24–25. Copyright © 2007 Cambridge University Press. Reprinted with the permission of Cambridge University Press.

"Ta'rīkh Ghunjā," edited by Ivor Wilks, Nehemia Levtzion, and Bruce M. Haight, previously published as "'Ta'rīkh Ghunjā' as originally told by Mahmud d. Abdallah," in *Chronicles from Gonja: A Tradition of West African Muslim Historiography* (Cambridge: Cambridge University Press, 1986), 158–63. Copyright © 2008 Cambridge University Press. Reprinted with the permission of Cambridge University Press.

Part III. Commerce and the Scrambles for Africa, 1700–1900

"The Various Nations of Blacks in Guinea," by Christian G. A. Oldendorp, from *Historie der caribischen Inseln Sanct Thomas, Sancy Crux und Sanct Jan : Insbesondere der dasigen Neger und der Mission der evangelischen Brüder unter denselben*, edited by Gudrun Meier et al. (Berlin: VWB, 2000), 383–84, 386–87.

"Revolt on a Danish Slaving Voyage," by Paul Erdmann Isert, from *Letters on West Africa and the Slave Trade: Paul Erdmann Isert's Journey to Guinea and the Caribbean Islands in Columbia (1788)*, translated and edited by Selena Axelrod Winsnes (New York: Oxford University Press, 1992), 175–81. Used by permission of Peer Heltberg Winsnes.

"Journal and Correspondences of H. W. Daendels," by Herman Willem Daendels, from *Journal and Correspondences of H. W. Daendels* (Legon: Institute of African Studies, University of Ghana, 1964), 253, 260. Used by permission of the University of Ghana (Institute of African Studies).

"The 'Bowdich' Treaty with Asante and the Oath at Nyankumasi," from *Great Britain and Ghana: Documents of Ghana History, 1807–1957*, edited by G. E. Metcalfe (London: Thomas Nelson & Son, 1964), 46–47, 87.

"She Who Blazed a Trail: Akyaawa Yikwan of Asante," by Ivor Wilks, from *Forests of Gold: Essays on the Akan and the Kingdom of Asante Book* (Athens: Ohio University Press, 1993), 331, 333–34, 337, 341, 346, 353–55.

"Plantations and Labor in the Southeast Gold Coast," by Ray Kea, from *From Slave Trade to "Legitimate Commerce": The Commercial Transition in Nineteenth-Century West Africa*, edited by Robin Law (Cambridge: Cambridge University Press, 1995), 120–22, 124–25, 132, 136. Copyright © 1995 Cambridge University Press. Reprinted with the permission of Cambridge University Press.

"Petition of the Principal Mulatto Females of the Gold Coast," from Petition of the principal mulatto females of the Gold Coast submitted to the Right Honorable Lord John Russell, Cape Coast Castle, March 29, 1841, in *House of Commons Papers*, vol. 12 (London: H. M. Stationery Office, 1842), 138.

"Grievances of the Gold Coast Chiefs," letter from Richard Pine to Cardwell, Cape Coast, 1864. Housed at The National Archives of the United Kingdom at Kew, PRO, CO 96/64.

"Proclamation of George Cumine Strahan," by George Cumine Strahan, from *Correspondences relating to the Queen's Jurisdiction on the Gold Coast, and the Abolition of Slavery within the Protectorate*, vol. 52, *Parliamentary Papers* (London: House of Parliament, 1875), 42–43.

"Gold-Mining and Colonial Capitalism in the Gold Coast," by Raymond E. Dumett, from *El Dorado in West Africa: The Gold-Mining Frontier, African Labor, and Colonial Capitalism in the Gold Coast, 1875–1900* (Athens: Ohio University Press, 1998), 72–74, 100–106. Copyright © 1998 Ohio University Press. This material is used by permission of Ohio University Press.

"Between the Sea and the Lagoon: The Anlo-Ewe of Southeastern Ghana," by Emmanuel Akyeampong, from *Between the Sea and the Lagoon: An Eco-Social History of the Anlo of Southeastern Ghana, c. 1850 to Recent Times* (Athens: Ohio University Press, 2001), 23–25, 215–17. Copyright © 2002 Ohio University Press. This material is used by permission of Ohio University Press.

"One Hundred and Fifty Years of Christianity in a Ghanaian Town," by John Middleton, from *Africa* 53, no. 3 (1983), 2–7, 13–14. Copyright © 1983 Cambridge University Press. Reprinted with the permission of Cambridge University Press.

"The Peoples of the Gold Coast Hinterland," by George Ekem Ferguson, from *The Papers of George Ekem Ferguson: A Fanti Official of the Government of the Gold Coast, 1890–1897*, edited by Kwame Arhin (Afrika-Studiecentrum, 1974), 115–19, 126, 128, 131. Housed at The National Archives of the United Kingdom at Kew.

"For the Safety of the Public, and the Welfare of the Race," from *Gold Coast Aborigines*, January 1, 1898, 2–3.

"To the Educated Community in the Gold Coast Colony," by Carl C. Reindorf, from *History of the Gold Coast and Asante* (Basel: Carl C. Reindorf, 1895), iii–vii.

Part IV. Colonial Rule and Political Independence, 1900–1957

"The Petition of 1913," by King Asantehene Agyeman Prempeh I, from *History of the Ashanti Kings and the Whole Country*, edited by A. Adu Boahen et al., transcribed by Nancy Lawler, T. C. McCaskie, and Ivor Wilks (New York: Oxford University Press for The British Academy, 2008), 148–49. Used by permission of The British Academy.

"Fathering, Mothering, and Making Sense of *Ntamoba* in Colonial Asante," by Jean Allman, from "Fathering, Mothering and Making Sense of *Ntamoba*: Reflections on the Economy of Child-Rearing in Colonial Asante," *Africa* 67, no. 2 (1997): 298–300, 302–5, 309–11. Copyright © 1997 Cambridge University Press. Reprinted with the permission of Cambridge University Press.

"The Blinkards," by Kobina Sekyi, from *The Blinkards and the Anglo-Fanti* (Accra: Readwide Publishers / Heinemann International Literatu, 1997), 4–9. *The Blinkards* © W. E. G. Sekyi 1974. Used by permission of Pearson Education Ltd.

"The Trial of Akrofi," by R. E. Obeng, from *Eighteen Pence* (Accra: Sub-Saharan Publishers, 1999), 133–43. Used by permission of Sub-Saharan Publishers.

"Of Water and Spirits," by Sandra E. Greene, from *Sacred Sites and the Colonial Encounter: A History of Meaning and Memory in Ghana* (Bloomington: Indiana University

Press, 2002), 35, 37–38, 40–42, 43–46. Courtesy of Indiana University Press. All rights reserved.

"AFRINHYIA PA O-O-O!," by T. E. Kyei, from "AFRINHYIA PA O-O-O," in *Our Days Dwindle: Memories of My Childhood Days in Asante*, 123–31, 133–37, 142–44. © 2001 by T. E. Kyei. Published by Heinemann, Portsmouth, NH. Reprinted by permission of the publisher. All rights reserved.

"Reminiscences: The Hill of Knowledge," by Kosi Kedem, from *The Chance of a Lifetime* (Accra: Governance and Electoral Systems Agency, 2008), 231–39. Used by permission of the author.

"The ARPS and the National Congress, 1901–30," by David Kimble, from *A Political History of Ghana: The Rise of Gold Coast Nationalism 1850–1928* (Oxford: Clarendon Press, 1963), 358, 374–78, 380–81, 383. Copyright © 1963 Oxford University Press. By permission of Oxford University Press.

"Women's Conjugal Strategies in a World of Cash and Cocoa," by Jean Allman and Victoria Tashjian, previously published as "'Serving a Man Is Wasted Labor': Women's Conjugal Strategies in a World of Cash and Cocoa," in *I Will Not Eat Stone: A Women's History of Colonial Asante*, 133–40, 143–45, 147–48. Copyright © 2000 by Jean Allman and Victoria Tashjian. Published by Heinemann, Portsmouth, NH. Reprinted by permission of the publisher. All rights reserved.

"Report on the Riots of 1948," by the Commission of Enquiry into Disturbances in the Gold Coast, from *Watson Commission Report and White Paper, 1948 Jan 01–1948 Dec 31*. Housed at The National Archives of the United Kingdom at Kew, FCO 141/5082, 682–86.

"History and National Development: The Case of John Mensah Sarbah and the Reconstruction of Gold Coast History," by D. E. Kofi Baku, from *Research Review* 6, no. 1 (1990): 36–48, 36–37, 39, 41–44. Used by permission of the author.

"The Administrative Problem," by J. E. Casely Hayford, from *Gold Coast Native Institutions: With Thoughts upon a Healthy Policy for the Gold Coast and Ashanti* (London: Sweet and Maxwell Ltd., 1903), 3–15.

"The Employment of Men: Clerks, Police, Soldiers, and Teachers, 1930–1951," by Stephan F. Miescher, from *Making Men in Ghana* (Bloomington: Indiana University Press, 2005), 84–91, 112–13. Courtesy of Indiana University Press. All rights reserved.

"Achimota: From the Story My Mother Taught Me," by Abena P. A. Busia, from *Testimonies of Exile* (Trenton, NJ: Africa World Press, 1990), 30–32. Used by permission of Africa World Press.

"Women and Their Organizations during the Convention People's Party Period," by Takyiwaa Manuh, from *The Life and Work of Kwame Nkrumah* (Accra: Sedco Publishing, 1991), 108–9, 113–17, 119, 124–28. Courtesy of Sedco Publishing Ltd.

"Ghana: The Pioneer Guards the Gate," by Frederick Cooper, from *Africa since 1940: The Past of the Present (New Approaches to African History)* (New York: Cambridge University Press, 2002), 161–63. Copyright © 2002 Frederick Cooper. Reprinted with the permission of Cambridge University Press.

"Birth of Ghana," by Lord Kitchener, 78 r.p.m. (London: Melodisc Records, 1956). Courtesy of Quweina Roberts.

Part V. Independence, Coups, and the Republic, 1957–Present

"Independence Speech," by Kwame Nkrumah, from *I Speak of Freedom* (London: Panaf, 1961), 106–7. Used by permission of Panaf Books.

"The Nkrumah Government and Its Opposition," by Kwame A. Ninsin, from *The Life and Work of Kwame Nkrumah* (Accra: Sedco Publishing, 1991), 221, 223, 226, 228, 232. Courtesy of Sedco Publishing Ltd.

"Africa's Resources," by Kwame Nkrumah, from *Neo-Colonialism: The Last Stage of Imperialism* (New York: International Publishers, 1966), 1–2, 4–7, 9, 11, 14. Used by permission of Panaf Books.

"Ordained by the Oracle," by Samuel Asare Konadu, from *Ordained by the Oracle* (London: Heinemann, 1969), 58, 60–68. Used by permission of Pearson Education Ltd.

"Flight," by Kwame Dawes, from *Prophets* (Leeds: Peepal Tree Press, 1995), 151–59. Courtesy of Peepal Tree Press Ltd.

"Everything Counts," by Ama Ata Aidoo, excerpts from *No Sweetness Here and Other Stories*. Copyright © 1970 by Ama Ata Aidoo (New York: Feminist Press at the City University of New York, 1995), 1–7. Reprinted with the permission of The Permissions Company, Inc., on behalf of The Feminist Press at the City University of New York, www.feministpress.org. All rights reserved.

"Story: Patience and Pleading," by Gracia Clark, from "Abenaa Adiiya," in *African Market Women: Seven Life Stories from Ghana* (Bloomington: Indiana University Press, 2008), 32–34. Courtesy of Indiana University Press. All rights reserved.

"Rebellion, Revolution, and Tradition: Reinterpreting Coups in Ghana," by Maxwell Owusu, from *Comparative Studies in Society and History* 31, no. 2 (1989): 372–73, 382, 384, 390, 392. Copyright © 1989 Cambridge University Press. Reprinted with the permission of Cambridge University Press.

"Miracles and the Message (1983 Drought in Ghana)," by Kwesi Brew, from *Return of No Return and Other Poems* (Accra: Afram Publications Ghana Ltd., 1995), 33–35. Used by permission of Afram Publications (Ghana) Ltd.

"Win the Match and Vote for Me," by Kevin S. Fridy and Victor Brobbey, from *Journal of Modern African Studies* 47, no. 1 (2009): 21–28. Copyright © 2009 Cambridge University Press. Reprinted with the permission of Cambridge University Press.

"The 1994 Civil War in Northern Ghana," by Artur Bogner, from *Ethnicity in Ghana: The Limits of Invention*, edited by Carola Lentz and Paul Nugent (New York: St. Martin's Press, 2000), 185, 188–89, 192–93, 195–96, 199. Reproduced with permission of Palgrave Macmillan.

"'That All Konkomba Should Henceforth Unite,'" by Benjamin Talton, from *Politics of Social Change in Ghana: The Konkomba Struggle for Political Equality* (New York: Palgrave Macmillan, 2010), 176–80. Reproduced with permission of Palgrave Macmillan.

"I Am Not Brainwashed," by Asirifi Danquah, from *Daily Graphic*, December 21, 2006. Courtesy of the Daily Graphic.

"Hydro-Power and the Promise of Modernity and Development in Ghana," by Stephan F. Miescher and Dzodzi Tsikata, from *Ghana Studies* 12/13 (October 2009): 15–19, 21, 23–25, 38–39, 48–49. Courtesy of University of Wisconsin–Madison, African Studies Program.

"The Ghanaian Media and National Unity," by George Sydney Abugri, from blog entry on *Sydney Abugri*, August 9, 2007, www.sydneyabugri.com/Web/. Courtesy of the author.

Part VI. The Exigencies of a Postcolony

"The Return of the Native," by Kwesi Brew, from *Return of No Return and Other Poems* (Accra: Afram Publications Ghana Ltd., 1995), 9–13. Courtesy of Afram Publications (Ghana) Ltd.

"Toward a Pan-African Identity: Diaspora African Repatriates in Ghana," by Obiagele Lake, from *Anthropological Quarterly* 68, no. 1 (January 1995): 21, 27, 29–30. Used by permission of The Institute for Ethnographic Research, Columbian College of Arts & Sciences.

"Slavery and the Making of Black Atlantic History," by Bayo Holsey, from *Routes of Remembrance: Refashioning the Slave Trade in Ghana* (Chicago: University of Chicago Press, 2007), 152–54, 156–57, 161–62, 164, 165–67. Copyright © 2007 University of Chicago Press.

"The Return through the Door of No Return," by Seestah IMAHKÜS, from "The Return—Thru the Door of No Return," in *Returning Home Ain't Easy but It Sure Is a Blessing!* (Bloomington, IN: Trafford, 2011), 51–54. Courtesy of the author.

"Citizenship and Identity among Ghanaian Migrants in Toronto," by Takyiwaa Manuh, from "Ghanaians, Ghanaian Canadians, and Asantes: Citizenship and Identity among Migrants in Toronto," *Africa Today* 45, nos. 3/4 (1998): 483–88. Used by permission of Indiana University Press.

"Chieftaincy, Diaspora, and Development," by George M. Bob-Milliar, from "Chieftaincy, Diaspora, and Development: The Institution of *Nkɔsuohene* in Ghana," *African Affairs* 108, no. 433 (2009): 543–46, 553–55, 557–58. © George M. Bob-Milliar, 2009. Published by Oxford University Press on behalf of Royal African Society.

"China–Africa Relations: A Case Study of Ghana," by Dela Tsikata, Ama Pokuaa Fenny, and Ernest Aryeetey (Legon: University of Ghana, 2008), 26–27. Sponsored by African Economic Research Consortium (AERC). Courtesy of the authors.

"Ghana Market Women Pay the Daily Micro Man," by Emily Bowers, from *Women's eNews*, February 26, 2007, http://womensenews.org/story/the-world/070226/ghana-market-women-pay-the-daily-micro-man#.UhZQNNKkopg. Accessed March 9, 2012. This article was originally published by *Women's eNews*.

"'The Slums of Nima' and 'Fading Laughter,'" by Kwesi Brew, (1) "The Slums of Nima," from *African Panorama and Other Poems* (Greenfield Center, NY: Greenfield Review Press, 1981), 39–41. Courtesy of The Greenfield Review Press. (2) "Fading Laughter," from *Return of No Return and Other Poems* (Accra: Afram Publications Ghana Ltd., 1995), 13–14. Courtesy of Afram Publications (Ghana) Ltd.

"Ghanaian Highlife," by E. J. Collins, from *African Arts* 10, no. 1 (1976): 66–68. Reprinted by permission of MIT Press.

"Profile of Five Ghana Emcees," by Msia Kibona Clark. Original essay, used with permission.

"Kumasi Realism: Alex Amofa," by Atta Kwami, from *Kumasi Realism: An African*

Modernism (London: Hurst & Co. Publishers Ltd., 2013), 220, 223, 225, 227–29, 283. Reprinted, with permission, from Atta Kwami, *Kumasi Realism*, copyright Atta Kwami, 2013.

"Paradigm Shift," by Paul Gifford, from *Ghana's New Christianity: Pentecostalism in a Globalising African Economy* (Bloomington: Indiana University Press, 2004), 20–27. Courtesy of Indiana University Press and courtesy of C. Hurst & Co. All rights reserved.

"The Funeral as a Site for Choreographing Modern Identities in Contemporary Ghana," by Esi Sutherland-Addy, from *Ghana Studies* 12, no. 13 (2009–10): 217–18, 224–27, 238–43. Courtesy of University of Wisconsin–Madison, African Studies Program.

"The United States, Ghana, and Oil: Global and Local Perspectives," by Tom C. McCaskie, from *African Affairs* 107, no. 428 (2008): 318–19, 322–24, 327–32. © Tom C. McCaskie, 2008. Published by Oxford University Press on behalf of Royal African Society.

"Obama's Visit as a Signifier of Ghanaians' 'Colonial Mentality,'" by Kwabena Akurang-Parry, from *GhanaWeb*, August 26, 2009, http://www.ghanaweb.com/GhanaHomePage/features/artikel.php?ID=167472. Accessed March 9, 2012. Courtesy of the author.

"Mobile Phones and Our Cultural Values," by Kwesi Yankah, from the *Ghanaian Times*, February 9, 2007, 26–27, and February 13, 2007, 27, http://www.ghanaculture.gov.gh/index1.php?linkid=338&archiveid=641&page=1&adate=19/02/2007. Accessed March 9, 2012. Courtesy of the author.

"Ghallywood or the Ghanaian Movie Industry," (1) from "90% of Kumawood Movies Are Destroying Movie Industry," by Ernest Dela Aglanu, Myjoyonline.com, September 17, 2013, http://www.myjoyonline.com/entertainment/2013/september-17th/90-of-kumawood-movies-are-destroying-movie-industry-ekow-smith-asante.php. Courtesy of Myjoyonline.com. (2) from "Ekow Smith-Asante in Big Trouble with Chiefs, People of Asankragua," by Samuel Nii Narku Dowuona, from OMGGhanna, 2013, http://omgghana.com/ekow-smith-asante-big-trouble/. Courtesy of OMGGhanna.com.

"Ghana's Philosophy of Survival," by Kwesi Brew, from *Return of No Return and Other Poems* (Accra: Afram Publications Ghana Ltd., 1995), 38–39. Courtesy of Afram Publications (Ghana) Ltd.

Every reasonable effort has been made to obtain permission. We invite copyright holders to inform us of any oversights.

Index

Note: Page numbers in *italics* indicate illustrations.